THE FOREIGN POLICY OF WEST GERMANY

FORMATION AND CONTENTS

THE FOREIGN POLICY OF WEST GERMANY

FORMATION AND CONTENTS

Editors

Ekkehart Krippendorff
Volker Rittberger

German Political Studies Volume 4
Sponsored by the German Political Science Association

SAGE Publications · London and Beverly Hills

SAGE Publications Inc
275 South Beverly Drive
Beverly Hills, California 90212

For information address
SAGE Publications Ltd
28 Banner Street, London EC1Y 8QE

British Library Cataloguing in Publication Data

German political studies.
Vol. 4: The foreign policy of West Germany
1. Germany, West — Politics and
government — Periodicals
I. Krippendorff, Ekkehart II. Rittberger,
Volker
320.9'43'087 JN 3971.A1 80-40149

ISBN 0-8039-9818-X
ISBN 0-8039-9819-8 Pbk
ISSN 0307-7233

Contents

1

WEST GERMANY'S FOREIGN POLICY: An Introduction

Ekkehart Krippendorff

INTERNATIONAL RELATIONS THEORISTS seem to have generally accepted some propositions with regard to the foreign policy of nation states in the international arena which make former 'models' or classical 'principles' appear outmoded. One of them was the principle of *Staatsraison* (not by chance a German invention, at least in its corollary of the *Primat der Aussenpolitik*), according to which states are basically autonomous units acting according to the laws of a 'state of nature' in the international arena, i.e. with survival as independent units as their primary political raison d'être. There are good reasons to suggest that in fact states never were such 'monads' in a world without rules and laws besides that of the 'survival of the fittest', and that the construction of the State/Prince never corresponded to the empirical reality even at the time when it was theoretically formulated as a guideline for the actions of statesmen. But, in any case, there exists by now a certain consensus among theorists that international politics in the second half of the 20th century are basically characterized by 'interdependence' rather than by 'sovereignty'.

In terms of terminological creativity, scholars of international relations have been impressively productive and have shown considerable intellectual fantasy, labelling this new reality at times 'transnational politics', 'multipolarity', 'international integration', 'interaction' etc. In many respects — even though for historically seemingly unique reasons — the emergence of West Germany's foreign policy can be considered from its beginning in the early 1950s to the present as a demonstration of the validity of those newly-found insights into the political structure of the international system: the Federal

Republic of Germany presents herself, as far as her foreign policy is concerned, from an analytical point of view as a rather fascinating 'model' (the fact, that leading West German politicians consider the FRG in quite different respects a 'model' for other nations, is purely a terminological coincidence).

For historically unique reasons, West Germany was forced into breaking new ground towards a modern foreign policy, adequate for the conditions of the second half of the 20th century. To begin with, the creation of the FRG as a new state was the result of World War II and, therefore, clearly a function of international politics: this new 'actor' on the stage of international affairs was created by others, and if not against the will of her population so at least without the expressed will of the Germans under Western occupation; her very constitution — unique by the standards of democratic principles — was never submitted to a popular referendum. But, more important and phrased in International Relations terminology, it was created by means of the most complete and comprehensive international 'integration' imaginable for any country in recent history (with only the GDR as its logical counterpart). Only to the degree that the FRG became ever more firmly an integral part of the 'Western system' was the original status of the occupational regime — that extreme form of integration — altered and finally legally abolished (even though it should not be overlooked that West Berlin still is, in terms of international law, an occupied territory rather than a sovereign unit or legally part of the FRG). *Integration*, therefore, became both in terms of the generally accepted terminology as well as in terms of theory the very key word for the political existence of the new West German state: for its *economy* (the Coal and Steel Community was created concomitant with the foundation of the republic), for its *ideological identity* (West Germans were urged by the media and by public opinion leaders to be Europeans first and foremost), for its *cultural orientation* (most prominent during the formative years was a myriad of international exchange programs on every possible level), in *military and defense* matters (West German rearmament was made acceptable by Adenauer's launching of the EDC idea, i.e. of West German soldiers under a European command system), and, last but not least, in the sphere of *politics*: this newly-born state was the first one to declare explicitly in its very constitution the possibility if not desirability of renouncing parts of its national sovereignty in favour of international organs and/or organizations in order to achieve a stable, more peaceful international order.

What was in the beginning the function of externally imposed political decisions, i.e. the 'Diktat' of the occupation powers to grant only a restricted, limited, 'conditional' sovereignty (and even the Emergency Laws of 1968 have not restored it fully, apart from the special case of West Berlin), was gradually transformed into a genuine foreign policy strategy, making virtue out of necessity: the integration of the West German economy into the larger West European context, the merger of her military forces into the Western defense system of NATO, the active participation in the creation of the Common Market first and the European Community later etc. — and it is not by accident that all these processes find their counterpart for East Germany within the Soviet-led system of similarly 'limited sovereignties'.

Most of the papers presented in this volume demonstrate the integration aspects of West Germany's foreign policy, the 'model' of subordinating so-called national interests to broader social, economic and strategic security interests. We, the editors, have not solicited the individual contributors to make this point — rather this turns out to be one of the results of independent research, starting from different methodological approaches or 'political biases' but leading to similar conclusions or observations in the context of a wide range of topics.

Haftendorn, for example, elaborates on what she calls the international bureaucratization of strategic decision-making, showing that the area of maneouvre of West German foreign policy makers is extremely limited. Or, to put it differently, at least in the field of strategic matters West Germany does not have a policy with a genuine national profile. In a completely different key, from a different angle, *Schlupp* argues the case of a German-American *Herrschaftssynthese*, i.e. the socio-political submission of the West German bourgeoisie under its American partner exactly because of the former's lack of national identity — at least in comparative terms, e.g. when compared with the nationally more self-assured (and therefore, less 'integrationist') bourgeoisies of France and England. Here we have the fascinating hypothesis that West Germany, for historical and political reasons, originating in the very conditions of its birth as a particularly vulnerable new state, is more bent on integration into an Atlantic socio-economic and cultural community than its most important European partners. At least some of the international strategies of the FRG become plausible against this background of the weakness of her bourgeoisie in terms of a lack in historical and national identity. Again, from a seemingly different perspective or, rather, in tackling a different problem — i.e. the broken national unity — *Schweigler* tries to demonstrate the deep erosion of an all-German national consciousness, the 'de-nationalization' of the issue of German unity: social and economic issues seem to have gained a decisive upper hand over the national variable as far as overall political consciousness is concerned as measured by public opinion data. It is, of course, possible to ask whether these empirically correct positions will remain unchanged in the long run: many sensitive observers suggest that the national issue is only at this point a dormant one and can be re-vitalized under different overall political and/or economic conditions, e.g. in case of a series of political crises. If, on the other hand, Schweigler's thesis is corroborated in the long run, we might interpret his findings as foreshadowing a more profound process of 'de-nationalization' to be observed with regard to the older and more stable bourgeoisies of the Western countries as well — hence, once again, our *Modell Deutschland*.

Looking at the FRG's foreign policy in terms of a model for supranational integration, even the much talked about *Ostpolitik* reveals itself not at all as a proof of West Germany's emancipation towards a more independent, self-assured role on the stage of international politics, but rather as its opposite. As *Kreile* points out, the real meaning of 'Ostpolitik' lies in the — so far successful — attempt to emancipate, to liberate the West German state from an historical heritage that had become increasingly self-defeating and counterproductive as far as pursuing full Western integration is concerned. 'Ostpolitik' should be interpreted, therefore, as a strategy to give the government a freer hand in solving the overall problems of the social and economic stability of West German society by means of an explicit renunciation of a political policy (renunciation of re-unification policy and renunciation of a special relationship with the GDR). In other words, West Germany is now free to put its priorities openly where they have always been: with West European or rather with Atlantic integration and interdependence. While the pre-'Ostpolitik' foreign policy might be considered the negation of a political policy because it had defined its own strategies and options in terms of denying East Germany's right to existence and had led, therefore, to painful paralyses and deadlocks on almost every level, now West Germany's foreign policy is moving towards the full normality of being part of the Western security system. And by 'security system' we have in mind, obviously, the broad meaning of the concept which includes social, economic and political stability far beyond the more narrow military aspects.

Normality means that only now is the full weight of the FRG's economy within the broader context of the capitalist world economy going to be felt by her allies and partners, uncrippled by World War II legacies and politico-ideological bonds. When *Albrecht* states that, until a few years ago, only a minority of radical and marxist analysts had pointed out that the FRG had, in effect, become a powerful partner in the United States' imperial strategy while officially and in terms of public opinion West Germans still considered themselves a minor power with hardly any significant role in world politics, one might have to qualify this statement: it did indeed need the break-through of the Grand Coalition to cut that umbilical cord and give the West German economy a foreign as well as an economic policy which corresponded to its very dynamics, and develop the instruments to deal with the crises resulting from capitalist normality. Such normality, which makes West German foreign policy decision-making quite comparable to structurally similar processes in Western Europe and the United States, is formulated by *Krause/Wilker* as the principle, 'that the importance of economic interests in comparison with those of a "political" nature will increase to the extent that the management of internal economic crises (unemployment, inflation etc.) — threatening the legitimacy of the government — has become a problem'. Against this general background one should, finally, read the essay by *Gantzel-Kress*, which traces the slow and tortuous evolution of the discipline of International Relations in West Germany. It had started as narrowly as most West Germans had perceived the role of their new state in international affairs: as the result of the East-West conflict which meant that for them as well as for the academic community a proper understanding of the division of Germany, or even of the Berlin problem, seemed sufficient for the understanding of world politics altogether. Now, however, some thirty years later, a new generation of scholars has emerged and is trying to look at its own country's role in international relations with fresh and often critical eyes, a process to which some of the contributions to this volume testify.

1

WEST GERMANY AND THE MANAGEMENT OF SECURITY RELATIONS:
Security Policy Under the Conditions of International Interdependence

Helga Haftendorn

INTRODUCTION

KONRAD ADENAUER'S DECISION TO INTEGRATE the Federal Republic of Germany into the Western community facilitated the development of transnational policy-making processes.[1] His decision was based on choice as well as necessity: due to the direct and authoritative participation of the Allied High Commissioners in the planning, management, and resolution of security matters, the Federal Republic could justifiably be classified as a 'penetrated' system[2] during the period of occupation. After the Paris and Bonn Treaties entered into force in 1955, this direct participation was replaced by a coordinated, partially integrated international decision-making network of NATO, WEU, the Common Market, and bilateral German-American, German-British, and German-French relations. Control of the FRG, the dominant aspect of the early years, gradually became less important, and West Germany began to play a more independent and confident role in the Western community. Thus, the historically determined dependence of the FRG in security affairs has steadily decreased, while the level of interdependence with her Western partners has constantly increased. This resulted in the simultaneous growth of German influence *and* dependence along the entire spectrum of joint political, military, and economic affairs.

At the same time security affairs themselves became significantly more complex, involving, in addition to defense and deterrence, an extensive network of bilateral and multinational foreign relations. Détente,[3] which together with defense policy has become the second 'pillar' of security policy, provides a good example. Furthermore — and not only since the oil crisis — issues of international or domestic economic policy have a growing impact on national security.[4] From the complexity of security affairs follows both a functionalization and a specialization of foreign policy decision-making processes. The development of factual expertise by traditional institutions such as the Foreign Office (*Auswärtiges Amt*) and the Ministry of Defense (*Bundesministerium für Verteidigung*) has been encouraged. At the same time other departments, such as the Ministry of Economics (*Bundesministerium für Wirtschaft*), have enlarged their role in security affairs. Though the main task of the MoD to protect the territorial integrity of the FRG through military means has remained intact, its once dominant position in the area of security relations has been circumscribed. It now shares the overall handling of security affairs with a number of other agencies, contributing its expertise to military-political questions. The necessity to produce adequate strategies for problem-solving leads to the development of new interagency and interdepartmental procedures for processing information and making decisions. No structure, however, has yet been created in which the various issue-areas of security policy — defense, alliance, and détente policy, as well as certain aspects of international economic policy — can be combined to allow for coordinated conceptual planning. The Federal Security Council (*Bundessicherheitsrat*) is purely a cabinet committee with minimal administrative support, while the Chancellor's Office (*Bundeskanzleramt*) normally confines itself to functioning as a support staff rather than assuming overall planning tasks.

Security policy is influenced, determined, and legitimized by a variety of forces acting within the political system. During the first half of the 1970s in the FRG, détente policy was caught in the crossfire of divergent aims and values which were reflected in the polarization of interests and opinions between government and opposition. The increased interest in security problems and the politization of public discussion was accompanied, however, by a reduction of opportunities for the legislature, political parties, and interest groups, to influence the security policy-making process. It had become so complex that special expertise was needed to understand and to cope with the problems involved which in turn led to its referral to various functional units within the administration. This increased functionalization caused an increase in the international bureaucratization of the decision-making process and thus a decrease in the possibilities for political control as well as to a loss of democratic accountability.

The close integration of the FRG into its international environment, the much more complex nature of security affairs, and the high level of politization are most visible in the area of security and détente policy, as shown in the following examples of decision-making processes.

DECISION-MAKING IN THE AREA OF SECURITY AFFAIRS

Decision-making processes cannot be studied apart from their subject matters. Depending on the international and domestic framework, the specific nature of a problem, and the available institutional facilities, as well as the personality of the actors concerned, specific patterns of opinion-formation, coordination, and decision-making emerge. These patterns exist for a time and may even serve as examples for similar decision-making processes before adapting to different problems and changed external circumstances. Thus, the formal organizational structures of the political administration in Bonn can serve only as initial reference points. More important is the international involvement of the FRG and the evolving transnational patterns (NATO, EC, bilateral agreements, etc.), as well as the integration of the political-administrative system into the society as a whole. Thus, numerous informal processes are superimposed upon the formal structures.

Due to the complexity of security affairs, there is no single security policy decision-making process. In addition to the overall goal of insuring the territorial integrity of the FRG and her freedom to realize her own identity,[5] the various issue-areas of security policy are characterized by their own intermediate goals. Military force planning is concerned with manpower and equipment (supplies, fuel, stockpiles in case of attack); its primary purpose is to guarantee defense readiness. Factors to be considered include threat perception, the military-strategic concept, and the availability of material and manpower resources. This task falls within the responsibility of the MoD, which is, however, dependent on the financial resources available. As the German defense contribution is made within the framework of an integrated defense alliance, it is therefore also a part of Germany's alliance policy. From an alliance standpoint, coordinated force plans are a necessary prerequisite for a joint military strategy. Parallel to and closely coordinated with the national planning processes, the alliance itself therefore sets up force goals. The development of defense policy principles (*Verteidigungspolitische Richtlinien*) and a military-strategic concept for the German Armed Forces (*Bundeswehr*) can thus not be considered separately from the evolution of alliance strategy as recorded in the Military Committee document '14/3', and in the 'guidelines' which are approved every two years.[6] The formulation of defense principles within an alliance implies the setting of priorities which predetermine national security policy options, and have wide ramifications for the German political system as a whole.

In the case of the East-West negotiations on mutual and balanced force reductions (MBFR) in Vienna, the West German decision-making system was faced with completely different problems. The MBFR 'signal' issued by the NATO Council in June 1968 in Reykjavik had to be seen as a counterproposal to the East European drive for a European security conference (CSCE). Its purpose was to inject matters of military-political substance into such a conference. It was also hoped that unilateral Western troop reductions — a definite possibility as a result of several Mansfield resolutions debated in the US Congress — could be avoided, and the importance of US-Canadian involvement (in Europe) for European security could be emphasized. MBFR and CSCE also seemed to offer a common framework for the détente policies of the NATO partners. For Bonn and its 'Ostpolitik', this aspect was particularly impotant. The MBFR negotiations themselves were designed to reach a conventional force balance in Central Europe at a lower level, and thus to eliminate the conventional superiority of the Warsaw Pact. This new security ratio, balanced according to numbers, types, deployment of troops and armaments, and taking into account redeployment possibilities, was to be supplemented by a system of confidence-building measures.[7] As in the case of force goals, the national MBFR decision-making process was closely coordinated with multilateral processes, particularly within NATO. The complex issues and priorities involved in MBFR led in turn to a proliferation of instititional structures within the political system of the FRG. The FO and the MoD worked together on a practically equal basis, though at times competitively, to develop a German position for MBFR. An even more extensive and diversified institutional structure evolved during the preparations for the CSCE. At the international level, the group 'European Political Cooperation' (EPZ = *Europaeische Politische Zusammenarbeit*) functioned as a West European clearing house. In Bonn, as many as fifteen departments, including the Chancellor's Office, were at one time or another involved, requiring the creation of new interagency coordinating structures and processes.

Depending on the range of problems involved, specific patterns of opinion-formation and decision-making develop, which in the area of foreign and security policy illustrate clearly the extensive integration of the FRG into the Western community. In the case of a recurrent problem such as the formulation of force goals, the existing organizational routine is employed. From time to time, this routine is adjusted to account for changing political, organizational, and personnel conditions. New types of problems, on the other hand — as in the case of MBFR — for which no established problem-solving processes exist, foster the development of functional innovative processes[8] and lead to redistribution of responsibilities within the organization and new patterns of coordination. Domestic political forces within the FRG — interest groups, media, public opinion, even the Bundestag and political parties — have, as a rule, relatively little influence on security policies and the decision-making processes which produce them.[9] Although there is no omnipotent military-industrial complex in existence, there have been instances where organized industries have pushed a specific policy. This has been the case with the German-Brazilian nuclear agreement, where highly sensitive domestic questions were involved, and a technological-industrial-bureaucratic coalition had its way, shunning alliance and security considerations.[10]

THE DECISION-MAKING PROCESS WITHIN THE FRG

Most discussions of the political system of the FRG concentrate on the normative, constitutional aspects, an approach which is only gradually being abandoned in favor of a more functional view.[11] As a result, the extent to which a problem-oriented functional system is being superimposed over the formal legal and administrative system is often overlooked. This functional system centers at the working level on the individual desks and divisions, not on the department heads. Information is transmitted as often over the telephone as via the more traditional memorandum process. The complexity of this system is further underlined by a variety of organizational routines, bureaucratic 'games', party loyalties, and individual idiosyncracies.

The center of decision-making for all international matters — whether in the area of foreign or security policy — is the Foreign Office. This ministry is, according to Article 73 of the Basic Law (*Grundgesetz*) and § 11 of the rules of procedure (*Geschaeftsordnung*) of the government, responsible for all international relations (although in the case of foreign economic policy its responsibility is limited). The majority of German representatives in NATO, the European Community and the United Nations, as well as delegates to international conferences like MBFR and CSCE, are staff members of the FO. Other government departments also have delegates, but their instructions are coordinated and transmitted through the FO. The MOD attempted at one time to curtail the dominance of the FO and to expand its own role beyond that of military advisor, to achieve a specific departmental responsibility in security affairs, similar to the role of DOD/ISA (International Security Affairs) in the US Department of Defense. This attempt, which occurred during the MBFR preparations in 1972/73 and which was based on recommendations of the MoD Planning Staff and Political Division of the Armed Forces Staff (Fü S = *Fuehrungsstab Streitkraefte*), was blocked by the FO, although the matter was never fully discussed by the departments involved. The instructions to the German delegation in NATO as well as to representatives at international conferences are formulated by and channeled through the FO, in close coordination with the MoD. The reporting procedures take a similar course in reverse. The NATO or MBFR delegations report to the FO (either to the NATO desk or to the European Security desk), but the telegrams are marked 'also for MoD', and are routed directly to the relevant desks in that ministry, although this takes place through the communications system of the FO. Instructions and reports which go directly from the MoD to Brussels or Vienna — these normally involve military questions or direct communications to the MoD delegates — must be approved by the FO in advance and are then accordingly marked 'approved by FO'. All instructions or reports are prepared at the desk level and then signed off by the *Staatssekretaer* or his deputy.

This system of preparing and coordinating decisions at the working level is so complex that both top officials and political leaders, although kept informed on most matters, are seldom involved in routine processes (or in cases of decisions which are considered to be routine), except for formal confirmation. The advantage of this system is the greater capacity of the bureaucracy to process problems and its relatively smooth operation. Its weakness is, however, that only one or a limited set of policy options is made available to the political leaders. For this reason, the responsibility of the Chancellor (*Bundeskanzler*) for policy guidance is in practice limited to the establishment of an overall security policy concept. The extent to which the bureaucracy respects this concept is in turn monitored by the Chancellor's Office which also oversees regular coordination with the other government departments.

Decisions affecting security policy are relatively seldom made by the Chancellor himself, in the Cabinet, in the Federal Security Council, or in a *Chefgespraech* (a meeting of top government officials, comparable to the 'Tuesday lunches' of the Johnson era). Examples of such exceptions to the rule are the declaration of Chancellor Schmidt in the summer of 1976 that the FRG would contribute to the costs of stationing American troops in Garstedt, North Germany; the passage of government guidelines for handling the CSCE by the Cabinet in May 1972, the approval of the German MBFR position by the Federal Security Council in October 1973, and the deliberation of the third American MBFR negotiating option in May 1975. In most other cases, such as preparations for NATO Meetings, the role of the Cabinet is confined to the approval of position papers which have been prepared by the government departments.

The working level consists primarily of the *Fachreferate* or desks. In the FO, questions of security policy are primarily the responsibility of the NATO desk, Referat 201, 'Atlantic Alliance and Defense', the East European division (espec. 212 'General East-West Relations', charged with CSCE), the arms control division (with its three desks: 220, 'World-wide Disarmament and Arms Control', which keeps track of, among other things, the SALT negotiations, 221, 'Security in Europe', where MBFR is the main project; and 222, 'Verification, Prohibition of B- and C-Weapons, and Technical Matters', which includes non-proliferation). The latter division, created by an initiative of the Bundestag in 1965[12] and headed by a special ambassador for disarmament and arms control, does play an important role, along with the NATO desk, in questions of security policy. Until 1969, the CSCE project was handled by its European security desk (221), along with MBFR. Partly because of the extremely heavy work load at this desk and partly due to other, personnel considerations, but mostly because of the realization that CSCE would have important implications for inter-German policy and therefore required coordination with the 'Ostpolitik' as well as with other ongoing

Figure 1
Institutional Structure for Security Policy Decision-making

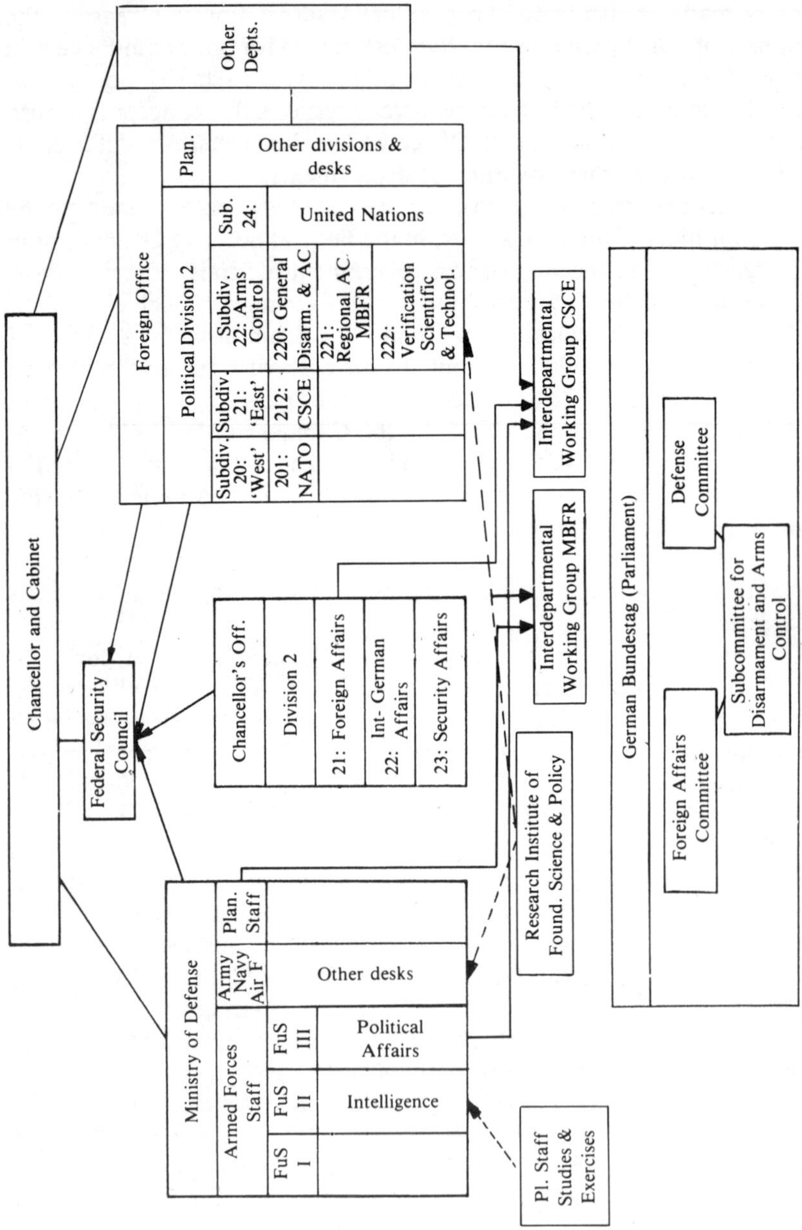

negotiations with the Soviet Union, Poland, Czechoslovakia, and East Germany, the primary responsibility for CSCE was shifted to a desk in the Eastern Division (then known as Referat II A3, 'Structural Problems Concerning the East') which at that time had a relatively light work load (see Fig. 1).

In the MoD, the Division III of the Armed Forces Staff (Fü S/III 'Military Policy and Leadership') functions as a staff for all questions of military policy and strategy. Its desk No. 1 is charged with general questions of military policy, desk No. 2 with military strategy (for example, military-political guidelines and military-strategic concepts), No. 3 handles NATO questions including force goals, and No. 5, arms controls (for example, SALT and MBFR). Close contact is maintained between these groups and Division II, which is responsible for military intelligence, as well as with the command staffs of each of the military services.

The third organization involved with security questions is the Chancellor's Office. Its functions, however, are limited to the coordination of the other departments and to insure that the general political concepts formulated by the administration in power are respected at the working level by the various departments. Primary responsibility for security affairs lies with Division II, specifically with the desk 'East-West Relations, Bilateral Relations with Eastern Europe, the Soviet Union, and North America'. This desk is part of Group 21, which is responsible for coordination with the FO. Group 23, 'Security-political/defense Questions, Disarmament and Arms Control', is a second focus for security affairs within the Chancellor's Office and, in addition, functions as a secretariat for the Federal Security Council. This council is primarily a cabinet committee without a formal organzational structure. The administration has delegated certain tasks to the council (for example, the approval of arms export agreements), but above all it serves as a forum for the formulation of military-political guidelines. It also approves the 'White Papers', the bi-annual reports of the Defense Minister.

A somewhat disputed point is the role of the planning staffs in the various organizations.[13] The planning division of the Chancellor's Office does not engage in conceptual planning in the area of security policy. Its duty lies mainly in the day-to-day planning of government operations. For several years (1970-74), the planning staff in the MoD played an important role in the development and formulation of security policy. This group was created and staffed by the then Defense Minister Helmut Schmidt to provide direct support for his office, especially in dealing with political questions. It was also seen as a counterweight to the essentially military approach dominant throughout the existing structure of the ministry. This planning staff, under the direction of Hans-Georg Wieck, participated directly in German MBFR policy-making, in part through use of the right of concurrence (*Mitzeichnungsrecht* — whereby a second organization is assured an input into policy formation, although primary responsibility remains with the department officially charged with the project) and in part through direct initiatives by the Wieck staff within the government, as well as through public statements. This led to a certain amount of competition within the MoD, as well as between the planning staff of the MoD and the relevant divisions of the FO. At that time, the planning staff of the FO was not engaged in security policy. In 1973, as the problem of appointing a delegation head for the first round of the CSCE in Helsinki arose and Foreign Minister Scheel selected Guido Brunner for this post, it was necessary to find a suitable position at ambassadorial level for him in Bonn. For various reasons it was decided to name Brunner successor to the head of the FO planning staff, who was up for transfer, rather than to make him ambassador-at-large. Similarly, Brunner's successor, Dr Klaus Blech, was made delegation chief at the Geneva CSCE negotiations and head of the planning staff. Primarily, this staff functions as a working staff or cabinet for the Foreign Minister and reports directly to him. Its six-eight staff members, senior civil servants, write speeches, deal with certain important problems which require coordination between different departments, and attempt to develop foreign policy for upcoming issues.

Research and analyses in the area of security affairs are provided by two 'think-tanks': the Research Institute of the Foundation for Science and Policy (*Forschungsinstitut der Stiftung Wissenschaft und Politik*) in Ebenhausen near Munich, a government financed institution working primarily for the FO; and the Armed Forces Planning Staff for Studies and Exercises (*Amt fuer Studien und Uebungen der Bundeswehr*), an agency of the MoD in Bensberg. Within a program outlined by the planning staff of the FO, as well as in response to estimates of upcoming needs made at the institute itself, the *Stiftung Wissenschaft und Politik* prepares research papers on a variety of foreign and security policy topics. These studies are mainly designed to provide desk officers with background information. The professional staff of the institute is also engaged in direct political counseling. Its actual input into the conceptual policy planning process of the administration, however, is somewhat marginal. One exception has been the proposal for a Force Limitation

Agreement as part of the German MBFR policy. The Bensberg group has even less influence. This organization was involved in the German MBFR project through its review of various negotiating options and positions. In addition, detailed operations research studies were developed by its MBFR Working Group in Ottobrunn and its Central Operations Research Group (*Zentrale Operations Research-Stelle*) in Trier.

More significant to the formation of opinion within the government than extensive and detailed research papers have been occasional newspaper articles by such well-informed journalists as Lothar Ruehl, Theo Sommer, and Günter Gillessen. They have been successful both in signaling changes in the international situation and in discussing alternative options.

The proliferation of responsibilities in the area of security policy makes the problem of interagency coordination especially critical. At the working level, three instruments are available for coordination: the telephone, the right of concurrence, and the possibility of establishing interdepartmental working groups. The telephone has proved to be the most effective of these, allowing for personal contact between desk officers or their assistants and their counterparts in other departments or divisions. A good example is, on the MBFR project, the coordination between the arms control desks in the FO and in the MoD. The right of concurrence is also used regularly. In this way, the two desks mentioned above cooperated on the confidence building measures of 'Basket 1' in the CSCE agreements. While the responsibility for the CSCE rested exclusively with the FO, the MoD through its *Mitzeichnungsrecht* was able to insure a defense department input. Similar arrangements have been made with other departments to handle questions of interdepartmental interest regarding the CSCE. Interagency working groups (IMAG) exist, or did exist, for the MBFR as well as for the CSCE negotiations, mostly representing the desks directly involved in the FO, and the Chancellor's Office. The IMAG-MBFR was charged with the development of a common German MBFR position until the fall of 1973, when a joint NATO proposal was adopted. The IMAG-CSCE was created in May 1972 by a Cabinet decision. Altogether, some fifteen departments with an even greater number of working units belong to this group — a total of approximately forty-five persons, chaired by the head of the Political Division of the FO. The success of this group was due to its adept performance as an interdepartmental coordinating organization and to its low personnel turnover. Nevertheless, such groups tend to be exceptions rather than the rule. The *Ressortprinzip*, by which preparatory work and decision-making are largely confined to the agency in charge, as well as the hierarchical structure of the ministries and the resultant autonomy on the part of the individual desks, introduces an element of chance into the exercise of responsibilities. It also contributes to a struggle for influence, fostering competition among the desks and encouraging isolated decision-making. A good example is provided by the nuclear export policy, whereby the negotiations over the treaty with Brazil were handled by the Ministry for Research and Technology (*Bundesministerium für Forschung und Technologie*) with little input by the FO and its disarmament division, which technically is responsible for non-proliferation. As a result of this lack of coordination, security and alliance aspects of the Brazilian project were completely neglected until shortly before the treaty was to be signed. At that point, a thorough review no longer seemed possible without causing considerable trouble with Brazil. This case illustrates the need for a creative and forward-looking planning unit at the Cabinet level.

The legislature and its committees are only marginally involved in the formation and management of security policy.[14] From time to time, they are informed on the progress of international negotiations, and legislators have made some written requests for information from the government. There have been, less than a dozen meetings of the foreign and defense committees on security policy, and during the tenure of the 7th German Bundestag only two debates took place on the floor. Only a few legislators are well informed and follow the negotiations with interest and comprehension. CSCE has domestically been considered within the overall context of 'Ostpolitik', which in turn led to a division of support and opposition along more or less established party lines. MBFR has been regarded by the CDU/CSU opposition with ambivalence. Its position on the negotiations differs from that of the SPD/FDP coalition in the estimation of relative force capabilities and in the assessment of the political possibilities of MBFR. Agreement between government and opposition is limited to the support of the common NATO-MBFR position. In contrast, the determination of force goals is seen as a bipartisan exercise.

Reports in the national press, on the radio, and on television deal mainly with isolated incidents and points of disagreement, although many of the larger magazines and newspapers, as well as the radio and television networks, have knowledgeable journalists. Approximately a dozen of these are members of the small political-academic community of security experts, which also includes a handful of politicians from the

Bundestag parties, a number of university professors, and members from several research institutes. Among these experts close contact is maintained and a regular exchange of ideas takes place. Similar to the decision-making structure within the administration, this community of experts is closely linked with its peers in NATO and other countries. With the exception of the debate over German rearmament in the 1940s, questions of security policy normally are of limited public interest, despite their possibly extensive ramifications for the society as a whole.

TRANSNATIONAL COOPERATION AND DECISION-MAKING STRUCTURES

A study limited to the opinion-formation and decision-making processes within the national system would be incomplete if it did not take into account the high level of integration of the FRG with its international environment.[15] Interdependence exists not only within the framework of such international organizations as the European Community and the North Atlantic Alliance, although there it is particularly strongly developed. A number of important security policy decisions are also taken bilaterally as, e.g., by meetings of heads of government, by bilateral commissions, by regularly scheduled conferences of representatives of the General Staffs of two countries, or by direct contacts between desk officers. Regular contacts also exist between legislators of the Western nations, especially through such organizations as the European Parliament and the Parliamentary Conference of NATO. Finally, the contribution of the mass media with their worldwide range to the internationalization of the opinion-formation process should not be ignored. The overall result has been the evolution of complex transnational cooperation and decision-making structures.

This became more evident in the case of MBFR. For the FRG, MBFR has always been a joint alliance project, despite the fact that the partners have often differed in their goals, interests and expectations. Bonn's MBFR policy has in most instances been directed at NATO or the most important NATO partners, rather than at the Warsaw Pact or its members. Thus MBFR policy has to be seen primarily in the framework of alliance and security policy and only secondarily in that of 'Ostpolitik'. At the same time, it is a component of an overall East-West interaction pattern, whose main actors are the USA and the USSR.

For the conduct of the MBFR negotiations in Vienna, NATO has developed a complex institutional structure. All instructions to the NATO delegations in Vienna are given by the North Atlantic Council (NAC)/Defense Planning Committee (DPC) or by the permanent political organ of the NAC/DPC, the Senior Political Committee (SPC), which acts on behalf of the national governments. The preparation of position papers or the evaluation of negotiating proposals, especially in cases involving military aspects, takes place within the MBFR Working Group, which is under the supervision of the SPC, though chaired by the Deputy Chairman of the Military Committee. In this group, the member nations are represented by civil servants or military officers attached to the permanent missions in Brussels, or by representatives of national FOs or MoDs. Members of the Political Division of the International Staff and members of the International Military Staff function as advisors to the Working Group. The MBFR-Working Group thus constitutes a contact point at the working level for the civil and military elements of the NATO organization as well as for the national governments. Not only can national positions thus be developed in coordination with one another, but also the groundwork for alliance positions can be laid.[16] In Vienna, Western consultation takes place within the ad hoc group, which thus constitutes an extension of the SPC (see Fig. 2).

A similarly complex system of intra-Western coordination exists for the CSCE negotiations. Its focus during the Geneva phase of the talks was the European Political Cooperation Group (EPC — consisting of the nine countries of the European Community)[17] and its CSCE subcommittee, as well as the ad hoc group, which included a member of the EC Commission, and which was responsible for the economic questions of 'Basket 2'. Agreement was also reached within a NATO caucus in accordance with common alliance guidelines, which had been developed within the NAC or the SPC. Questions involving Germany or Berlin were handled by the 'Bonn Group', consisting of representatives of the FRG, France, Great Britain and the United States (see Fig. 3).

Compared to the situation at the MBFR negotiations, the delegations in Geneva had greater freedom of action in relation to the decision-making centers in the national capitals and at Brussels. This was due mainly to two factors: first, the CSCE agreements would not be binding under international law, and, second, the subjects under discussion were complex and broad, involving political, military, legal, economic, and cultural aspects. In order to reach the necessary compromises among the Western delegations, and to successfully negotiate with the neutral and Eastern members of the CSCE on the basis of these positions, coordina-

Figure 2
The NATO MBFR System

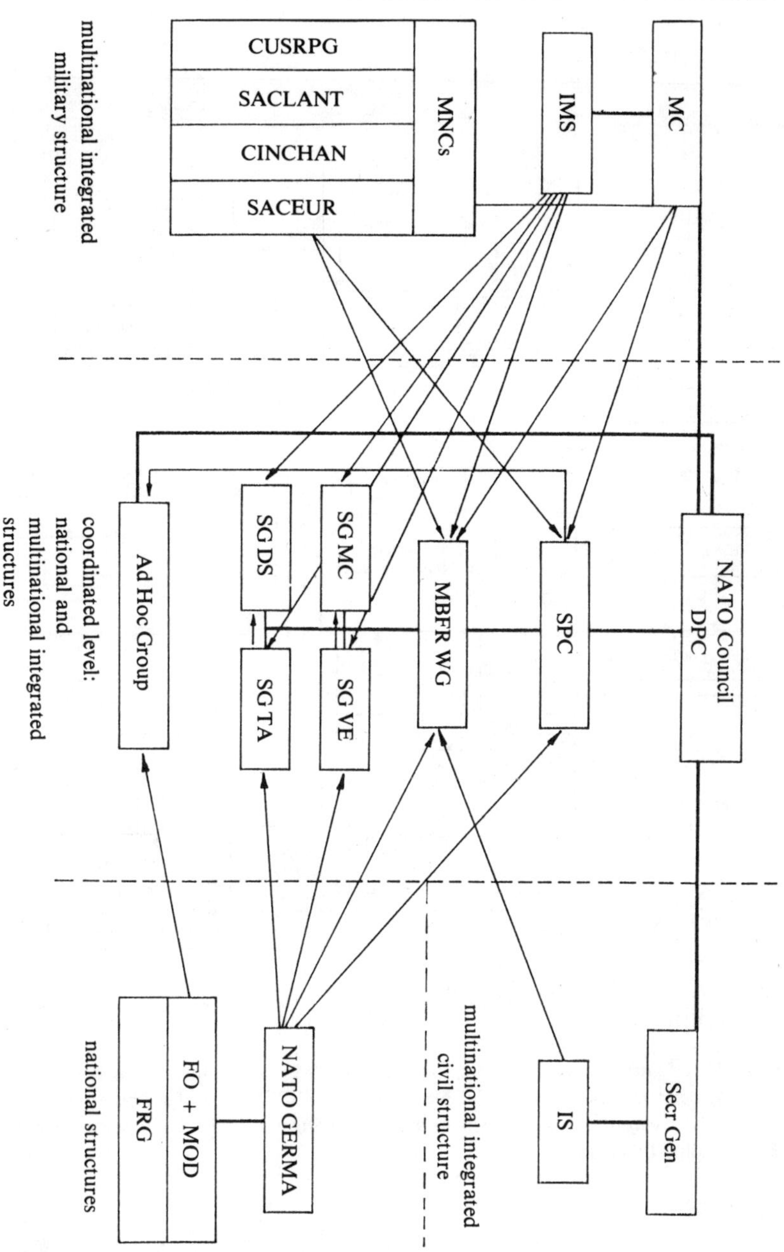

Figure 3
The European Political Cooperation at the CSCE

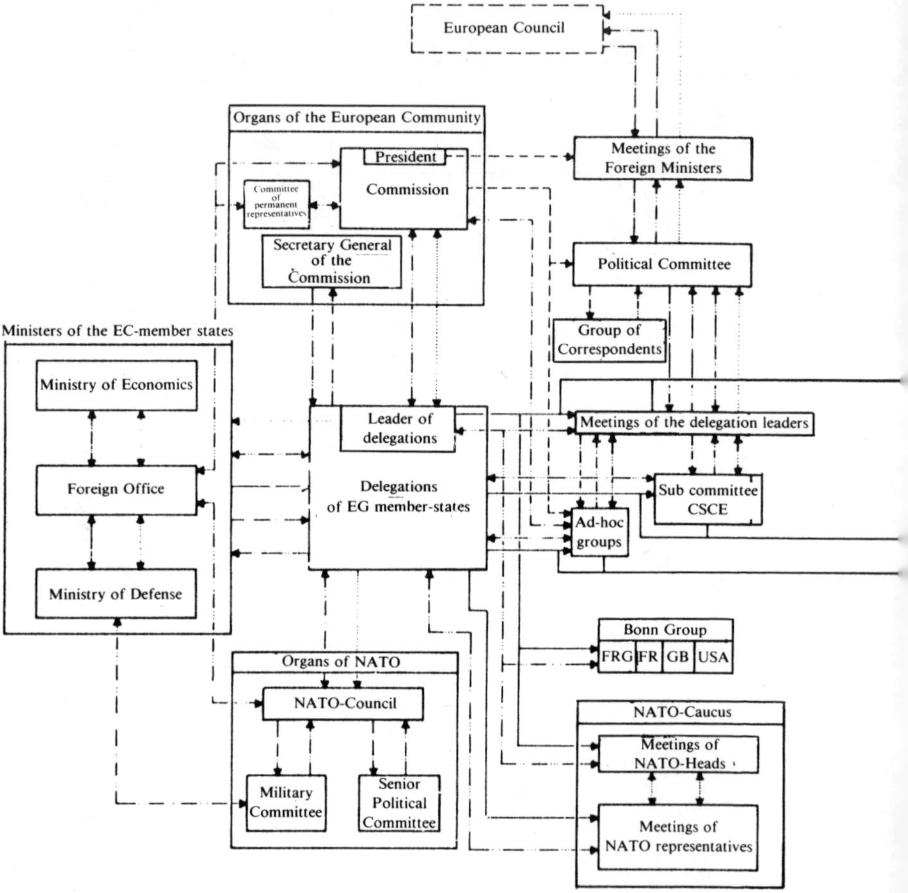

Source: This figure is adapted from that on pp. 90-91 of Hanns-Jürgen Küsters, 'Die aussenpolitische Zusammenarbeit der Neun und die KSZE', in: Helga Haftendorn et al., *Verwaltete Aussenpolitik. Sicherheits-und entspannungspolitische Entscheidungsprozesse in Bonn* (Köln, 1978).

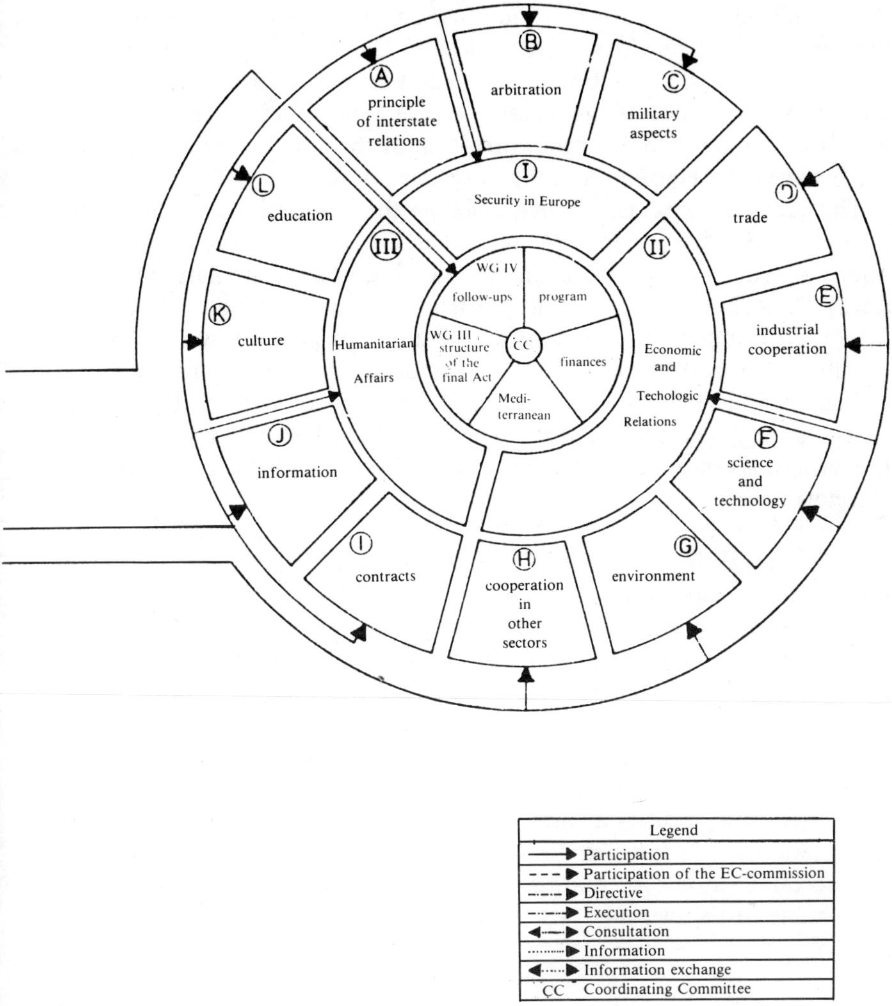
A
principle of interstate relations
B
arbitration
C
military aspects
D
trade
E
industrial cooperation
F
science and technology
G
environment
H
cooperation in other sectors
I
contracts
J
information
K
culture
L
education
I
Security in Europe
II
Economic and Techologic Relations
III
Humanitarian Affairs
WG IV
follow-ups
program
finances
Medi-terranean
WG III structure of the final Act
CC
Legend
Participation
Participation of the EC-commission
Directive
Execution
Consultation
Information
Information exchange
CC Coordinating Committee

tion had to take place in Geneva. The international bodies (EC Council/EPC and the NAC/SPC) as well as the national governments (through their foreign offices) were regularly informed on the status of negotiations. (This took place in addition to reports by the commuting delegation chiefs.) In the final phase of the conference, however, the foreign ministers intervened directly through instructions pertaining to the summit-level conclusion of the CSCE, as well as to various aspects of the agreements. The close coordination on CSCE among the 'Nine' (the EC nations) led to a CSCE result that can be regarded as a joint achievement. The coherence of the position of the Nine was further underlined by a joint 'commentary' or interpretation of the CSCE agreements written between the Helsinki and the Belgrade conferences.

The question remains, however,whether the international bodies (SPC in the case of MBFR and EPC at the CSCE) truly function as planning units, or whether they are primarily clearing houses for national positions. The suspicion that the latter is true is supported by the example of MBFR. All important proposals and changes of position were initiated by alliance members, and the most important coordination took place in bilateral and trilateral discussions. In the case of the CSCE negotiations, the EC had no administrative apparatus. The country which for the term of six months occupied the presidency provided the services of a secretariat.

The influence and latitude of a single nation like the FRG in intra-alliance bargaining processes depends on three factors: the ability to make realistic proposals which are supported by an interdepartmental consensus within the national administration; the status and the personality of the delegates as well as their persuasive ability and their skill in the conduct of negotiations; and the extent to which the national position correlates with that of the most important partners, mostly the United States. Normally — and CSCE was an exception due to the relative disinterest of the United States — Bonn has been most successful in international security affairs when it has concentrated on influencing the positions of its partners (especially the US) to take German interests into account, or on subtly adjusting to these positions, sacrificing as little as possible of its own interests.[18]

THE COORDINATION OF NATIONAL AND INTERNATIONAL PLANNING PROCESSES

The determination of force goals, on the other hand, involves two separate although parallel and extensively coordinated processes in Bonn and Brussels. The size and structure of the Bundeswehr are set by the federal budget, as provided for in Article 87a of the Basic Law, and are determined in accordance with the overall force goals established by the NATO partners. The national force planning exercise produces proposals as to size, structure, and mission of the Bundeswehr in accordance with German alliance policy and the available financial resources. Force planning is based, first, on national defense policy guidelines and the military-strategic concept of the Bundeswehr,[19] and second, on the force proposals for each country, developed within NATO as part of the NATO five-year Force Plan, which is revised every two years. The national planning data of the FRG form an input into the NATO planning process, which eventually results in the determination of NATO force goals. NATO can, however, only make recommendations. Legal limits for the FRG are set by the appropriations granted in the federal budget, which are determined after detailed negotiations between the MoD, the Minister of Finance, and members of the Appropriations Committee of the Bundestag.

In Bonn, the MoD is responsible for all decisions regarding force planning and military-strategic concepts. Coordination with military and political groups in NATO is effected via two channels: one between the MoD and the Military Committee; a second between the FO and the Defense Planning Committee. Within the MoD, the following organizations cooperate on the plans: the Command Staff of the Armed Forces and the Command Staffs of the three services are responsible for the overall concept of military defense; the Budget Division is in charge of finance planning and drawing up a proposal for the defense budget; and the Armament Division handles research, development, and procurement of weapons systems and other armaments. The representation of national interests during the NATO force planning process is the responsibility of the NATO desk within the Political Division of the Command Staff. This desk serves as liaison between the MoD and the NATO Military structure, as well as between the MoD and the planning organizations within the civil organization of the alliance. It is supported by other desk officers of the Armed Forces Staff, by the services' planning staffs, and by the Budget Division. Every major decision must be approved at the political level of the government (*Minister and Staatssekretaere*). The Cabinet as a whole is therefore informed of all important steps in the planning process as decisions on defense policy often have consequences for other departments as well. For example, weapons procurement encroaches upon the responsibilities of the Ministry of Economics, just as questions regarding the stationing of allied troops do in the province of the Finance Ministry. Thus the role of the administration, or of administrative heads, is stronger in the case of force planning than in MBFR or CSCE, because defense plans must be approved annually by the Cabinet, on both budgetary and political merits, in addition to meeting NATO approval. In the international debate on burden sharing and the size of the German defense contribution, Chancellor Schmidt is known to have said 'Not one soldier more than 495,000'.[20] This quote illustrates the importance of political considerations involved in the force planning exercise above and beyond the essentially military aspects, as seen by the MoD, and the alliance needs, as reflected by the FO.

Defense planning within NATO is conducted on the basis of, first, an assessment of the military situation, the consideration of economic factors, and an evaluation of the likely political conditions throughout the period under consideration (e.g. a planning process of two years and a planning period of five years). Second, defense planning is based on the force proposals made by the NATO military commanders, according to military-strategic and operational factors; third, on the NATO force goals, the attainment of which is monitored each year through the use of a Defense Planning Questionnaire. Within NATO, the Defense Planning Committee (DPC) is responsible for NATO planning, supported by the recommendations and review procedures of the Defense Review Committee and the Division of Defense Planning and Policy of the International Staff. A characteristic of alliance defense planning is the high degree of interdependence between civil and military, joint and national elements of the alliance organization. This defense planning cycle leads to the approval of a new five-year plan every two years.[21]

When one compares the two decision-making processes — MBFR and force planning — the low level of coordination between them is striking, especially since essentially the same subject matter — the size and deployment of forces — is under consideration. Within the FRG, MBFR is handled mainly by the arms control desks of the FO and the MoD, while the NATO desks of the two departments are in charge of force planning. Within NATO, the responsibility for the two projects also lies in different organizations. MBFR is under the direction of the SPC and force planning falls within the province of the DPC.

The first opportunity for coordination on the two projects is at the political level. Within the German government, this takes place in the intra-departmental conferences of division heads; and in NATO, in the NAC/DPC. Since the majority of decisions are made at the working level (though within the context of a long-term security policy concept developed by the political leaders), the result is that MBFR policies and force planning are processed essentially in isolation from one another. While national force planning takes place according to established defense policy guidelines (which are formulated by the Planning Staff of the MoD in cooperation with the Command Staff and the Armaments Division and are approved by the Federal Security Council), no comparable framework, such as might be provided by overall security guidelines, has yet been developed to encompass both defense and arms control considerations.

DISADVANTAGES OF THE PRESENT SECURITY POLICY-MAKING SYSTEM

There are a number of liabilities inherent in the security policy-making process in the FRG, which serve to illustrate the conflict between the requirements of interdependence within an international environment and the relatively formal and hierarchical administrative structures of the national government.

— The low level of public interest in security policy, especially in détente policy, results in the confinement of security questions to the sphere of 'experts'. (There is apparently more public interest in defense policies as such, or for 'straight' *Ostpolitik*.)

— The high level of bureaucratization and compartmentalization within the departments. The concentration of decision-making at the working level insures a high problem-solving capacity for routine matters, but at the same time narrows the flow of information and the strategies available. The result is a tendency to produce solutions to problems rather than to develop political options. Many possible alternatives are excluded from the decision-making process without being seriously considered.

— The work load of each staff member is heavy, which necessitates a selective processing of information. Research papers are either totally disregarded or only superficially studied. The majority of scholars are unable to tailor their analyses to the operational needs of the practice-oriented staff members.

— The system of job rotation hinders the development of expertise within the bureaucracy. Since every new staff member must start essentially from scratch, a transition period, characterized by repetition and amateurishness, is often inevitable. This disadvantage, however, is somewhat offset by the fact that security policy is not wholly in the hands of narrow-minded experts.

— A primarily legal or military disposition on the part of many staff members leads to a certain narrowness of approach, either decidedly legalistic (in contrast to the more pragmatic approach of the alliance partners) or dominated by threat perceptions and thus emphasizing relative force capabilities. Many staff members have little international experience before assuming their duties in this highly interdependent transnational setting.

— The lack of high-level planning and coordinative structures, justified by the fact that the FRG cannot pursue an independent security policy, is also due to the historical and political traditions of departmentalization and interdepartmental competition. It impedes the constructive adaptation of national interests to alliance policies, hinders the determination of national priorities, and leads to the neglect of adequate, forward-looking security policy planning.

The decision-making system of the FRG in the area of security affairs is thus characterized, first, by the dichotomy between the constitutional system, anchored in the Basic Law, and the functional, problem-oriented system which has developed alongside and is superimposed upon the formal structure, in response to the need to increase the problem-solving capacity above and beyond that offered within the formal framework. The second important point concerns the complexity of security policy and its myriad political, economic, and social aspects, a result of the growing interdependence of the foreign policy decision-making processes in the Western industrial nations. Although the FRG is aware of, and has accepted, her limited international freedom of action in the area of security and détente affairs, she has not yet fully taken account of this growing complexity, and certainly has yet to master it.

NOTES

1. This article offers some preliminary findings of a research project which has been conducted by a group of scholars at the Hochschule der Bundeswehr in Hamburg. The results of this project have been published under the title *Verwaltete Aussenpolitik. Sicherheits und entspannungspolitische Entscheidungsprozesse in Bonn* by Helga Haftendorn, Wolf-Dieter Karl, Joachim Krause and Lothar Wilker, Verlag Wissenschaft und Politik (Köln, 1978). An earlier, German version has been published under the title: 'Management der Sicherheitspolitik. Ein Beitrag zum Entscheidungsprozess der Bundesrepublik Deutschland', in: Klaus-Dieter Schwarz (ed.), *Sicherheitspolitik* (Bad Honnef 1977), pp. 339-355.

The author would like to express her appreciation for the many suggestions which she received on the draft of this article to her colleagues at Hamburg, and to a number of staff members — military and civilian — in the *Bundeskanzleramt*, in the *Auswärtiges Amt* and in the *Bundesministerium der Verteidigung*, as well as at the German Mission in Brussels and the MBFR Delegation in Vienna.

2. For a discussion of 'penetrated systems' see James N. Rosenau, 'Pre-Theories and Theories of Foreign Policy', in: *The Scientific Study of Foreign Policy* (New York and London 1971), pp. 95ff; and Wolfram F. Hanrieder, 'Compatibility and Consensus: A Proposal for the Conceptual Linkage of External and Internal Dimensions of Foreign Policy', in: Wolfram F. Hanrieder, *Comparative Foreign Policy* (New York 1971), pp. 242ff.

3. For a discussion of détente policy, see Helga Haftendorn, *Abrüstungs und Entspannungspolitik zwischen Sicherheitsbefriedigung und Friedenssicherung. Zur Aussenpolitik der Bundesrepublik Deutschland 1955-1973* (Düsseldorf 1974); see also Ruediger Juette (ed.), *Détente and Peace in Europe* (Frankfurt/New York 1977).

The complementary nature of defense and détente policies was emphasized for the first time in the 'Harmel Report' of 14 December 1967, which dealt with the future tasks of the NATO alliance. This joint goal appeared in the 1970 White Paper as an official German position.

4. This point was well taken by Chancellor Schmidt in his 1977 Alastair Buchan

Memorial Lecture. See *Survival*, January/February 1978, pp. 2-10.

5. Richard Löwenthal, 'Freiheit der Eigenentwicklung', in: *Aussenpolitische Perspektiven des westdeutschen Staates*, Vol. 1: *Das Ende des Provisoriums* (München/Wien 1971), pp. 11ff. Concerning the goals of security policy, see the article by Dieter Mahncke, 'Die Sicherheitspolitik der Bundesrepublik Deutschland', in: Klaus-Dieter Schwarz (ed.), *Sicherheitspolitik* (Bad Honnef 1976), pp. 307ff.

6. For a discussion of the military-strategic doctrine of NATO, see Helge Hansen, 'Militaerstrategische Konzepte', in: Karl Carstens and Dieter Mahncke, *Westeuropaeische Verteidigungskooperation* (München/Wien 1972), pp. 56ff, as well as the article by Klaus-Dieter Schwarz, 'Die sicherheitspolitische und militärstrategische Zukunft der NATO', in: Schwarz, op. cit. note 1, pp. 263ff. The Ministerial Guidance 1975 is printed in the Annex to the Communiqué of the Ministers' Conference of the Defense Planning Committee of NATO, 22 and 23 May 1975, in Brussels, see *NATO — Facts and Figures* (Brussels 1976), pp. 344-349.

7. For a discussion of the developmental history of MBFR and CSCE, see Haftendorn, op. cit. note 3; Christoph Bertram, 'Mutual Force Reductions in Europe: The Political Aspects', *Adelphi Papers No. 84* (London 1972); Lothar Rühl, 'Beiderseitige Truppenverminderungen in Europa. Grundlagen, Moeglichkeiten und Grenzen von MBFR-Verhandlungen', in: *Europa-Archiv* 10/1973, pp. 325ff; ibid., 'Die Truppenabbauverhandlung und die Europaeische Sicherheit zwischen 1973 und 1976', in: Karl Kaiser and Karl Markus Kreis (eds.), *Sicherheitspolitik vor neuen Aufgaben* (Frankfurt 1977), pp. 103ff; Lothar Rühl, 'Origines et perspectives de la negociation de Vienne sur les MFR', in: *defense nationale*, 12/1975, pp. 69ff; Götz von Groll, 'Ost-West-Gespraeche in Helsinki', in: *Aussenpolitik* 9/1972, pp. 513ff; ibid., 'Die Helsinki-Konsultationen', in: *Aussenpolitik* 2/1973, pp. 123ff; ibid., 'Die Aussenminister in Helsinki', in: *Aussenpolitik* 3/1973, pp. 255ff; ibid., 'Die Genfer KSZE-Verhandlungen', in: *Aussenpolitik* 2/1974, pp. 159ff; ibid., 'Die KSZE—Debatte im Deutschen Bundestag', in: *Aussenpolitik* 4/1974, pp. 375ff; ibid., 'Die Schlussakte der KSZE', in: *Aussenpolitik* 3/1975; ibid., 'Die KSZE und die Europaeische Gemeinschaft', in: *Aussenpolitik* 3/1976; Karl E. Birnbaum, 'Die Konferenz ueber Sicherheit und Zusammenarbeit in Europa: eine Zwischenbilanz der Genfer Kommissionsphase', *Arbeitspapiere zur Internationalen Politik der DGAP*, No. 2 (Bonn 1974).

8. The phrase 'functional innovative processes' indicates new processes which evolve gradually as a result of pressure caused by an unsolved problem; they are not official organizational structures. For an introduction to the functions and problems of the ministerial bureaucracy, as well as bibliographical references to further literature on the subject, see Günther Schmid and Herbert Treiber, *Bürokratie und Politik* (München 1975).

9. A possible exception lies in the area of military conscription, and the right of conscientious objection, as well as in the particular sensitivity in the Bundeswehr to political incidents. This was demonstrated in late 1976 by the case of Generals Krupinski and Franke. See the article by Christian Potyka, 'Die vernachlässigte Öffentlichkeit', in: *Sicherheitspolitik vor neuen Aufgaben*, op. cit. note 7, pp. 365ff. On the role of the Bundestag and the political parties, see Reinhold Roth, *Aussenpolitische Innovation und politische Herrschaftssicherung* (Meisenheim 1976), as well as Heribert Schatz, *Der parlamentarische Entscheidungsprozess* (Meisenheim 1970).

10. For a critical discussion of the goals and functions of the arms policy, see Carola Bielfeldt, *Rüstungsausgaben und Staatsinterventionismus. Das Beispiel der Bundesrepublik Deutschland 1950-1971*, Gesellschaftswissenschaftliche Diss. (Frankfurt 1976); Peter

Schlotter, *Rüstungspolitik in der Bundesrepublik. Die Beispiele Starfighter und Phantom* (Frankfurt 1975). On decision-making patterns in the area of arms transfer policy, see Helga Haftendorn, *Militärhilfe und Rüstungsexporte der BRD* (Düsseldorf 1971).

11. This development can be easily traced with the help of the various editions of the book by Thomas Ellwein, *Das Regierungssystem der Bundesrepublik Deutschland* (Köln and Opladen 1963, 1965, 1973, 1977) as well as in: Thomas Ellwein, *Regieren und Verwalten* (Opladen 1976). See, in addition, Renate Mayntz and Fritz W. Scharpf, *Policy-Making in the German Federal Bureaucracy* (Amsterdam 1975).

12. See Haftendorn, op. cit. note 3, pp. 79ff.

13. For a discussion of the role of planning staffs see Guido Brunner, 'Wozu Außenpolitischen Planungsstab?' in: *Aussenpolitik* 7/1972, pp. 546ff; Swidbert Schnippenkötter, 'Planung in der Außenpolitik', in: *Aus der Schule der Diplomatie. Festschrift für Peter Pfeiffer* (Düsseldorf 1965), pp. 161ff.

14. On the role of the Bundestag in the foreign policy decision-making process, see Ernst Majonica, 'Bundestag und Außenpolitik', in: Hans-Peter Schwarz (ed.), *Handbuch der deutschen Außenpolitik* (München und Zürich 1975); Günther Patz, *Parlamentarische Kontrolle der Außenpolitik* (Meisenheim 1975); Reinhold Roth, *Parteiensystem und Außenpolitik* (Meisenheim 1973).

15. This is a weakness of most political science and administrative science treatments. See Mayntz and Scharpf, op. cit. note 11, or Winfried Steffani, *Parlamentarismus ohne Transparenz* (Opladen 1973).

16. On the decision-making process in NATO, see Wilfried Hofmann, 'Die Beteiligung der Bundesrepublik Deutschland an den Entscheidungsprozessen der NATO', in: *Regionale Verflechtung der Bundesrepublik Deutschland. Empirische Analysen und theoretische Probleme* (München and Wien 1973), pp. 143ff.

17. For a discussion of the various forms of West European cooperation see the articles by Ulrich Everling, Ernst-Ulrich Junker, Reinhold Lohrmann and Theodor Holtz, in:. *Regionale Verflechtung*, op. cit. note 16, as well as the articles by Helge Hansen and Jürgen Schwarz, and Thomas Jansen in: Karl Carstens and Dieter Mahncke (eds.), *Westeuropäische Verteidigungskooperation* (München and Wien 1972).

18. On the effects of transnational interdependence on the foreign policy and political system of the FRG, see Karl Kaiser and Roger Morgan (eds.), *Strukturwandlungen der Aussenpolitik in Grossbritannien und der Bundesrepublik* (München and Wien 1970); Forschungsinstitut der Deutschen Gesellschaft für Auswärtige Politik (ed.), *Aussenpolitische Perspeektiven des Westdeutschen Staates*, 3 vols (München and Wien 1972).

19. See *Weissbuch 1973/1974* (Bonn 1974), pp. 29ff.

20. See Zeichen setzen, in: *Der Spiegel*, No. 1-2/1977, pp. 18ff.

21. On force goal planning, especially within the NATO alliance, see *NATO Facts and Figures* (Brussels 1976), pp. 111-115.

2

MODELL DEUTSCHLAND AND THE INTERNATIONAL DIVISION OF LABOUR:

The Federal Republic of Germany in the World Political Economy

Frieder Schlupp

INTRODUCTION

DURING THE 1970s, marked by the lasting 'second crisis of the world economy in this century' and by accelerated structural changes of the world political system, the international economic position and internal situation of the Federal Republic of Germany (FRG) has received substantial mass media attention, growing international economic relevance and political importance in the capitalist world economy and in world politics in general, and in Western European affairs in particular.

As a 'model' or 'nightmare', as an 'economic superpower' or 'political dwarf', as an 'island of stability' or a factor of international destabilization; as a privileged, 'bigemonic' American (junior) partner or principal, 'antagonist' American ally and competitor, West Germany has provoked heated and controversial evaluations in Western Europe and overseas with respect to her international economic position and domestic sociopolitical situation.

In this chapter an attempt will be made to elaborate, in a brief and simplified manner, analytical perspectives and empirical evidence for the investigation of West Germany's recent role and position in the intercapitalist division of labour.[1]

Section 1 begins with a short tour d'horizon (or rather tour de force) roughly outlining the contemporary global setting for West Germany's international economic position and political role. It continues with an account of the recent controversies about West Germany's role in Western Europe and in Euro-American affairs. The section concludes with a conceptual framework for the theoretical and empirical analysis of the inter-capitalist division of labour, and with a rudimentary operationalization. This should enable us to describe and explain basic historical patterns and structural dimensions of West Germany's specific 'model' of national accumulation and its relative position in the contemporary hierarchy of the capitalist world economy.

Section 2 is devoted to the presentation of empirical evidence illuminating various crucial aspects of the West German position in the inter-capitalist hierarchy of specialization and development, underlining the relative 'over-industrialization' and extreme world market orientation, the high level of inter- and de-nationalization as well as the high degree of concentration and centralization of capital.

Special reference will be made to the international position of the West German economy in the Western European system as well as in the capitalist world markets for capital goods industries. Together with considerable capacities for economic modernization and technological innovation, these aspects are viewed as the cornerstone of West Germany's relative strength and leading role in the capitalist world economy.

In section 3, some consequences of the West German international economic position for domestic politics are briefly outlined, many of which tend to lead to the proliferation of structural economic crisis and at least latent political conflicts.

In spite of, as well as because of West Germany's leading position in the inter-capitalist division of labour, the dynamics and dialectics of capitalist world market competition are expected to generate structural external dilemmas and internal contradictions for the reproduction of the German 'model'. Both 'stabilization' and 'modernization' strategies designed to overcome these dilemmas and contradictions will be shown to increase domestic as well as international conflicts.

Because of recent socio-economic and political changes in the capitalist world economy, and especially in Western Europe, the transformation of domestic socio-political relations, and the transition of foreign economic and political relations are deemed necessary to overcome the structural 'stability- and domination-dilemmas' of West Germany, and the corresponding destabilization- and dependence-dilemmas of other Western European societal formations.

The *Modell Deutschland* has meanwhile become a cardinal problem for the economic restructuring and political reorganization of Western European as well as Euro-American affairs. As recent scenarios of Western European 'futures' indicate, it has become a structural problem for strategies of Atlanticist cooperation as well as Euro-Capitalist integration, for bourgeois strategies of national independence as well as for reformist strategies of national autonomy in Western Europe. The longer the more, it will also become a structural problem for itself because of its internal contradictions and external dilemmas. Both developments indeed may converge in what could be properly called the 'new' (West) German problem and the 'new' (West) German question.

I.1 WORLD ECONOMY IN CRISIS, AND WORLD POLITICS IN TRANSITION — FROM THE 'PAX AMERICANA' TO A 'NEW' INTERNATIONAL ORDER?

The contemporary structural changes in all the main 'conflict formations of the world society' make the 1970s a period of global socio-economic and political transformation where the final 'end' of the post-war system — the era of 'Pax Americana' — and the gradual emergence of a 'new' global system based on a new diversity of international hierarchies seem to mutually interweave and overlap each other. With respect to the so-called North-South conflict, demands for a New International Economic Order[2] as well as real tendencies toward a 'new' international division of labour[3] imply not only an immediate adaption and long-term restructuring of the economic relationships between the underdeveloped capitalist peripheries and the developed capitalist centres of the world economy.

The growing international economic importance and political relevance of certain 'newcomer' nations in the Third World — the world's 'new middle class' of industrializing 'threshold' and 'nouveau riche' oil-countries also poses the problem of how to 'integrate' these new peripheral power centres into the institutional and procedural 'system' of international politics and policy making.

In the framework of East-West relations, the politics of detente and inter-systemic economic-technological cooperation have led to a significant expansion of East-West economic exchange. Increasingly, both Eastern and Western strategies seem to be oriented toward a structural reorganization of East-West competitive coexistence; eventually implying even a gradual re-integration of the Eastern system of international economic specialization and exchange into the capitalist world market.[4]

The recent 'second crisis of the world economy in this century' has also further accelerated structural changes in the inter- and intra-national power constellations of the developed capitalist centres of the world economy, and in world politics. From about 1967 on, in the course of only one decade, Euro-American and Japanese-American politico-economic relations have undergone remarkable transformations. They have been accompanied by substantial shifts in the balance of internal societal forces in the US, Japan and Western Europe which have left deep marks in domestic politics, indicated by growing socio-political polarizations.[5]

During this short time span, the turbulent economic developments and contradictory political tendencies of the inter-capitalist division of labour have increasingly cast doubts on the hegemonial role and dominating position of the US in 'metropolitan capitalism'. Western European fears of the growing US challenge of technological 'colonization' in the late 1960s[6] have only in the last decade been superseded in connection with Vietnam and Watergate, the Dollar crisis and the apparent erosion of US economic-technological superiority and political-military supremacy by growing European (and also Japanese) hopes of catching up, and even overtaking the US as a world political partner and rival.[7]

Following the Nixon-Kissinger shocks in US foreign economic policy and the accentuated emphasis on bipolar (or tripolar) relations with the Soviet Union and the People's Republic of China, fears of a global politico-diplomatic and military-strategic condominium have again replaced earlier, more hopeful European visions of Euro-American political partnership and economic rivalry in relative equality. Since the oil crisis and during the lasting world economic crisis, the higher structural vulnerability of the Japanese and Western European economies has led to perceptions of the US, in spite of large and lasting trade deficits, and of American concern over decreasing international competitiveness, in a more or less reconsolidated position of economic domination and political hegemony.

While the position of the US may have somewhat declined in relative terms, limiting the American capacity for strictly unilateral hegemonic strategies, the US — because of its persisting economic weight and political importance in international politico-economic affairs — can still successfully 'require the rest of the world to help to solve any problems that arise from the seeming weakness of the US economy'.[8]

Thus there is a considerable agreement about the gradual termination of the post-war 'Pax Americana'. While total US domination may belong to the recent past, the US still remains the central, dominating and hegemonial power, capable of persuading, or forcing, 'the rest of the (capitalist) world' into dependent strategies of 'cooperative' world political 'management' and world economic 'burden sharing' according to American priorities.[9] The Carter Administration, in particular, has stressed the necessity for such a 'sharing' of international political 'responsibilities' and economic and financial burdens in the framework of a 'trilateral' cooperation between the US, Western Europe and Japan because of the envisaged end of (absolute) US domination and hegemony.[10] The relative increases in Western European and Japanese economic capacities and political potentials are here seen, along with the increasing international importance of the world's 'new middle class' in the Third World, as the principal elements of a postulated 'new' world economic and political diversity, as an indication of a new and far more complex international hierarchy in comparison to the post-war era.

Therefore, whereas the traditional forms and functions of Atlanticist cooperation may have become undermined by the political conflicts and economic changes of the past decade, the developing 'trilateralism' is seen not only as a new and adequate expression of the new international diversity in hierarchy in Euro-American affairs, but also as an adequate political form to cope with the lasting international economic crises and political transformations.

I.2 WESTERN EUROPE AND THE CRISIS OF THE WORLD ECONOMY: FROM 'EURO-CAPITALIST' INTEGRATION TO WEST GERMAN DOMINATION?

As the recent developments of Japanese-American relations indicate, there is a wide and broadening gap between trilateralist ideologies and reality. As partners and rivals caught in conflictive economic competition and political cooperation, only Japan's continuing structural dependence on the US appears to prevent, at least for the time being, an open clash between the 'antagonistic allies'.[11]

Although the Euro-American relationship is far more complicated, quite similar conflicts and structural contradictions seem to mark its two pillars — Atlanticist cooperation and European 'unification'.[12] During the past decade, conflicts and tensions between Europe and the US have preoccupied public attention and political perceptions. The erosion of the socio-economic and political bases of traditional Atlanticist cooperation has led to mourning over the (legendary) 'Atlantis Lost'.[13] Only recently, however, do the structural intra-national economic heterogenizations, political polarizations, and societal factionalizations within the Western European system seem to have gained the political, and also analytical, attention they deserve.[14]

As a direct effect of the world economic crisis, an international synchronization of inflation, rising unemployment and severe payments imbalances characterizes the contemporary situation of Western Europe in general and — with significant modifications — also that of each national economy. But in this context, precisely these significant international differences should not be ignored. The divergencies of national economic trends and socio-political prospects do in fact cause a deep and structural international discrepancy in terms of economic stability and political cohesion among the national economies in Western Europe which have, however, turned out to be very durable during the conflict and crises ridden period beginning in the late 1960s.[15]

Also in the 'integrative' context of the EEC, international divergence, instead of convergence, international hierarchies of domination and dependence instead of symmetrical constellations of interdependence mark the actual situation. Even in official evaluations the EEC is described as an 'international class society' (EEC Commissioner Haferkamp) because of the severe international discrepancies between the many 'problem' and deficit-countries, on one hand, and the few more or less stable surplus-countries, on the other (see Table 1).[16]

The superior weight and technological lead of the West German economy in the framework of the EEC in particular has evidently reached a level which prohibits the maintenance of the still cherished image of the EEC as a well balanced regional system of economic integration and political interdependence. The West German economy alone accounts for more than one-third of the total EEC GNP. Its central position in the EEC trade network surpasses that of the US and Japan taken together in the OECD area. Its trade surplusses and currency reserves in the 1970s are the highest in the world, and overshadow the trade balances and currency situations of the other Western European countries. The strong international position of the DM indeed transforms the European 'currency snake' into nothing more than a defacto DM reptile. The financial contributions to the EEC budget on the part of the West German Government accounted in 1976 for over 80% of the total net financial transfers between the member countries. In addition, West German

TABLE 1
The EEC in the World Economic Crisis: International Divergencies of National Economic Developments in the 1970s

Country/ area	GDP-annual change in % volume terms				Implicit prices, private consumption, annual % change				Unemployment in % of total workforce				Unit labour costs annual changes in %			
	1970/ 1974	1975	1976	1977	1970/ 1974	1975	1976	1977	1970/ 1974	1975	1976	1977	1970/ 1974	1975	1976	1977
FRG	3.6	-2.6	5.7	3.0	5.8	6.3	4.4	4.0	1.1	4.1	4.1	4.0	9.5	7.0	1.7	4.0
France	5.1	0.1	5.2	2.8	8.3	11.6	9.9	9.0	2.7	4.0	4.4	5.4	13.4	17.6	9.7	9.1
Great Britain	2.5	-1.7	1.6	0.5	7.5	23.6	15.3	15.3	2.8	3.9	5.2	5.9	21.3	32.9	12.1	10.0
Italy	4.1	-3.5	5.6	2.0	8.7	17.6	17.5	18.5	(5.2)*	(5.6)*	(5.9)*	(6.8)*	20.7	25.6	16.1	20.3
Netherlands	4.7	-1.1	4.4	2.5	8.0	10.3	9.2	7.3	2.1	4.0	4.3	4.3	11.5	14.3	6.0	5.5
Belgium	5.2	-2.0	3.0	2.8	6.3	12.1	9.0	7.3	2.3	4.5	6.1	6.9	14.6	16.2	6.9	6.3
Luxenbourg	4.1	-8.4	2.7	1.3	6.0	10.7	9.8	7.0	0.0	0.2	0.4	0.5	21.8	23.7	5.6	8.2
Denmark	2.9	-1.1	4.8	1.0	7.9	8.8	8.5	10.5	1.3	5.0	5.1	6.2	17.0	13.7	8.8	6.0
Ireland	3.6	0.4	3.2	5.0	10.8	21.8	17.0	14.0	5.9	7.9	9.4	9.6	18.2	29.2	14.3	10.0
EEC	4.0	-1.8	4.7	2.5	7.8	12.8	9.9	9.5	(2.8)*	(4.4)*	(4.9)*	(5.5)*	15.5	17.4	7.6	8.5
Maximum spreads	2.7	8.8	4.1	4.5	5.0	17.3	13.1	14.5	5.9	7.7	9.0	9.1	12.3	25.9	14.4	16.3

Source: Author's own calculations based on data from EEC Commission, *Annual Economic Report,* October 1977.

* According to national data underestimating significantly the effective volume of unemployment.

credits and other financial aids to Western European countries have established the FRG as the major creditor country and 'Europayer'.[17]

For many observers, the FRG has become the *économie dominante*[18] in Western Europe. Today, this dominating position of the West German economy increasingly attracts a degree of political attention which had been reserved, at least until very recently, exclusively for the US.

Closely connected with a tendency toward a deepened international politico-economic hierarchization in Western Europe, most clearly reflected in the dominating position of the FRG, tendencies toward increased intra-national economic heterogenization, societal factionalization and political polarization have also become highly visible and consequential in Western Europe, particularly in Western European 'problem'- and deficit-countries.

Evidently, the lasting international economic crisis has deepened the existing socio-political cleavages and confrontations within most Western European countries. The many national governmental, even systemic crises, particularly in Italy and France, seem to reflect — beyond purely short-term difficulties — fundamental shifts in the societal relations of forces which openly threaten the systemic stability and political legitimacy of the national bourgeois power blocs.

In Southern Europe, these tendencies have converged in the emergence of a rather new kind of transnational Western European confrontation between the established 'Euro-Capitalist' system on one side, and the rising 'Euro-Socialist' and 'Euro-Communist' perspectives and political groupings on the other.

These changes in the internal societal constellations, opening up possibilities of new political affiliations and coalitions in party politics and government, have gained a political relevance transcending to some extent the purely national context. The recent formal coalitions and informal party alliances show this clearly: although conflict- and crisis-ridden, the Left in France, a possible 'historic compromise' in Italy, ambivalent affiliations and coalitions as well as changing power blocs in Portugal, Spain, and Greece may be viewed as components of a new, and qualitatively different transnational societal situation in Western Europe. They even point to the latent possibility of future 'Euro-Socialist' policies at the international level, thus confronting the 'Euro-Capitalist' status quo with alternative domestic policies and, subsequently, with new options for foreign policies and international politics in Western Europe.[19]

I.3 'MODEL' OR 'NIGHTMARE'? WEST GERMANY IN THE 1970s — AMBIGUITIES AND CONTROVERSIES OF AN 'ISLAND OF STABILITY'

At first glance, the FRG must indeed appear as a rather exceptional case in the recent global setting as well as in the regional Western European system. In spite of her below average real growth rates in the years following the oil crisis (see Tale 2), West Germany is nevertheless praised abroad as well as at home as an extraordinary 'economic miracle' and unique 'island of stability', as an exceptional 'export wonder' and a rare 'surplus country'. Compared with the other major developed capitalist economies, the West German performance in terms of inflation rates and (real) unit labour costs (see Table 3.1) and in terms of trade and payments balances (see Tables 3.2 and 3.3), indeed makes the FRG (and to a certain extent also Japan) appear as a somewhat deviant national case in any international economic comparison.

TABLE 2
Real Growth in Major Capitalist Developed Countries, 1974-1978

	GNP at constant prices: annual changes in %					
Country	**1974**	**1975**	**1976**	**1977**	**1978**	**cumulated 1974-1978**
FRG	+0.7	-2.5	+5.7	+2.5	+2.5	+9.4
France	+2.3	-1.4	+5.2	+2.5	+2.5	+11.1
Great Britain	+0.3	-2.0	+1.4	+0.5	+2.0	+2.2
Italy	+3.9	-3.5	+5.6	+1.0	+2.0	+9.0
USA	-1.6	-1.6	+6.1	+4.5	+3.5	+10.9
Japan	-1.1	+2.4	+6.3	+5.5	+5.5	+18.6
All capitalist developed countries	-0.1	-1.3	+5.5	+4.0	+3.5	+11.6

Sources: 1974-1976 OECD and national data, 1977 and 1978, estimates according to RWI, Essen; see *Handelsblatt,* 11 November 1977, 2.

TABLE 3.1
West Germany as a National 'Island of Stability': International Comparison of Inflation Rates and Annual Changes of Real Unit Labour Costs in Major Capitalist Industrialized Countries (in percent)

Country/area	Yearly inflation rates					Annual changes: real unit labour costs		
	1975	1976	1977*	1978*	1975/ 1978	1976	1977**	1978**
Capitalist industrialized countries	9.0	8.1	8.0	7.0	8.0	7.3	7.5	7.0
FRG	5.4	4.0	4.0	3.5	4.2	1.3	4.5	3.0
USA	7.1	4.7	6.8	5.7	6.1	5.1	5.5	6.0
Japan	8.2	10.6	7.0	6.0	8.0	6.0	6.0	5.5
France	9.6	9.9	9.0	10.0	9.6	9.6	8.5	8.0
Great Britain	24.9	15.1	14.0	12.0	16.5	11.5	10.5	11.5

*Estimates according to Morgan Guaranty Trust.
**Estimates according to Deutsches Institut für Wirtschaftsforschung.
Sources: USIS-Amerika Dienst, No. 32 (14 Dec. 1977) and: *DIW-Wochenberichte*, 3-4/1978.

TABLE 3.2
West Germany as a 'Surplus Country': International Comparison of Trade Balances of Major Capitalist Industrialized Countries

Country	Trade balances (Billion $)				
	1974-1976	1977*	1978*	1977-1978*	1974-1978
FRG	+57.1	+21.0	+23.0	+44.0	+101.0
USA	-5.4	-30.0	-35.0	-65.0	-70.4
Japan	+15.6	+17.0	+15.0	+32.0	+47.6
France	+1.8	-2.8	-2.0	-4.8	-3.0
Great Britain	-24.6	-4.0	-2.5	-6.5	-31.1

*Estimates according to Morgan Guaranty Trust.
Sources: International Economic Report of the President, 1977; OECD; *USIS-Amerika-Dienst*, No. 32.

TABLE 3.3
West Germany as a 'Surplus Country': International Comparison of Currency Reserves and Current Balances of Major Capitalist Industrialized Countries

Country	Currency reserves in % world total			Current Balances billion $					
	1974	1975	1976	1974	1975	1976	1977*	1978*	1974-1978
FRG	14.7	13.6	13.5	+9.7	+3.8	+3.0	+2.5	+2.5	+21.5
USA	7.3	7.0	7.1	-0.9	+11.7	-0.6	-14.0	-13.0	-16.8
Japan	6.1	5.6	6.4	-4.7	-0.7	+3.7	+7.0	+4.5	+9.8
France	4.0	5.5	3.8	-6.0	-0.1	-6.1	-4.3	-3.3	-19.8
Great Britain	3.1	2.4	2.6	-8.7	-3.7	-2.7	0.0	+2.5	-12.6

*OECD Estimates July 1977.
Sources: OECD; IMF; author's calculations.

Moreover, considering the deep societal conflicts and manifest political confrontations in many other Western European 'problem' countries, the apparent stability of the FRG has abroad induced flattering perceptions of West Germany as an exemplary socio-economic and political 'model' combining economic strength and competitiveness with societal cohesion and domestic political balance.[20]

With the third largest GNP in the capitalist world and the second largest trade volume; with the highest trade volumes in manufactured and industrial goods; with the highest shares in important sectoral and regional segments of the world market, the West German economy must indeed appear as a world economic 'superpower'[21] (see Tables 4.1 and 4.2).

Because of the growing economization of international politics and the corresponding politicization of international economics, the FRG — formerly seen as an 'economic giant', yet a 'political dwarf' — also seems to have become a (perhaps not so 'timid') world political 'giant',[22] gradually outgrowing its earlier role as a 'free rider' in the shadow, and under the umbrella, of unilateral US hegemony.

Today, West Germany plays a much more active and visible international role not only in Western European affairs but also in Euro-American and trilateral relations. According to American, and trilateral

TABLE 4.1
The 'Trilateral' Powers in the World Economy: Indicators of Absolute and Relative Relevance

Country	GNP	(1975) Exports	% Share in world total GNP	% Share in world total Exports	Foreign direct (1975) investment	% Share in world total	Trade balances 1974/76	Trade balances 1977/8	Current balances 1974/76	Current balances 1977/8	% Share in world total currency reserves
	(Billion $)		(%)		(Billion $)	(%)	(Billion $)		(Billion $)		(%)
USA	1516	107.2	24.5	11.8	133.2	52.0	—5.4	—65.0	+10.3	—27.0	7.0
FRG	423	90.1	6.8	9.9	16.0	6.3	+57.1	+44.0	+16.5	+5.0	13.6
Japan	488	54.8	7.9	6.0	15.9	6.2	+15.6	+32.0	—1.7	+11.5	5.6
1-3	2427	252.1	39.2	27.7	165.1	64.5	+67.3	+11.0	+25.1	—10.5	26.2

Sources: Author's calculations based on: *International Economic Report of the President,* 1977; IMF; OECD; *Survey of Crrent Business*; BMWI; MITI; Estimates for 1977/8 according to Morgan Guaranty Trust in: *USIS-Amerika Dienst*, No. 32, 14 December 1977.

TABLE 4.2
Relative Changes of National Economic Potentials, 1960-1975: The Federal Republic of Germany and Japan in Relation to the United States

	USA = 100															
	GNP				Exports				Foreign direct investment				Currency reserves			
	1960	1965	1970	1975	1960	1965	1970	1975	1960	1965	1970	1975	1960	1965	1970	1975
USA	100				100				100				100			
FRG	13.8	16.3	18.9	27.5	55.3	65.1	79.1	84.1	2.4	4.2	7.4	12.0	36.4	48.2	94.2	194.3
Japan	8.5	12.4	20.0	32.2	20.4	30.9	44.7	51.1	0.9	1.9	4.6	12.0	10.2	13.8	33.6	80.0
	1975/1960: Multiplicators-relative to USA (USA = 1)															
FRG	2.0				1.5				5.0				5.3			
Japan	3.8				2.5				13.3				7.8			

Sources: Author's calculations based on: *International Economic Report of the President,* 1977; IMF; *Survey of Current Business*; BMWI; MITI. Calculations in current Dollar values.

world political concepts and strategies, the FRG has even to be seen as the principal, and privileged (junior) partner of the US in a German-American 'joint leadership' and 'bigemony' in Euro-American relations.[23]

This international economic position and political role has induced both international expectations and pressures with respect to West Germany's 'responsibilities' in the framework of the international economy. Official economic policy programmes and projections worked out in the US as well as by international organizations like IMF, OECD or EEC expect the FRG to perform the function of a world economic 'locomotive' which should follow an economic policy of reflation and import stimulation in order to help to pull other countries out of their acute economic recession and payments difficulties.[24]

In the North-South conflict and 'dialogue', as well as in East-West trade and industrial cooperation, in the context of IMF and GATT as well as of OECD and IEA, in formal economic summits and in the informal coordinations between the major capitalist countries (the 'Big Three', or 'Big Five', or 'Big Seven', etc.), West Germany is expected to show a higher 'political profile' and a greater willingness to take over international political responsibilities and financial burdens in accordance with its leading economic position and political status.

Above all, the Carter Administration has invited, admonished, and pressured the West German Government to move in such a direction. Together with the US and Japan, the FRG is expected to join in a trilateral effort of the leading capitalist powers to defend the 'open and free' capitalist world economy against the 'economic nationalism' proliferating during the recent international economic crisis. Because of its exemplary 'open' market economy, the FRG is considered the main partner of the US in such an attempt at an internationally coordinated capitalist 'systems policy' in terms of continuing efforts to strengthen the global 'systemic interests', to promote 'internationalist' transnational coalitions in order to 'check the intrusion of national governments into the international exchange of economic and non-economic goods', and finally to 'limit the degree to which national governments can distort the international investment process' — in short, 'to work against all those governments or political forces willing to pay a price for more national autonomy'.[25]

Against nationalist and protectionist tendencies threatening the intensive international division of labour and the open and free international flow of goods and services, capital and technology, the FRG is expected to throw all her economic weight and political standing into a cooperative international campaign 'to make the world safe for interdependence' and 'to make the world safe for the multinational corporation'[26] — the main agent and vehicle of international specialization and exchange in the contemporary capitalist world economy.[27]

According to such ideological concepts and political strategies, an internationally concerted capitalist 'systems policy' is required to secure and stabilize the effective functioning of the open 'liberal' capitalist world economy, especially in these times of international economic crises. Since (in these terms) history is believed to have shown that only hierarchically organized international economic (and political) systems can be considered relatively stable, West Germany is expected to join the US at the top, and in the centre of 'concentric circles' of hierarchical international policy making in the 'systemic' task to reorganize and restabilize the 'liberal' inter-capitalist division of labour.[28]

In sharp contrast to such ideological perspectives and political strategies, the very same indicators of West Germany's economic strength, socio-political stability, and (postulated) international stabilization efforts and effects are considered by others to present the FRG as not at all an economic example to be followed, nor as a socio-political 'model' to be imitated, nor as a factor of international 'systems policy' and stabilization to count on and get support from.

To many observers the FRG has instead become a political 'nightmare' to be feared and a deterring example of authoritarian domestic politics to be avoided, even a dangerously expansionist, and destabilizing *économie dominante* as well as a hegemonial power to be resisted by all means.[29]

Thus, West Germany's economic 'miracle' and socio-political 'model' is praised, on the one hand, as the result of a national, and simultaneously international 'success story' in terms of an economically reconstructed, societally restored, internationally reorganized system of Western European unification and Atlanticist cooperation, established under 'benign' and 'consensual' US leadership and embedded in a more and more 'open and free' inter-capitalist division of labour.[30]

But on the other hand, West Germany's post-war development as well as contemporary international position and internal situation is heavily criticised (along with the principles and realities of the international economic and political system which allowed, and induced, this specific national development and position) as West German 'expansionism' and even 'imperialism' in an international capitalist system marked by a structurally unequal international division of labour, and a structurally hierarchical international power constellation.

I.4 THE FEDERAL REPUBLIC OF GERMANY AS A DOMINATING ECONOMY IN WESTERN EUROPE: WEST GERMAN 'STABILITY- AND DOMINATION-DILEMMAS'

In the framework of bourgeois concepts and theories of international domination and hegemony — as well as in marxist approaches to capitalist development as an essentially international, and 'imperialist' system based on the centralization and internationalization of capital — the FRG today appears in the international position and role of a 'dominating' or 'imperialist' national system in Western Europe.

Increasingly, in official — national as well as 'European' — circles in Western Europe, West German economic strength and political 'stability' the longer the more is considered a mixed blessing at best, even a case of internationally destabilizing national 'over'-stability. Here, West Germany's economic stability and domination is indeed seen to force the other Western European societies into an instability- and dependence-dilemma — thus making the stability and domination-'Modell Deutschland' appear as an international villain, and *scandalon* instead of a factor of international stabilization and balancing. In addition, the international role and position of the FRG in Euro-American relations and in the framework of trilateral world economic management have significantly reinforced critical evaluations and counter-reactions with respect to the West German 'model'.

In West Germany, such ambivalences and ambiguities, controversies and criticisms concerning the international economic position and political role, the internal situation and external consequences of the 'Modell Deutschland' have mostly been put aside or played down. Official declarations present the FRG instead as a national 'model' of domestic stability, and an international example of stabilizing foreign (economic) policy; deeply dedicated to close multilateral political cooperation and intensive, mutually advantageous international economic exchange. The proper role and actual function of the FRG is seen as that of an equally modest and honest international broker in Western European as well as Euro-American affairs. The 'exemplary', even privileged bilateral relations with both France and the US, the fundamental West German orientation both to West European unification and Atlanticist cooperation is underlined as an existential necessity for the FRG and as an important contribution to international balance and compromise.

The division of Germany (and its strategic and diplomatic implications) as well as the dependence of the West German economy on the overall stability and principal 'openness' of the capitalist world economy are presented as reasons why West Germany's 'enlightened national interest' — and actual domestic politics and foreign policies — are seen as parallel, even identical to the (postulated) 'systemic' interests of all developed capitalist countries: even West German 'patriotism' is officially defined as 'internationalism'.[31]

The considerable bilateral aids and multinational financial transfers in the framework of the IMF or EEC are here presented as a striking proof of West Germany's active international political cooperation and financial solidarity. Correspondingly, West Germany's domestic socio-political stability and stabilization policies are held as fundamental and effective contributions to international and, above all, Western European stability and stabilization.

Against international pressures demanding reflationary economic policies to stimulate West Germany's growth and imports, the West German 'stabilization policy' is not only defended but also aggressively recommended as a cure for other countries. In fact, according to the ruling consensus in the FRG, the reconstruction of both inter- and intranational stability in Western Europe, the eventual completion of Western European unification by an Economic and Monetary Union, and finally even European Union, is said to become a realistic option only if it will be designed as a 'European Stability Community' in conformity with the 'Modell Deutschland'.[32]

Thus, in spite of all other affirmations, the ruling West German consensus in effect demands that other Western European countries follow the stability- and stabilization-'model' of the FRG. Thus, Western European conformity to West German priorities and policies is made the essential West German prerequisite for any further (political as well as financial) support for Western European economic integration and political cooperation.

In my view, it is that fundamental West German policy orientation which is responsible for the recent stability- and domination-dilemma of the FRG and the corresponding instability- and dependence-dilemma of the other Western European countries.[33]

Instead of a European 'stability community, this political strategy, on the contrary, may induce a further international escalation of socio-economic destabilization. In the context of deepened international hierarchies and intra-national polarizations in Western Europe, such an insistence on a European 'imitation' of the 'Modell Deutschland' will rather provoke nationalist and protectionist reactions against West German economic domination and political hegemony.

Viewed in this perspective, the stubborn West German insistence upon Western European conformity with the German 'model', in spite of such manifest risks and latent dangers, requires an explanation.

Apologists for the 'model', and critics of the 'nightmare' West Germany, tend to evaluate this stubborn and demanding insistence as a clear indication of the eminent strength and superiority of the FRG in the Western European system: confident of her power, West Germany seems to assume that she is able to subordinate the other Western European economies and societies under her political priorities. Even if such a strategy was unsuccessful in Western Europe, these evaluations would tend to underline another option for West Germany, particularly in the face of increasing nationalist and societal confrontations. While the FRG may suffer considerable damage economically and politically in such a conflictive escalation, the other Western European societies would suffer even more. While the West German economy may in such a constellation successfully expand in other world markets to find compensation for the possible losses in Western European markets, other Western European countries may not be able to exercise this option to a similar extent. Even if some Southern West European countries may succeed in ganging up against the FRG, there is still the 'American option' left for West Germany as a viable alternative of foreign economic and political orientation...

II.1 CRITICAL THEORIES OF THE INTER-CAPITALIST DIVISION OF LABOUR: STRUCTURAL INTERNATIONAL AND INTER-SECTORAL HIERARCHIES

As this tour de force may already indicate, the FRG (together with the US) as a leading, even dominating, capitalist economy is closely identified by apologists for the 'model' as well as by critics of the 'nightmare' West Germany with the logic and principle, history and reality of the contemporary inter-capitalist division of labour. Therefore, evaluations of West Germany's role and position in the international economic and political system are at the same time evaluations of the rationality and acceptability of this international system itself.

The more the basic rationality of this system is questioned, the more also the international position and function of the West German economy is criticized. The more the dominating ideology of free trade and the prevailing neo-classical doctrine of collectively, more or less equally shared 'gains' from international specialization and trade are resisted on theoretical as well as political grounds, the less will be the political willingness to accept the economic effects and political consequences of such an international division of labour.

Following the political conflicts and theoretical debates over the determinants and consequences of the liberal inter-capitalist division of labour with respect to exploitative underdevelopment and structural dependence in the capitalist peripheries,[34] heretical and critical theoretical approaches have been advanced with respect to the structurally unequal and hierarchical character of the relations among the developed capitalist economies in the 'centre' of the world economy.

In reaction to the famous 'Leontief paradox' and to a body of other theoretical and empirical studies showing the inability of the neo-classical factor-proportions theorem(s) to describe and explain both the patterns of trade between the developed capitalist economies (accounting for about 75% of total world trade) and the interrelations between international trade and international investment,[35] both bourgeois-heretic[36] and neo-marxist paradigms[37] have been developed as either complementary or alternative explanations of the contemporary inter-capitalist division of labour, characterized by the world market movement of capital, the relevance of absolute technological advantages and monopolist positions, the importance of 'human skills' and the dynamics of sector-, industry- and product-cycles with respect to the development of trade patterns.

In spite of considerable theoretical differences and incompatibilities, all these frameworks also commonly view the 'metropolitan' division of labour as a structurally unequal and hierarchical system of domination and dependence. Most of these heretical (i.e. neo-factor proportions-; neo-technology; product-cycle) bourgeois and alternative neo-marxist approaches have been predominantly concerned with the explanation and description of American absolute technological advantages and monopolist positions in the post-war era.

Only recently have these approaches been applied also to the Japanese[38] and West German[39] positions in the structural hierarchy of the inter-capitalist division of labour. In most of these theoretical and political approaches the explicit or implicit 'imperial bias' of neo-classical theoretical explanations and of liberal political strategies with respect to an open and free capitalist world economy to be made 'safe for the multinational corporation' has been very apparent. The hierarchical, imperialist logic of the established system of international specialization and exchange has been described and explained very convincingly in particular by neo-marxist approaches developed in close connection to and critical of heretic product-cycle-paradigms.

According to such structural-historical concepts, the development of capitalism, and capitalist development as an international system, is marked by a systemic logic of imperialist hierarchy in terms of a structurally uneven and unequal development of capitalism on the national as well as the global scale. The 'Pax Britannica' as well as the 'Pax Americana' here reflect historical periods of such structural inter-capitalist hierarchies, the material bases of which can be defined in terms of cyclical sector-, industry-, product- and technology-hierarchies.[40]

Very simplified, this analytical perspective of inter-capitalist hierarchies in terms of cyclically reproduced sectoral hierarchies in the inter-capitalist division of labour can be superficially illustrated by a short review of the historical genesis of the capitalist world economy during the period of the second industrial revolution in the latter part of the 19th century.

During this period, the structural differentiation between the national accumulation patterns of Great Britain and France on one hand, and the US and Germany on the other became intensified decisively by the emergence of 'modern' industries, the introduction of new products and production techniques on a mass scale. While Great Britain and France — with a relative lead in traditional industries, and control over their formal colonies — experienced a relative structural retardation in terms of the inter- and intra-sectoral modernization of their national production and trade profiles during this period, above all the US, but also Germany, with their prevailing developmental orientations toward modern industries and the open world market, were led by their specific domestic societal conditions of production as well as by the mechanism of world market competition to a very accentuated, and intense national specialization in new products and modern production processes.[41]

The development of these modern industries (mainly electrical and non-electrical machinery, later automobiles and the chemical industry) went hand in hand with a rising tide of concentration and centralization of capital as well as with a profound technological reorganization and socio-political restructuring of the immediate production and labour processes, above all reflected by the transition from 'Taylorism' to 'Fordism'.[42] In addition, the development of capital goods industries has led to a continuing intensification of inter- and intra-sectoral forward and backward linkages, and to a proliferation and diffusion of new products and production processes into other industries and branches of the national economy.

Both theoretical reflections and empirical investigations show[43] that the higher the absolute and relative national specialization in modern industries and technologies and especially in capital goods production, the higher the structural 'coherence' of the national production apparatus, the higher the relative completeness of technological, financial and commercial product- and production- chains, and also the higher the relative homogeneity of economic modernization and productivity in all sectors and industries.

Such a national specialization pattern of modern industries and capital goods production tends to favour, by multiple spin-off effects, a relatively 'autocentred' socio-economic national development. A contrasting specialization in traditional industries and production-chains in turn tends to result in a much less autocentred, even structurally dependent national development pattern because of absolutely or relatively incoherent, incomplete and heterogenous inter- and intra-sectoral linkages within the framework of the national economy.

II.2 WEST GERMANY'S POSITION IN THE INTER-CAPITALIST HIERARCHY: SOME STRUCTURAL ASPECTS AND HISTORICAL ELEMENTS

Applying this broad analytical perspective to the investigation of the structural-historical essence of the German specialization profile, four principal elements of the German 'accumulation model' can be selected to define the structural core of the (West) German position in the historical dynamics and structural dialectics of the inter-capitalist division of labour:[44]

1. The extreme national specialization in *industrial* production (and trade) in general, and in capital-goods in particular;

2. The overwhelming 'outward' trade orientation toward the world market in general, and to the most 'central', more developed foreign markets in particular;

3. The considerable level of concentration and degree of centralization of capital as well as the specific interrelations, even 'symbioses' between industrial and finance capital;

4. The gradual 'negative' and latent — as ambivalent as contradictory — 'positive' integration of the labour movement into the bourgeois-capitalist economic and political system.

We have elaborated elsewhere[45] why and how these different structural dimensions of the German 'accumulation model' have tended to reinforce each other. Thus (to give only one example) both the specific pattern of industrial specialization and the orientation toward the most central world markets have allowed a very significant degree of sectoral coherence and a considerable level of international competitiveness — in turn inducing a highly 'organized capitalism'. In addition, such developments have also structurally eased the relative integration and discipline of the German labour movement, decisively pushed forward by the political consequences of the two World Wars, the world economic crisis of the late 1920s and 1930s, as well as by fascism, and after 1945 by the effects of bourgeois restoration, the mass-integrative ideology of 'social market economy' and the reality of relative prosperity during the period of the West German 'economic miracle'.

In recent publications[46] we have used this framework for comparisons of the French and West German international economic positions and for an investigation of their bilateral relationship in the context of the contemporary capitalist world economy. In the following an attempt is made to concentrate the analytical perspective on several crucial aspects of West Germany's recent position in the inter-capitalist division of labour. Obviously, this can be done here only in a highly superficial and merely illustrative way. More stringent and complete elaborations will be found in other publications in preparation.[47]

Here it must suffice to present selected empirical evidence which may give a first descriptive indication of the qualitative importance and quantitative extent of several core elements of the German 'accumulation model' and its relative position in the inter-capitalist hierarchy.

II.3 'OVER-INDUSTRIALIZATION' AND WORLD MARKET ORIENTATION: A SECTORAL PROFILE OF WEST GERMAN ECONOMIC SPECIALIZATION

As many studies have shown, the historical pattern of German industrial specialization has become even more pronounced for West Germany since 1945 due to the division of Germany as well as due to deliberate domestic and foreign economic policies in the 1950s and 1960s.[48] Diverse state interventions and especially subsidies, a determined export policy[49] and a 'protectionism by stealth' based on a undervalued DM parity have effectively contributed to the marked 'over-industrialization'[50] of the West German economy in comparison to all major capitalist economies (see Table 5.1).

TABLE 5.1
The 'Over-Industrialization' of the West German Economy: International Comparison of the Share of Manufacturing in Gross Domestic Product of Major Capitalist Industrialized Countries, 1963 and 1973
(Current Prices)

Country	Per Capita Income ($)		% Share of manufacturing in GDP	
	1963	1973	1963	1973
FRG	1676	5614	41.15	40.39
USA	3151	6267	28.01	25.26
Japan	710	3755	34.33	35.13
France	1743	4904	36.13	35.37(1971)
Great Britain	1583	3096	29.67	27.11

Source: OECD National Accounts of OECD Countries; div. issues.

As an inter-temporal comparison indicates, this relative 'over-industrialization' has significantly been increased even in real terms in spite of rising per capita income (see Table 5.2). That development at first glance runs counter to prominent theorems postulating a secular, even causal interrelationship between rising per capita income, relative de-industrialization and corresponding 'tertialization' of developed national economies.

TABLE 5.2
Changes of the % Shares of the Main Economic Sectors in the West German Gross Domestic Product, 1950-1974 (in real terms)

Sector	Average Annual % Share in GDP 1950/1959	1960/1969	1970/1974
Agriculture and forestry	8.3	4.8	3.9
Industry	49.5	55.2	57.1
of which:			
Energy, mining	5.4	4.4	4.2
Manufacturing	37.4	43.1	45.6
Construction	7.7	7.7	7.3
Distribution and services	42.2	40.0	39.0

Source: WSI-Mitteilungen, 10/1976, 564.

Table 6 indicates the increasing world market orientation of the West German economy since 1950 in terms of 'direct' foreign trade only:

TABLE 6
World Market Orientation of the West German Economy: The Development of Foreign Trade, 1950-1976

Year	Export (Billion DM) (1)	Import (Billion DM) (2)	Balance (Billion DM) (3)	Export/capita (DM) (4)	Import/capita (DM) (5)	Export (in % GNP) (6)	Import (in % GNP) (7)	Export % Share in cap. world total (8)	Import % Share in cap. world total (9)
1950	8.4	11.4	—3.0	170	232	8.5	11.6	3.5	4.6
1960	47.9	42.7	+5.2	865	771	15.8	14.1	10.1	8.5
1965	71.7	70.4	+1.2	1214	1194	15.6	15.4	10.9	10.1
1970	125.3	109.6	+15.7	2066	1807	18.5	16.1	12.3	10.2
1971	136.0	120.1	+15.9	2219	1959	18.0	15.9	12.5	10.5
1972	149.0	128.7	+20.3	2416	2088	18.0	15.6	12.4	10.4
1973	178.4	145.4	+33.0	2879	2346	19.4	15.8	12.9	10.3

TABLE 6 (continued)

1974	230.6	179.7	+50.8	3716	2896	23.4	18.2	11.7	9.0
1975*	221.6	184.3	+37.3	3595	2981	21.5	17.9	11.5	9.3
1976*	256.6	222.2	+34.5	4172	3612	22.8	19.8	11.6	9.8
1977*	273.4	235.1	+38.3	—	—	—	—	—	—

*Preliminary.
Source: Bundesministerium für Wirtschaft (BMWi), *Leistung in Zahlen '76; own calculations.*

Table 7 allows a comparison of the relative world market integration of major capitalist economies in terms of goods and services.

TABLE 7
International Comparison of the Relative World Market Orientation of the 'Trilateral' Economies, 1960-1975

% Shares of exports and imports (goods and services, without factor incomes) in GDP; at current prices and parities.

Country	1960		1965		1970		1975		1975/1960 Multiplicator	
	EXP	IMP	EXP	IMP	EXP	IMP	EXP	IMP	EXP	IMP
FRG	18.1	15.9	17.4	17.2	20.2	18.1	24.0	20.6	1.33	1.30
EEC	19.8	19.3	18.9	18.7	22.1	21.4	26.8	25.9	1.35	1.34
Japan	11.1	10.4	10.6	9.2	11.0	9.7	14.0	14.1	1.26	1.36
USA	4.5	3.8	4.7	3.8	5.5	4.9	9.9	8.4	2.20	2.21

Source: EC Commission, *Lage und Perspektiven der Weltwirtschaft* (Lettenhove Report), Brussels, Dec. 1976, 34; own calculations.

If direct and indirect exports of both goods and services are taken into account the fundamental export orientation of the West German economy emerges even more clearly (see Table 8).

TABLE 8
World Market Orientation of the West German Economy, 1972-1975: Relative Overall (Direct and Indirect) Export Dependence (Goods and Services) of the Main Economic Sectors

	% Share of exports in total sales			
Sector	**1972**	**1973**	**1974**	**1975**
All sectors	20.2	21.5	25.2	24.1
Agriculture, forestry	13.4	14.9	16.5	15.2
Total industry	32.3	34.1	39.2	39.0
Mining	37.8	40.8	43.9	44.3
Basic materials and production goods	36.7	38.3	44.0	43.7
Capital goods industries	40.2	41.5	46.7	47.4
of which:				
Machinery	47.2	48.9	55.8	56.1
Automobiles	47.7	48.9	54.6	52.0
Electrical machinery	32.9	34.2	38.9	39.8
Consumption goods	20.8	23.6	27.4	26.6
Food	11.9	13.2	16.2	15.6

Source: DIW-Wochenberichte, 22, 1976, 221 based on input/output calculations of the DIW.

In addition, as the sectoral differences of foreign trade orientation show, the capital goods industries, in particular, are characterized by a remarkably high export orientation (or even dependence); in several important cases reaching about 50% of total sales.

With respect to the central theoretical and historical relevance of the capital goods industries in the German 'accumulation model' already alluded to above, Table 9 gives a first indication of the quantitative importance of these industries in recent West German exports. The domi-

TABLE 9
Sectoral Profile of West German Industrial Specialization: The Relevance of Capital-Goods-Industries in West German Exports, 1976*

Sector and industry	Exports Million DM	% Share in total Exp.	*of which:* capital goods (1) Million DM	% Share	Consumption goods (2) Million DM	% Share	Others (3) Million DM	% Share
I. Capital goods industries	(1)	(2)	(3)	(4)	(5)	(6)	(7)	(8)
Total	136360	54.4	66781	47.9	20422	14.7	52158	37.4
Non-electrical machinery	47960	18.7	34278	71.5	95	0.2	13587	28.3
Automobiles	37543	14.7	10972	29.2	12723	33.9	13848	36.9
Electrical machinery	25798	10.1	9048	35.1	5461	21.1	11289	43.8
Manufactured metal goods	7665	3.0	834	10.9	1135	14.8	5696	74.3
Instruments	5029	2.0	1306	26.0	831	16.5	2892	57.5
Shipbuilding	3827	1.5	3650	95.4	177	4.6	—	—
Computers, bureau machinery	4123	1.6	2725	66.1	—	—	1398	33.9
Steel construction	3005	1.2	2772	92.3	—	—	233	7.7
Aircraft and parts	2166	0.8	1196	55.2	—	—	970	44.8
Steel rolls and foundries	2245	0.9	—	—	—	—	2245	100.0
II. Other Sectors and industries total	116814	45.6	945	0.8	12332	10.6	103534	88.6
of which: Chemical industry	33710	13.2	—	—	1000	3.0	32710	97.0
III. All sectors and industries	256172	100	67726	26.4	32754	12.8	155692	60.8

(1) excluding building construction capital goods
(2) excluding food
(3) including food, raw materials, intermediate goods, etc.

*Source: Own calculations, based on official data, and *Commerzbank-Aussenhandelsblätter, 7, 1977.*

nant role of (electrical and non-electrical) machinery and automobiles is reflected by their combined share of 42.5% in total West German exports. If, in addition, the exports of the chemical industry are also included, these four industries together account for 55.7% of West Germany's total exports.

The share of 'proper' capital goods in the export of the (so-called) capital goods industries (Table 9, col. [4]) does merit special attention because it must be considered as the highest in any international comparison.[51]

II.4 THE REGIONAL ORIENTATION OF FOREIGN TRADE: WEST GERMANY'S DOMINATING CENTRALITY IN WESTERN EUROPE AND WORLD MARKET 'INFLUENCE ZONES'

Turning to the regional distribution of West German foreign trade in the 1970s, Table 10 indicates West Germany's basic economic exchange orientation toward the most central and more developed world markets. About three-quarters of the total exports (imports) go to (come from) developed capitalist world markets, mostly to (from) Western European countries. A considerable part of West Germany's exports to underdeveloped countries is concentrated in the so-called 'threshold countries', and OPEC. Between 1972 and 1976, the share of OPEC countries in West German exports to underdeveloped countries has risen from 27.5% to 49.6%.[52]

The political controversies over West Germany's — quantitatively as well as qualitatively — dominant trade position in Western Europe mentioned above appear to be justified and supported by the data presented in Table 11. In 1975 (the last year for which UN data are available) West Germany ranks first (second) in eleven (five) out of a total of seventeen cases as a major trading partner in Western Europe — indeed reflecting a central and dominant position.

This quantitative indication of structural inequalities and hierarchies in the Western European trade network marked by the dominant centrality of West German exports is complemented by the structural dimension of the sectoral and industry distribution of West German exports to Western European countries. We have already stressed the decisive importance of the capital goods sector for the inter-capitalist hierarchy of specialization in production and trade as well as for the degree of relative auto-centredness and coherence of developed capitalist economies.

TABLE 10

The Regional Distribution of West German Foreign Trade in the 1970s

Year	Developed capitalist countries							Underdeveloped capitalist countries	'Communist' countries	Not allocable
	Total	Western Europe				Overseas of which:				
		EEC	EFTA	Others	All	All	USA			
EXP	83.6	40.1	22.6	6.7	69.4	14.2	9.1	11.9	4.3	0.2
1970 IMP	79.8	44.2	15.2	4.0	63.4	16.4	11.0	16.1	4.0	0.1
EXP	83.5	40.1	22.4	6.6	69.1	14.4	9.7	12.0	4.3	0.2
1971 IMP	80.0	46.6	14.1	3.9	64.7	15.3	10.3	15.9	4.0	0.1
EXP	83.3	39.9	23.0	6.7	69.7	13.6	9.3	11.4	5.1	0.2
1972 IMP	80.5	48.6	13.7	4.5	66.9	13.6	8.4	15.3	4.1	0.1
EXP	82.2	47.1	15.7	6.4	69.2	13.0	8.5	11.5	6.1	0.2
1973 IMP	78.9	51.9	8.8	4.6	65.3	13.6	8.4	16.5	4.5	0.1
EXP	78.9	44.9	14.9	6.7	66.5	12.4	7.5	13.9	6.9	0.3
1974 IMP	72.9	47.9	8.4	4.0	60.3	12.6	7.8	22.3	4.7	0.1
EXP	75.4	43.5	14.5	7.2	65.2	10.2	5.9	16.4	7.9	0.3
1975 IMP	75.2	49.5	8.7	4.1	62.3	12.9	7.7	20.0	4.7	0.1
EXP	76.6	45.7	15.0	6.4	67.1	9.5	5.6	16.3	6.8	0.3
1976 IMP	74.5	48.2	8.9	4.2	61.3	13.2	7.9	20.5	4.9	0.1

Source: BMWi.

TABLE 11
The Dominating Position of the West German Economy in the Western European Trade Network, 1975: % Shares of the Major Trading Countries in the Imports of Western European Countries

Importing country	Major trading partners and their % share in total imports: 1st Rank		2nd Rank		3rd Rank		4th Rank	
FRG	NTH	14.1	FRA	12.2	ITA	9.4	BEL/LUX	8.6
France	FRG	18.0	BEL/LUX	9.6	ITA	8.9	USA	7.6
Italy	FRG	17.3	FRA	13.5	USA	8.8	NTH	4.7
GBR	USA	9.6	FRG	8.3	NTH	7.6	FRA	6.7
Netherlands	FRG	25.7	BEL/LUX	12.4	USA	10.1	FRA	7.7
BEL/LUX	FRG	22.4	FRA	17.7	NTH	17.0	USA	6.4
Switzerland	FRG	27.9	FRA	13.9	ITA	9.9	USA	7.6
Austria	FRG	40.0	ITA	8.1	SWZ	6.7	FRA	4.1
Sweden	FRG	19.2	GBR	10.9	ITA	8.2	USA	6.6
Norway	SWD	19.2	FRG	15.7	GBR	9.7	USA	7.1
Denmark	FRG	19.7	SWD	14.3	GBR	10.3	USA	6.0
Finland	SWD	15.9	FRG	14.2	GBR	8.7	USA	5.5
Iceland	FRG	10.7	GBR	10.7	NOR	10.6	DEN	10.0
Ireland	GBR	48.7	USA	7.2	FRG	7.0	FRA	5.1
Portugal	USA	12.4	FRG	11.4	GBR	8.7	FRA	7.6
Spain	USA	16.1	FRG	10.4	FRA	8.4	ITA	5.2
Greece	FRG	15.9	ITA	8.2	USA	7.4	FRA	6.0
Yugoslavia	FRG	18.7	ITA	11.3	USA	5.4	FRA	4.6

Source: Based on computations by Josef Staud of UN trade data.

Among the capital goods industries in general, machinery — and especially those branches producing ‘production means destined for the production of production means’ — must be considered as the most central and also the most hierarchical factor in the inter-capitalist division of labour because of its cross-sectoral and international impact on the general ‘norms’ of production and overall terms of economic exchange. Indeed, overall sales — and specifically exports — of machinery may be taken as a most direct indicator of the hierarchical ranking of developed capitalist economies in the world economy.

As Table 12 shows, the latter are especially heavily concentrated in only six leading capitalist economies. With only about one-third of total (domestic and foreign) US sales in machinery, West Germany nevertheless accounts for about the same volume in machinery exports as the US.

TABLE 12
Capitalist World Production and World Trade of (Non-electrical) Machinery: The Main Producing and Exporting Countries, 1975/6

Country	Sales of machinery 1976		Exports of machinery 1975
	Billion DM	% Share	% Share
Cap. Total	753.5	100	100
USA	275.3	36.5	24.6
FRG	93.8	12.5	23.2
JAPAN	82.8	11.0	7.7
GBR	48.3	6.4	10.3
FRANCE	29.4	3.9	8.2
ITALY	26.6	3.5	6.9

Source: Own calculations based on data from VDMA (Association of German Manufacturers of Machinery) and *Handelsblatt,* 25 November 1977.

With respect to international trade in machinery in Western Europe (see Table 13), the FRG, with an overall share of 30% (about twice the US share, and three times the share of Great Britain and France) evidently stands out as by far the dominant supplier of this region.

This qualitatively dominant West German position in the Western European trade network is amply documented by a bulk of other studies. In an especially refined empirical analysis of the international and intersectoral hierarchy of specialization in production and trade in the EEC, including highly disaggregated product classes as the level of analysis, the dominant centrality, often even monopolistic position of West German capital goods exports in Western European trade emerges in still more detail and more clearly.[53]

TABLE 13
The Dominating Position of the West German Economy in Western European Trade in (non-electrical) Machinery, 1975: % Shares of the Main Capitalist Exporting Countries in the Machinery Imports of Western European Countries

Importing Country	Major machinery exporters and their rank and % share in imports of: 1st Rank	%	2nd Rank	%	3rd Rank	%	4th Rank	%
Western Europe	FRG	30.4	USA	15.8	GBR	10.0	FRA	9.2
FRG	USA	17.2	FRA	16.5	ITA	11.1	GBR	10.0
France	FRG	39.1	USA	14.4	ITA	12.2	GBR	10.6
Netherlands	FRG	41.0	USA	15.7	GBR	12.3	FRA	7.4
BEL/LUX	FRG	33.6	USA	29.3	FRA	15.6	GBR	10.2
Switzerland	FRG	48.7	USA	10.0	FRA	9.6	ITA	9.2
Austria	FRG	59.0	ITA	6.6	GBR	6.1	FRA	4.1
GBR	USA	29.0	FRG	25.3	FRA	10.7	ITA	6.3
Ireland	GBR	50.0	FRG	14.4	USA	12.5	FRA	4.0
Italy	FRG	42.4	FRA	15.4	USA	12.4	GBR	10.9
Spain	FRG	27.3	USA	22.1	FRA	12.0	ITA	11.6
Portugal	FRG	21.4	FRA	17.9	GBR	15.8	ITA	10.0
Greece	FRG	27.4	ITA	19.0	USA	11.2	GBR	10.0
Turkey	FRG	33.4	USA	19.7	ITA	12.6	GBR	11.4
Sweden	FRG	32.8	GBR	13.4	USA	11.7	FRA	5.2
Norway	FRG	34.0	USA	21.1	GBR	19.3	FRA	11.3
Denmark	FRG	32.1	GBR	14.8	USA	7.4	FRA	4.2
Finland	FRG	27.6	GBR	14.3	USA	8.0	FRA	4.5
Yugoslavia	FRG	43.6	ITA	14.6	USA	8.6	FRA	8.3

Source: Calculations by Udo Rehfeldt based on data from VDMA, 1977; see also Table 16.

As our own investigations have shown,[54] in the bilateral Franco-German economic relationship this dominant West German trade position has decisive consequences in terms of structural dependence and structural incoherence for the French economy — itself the second largest economy in Western Europe and one of the six major capitalist exporters of machinery.

Beyond the regional Western European trade network where the FRG (from the 1950s on) has gradually increased its central trading position (correspondingly causing relative decreases of the American, British, and French positions), the FRG also accounts in the wider OECD area and at the world market level for significant absolute trade volumes and relative market shares.

With a share of 11.6% of total capitalist exports (all sectors) in 1976, the West German economy accounts for about twice this share in the world trade of manufactured and finished industrial goods — a share even surpassing that of the US (see Table 14). Thus the FRG must be seen — at least in the world market competition of capital goods industries — as the main competitor of the US with about the same share as the American economy in capitalist world trade in electrical machinery (see Table 15) and non-electrical machinery (see Table 18).

If the world market shares of the major machinery exporters are investigated on a less global and more disaggregated macro-regional level, rather clearcut international 'influence zones' of the major exporting countries do appear. Clearly, Western Europe emerges above all as West Germany's 'influence zone' — alone accounting for more than half (12.8%) of West Germany's overall world market share (23.2%) because of its absolute and relative market size in machinery (42% of world total).

II.5 INTERNATIONAL TRADE AND INTERNATIONAL INVESTMENT: THE RELATIVE DE-NATIONALIZATION AND INTERNATIONALIZATION OF WEST GERMAN CAPITAL

The trade data presented here, however, do not tell the whole story of West Germany's recent international economic position in the hierarchical inter-capitalist division of labour. In fact, they are misleading if used without reference to other important dimensions of international competitiveness in the capitalist world economy.

While the West German trade position surpasses — at least in several sectoral and regional segments of the world market — that of the US, this position undergoes decisive changes if international transfers of technology, international investment and foreign production are taken into account to cover that other most important aspect of international market shares.

As the American case makes very clear, international investment and foreign production have become factors of even greater economic relevance and also political importance than international trade in the

TABLE 14
Indicators of International Competiveness of the Major Capitalist Industrialized Countries: National Shares in Total Exports, 1964 (1966)-1976

Country	% Share in total cap. GNP (Centre)	% Share in total exports of finished industrial goods of the 11 leading capitalist countries								Relative export performance in the OECD area		
		1964	1966	1970	1972	1973	1974	1975	1976/(in)	1960-73	1973-76	1977
FRG	11.3	19.3	19.3	19.8	20.2	22.1	21.7	20.3	21.1	+0.75	+0.50	+0.0
USA	40.9	21.5	20.1	18.5	16.1	16.1	17.2	17.7	17.5	—2.00	—1.75	—1.5
Japan	13.2	8.1	9.7	11.7	13.2	12.8	14.5	13.6	14.7	+7.5	+7.0	—1.5
France	9.0	8.7	8.6	8.7	9.3	9.5	9.3	10.2	9.7	+2.5	—1.25	—1.5
Great Britain	6.2	14.4	13.4	10.8	10.0	9.4	8.8	9.3	8.7	—3.25	—1.75	+0.5

Source: DIW-Wochenberichte; Europe Weekly Statistics, No. 66 (21 January 1977); *OECD-Economic Outlook, July 1977; own calculations.*

TABLE 15
Capitalist World Trade in Electrical Machinery, 1913-1975: The Main Exporting Countries and their % Share

Exporting country	% Share in capital exports of electrical machinery 1913	1928	1938	1950	1958	1966	1974	1975
				(%)				
Germany/ West Germany	46	29	28	6	21	20	20.3	19.2
USA	16	24	23	34	29	24	21.5	20.8
Great Britain	22	20	21	30	20	12	8.4	8.8
Netherlands	—	6	8	6	7	8	5.6	6.0
Japan	—	—	4	—	3	10	15.6	14.9

Source: '50 Jahre ZVEI', Frankfurt 1968, 92 (for 1913-1966); *ZVEI-Die Elektrotechnische Industrie, Statistischer Bericht 1975*, Frankfurt 1976.

contemporary world economy. Already in the early 1970s the (estimated) world total of 'foreign production' has surpassed that of total world trade.[55] If, therefore, the international trade of US-foreign affiliates in the OECD area is taken into account in addition to the proper foreign trade directly from the US, the respective 'national' shares in OECD area trade are considerably reversed.[56]

To a remarkable extent the foreign penetration and relative denationalization of the West German economy due to inflows of productive capital and foreign technology has contributed to its strong position in the inter-capitalist trade system.

Multinational corporations from abroad account for a very sizeable absolute volume of, and relative shares in West German domestic production and foreign trade, particularly in those industries where they are heavily concentrated.[57] Unfortunately, the available official data on international investment do not allow systematic and satisfactory empirical investigations.

Beyond the statistics published by the Bundesministerium für Wirtschaft (Table 16); and by the Deutsche Bundesbank (Table 17), only very limited (and biased) sample data have been collected with respect to foreign MNCs' participation in West German foreign economic and monetary exchanges.[58]

TABLE 16
Stock of Foreign Direct Investment in the FRG on 30 June 1977, by Selected Economic Sector and Country of Origin

Sector/ industry	USA	SWZ	NTH	GBR	in Million DM FRA	BEL/ LUX	JAP	SWD	CAN	ITA
All sectors	18452	7609	5768	4545	2685	2658	984	966	570	554
Mining										
Oil, gas extract.	769									
Building material		167								
Basic materials and production goods										
Iron and steel	134	316	1314			289		45		
Petroleum process.	3357	296	576	737	415	495				268
Chemical industry	1528	921	223	336	87	580				
Pharmaceutical ind.	255	233								
Paper, pulp, wood		105						221	40	
Rubber and asbestos	499	310		98						71
Non-iron metals	354		153						57	
Plastic process.	151	135								
Capital goods industries										
Non-electrical machinery	2082	805	300	380	99	70	80	209	94	50
Automobiles	1331	94	343	119	96	167		42		20
Aircraft, parts			1 5 0							
Electrical machinery	2368	613	373	146	310		51	88		
Instruments	311	173								
Metal works	413				66					
Steel construction	120				66			68		

TABLE 16 (continued)

Consumer goods										
Textiles		254	188	90					97	33
Food, tobacco	867	544	367	409		214		38	48	34
Trade and services										
Banking	1443	182	140	309	339	168	657		76	
Insurance		128		134						
Immobiles		116	219	129		96				
Hotels	156									
Holdings	1060	744	595	1164	664	107	35		62	
Shipping			101				89			
Retail trade	338						89			

Source: BMWi.

TABLE 17

The Absolute and Relative Relevance of Enterprises with Foreign Participation in West German Manufacturing and Trade, by Economic Sector or Industry, at Yearend 1972

Shares of enterprises with foreign participation in:

Economic sector or industry	Balance sheets: domestic and foreign enterprise total (Billion DM)	Balance sheets: foreign only (Billion BM)	Balance sheets: enterprises share in total (%)	Annual sales: domestic and foreign enterprises total (Billion DM)	Annual sales: foreign only (Billion DM)	Annual sales: enterprises share in total (%)	Employment: domestic and foreign enterprises total (1000s)	Employment: foreign only (1000s)	Employment: enterprises share in total (%)
Total manufacturing and trade	1059.8	184.2	17.4	1529.9	265.7	17.4	16532.2	2195.6	13.3
of which:									
Mining	24.2	3.7	15.3	19.5	4.7	24.1	277.8	34.7	12.5
Chemical industry, Asbestos, rubber, plastic processing	76.5	22.5	29.4	82.1	26.1	31.8	922.8	231.2	25.1
Petroleum processing	19.3	14.7	76.2	27.3	21.5	78.8	37.2	27.5	73.9
Metal production and processing	60.8	23.9	39.3	68.3	25.1	36.7	763.0	235.3	30.8
Machinery, automobiles, steel constr.	124.5	28.9	23.2	164.1	36.4	22.2	2034.6	475.2	23.4

TABLE 17 (continued)

Electrical machinery, instruments, etc.*	89.2	26.0	29.1	119.4	35.3	29.6	1746.2	502.6	28.8
of which:									
Electrical machinery	(58.0)	(21.4)	(36.9)	(73.4)	(29.0)	(39.5)	(1096.2)	(399.5)	(36.4)
Food, tobacco	66.3	12.0	18.1	120.2	23.2	19.3	531.3	139.1	26.2
Retail trade	234.4	26.0	11.1	582.0	64.8	11.1	3239.0	208.1	6.4

Excluding agriculture and forestry, services, banking and insurance.
*Including musical instruments, sporting gear, toys, jewelry.

Source: Deutsche Bundesbank-Monatsberichte, No. 11, 1974, 30.

TABLE 18
World Trade in (Non-electrical) Machinery, 1975: The Main Capitalist Exporting Countries* and their 'Influence Zones'

Importing region	(Machinery) % Share in total exports	National Ranks and % shares in total capitalist machinery-exports* to each importing region 1st Rank	%	2nd Rank	%	3rd Rank	%	4th Rank	%	5th Rank	%	6th Rank	%
WORLD	100.0	USA	24.6	FRG	23.2	GBR	10.3	FRA	8.2	JAP	7.7	ITA	6.9
Western Europe	42.0	FRG	30.4	USA	15.8	GBR	10.0	FRA	9.2	—	—	—	—
USA	6.2	CAN	26.0	FRG	20.4	JAP	17.1	GBR	13.4	ITA	5.3	FRA	4.6
Canada	6.2	USA	81.5	GBR	5.6	FRG	4.2	JAP	2.6	SWD	1.7	ITA	1.2
Japan	1.7	USA	53.6	FRG	17.1	GBR	8.3	SWZ	7.6	SWD	7.5	ITA	7.1
Australia/Oceania	2.3	USA	37.0	GBR	22.8	JAP	11.0	FRG	10.8	ITA	3.8	SWD	2.9
Rep. South Africa	2.2	USA	26.0	GBR	23.0	FRG	20.7	ITA	5.7	—	—	—	—
Eastern Europe	7.9	FRG	33.9	FRA	12.0	ITA	10.2	USA	10.0	—	—	—	—
Africa (excl. SAR)	6.0	FRA	23.2	FRG	18.6	USA	17.8	GBR	14.4	ITA	9.8	—	—
Latin America	9.7	USA	48.5	FRG	14.3	JAP	8.1	ITA	7.4	GBR	6.8	FRA	4.1
Asia (excl. Japan)	15.1	USA	26.1	JAP	22.1	FRG	17.8	GBR	11.4	FRA	6.7	ITA	5.2

Source: Calculations by Udo Rehfeldt based on data from Verein Deutscher Maschinenbau-Anstalten (VDMA 1977)
* Exporting countries include: EEC, EFTA, USA, Canada, Japan and Finland.

Because of the considerable concentration of direct foreign investment in West Germany on very large MNCs (of the world largest 100 corporations, seventy-eight have direct investments in the FRG accounting for over 40% of total direct foreign investment in West Germany)[59] these very large foreign MNCs play an especially central role not only in several economic sectors and industrial branches (see Table 19), but also in the league of West Germany's largest enterprises. In 1974 (1972), thirty-five (thirty-two) of the 100 largest enterprises in the FRG showed 'significant' foreign capital participation and account for 33.3% (29.5%) of total sales of the largest 100 enterprises.[60] According to our own calculations, at least twenty-five of the 100 largest West German *Aktiengesellschaften* and at least fifty of the 100 largest *GmbH* have sizeable foreign capital participation.[61] US-based MNCs own by far the greatest share (39.3%) of the total stock of direct foreign investment in the FRG (see Table 20). Since the official statistics have only been compiled since 1961, they do underestimate significantly the real volume of direct investment in the FRG by excluding direct investments undertaken before that date (and in very important cases — like automobiles and electrical machinery — dating well back to the 1920s).[62]

TABLE 19
Sectoral Distribution of Foreign Direct Investment in West Germany, 1977 (first half)

Sector/industry	Foreign direct investment in West Germany		
	(Million DM)	(% Share in total)	(% Share, cumulated)
Petroleum	6229	13.3	13.3
Holdings	4617	9.8	23.1
Machinery	4275	9.1	32.2
Electrical machinery	4080	8.7	40.9
Banking, etc.	3825	8.1	49.0
Chemical industry	3816	8.1	57.1
Automobiles	2430	5.2	62.3
Iron and steel	2287	4.9	67.2
Food	1917	4.1	71.3
Rubber, asbestos	1107	2.4	73.7
Together	34589	73.7	—
Others	12418	26.3	—
Total	47007	100	100

Source: Own calculations based on BMWi data.

TABLE 20
Countries of Origin of Foreign Direct Investment in West Germany, 1977 (First half)

Country of Origin	FDI in West Germany		
	(Million DM)	(% Share in total)	(% Share, cumulated)
USA	18452	39.3	39.3
Switzerland	7609	16.2	55.5
Netherlands	5768	12.3	67.8
Great Britain	4554	9.7	77.5
France	2658	5.7	83.2
Belgium/Luxembourg	2658	5.7	88.9
Japan	984	2.1	91.0
Sweden	966	2.1	93.1
Canada	570	1.2	94.3
Italy	554	1.2	95.5

Source: Own calculations based on BMWi data.

Due to the historically strong position of a small number of very large MNCs from the Netherlands and Great Britain in West Germany, the direct foreign investments of these countries in the FRG today still surpass total West German investments in these respective countries.[63]

While direct foreign investments in West Germany have to be taken into account in order to outline the share of foreign MNCs in West Germany's production and trade, correspondingly West Germany's investments abroad also have to be included in an analysis of West Germany's international position in the world economy. According to official data inflows of direct foreign investments surpassed outflows until 1973 (except 1968/70). Since 1974, however, the reverse has been the case.

At the end of 1976 the accumulated stock of West German direct foreign investment was for the first time larger than the stock of direct foreign investment in the FRG (see Table 21). The regional and sectoral distribution of West German foreign direct investment shows a rather close similarity with the sectoral and regional patterns of West Germany's exports (Tables 22-24). The main industries accounting for

55.7% of West Germany's total exports also account for (at least) 43.4% of total West German direct investment abroad.

TABLE 21
The Inter-and De-nationalization of the West German Economy: In and Outward Foreign Direct Investment, 1952 (1961)-1977(I)

Year	West German FDI outflow (net) Million DM	West German FDI stock (yearend) Million DM	FDI in West Germany inflow (net) Million DM	FDI in West Germany stock (yearend) Million DM
1952-1955	421	421	—	—
1956	410	831	—	—
1957	518	1349	—	—
1958	509	1859	—	—
1959	564	2422	—	—
1960	740	3162	—	—
1961	984	4110	296	296
1962	846	4956	1391	1687
1963	1115	6071	1504	3190
1964	1134	7205	2005	5195
1965	1112	8317	2549	7744
1966	1678	9995	2885	10629
1967	2063	12058	3890	14518
1968	2292	14349	2249	16767
1969	3269	17618	2104	18871
1970	3495	21113	2729	21600
1971	2668	23781	3986	25586
1972	2816	26597	3729	29314
1973	5638	32235	6128	35442
1974	4530	36765	4484	39926
1975	5227	41992	2528	42454
1976	5057	47048	3064	45518
1977(I)	2572	49620	1489	47007

Source: BMWI.

TABLE 22
Sectoral Distribution of West German Direct Foreign Investment, 1977/I:

Sector/industry (ranked according to volume)	Stock of foreign direct investment (Million DM/%) Domestic industry's FDI	% Share in total FDI	Industry invested in abroad	% Share in total
Chemical industries	9152.8	18.4	6421.2	12.9
Electrical machinery	5470.9	11.0	4058.3	8.2
Machinery	3975.8	8.0	3314.5	6.7
Iron and steel	3896.3	7.9	1503.2	3.0
Banking, etc.	3494.5	7.0	2542.1	5.1
Automobiles	2977.8	6.0	2916.1	5.9
Petroleum	2508.3	5.1	2580.6	5.2
Land, buildings	1553.6	3.1	1971.5	4.0
Food	1234.6	2.5	521.6	1.1
Pharmaceuticals	1119.4	2.3	989.2	2.0
Hotels	1053.2	2.1	1720.0	3.5
Holdings etc.	337.4	0.7	9338.4	18.8
Together	36774.6	74.1	37876.1	76.3

Source: Own calculations based on BMWi data.

Western Europe, receiving 67.1% of West German exports, also accounts for 57.3% of total foreign direct investments. There are, however, several significant deviations. Thus, Canada, Brazil, and also the US receive a higher share of West German direct foreign investments than exports; during recent years the US has even become the most important 'host' country for West German direct investments abroad[64] (see Table 25).

Especially during 1968/69, and again since 1973/74, West German direct foreign investments have exhibited explosive growth rates. Between 1973 and 1977 (first half), total stock nearly doubled. The severe limitations of the available statistics fundamentally distort the real amount of West German direct foreign investments and do preclude any reliable international comparison.

TABLE 23
Regional Distribution of West German Direct Foreign Investment 1977/I

Country of destination	Stock of West German direct foreign investment (Million DM)	(% Share in total)	(% share, cumulated)
USA	6114	12.3	12.3
Belgium/Luxembourg	5976	10.0	22.3
France	4813	9.7	32.0
Switzerland	4694	9.5	41.5
Brazil	3747	7.6	49.1
Spain	3693	7.4	56.5
Canada	3408	6.9	63.4
Netherlands	3205	6.5	69.9
Great Britain	2103	4.2	74.1
Italy	1680	3.4	77.5
Austria	1635	3.3	80.8
Curacao	—	2.0	82.8

Source: Own calculations based on BMWi data.

TABLE 24
Regional Concentration of West German Direct Foreign Investment and Exports, 1976

Country of destination	West German FDI Stock (Billion DM)	% Share (%)	West German exports Volume (Billion DM)	% Share (%)
USA	5.4	11.4	14.4	5.6
Belgium	5.0	10.0	20.3	7.9
France	4.7	9.9	33.7	13.1
Switzerland	4.6	9.7	11.6	4.5
Brazil	3.4	7.3	2.7	1.1
Canada	3.2	6.8	2.0	0.8
Netherlands	3.1	6.6	24.8	9.7
Spain*	2.9*	6.2*	4.3	1.7
Great Britain	2.0	4.2	12.2	4.7
Italy	1.7	3.5	19.9	7.4
Together	36.0	75.6	112.2	56.5
Total Western Europe	30.0	57.3	172.1	67.1

Ranked according to the Share in West German Foreign Investment abroad.
* Canary Islands excluded.

Source Own calculations based on BMWI and Bundesbank data.

TABLE 25
Stock of West German Direct Investment Abroad, on 30 June 1977; by Selected Economic Sector and 'Host' Country

Sector industry	'host' country	USA	BEL/ LUX	FRA	SWZ	BRA	CAN (Million DM)	NTH	SPA*	GBR	ITA	AUS
All sectors		6114	4976	4813	4694	3747	3408	3205	2880*	2103	1680	1635
Mining												
Coal		93										
Iron ore							6 8					
Salt							141					
Stone, clay				105					46			45
Oil, gas extraction			133		215	53						
Energy			75		90							107
Basic materials and production goods												
Iron and steel		427		166		232	208	155				
Petroleum processing			53					81	77	750		
Chemical industries		1486	863	815	85	421	219	478	309	360	233	136
Pharmaceuticals		83		218		89				45	158	
Paper, pulp,							97					
Rubber-, asbestos									61			
Steel works				312			136					
Non-iron metals				91								

TABLE 25 (Continued)

Capital goods industries											
Machinery (non-el.)	455	80	516	185	589	89	64	214	185	328	176
Automobiles	275	830	237		677			120			41
Aircraft, parts							150				
Electrical machinery	708	163	425	96	716		108	232	85	378	164
Instruments											
Metal works					83						
Consumer goods											
Textiles		89		85							129
Ceramics			92								
Agrobusiness, food					205						
Trade and services											
Banking	114	1261	137	182	73			45	181		
Insurance	152								178		
Immobiles	267			76		740		137		55	
Hotels								1130		32	
Holdings	1012	644	532	3127	115	906	1455		34	60	
Financing	97	172		119							

* Excluding Canary Islands (813 Million DM)

Source: BMWi.

Rough estimates of the total book value of West German direct investment abroad expressed in current Dollar prices result in figures comparable to the total stock of British direct foreign investment, thus making the FRG today appear the third ranking country in terms of foreign investment.[65] According to Japanese projections,[66] both West German and Japanese direct foreign investments will surpass British investment by the early 1980s. Thus it seems that Japan, as well as the FRG, will soon reach an international investment position in concordance to its international ranking in terms of GNP and international trade — thereby again underlining the structural hierarchy in the framework of the inter-capitalist division of labour.

11.6 R&D AND TECHNOLOGY: THE WEST GERMAN ECONOMY IN THE INTERNATIONAL PRODUCT-CYCLE-COMPETITION

Because of the explosive growth of West German direct foreign investments in the 1970s the often mentioned relative lag and gap in terms of outward directed investments (if compared to the West German ranking in terms of GNP and foreign trade) may well become closed in the very near future. A similar gap has often been described in terms of West Germany's R & D expenditures and technological capacity, usually seen to be indicated by steadily rising deficits in international transfers of technology as measured by the patent- and licence-balance.[67]

In a broader perspective this deficit is even understood as only one reflection of a fundamentally 'wrong', misdirected overall development of West Germany's production- and trade-structure since the 1960s. According to several recent studies[68] West Germany's ever increasing 'over-industrialization' is caused by a hypertrophic expansion of more or less standardized and mature industrial production made possible only by a 'wrong', undervalued DM-parity prevailing during the 1950s and 1960s. To a considerable extent the 'wrong' DM-parity is seen here to have resulted in an overreliance on imported (or imitated) technology and know-how.

Thereby the West German economy is seen in effect to risk a dangerous lag and gap in terms of own and independent technological innovations. According to these evaluations, West Germany's competitive position in the capitalist world market the longer the more requires larger and more independent national capacities for economic modernization and technological innovation if the leading position in the hierarchy of inter-capitalist competition is to be maintained. Instead of an extended specialization in products and technologies in the late and mature stages of industry- and product-cycles favoured by the undervalued DM-parity and subsequently by inflows of foreign technology and foreign workers,[69] West Germany's 'real' comparative and qualtitative 'factor-proportion advantages' are seen — in the context of recently accelerated structural changes in the capitalist world economy — above all in innovative technologies and intelligent, highly sophisticated and differentiated products in the 'early' industry- and product-cycle-stages.[70]

Because of the highest industrial labour costs among the major capitalist countries[71] the West German economy is therefore recommended to intensify its future specialization in those products and technologies that make the best use of the 'human' and 'research' capital as embodied in the highly qualified work force, the innovative capacities of industry and its specific capability to organize the production of complex, tailor-made, turn-key plants, other complete industrial equipment and industrial 'problem solutions'.[72]

Actually, both business strategies and governmental policies have increasingly become directed toward the development of modern, high technology 'key'-industries.[73] Since West Germany's first post-war recession in 1966/67, private as well as public R & D expenditures have shown growth rates steadily above the international average. In the late 1970s the FRG — together with Japan — ranked second only to the US in terms of absolute volume of R & D expenses in the capitalist world economy, in real and relative terms meanwhile surpassing even American expenditure (R & D in % of GNP).[74]

While the US has become increasingly concerned since the early 1970s with the seeming erosion of its absolute technological lead and relative economic competitiveness,[75] especially with respect to Japan and its 'invasion' of the US domestic markets;[76] while an increasing number of studies have investigated the Japanese tendency to 'ride out' product-cycles, and to catch up with the US lead in certain (mostly consumer-) goods,[77] only a few studies are available on the relative development of technological competition between the US and the FRG.[78]

The fact that the expansion of West German high technology exports has not specifically concentrated on the US domestic market may go a long way to explain this gap. However, as the recent German-American controversies over the exports of nuclear power systems indicate,[79] it may well turn out that a considerably intensified technological Germano-American competition in new products and production techniques especially in (Third) World markets will characterize their bilateral economic relationship in the next decades.

Since the late 1960s accelerated concentration, centralization and internationalization processes have definitively strengthened the (domestic and foreign) commercial, technological, and financial position of West Germany's 'national champions' and 'multinational giants' relative to their major international competitors. Between 1967 and 1975, the fifty (100) largest West German industrial enterprises have increased their share in total sales of West German industry from 41.9% (69.1%) to 52.2% (62.7%); in 1975, the added volume of foreign sales of the largest twenty (fifty) corporations (for which data are available) corresponds to 55.2% (69.1%) of West German industrial exports.[80]

The degree of concentration of West German direct foreign investment, and private R & D expenditure on the very largest West German enterprises is even higher. Because of the dominant position of the largest West German corporations in industrial production and exports, R & D expenses, direct foreign investment, and foreign production especially in the most central, and internationalized industries and branches, a very large part of the international economic transactions of West German industry is in effect accounted for by the intra-corporate exchanges of West German MNCs.[81]

Based on these accelerated concentration and centralization processes, West German big business during the 1970s has continuously increased its relative position among the world's (and above all, Western Europe's) largest corporations.[82] Mergers and acquisitions, joint ventures and cooperation contracts, export cartels, consortia, and other — formal or informal — agreements and understandings between the very largest enterprises have further intensified the formation of (at least de facto) organized capital groupings and industrial complexes. Often the very same largest, and most central, big corporations are at the core of several such mutually overlapping industrial complexes (including considerable financial participations by the big banks).

These processes have been most pronounced in the modern capital goods sectors, and in key industries. The development of the Siemens Corporation may serve here as an example:[83] Due to internal and external growth, Siemens (including all its major financial participations) has become not only West Germany's largest private corporation in terms of employment and sales, but also the corporation with by far the largest absolute R & D expenditures, alone accounting for over 10% of the total private R & D expenses of the West German economy. In addition,

Siemens and its major financial participations together regularly receive well over 25% of public expenditures for 'civilian' technologies; moreover, Siemens also receives considerable shares of public spending for military R & D. Indeed, Siemens is active in nearly all priority areas of public technology policy; today, Siemens is considered even by the American electrical machinery industry as the main competitor on the world markets in several areas, including nuclear power plants.

Beyond this singular and merely illustrative example of Siemens, the highly intensified German-American competition in the Eastern,[84] and OPEC markets,[85] and especially in the markets of the most important 'threshold countries' in the Third World[86] does not only indicate a relative increase in the West German international competitiveness in high technology industries, but also implies a growing potential for conflict between the trilateral powers.

According to Leontief,[87] West Germany today has to be evaluated as a country with a considerable capacity for independent economic modernization, technological innovation, and with a remarkable degree of sectoral coherence, completeness and homogeneity. According to Leontief, it is also the only economy besides the US and USSR in the world economy which is seen as capable of a more or less autocentred and independent national policy of technological innovation.

Because of its sectoral specialization profile, its innovative technological capacities, and its well organized Western European 'influence zone', even official Japanese policy considers the West German economy as an economic-technological 'model' of future-oriented specialization to be followed closely by Japan's new strategic orientations of industrial and technology policy.[88] Together with the increasing foreign expansion of West German banking,[89] the international position of the FRG in the structural hierarchy of the inter-capitalist division of labour today is marked by remarkable strength and competitiveness.

Viewed in perspective, the trade and payment, technology, international investment, and financial position together give an overall picture of the West German economy as the dominant economy not only in the Western European system, but also, at least partially, in several other rather central sectoral and regional areas in the capitalist world market.

However, this relative international position does not really compare with the overall economic domination and political hegemony of the US. As we have stressed earlier,[90] the FRG is still structurally dependent on the US in every aspect, be it political, diplomatic, military, economic-technological or socio-cultural. This bilateral relationship of structural domination-dependence is built-in in many ways, not least by the level and degree of American penetration of the West German economy in terms of international investment and technology.

That penetration should not only be viewed in narrow economic terms. To use concepts developed by Nicos Poulantzas,[91] the German-American relationship, in the last consequence, is anchored in, as well as based on a transnational coalition of hegemonial, and ruling class factions in both national societal formations. Corresponding to the relative structural de-nationalization of West German capital due to the American penetration, there seems to exist no manifest West German 'national' bourgeoisie any more in terms of a political formation of class factions representing an autonomous national power bloc, but only an 'internal' bourgeoisie, dependently linked to the hegemonial 'outward looking', world market oriented class factions in the US, but still disposing of their own politico-economic bases for regional domination in Western Europe.

This bilateral and transnational, German-American *Herrschaftssynthese* or 'synarchy', in effect has to be seen as the essential societal base, and principal political framework of the seeming West German post-war 'success story'. West Germany has profited considerably from the institutionalized opening-up of the Western European, as well as the capitalist world markets overseas; the US, in turn tends to consider West Germany as an ally especially useful with respect to the principal American goal of preventing a possible neutralist, or anti-American Western European 'ganging up'.[92]

As a pivot of the capitalist world economy, an anchor of NATO and a dominant economy in Western Europe,[93] West Germany indeed may be well equipped (viewed from an official American, as well as West German perspective) to play the role of a (not so 'modest' and 'honest') broker and go-between in Western European, and Euro-American affairs, following both the 'bigemonic' US, and the regional, Western European option.

While the logic of the official West German foreign policy strategy has always been to prevent any political split which would force West Germany to have to choose between the United States and Western Europe, it has up to now always been made clear (explicitly or implicitly) that the US option is indeed considered as an 'alternative without alternative' for West Germany, even in the face of recent Western European reorientations in domestic politics as well as foreign policies. The recently renewed Franco-German cooperation toward a 'European Option' for a Western

European 'zone of (monetary, economic and socio-political) stability' besides, partially also against the Dollar area; the — at least from time to time indicated — American fears of a possible future 'Self-Finlandization' of West Germany; the recently intensified American demands for a (re-)politization of East-West trade and economic cooperation (de facto directed politico-economically against the FRG and Japan as the leading capitalist economies in East-West exchange); the increasing economic competition between American, West German and also Japanese corporations in the growing markets of OPEC- and Third World-'threshold' countries; the rising international competition of corporate strategies and national public programmes of industrial policies in innovative and 'strategic' sectors and branches (i.e. aircraft and armaments, computers, telecommunications and 'compunications'; electronic steerings and numeric-controlled machine tools; nuclear power plants, offshore technologies and the like) will increasingly burden this still cherished West German 'US-option' as a presumed 'alternative without alternative' with mounting problems and political conflicts.

Clearly, these economically competitive and politically conflictive tendencies will require strong efforts and institutionalized mechanisms for economic crisis and political conflict management in the very near future. It is an open question if these can be worked out successfully against the background of directly conflictive national monetary and 'industrial' policies.

III.1 THE 'MODELL DEUTSCHLAND' IN CRISIS? DILEMMAS OF STABILIZATION- AND MODERNIZATION-STRATEGIES

In spite of the relative economic strength, social cohesion and political stability which has characterized the West German economic 'miracle' and political 'model' during the recent world economic crisis; in spite of the privileged international political role, and profitable international economic position of the FRG, manifestations of structural external dilemmas and internal contradictions[94] of the West Germany societal formation are increasingly breaking through the surface of all those apologetic images picturing the FRG as a model and a success story of the 'New Europe'.

In fact, it may well turn out that just this 'systemic' model will indeed become an exemplary case — but rather in terms of a prototypical reflection of the inter- and intra-national contradictions of modern post-war capitalism as an 'international regime'.

Thus, the recent crisis manifestations, crisis perceptions, and attempted crisis managements prevailing in West Germany may be understood also as a national paradigm of these systemic dilemmas and contradictions. Only on the surface can West Germany then be viewed as a deviant case; instead the FRG may be seen here as an example where the systemic restrictions and contradictions have up to now been developed even further than in other Western European countries. As the most developed national capitalism in Western Europe, West Germany may show structural specifics in terms of the very forms and the timing of crisis manifestation; in the final analysis, the West German case may, however, only exemplify developments which will also become relevant for other Western European societal formations in the near future.

Since early 1973, even before the manifest outbreak of the 'oil' and later world economic crisis, increasing socio-economic difficulties have been felt in the FRG. At first they were viewed as a purely short-term, cyclical consequence of the super-boom and the over-accumulation of the early 1970s following the first post-war recession in 1966/67. With the intensification of the international recession, later on 'wrong' social and economic policies (especially in other 'problem'- and deficit countries) have been held responsible, in addition to merely cyclical phenomena, for the lasting economic crisis manifestations, requiring a correction in terms of deliberate and more pronounced stabilization policies.

Then, as a reaction to the apparent ineffectiveness and dilemmas of such stabilization efforts, the longer the more 'structural problems' have also been recognized as more significant than purely short-term difficulties. Structural adaptions have consequently been considered necessary for the world economy in general, and the Western European, and West German economy in particular.

Finally, as the prominent rhetoric of the 'second crisis of the world economy in this century' indicates, the official evaluations of the recent economic crisis have gradually taken on a new tone: now, with the end of the post-war era of secular growth and prosperity, West Germany, in effect, is also seen in a new, historical development stage 'beyond growth and the economic miracle' — or rather in an era of lasting crisis and structural transitions.

In line with the continuously reduced mid- and long-term growth expectations, unemployment has become the main manifestation of West Germany's structural economic crisis. Because of secularly reduced growth forecasts, and demographic trends alone, recent economic projections postulate rising, and lasting unemployment until well into the 1980s and 1990s.[95] Along with the mounting political demands of a 'new international economic order', and accelerated developments toward a 'new' international division of labour, recent ecomomic projections and models foresee decisive structural changes for the West German economy in the near future, and new structural problems because of the long-term domestic implications of such world economic tendencies. The rising import and export competition, especially in labour-, energy- and pollution-intensive productions as well as mature standardized products by export oriented Less Developed Countries (LDCs), Eastern countries, and, last but not least, by less developed industrial newcomers from the peripheries of the capitalist system will require severe structural transformations and may cause lasting sectoral and regional crises in West Germany.

Because of the highly intensified international competition of import restrictions, export subsidies, and currency manipulations between the developed capitalist economies, West Germany's international competitiveness, in spite of the still enormous trade surplusses, and in spite of the still predominant DM-facturation of West German foreign trade, will gradually become eroded from above (by the competition with developed countries) as well as from below (by the competition with export-oriented countries of the Third Word, especially from South-East Asia). Narrowing export markets and saturated domestic markets, on one side, a (postulated) profit squeeze, and 'too high' industrial labour costs (among the highest in the world), on the other, are often seen as the main consequences of such a world economic constellation for the FRG. It seems that the West German economy and society has arrived at the crossroads, confronted with only two basic future development patterns, and two basic strategy options:

1. An even more pronounced, conservative *stabilization policy*,[96] with the primary goal of correcting the existing absolute wage level, and the relative share of working class income downward to proportions prevailing in the early 1960s. This is believed to be sufficient to reach, on the basis of the existing production apparatus, the former degree of international competitiveness.

2. Some sort of a (still very vaguely outlined) *modernization policy*[97] which is based on the toleration of the existing wage levels and distribution patterns and which is basically oriented toward a modernizing reorganization and restructuring of the sectoral and product mix of the

West German economy toward new production technologies and new products in order to bring the national economy again in line with the changed socio-political conditions of production and labour and the new pattern of the international division of labour.

III.2 RATIONALIZATION- AND INTERNATIONALIZATION-DILEMMAS— TOWARD A 'SYSTEM-CRISIS' OF LEGITIMACY AND MASS-INTEGRATION?

While the latter option has gained increasing public attention and cautious consideration in governmental declarations, obviously the 'stabilization' option is the predominant choice of all official and quasi official recommendations for the future economic policy of West Germany. But the ongoing attempts to correct the income levels and patterns labour has received through collective bargaining and *Mitbestimmungs-Politik* in the institutionalized framework of the *Konzertierte Aktion* have already brought about intensified social tensions and political conflicts, especially in industrial relations.

In addition, the prevailing policies toward dismantling the (modest) results of social and economic policy initiated in the early 1970s under Willy Brandt's slogan 'To wage more democracy', and to make West Germany — and subsequently also the whole of Western Europe — 'the socially most progressive territory of the world' have led to a domestic climate of illiberal authoritarianism and restrictive, even repressive policies endangering (often in the name of the *'Rechts- and Sozialstaat'*) the very foundations of the liberal-democratic political process in FRG.

Beneath the manifest surface of such restrictive, partially even repressive domestic policies, the socio-economic determinants of such political developments become more and more visible — and at the same time contradictory.

The structural economic heterogenization of capital in terms of sectoral divergencies, and its further dichotomization into a highly concentrated and centralized, diversified, as well as internationalized 'meso'-economic plan- (or quasi-monopolist) sector on the one side, and a 'micro'-economic, non-monopolistic market-sector of small and middle, more or less dependent, marginal or highly specialized enterprises on the other side (cutting across economic sectors and industrial branches) have further intensified the structural differentiations of profit rates, and the divergencies of relative competitiveness of strong and weak industrial branches. The recent developments of production costs and world market competition have further differentiated the inter- and intra-sectoral divergencies of productivity, as well as the financial capabilities and technological potentials for investment for rationalization, modernization and foreign production.

While domestic investment for new plants and equipment has lagged for years in absolute and relative terms, investment for rationalization and modernization has reached unprecedented absolute levels and relative shares and has caused massive lay-offs and structural, 'technological' unemployment.[98]

This domestic rationalization wave has decisively intensified the structural differentiations in the immediate production- and labour processes, and has thereby resulted in the structural socio-political polarization of the labour force in terms of a highly qualified minority of workers (and work functions) on the one side, and a less qualified majority of unskilled workers (and repetitive labour functions) on the other side, implying massive dequalification processes even for the large group of the famous German *Facharbeiter*.[99]

The resulting 'qualitative' differentiation, segmentation, and structural heterogenization of labour markets are in addition deepened by the quantitative and structural effects of the internationalization process on domestic labour markets. While a large investment gap is deplored domestically, at the same time direct foreign investments are mounting. These 'emigrated' investments and increasing numbers of runaway plants have already led to considerable unemployment, and job exports due to the adverse effects on domestic investment and production, as well as their indirect effects in terms of foreign production, i.e. substituting direct exports from the FRG, and increasing imports in place of domestic products.

Based on surveys, and econometric models, recent projections forecast domestic lay-offs in the range of about 1.5 million workers until 1985 due only to the increasing imports from export-oriented Less Developed Countries (most of which are induced by MNCs).[100] The recent parity changes will further intensify the remarkable growth of West German direct foreign investment not only in peripheral low wage countries, but also in other developed countries like the US, which today is also considered a low wage, and low cost country compared to the average West German labour and production costs.

Although since the 1920s the West German labour movement has in principle accepted the inherent logic of capitalist world market competition and its structural implications for domestic collective bargaining (giving priority to the maintenance of overall West German international competitiveness), recent developments have to some extent challenged new and differentiated patterns of labour strategy increasingly reflecting the structural differentiations and heterogenizations of the West German economy and labour 'markets'.

Corresponding to the intensified sectoral dichotomization, structural heterogenization and qualitative polarization of the production and labour processes, labour's socio-political interests and strategies have gradually become more differentiated and also more divergent. Beyond the union's unifying, general demands of re-distributive social policies, and re-allocative structural policies, sectorally divergent labour interests have already resulted in at least latent new 'sectoral' coalitions and inter-sectoral conflicts among, and between, capital and labour; making it still more difficult for the unions to represent, and compromise effectively the various interests of employed and unemployed, skilled and unskilled, young and old, male and female workers in the different industrial branches and in the different functions in the immediate production and labour process.

Labour's recent break with the established form of the *Konzertierte Aktion* indicates a changed climate in West German industrial relations. Correspondingly, the growing political polarization and factionalization within the established party system reflects an important, perhaps very consequential shift in the basic constellations of West German domestic politics.

Hand in hand with the apparent ideological erosion of the social-liberal coalition may even go a gradual erosion of the 'mass-integrative'[101] system — the core of the reform-capitalist 'model' West Germany — and a gradual fragmentation of the ruling ideological consensus which may give rise to cumulative developments toward a possible crisis of stability and legitimacy as well as to a further increase in authoritarian reactions and repressive tendencies.

III.3 WESTERN EUROPEAN 'FUTURES' AND THE FUTURE OF THE 'MODELL DEUTSCHLAND': CONTEMPORARY DILEMMAS, AND FUTURE CONTRADICTIONS

While these political tendencies within West Germany have induced critical evaluations from abroad (which tend to point to a certain continuity of [West] German history), the external, international effects of an even more pronounced West German 'stabilization' policy will further contribute to the conflictive international escalation of national reactions and counter-measures, above all in Western Europe. Already the stubborn West German insistence on Western European 'conformity' to the 'Modell Deutschland' has provoked cycles of internationally competitive national stabilization strategies; a further intensification could well result in an international deflationary spiral.

Similarly, the international competition of national 'industrial' policies and technological strategies, of import restrictions and export subsidies, is challenging an international escalation of competitive nation-state intervention.

Basically aimed at the 'national' development of primarily the same 'key industries' and 'new' technologies, these competitive national 'modernization'-policies may well result in an increased and conflictive 'politicization' of international economic relations and further erode the liberal system of international economic exchange.

Recent scenarios of possible, or probable Western European 'futures'[102] clearly reflect the basic national, as well as macro-regional dilemmas and contradictions of the prevailing 'Euro-capitalist' status quo. In all recent Western European 'prospectives', the FRG emerges as the central problem, and the cardinal point of any possible future system constellation: either in the context of a renewed Euro-capitalist status quo, or of an effectively re-organized hierarchical Euro-American system, the regionally dominant and contradictory role of the FRG will remain a destabilizing element. Even in a more 'neutralist', and more 'European' Western Europe, West Germany, and its apparently built-in US-orientation and 'option' must be considered a catalyst for intra-European, and Euro-American conflicts.

But as we have already alluded the seemingly 'ultra-stable' bigemonic Germano-American bilateralism[103] may also turn out to be much less 'cooperative', and lasting than is postulated by its proponents, and feared by the critics of this German-American bilateralism as 'Ultra-imperialism'.

Beyond all these prospective scenarios, and speculative future '(anti-)mondes', the new West German problem will remain the crucial open question of any reorganized future Western European system. In our view, only a structural transformation of the very economic base, and political superstructure of the 'Modell Deutschland' into a societal formation oriented not to systemic foreign economic expansion but to societal emancipation and political autonomy can establish favourable conditions for an internationally more balanced Western Europe. This restructuring must be based on political development toward more autonomous, and self-reliant democratic-socialist societal formations beyond the systemic deformations of both late capitalism and 'real socialism'.

Over the years, the SPD has been eager to proclaim, especially in the framework of the Socialist International, the strategy of a (so-called) 'Third Way' of 'democratic socialism' for Western Europe. However, neither the SPD, and much less any other party represented in the Bundestag, seems prepared for a structural transformation of the domestic, as well as international, foundations of the stability and domination 'Modell Deutschland'.

NOTES

1. This contribution (written in January 1978) is part of the research project 'Processes of Internationalization, State Intervention and Societal Development in Western Europe — with Special Reference to France and the Federal Republic of Germany', undertaken 1975-1977 by Prof. Gilbert Ziebura (Director), Christian Deubner, Gerd Junne, Udo Rehfeldt, Frieder Schlupp et al. at the Department of Political Science, University of Konstanz, and financed by the Deutsche Forschungsgemeinschaft.

To a certain extent, this project builds on approaches developed earlier at the Otto Suhı Institute at the Free University of Berlin, and presented in: G. Ziebura, F. Ansprenger and G. Kiersch, *Bestimmungsfaktoren der Aussenpolitik in der zweiten Hälfte des 20. Jahrhunderts*, Free University of Berlin, Department of Political Science, 1974; F. Schlupp, S. Nour and G. Junne, 'Zur Theorie und Ideologie internationaler Interdependenz', in: K.-J. Gantzel (ed.), 'Internationale Beziehungen als System', *Politische Vierteljahresschrift*, Special Issue No. 5, 1973, pp. 245-307; G. Junne, S. Nour and F. Schlupp, 'Zur Grobstruktur des internationalen Systems', in: E. Krippendorff (ed.), *Internationale Beziehungen*, Köln 1973, pp. 217-241; G. Junne and S. Nour, *Internationale Abhängigkeiten*, Frankfurt 1974.

First results of the recent research project are summarized in G. Ziebura et al., *Projekt-Zwischenbericht*, University of Konstanz, Department of Political Science, June 1976, mimeo; and further elaborated in C. Deubner, U. Rehfeldt and F. Schlupp, 'Deutsch-Französische Wirtschaftsbeziehungen im Rahmen der weltwirtschaftlichen Arbeitsteilung: Interdependenz, Divergenz oder strukturelle Dominanz?' in: R. Picht (ed.), *Deutschland-Frankreich-Europa*, München 1978, pp. 91-136. The complete results of the research project will be contained in the final project report (in preparation), and a Reader: C. Deubner, U. Rehfeldt, F. Schlupp and G. Ziebura, *Die Internationalisierung des Kapitals. Neue Theorien in der internationalen Diskussion*, Frankfurt 1979.

Specific aspects of the research project are treated in other working papers and publications, including:

C. Deubner, *West German Capital in the Foundation of Euratom*. Paper presented at the CSE conference, Coventry, 1976;

——, 'Neues Spaltmaterial: Die Nuklearpolitik der Europäischen Gemeinschaft', in: *AFK-Jahrbuch 1977*;

——, 'Die Expansion des westdeutschen Kapitals und die Gründung von Euratom', in: *Leviathan*, 2, 1978;

U. Rehfeldt, 'Investissements américains en France et politique gaulliste "d'indépendance nationale",' in: ACSES (ed.), *Sur l'Etat*, Brussels 1977;

——, *Zwei offizielle Strategien zur Überwindung der Strukturkrise der westdeutschen Industrie*, Paper presented at the DVPW conference, Bonn, October 1977;

——, 'Gemeinsames Programm, Krise und internationale Arbeitsteilung — Die Grenzen des Reformismus', in: *Leviathan*, 1, 1978;

F. Schlupp, 'Internationalisierung des Kapitals und ungleiche internationale Arbeitsteilung: Das "Modell Deutschland" und der "Euro-Kapitalismus" in der Krise', in: *Forum ds*, 5, 1978; pp. 84-114;

——, *Zur Position der Bundesrepublik Deutschland in der ungleichen westeuropäischen Arbeitsteilung-Stabilitäts- und Dominanz-Dilemmata des 'Modell Deutschland'*, Paper presented at the DVPW conference, Bonn, October 1977;

——, (with G. Junne), 'Internationale Wirtschaftsbeziehungen: Politisierung der Außenwirtschaft. Die Bundesrepublik in der weltweiten Arbeitsteilung', in: *Das Parlament*, 39, 1977, pp. 12f (abridged English translation in: *The German Tribune*, No. 809 [16 October 1977], p. 6;

——, 'Das deutsche Modell und seine europäischen Folgen', in: *EG-magazin*, 5, 1978, p. 8f;

——, *'Internationalisierung und Krise-Das "Modell Deutschland" im Metropolitanen Kapitalismus'*, in: *Leviathan*, 1, 1979;

——, (with C. Deubner and U. Rehfeldt), *'Die Internationalisierung der westdeutschen Wirtschaft'*, to appear (in French translation) in Deutsch-Französisches Institut (ed.): *Etudes sur l'Allemagne*, Paris 1980.

——, *West Germany in Western European Integration: Development-Dilemmas of a Dominating Economy*; Paper presented at the IDS conference on 'Integration and Unequal Development: The Experience of Western Europe', (May/June 1979)to appear in a Reader edited by Dudley Seers and Constantine Vaitsos);

——, 'Die Bundesrepublik in Westeuropa-heimliche Großmacht oder unheimliche Dominanzmacht?', in: *Gewerkschaftliche Monatshefte* 9, 1979;

——, *West Germany, the United States, and Western Europe: Contradictions of a Dominating Economy and Hegemonic Power in the Euro-Capitalist System*; Paper presented at the APSA Annual Meeting, September 1979, Washington DC;

——, *Die widersprüchliche Rolle der Bundesrepublik in der trilateralen*

'Welt'-Wirtschaftspolitik-Zur Ideologie-Kritik des Modell Deutschland; Paper presented at the DVPW conference in Augsburg, October 1979;

In direct succession to the terminated research project, further research efforts by C. Deubner and U. Rehfeldt, under the supervision of Prof. G. Ziebura, and in cooperation with F. Schlupp, will be directed toward the investigation of 'Mediterranean' affairs: C. Deubner, *Zum Stellenwert der westlichen Mittelmeerländer in der deutschen Politik*; and U. Rehfeldt, *Frankreich zwischen nordeuropäish-atlantischer Integration, nationaler Autonomie und Mittelmeer-Strategie (unter besonderer Berücksichtigung der wirtschaftlichen Beziehungen zu Italien, Spanien und Portugal)*; both University of Konstanz, Department of Political Science, September 1977 (mimeo).

2. Cf. G. Simonis, 'Die "Neue Weltwirtschaftsordnung"-Eine Chance für die Entwicklungsländer?' in: *Vierteljahresberichte, Probleme der Entwicklungsländer*, No. 71, March 1978, pp. 5-17; K. P. Sauvant and H. Hasenpflug (eds.), *The New International Economic Order*, Boulder 1977.

3. Cf. F. Fröbel, J. Heinrichs and O. Kreye, *Die neue internationale Arbeitsteilung*, Reinbek 1977.

4. Cf. C. Hosoya, H. Owen and A. Shonfield, 'Collaboration with Communist Countries in Managing Global Problems: An Examination of the Options', *The Triangle Papers*, 13, 1977; and R. Rotermundt, U. Schmiederer and H. Becker-Panitz, *Entspannung, Systemkonkurrenz und 'Realer Sozialismus'*, Nürnberg/Osnabrück 1977.

5. A recent publication contains, however apologetical, attempts at evaluation: K. Kaiser and H.-P. Schwarz (eds.), *Amerika und Westeuropa. Gegenwarts-und Zukunftsprobleme*, Stuttgart/Zürich 1977. For a critical analysis cf: E. Mandel and W. Wolf, *Ende der Krise oder Krise ohne Ende?*, Berlin 1978.

6. I.e. J. J. Servan-Schreiber, *Le défi americain*, Paris 1967; E. Mandel, *Die Widersprüche des Imperialismus*, Berlin 1971.

7. 'One possibility is that the overwhelming economic supremacy of the United States will collapse while the positions of the European Community and Japan will be elevated, causing big changes in the balance of power which may involve risks of giving rise to various political and economic confrontations'. Japan Economic Research Center, March 1972.

8. R. Vernon, 'Rogue Elephant in the Forest. An Appraisal of Transatlantic Relations', in: *Foreign Affairs*, April 1973, p. 586.

9. Cf. J. Petras and R. Rhodes, 'The Reconsolidation of US Hegemony', in: *New Left Review*, No. 97, 1976, pp. 37ff; D. P. Calleo, 'America, Europe and the Oil Crisis: Hegemony Reaffirmed?', in: J. Chace and E. C. Ravenal (eds.), *Atlantis Lost*, New York 1976, pp. 119ff.

10. Cf. F. C. Bergsten et al., 'The Reform of International Institutions', *The Triangle Papers*, 11, 1976; and above all the publications, and declarations of Z. Brzezinski.

11. Cf. J. Halliday and G. McCormack, *Japanese Imperialism Today*, Harmondsworth 1973.

12. Cf. F. Schlupp, *Some Notes on Capital, the State, and World Market Integration. Problems Regarding the Analysis of American Domination and Regional Integration in Western Europe*. Paper presented at the ECPR conference, Louvain-La-Neuve, April 1976 and also: *Der bürgerliche Nationalstaat und die Internationalisierung des Kapitals*. Paper presented at the DVPW conference, Duisburg, October 1975.

13. Chace and Ravenal, op. cit. note 9; cf. also E. O. Czempiel and D. A. Rustow (eds.), The *Euro-American System*, Frankfurt 1976.

14. Cf. Schlupp, 'Internationalisierung des Kapitals und ungleiche internationale Arbeitstellung...', op. cit. note 1; Deubner, Rehfeldt and Schlupp, op. cit. note 1.

15. Cf. the data contained in: EEC, *System von Strukturindikatoren*, Brüssel, June 1975.

16. Cf. EEC, *Lage und Perspektiven der Weltwirtschaft: Abhängigkeiten und Einflussmöglichlichkeiten der Gemeinschaft* (Lettenhove Report), Brüssel, December 1976.

17. Schlupp, *Zur Position der Bundesrepublik...*, op. cit. note 1.

18. The concept of the *économic dominante* has been developed mainly by Francois Perroux in the context of the French theoretical, as well as political, debate on the logic and history of the international division of labour. Cf. the overview by U. Rehfeldt, *Entwicklung der bürgerlichen und marxistischen Internationalisierungstheorie in Frankreich*, University of Konstanz, May 1977 (mimeo); and the overview in: Deubner, Rehfeldt, Schlupp and Ziebura, *Die Internationalisierung des Kapitals*, op. cit. note 1.

19. Cf. the references contained in Schlupp, 'Internationalisierung des Kapitals und ungleiche Arbeitsteilung...', op. cit. note 1. An analysis of the French Left is given in Rehfeldt, 'Gemeinsames Programm...', op. cit. note 1.

20. Cf. P. C. Ludz, *Deutschlands doppelte Zukunft*, München 1974, especially pp. 35ff; SPD, 'Weiterarbeiten am Modell Deutschland', *Regierungsprogramm 1976-80*, 1976.

21. Cf. F. C. Bergsten, 'The United States and Germany: The Imperative of Economic Bigemony', in: F. C. Bergsten, *Toward a New International Economic Order*, Lexington 1975, pp. 333ff.

22. Cf. A. Baring and M. Sase (eds.), *Zwei zaghafte Riesen? Deutschland und Japan seit 1945*, Stuttgart/Zürich 1977.

23. Cf. F. Bergsten, op. cit. note 21; ibid., 'Die amerikanische Europapolitik angesichts der Stagnation des Gemeinsamen Marktes. Ein Plädoyer für Konzentration auf die Bundesrepublik', in: *Europa-Archiv*, 4, 1974, pp. 115ff.

24. Cf. the recently intensified demands contained in the *International Economic Report of the President*, Washington 1978.

25. Cf. above all *The Triangle Papers*, 11, op. cit. note 10, and 12 (J. R. Schaetzel et al., 'The Problem of International Consultations', 1976).

26. A short case-study on German-American cooperation 'to make the world safe for the multinational corporation' is contained in F. Schlupp, *Internationalisierung des Kapitals, bürgerlicher Nationalstaat und Internationale Organisationen in den Metropolen: Die OECD und die Multinationalen Konzerne*. Paper presented at the workshop 'Internationale Organisation und Integration', Strasbourg, April 1977.

27. An elaboration of this assumption will be given in our Reader on new theories of internationalization of capital; cf. Deubner, Rehfeldt, Schlupp and Ziebura, op. cit. note 1.

28. This argument is at the core of all publications and declarations of the Trilateral Commission. Cf. *The Triangle Papers*, No. 1 (1973) - No. 15 (1978).

29. Several contributions in *Le Monde* have become especially prominent in this context. Cf. also 'Das Bild vom bösen Deutschland', in: *Der Spiegel*, 35, 1977, pp. 76ff; 'Ist Deutschland ein Alptraum?', in: *Die Zeit*, 36, 1977, p. 1; 'Bonn in der Rolle des Schurken', in: *Die Zeit*, 44, 1977, p. 20; 'Le nouvel imperialisme allemand', in: *Economia*, 35, 1977, pp. 80ff.

30. Cf. Chancellor Helmut Schmidt, Regierungserklärung, 19 January 1978.

31. Willy Brandt, 'Patriot muß Internationalist sein', in: *Südkurier*, 28 December 1977.

32. Cf. R. Dahrendorf, 'Themen, die keiner nennt. I. Außenpolitik: Die europäische und die amerikanische Option', in: *Die Zeit*, 39, 1976.

33. Cf. especially the articles cited in notes 14 and 17; and Schlupp, 'Das deutsche Modell und seine europäischen Folgen', op. cit. note 1.

34. Cf. the volumes edited by D. Senghaas: *Imperialismus und strukturelle Gewalt. Analysen über abhängige Reproduktion*, Frankfurt 1972; and: *Peripherer Kapitalismus. Analysen über Abhängigkeit und Unterentwicklung*, Frankfurt 1974.

35. Recent critical evaluations of 'the state of the art' concerning the theory of trade, investment, and the international division of labour are contained in: A. Lemper, *Handel in einer dynamischen Weltwirtschaft*, München 1974; H. Giersch (ed.), *The International Division of Labour. Problems and Perspectives*, Tübingen 1974; W. Bärtschi and H.-D. Jacobsen, *Kritische Einführung in die Außenhandelstheorie*, Reinbek 1976; R. Sohns, *Theorie der internationalen Arbeitsteilung*, Stuttgart 1976; H.-D. Meier, *Der Konkurrenzkampf auf dem Weltmarkt*, Frankfurt 1977.

36. Cf. the short overview in: L. T. Wells (ed.), *The Product Life Cycle and International Trade*, Boston 1972.

37. Cf. above all the works by C. Palloix: *Procès de production et crise du capitalisme*, Grenoble 1977; *L'Internationalisation du capital*, Paris 1975; and: *Les Firmes Multinationales et le procès d'internationalisation*, Paris 1973.

38. Cf. T. Ozawa, *Japan's Technological Challenge to the West, 1950-1974: Motivation and Accomplishment*, Cambridge 1974; M. Y. Yoshino, *Japan's Multinational Enterprises*, Cambridge 1976; Y. Tsurumi, *The Japanese Are Coming. A Multinational Interaction of Firms and Politics*, Cambridge 1976.

39. Cf. F. Wolter, 'Factor Proportions, Technology and West German Industry's International Trade Patterns', in: *Weltwirtschaftliches Archiv, 1977*, pp. 250-267; E. J. Horn, *Technologische Neuerungen und internationale Arbeitsteilung: Die Bundesrepublik Deutschland im internationalen Vergleich*, Tübingen 1976; H. Majer, *Die 'technologische Lücke' zwischen der Bundesrepublik Deutschland und den Vereinigten Staaten von Amerika*, Tübingen 1973; IFO/RWI, 'Die Entwicklung der Außenhandelsstruktur, der Industriestruktur und der Auslandsinvestitionen der deutschen Wirtschaft unter Berücksichtigung des Einflusses der Wechselkursänderungen', *Hauptbericht*, Gutachten im Auftrag des BMWI, München/Essen, July 1976; HWWA, *Der Einfluss Multinationaler Unternehmen auf Branchenstruktur und Aussenwirtschaft der Bundesrepublik Deutschland*, Gutachten erstellt im Auftrage des BMWI, Hamburg 1976.

40. A rather short overview on new theories of the sectoralization and hierarchization of the international division of labour, and national economies mainly developed in France is contained in: B. Mettler-Meibom and P. H. Mettler, 'Internationale Arbeitsteilung. Entwicklungstendenzen aus französischer Sicht', in: *Wirtschaftsdienst 1977*, pp. 360-365.

41. A recent synopsis of historical studies comparing, and explaining the development of Great Britain, and Germany in the 19th century, and until 1914 is given by C. P. Kindleberger, 'Germany's Overtaking of England, 1806-1914', in: *Weltwirtschaftliches Archiv 1975*, pp. 253-281 (Part I) and pp. 477-504 (Part II). Cf. also W. Spohn, *Weltmarktkonkurrenz und Industrialisierung Deutschlands 1870-1914*, Berlin 1977.

42. The early application of 'Taylorism' and (neo-)'Fordism' as modern reorganizations of relative surplus production in German industry is investigated in: E. Brockhaus, *Zusammensetzung und Neustrukturierung der Arbeiterklasse vor dem ersten Weltkrieg*, München 1975; P. Hinrichs and L. Peter, *Industrieller Friede? Arbeitskraft und Rationalisierung in der Weimarer Republik*, Köln 1976. Cf. also the case study by W. Ebach,

Moderne Fertigungsmethoden der deutschen Elektro-Industrie und ihre wirtschaftlichen Auswirkungen, Diss. Universität Köln, 1935.

43. Cf. the works by Palloix, op. cit. note 37.

44. Cf. also U. Rehfeldt, *Stärken und Schwächen der westdeutschen Wirtschaft*, University of Konstanz, January 1977 (mimeo).

45. Cf. the contributions cited in notes 14 and 17.

46. Cf. note 1.

47. Reference is made here to our final project report, and our Reader.

48. Cf. the earlier works by W. Michalski, *Export und Wirtschaftswachstum*, Hamburg 1970; A. Wagner, *Die Wachstumszyklen in der Bundesrepublik Deutschland*, Tübingen 1972.

49. Cf. M. Kreile, 'West Germany: The Dynamics of Expansion', in: *International Organization*, Vol. 31, 4, Autumn 1977, pp. 775-808.

50. Cf. E. J. Horn, 'Ist die BRD überindustrialisiert?', in: *Wirtschaftsdienst* 1976, pp. 345ff.

51. Cf. F. Wolter, *Die Bundesrepublik Deutschland als Standort für die Produktion von Investitionsgütern*, Kiel 1977 (Kieler Diskussionsbeiträge No. 49).

52. Cf. *DIW-Wochenberichte*, 5, 1978, p. 59. West German exports to countries of the Arab League meanwhile (in 1977) equal those to the US or Great Britain: cf. Commerzbank, *Berichte der Abteilung Volkswirtschaft*, 31 August 1977.

53. Cf. EEC, *Quinze Ans De Politique Communautaire* (Maillet Report), Bruxelles, 5 December 1972, especially Part I, Section 3.

54. Cf. Deubner, Rehfeldt and Schlupp, op. cit. note 1; and the project paper by J. Staud, *Art und Ausmaß der Einbettung der deutschen und französischen Ökonomie in den Welthandel*, University of Konstanz, December 1977 (mimeo).

55. Cf. UN, *Multinational Corporations in World Development*, New York 1973.

56. Cf. US Senate, Committee on Finance, *Implications of Multinational Firms for World Trade and Investment and for US Trade and Labour*, Washington (GPO) February 1973, especially Chapter III; F. Schlupp, *Multinational Corporations and the Inter-Capitalist Division of Labor: The Case of the 'Trans-Atlantic System'*, Paper presented at the ECPR conference in Strasbourg, April 1974.

57. Cf. the extensive bibliography on studies of direct foreign investment in West Germany included in G. Junne et al., *Die Regionalverteilung Ausländischer Investitionen in der Bundesrepublik Deutschland*, University of Konstanz, Fachbereich Politische Wissenschaft, August 1975 (the first study so far to analyze empirically the regional distribution of direct foreign investment in the FRG according to Bundesländer, and 'central' or 'peripheral' areas).

58. Cf. HWWA, *Die Rolle der Multinationalen Unternehmen im Zusammenhang mit der deutschen Währungspolitik*, Hamburg 1974; ibid., *Der Einfluss Multinationaler Unternehmen auf Branchenstruktur und Aussenwirtschaft der Bundesrepublik Deutschland*, Hamburg 1976.

59. According to Deutsche Bundesbank, *Monatsberichte*, 11, 1974.

60. Own calculations based on: Monopolkommission, *Hauptgutachten I*, Baden-Baden 1976.

61. Cf. F. Schlupp, *Konzentration, Zentralisation und Internationalisierung des westdeutschen Kapitals*, MS Universität Konstanz, March 1977.

62. Cf., i.e. M. Wilkins, *The Maturing of Multinational Enterprise*, Cambridge 1974; E. A. Philipps, 'American Direct Investment in West German manufacturing industries',

in: *Current Economic Comment*, 1960, pp. 29-43; *Directory of American Business in Germany*, München 1977[6].

63. Cf. German Chamber of Industry and Commerce (London), *List of Addresses — British Firms and Their German Subsidiaries*; Commerzbank, *Niederländische Beteiligungen in der Bundesrepublik*, September 1969.

64. Cf. 'Spiegel-Report über deutsche Investitionen in den USA', in: *Der Spiegel*, 41, 1977, pp. 119ff.

65. H. Krängenau, 'Deutsche Direktinvestitionen in den siebziger Jahren', in: *Wirtschaftsdienst*, 7, 1977, pp. 360ff uses only the official BMWI data which do not include reinvested profits, and direct investment financed by international credits and other foreign funds.

66. Cited in: *Entreprise*, No. 1015, 1975, p. 71.

67. As many observers have pointed out, the official statistics on international transactions in terms of patents and licences are not very useful because of severe limitations in coverage, and vague criteria for inclusion. Cf. 'Patent-und Lizenzbilanz. Der Saldo täuscht', in: *Wirtschaftswoche*, No. 29, 1977, pp. 57ff.

68. Cf. the short overview given in: Ziebura et al., *Projekt-Zwischenbericht*, Universität Konstanz, July 1976, Part. 3.

69. Cf. the summary: K. W. Schatz, 'Zum sektoralen und regionalen Strukturwandel in der Bundesrepublik Deutschland', in: WSI, *Mitteilungen*, 11, 1976, pp. 653ff.

70. V. Hauff and F. Scharpf, *Modernisierung der Volkswirtschaft. Technologiepolitik als Strukturpolitik*, Frankfurt 1975.

71. According to *Handelsblatt*, 18 January 1978, p. 2, in 1977 hourly labour costs per industrial worker in the FRG were DM 18.70, compared to DM 16.20 in the US, and DM 11.30 in France.

72. Cf. R. Dick, 'Wettbewerbsfähigkeitund Spezialisierung des westdeutschen Maschinenbaus', in: *Die Weltwirtschaft*, 1, 1975, pp. 159ff.

73. Cf. S. Tanski, 'Die Forschungs- und Entwicklungstätigkeit in der BRD', in: *Volks- und Betriebswirt*, 10, 1976.

74. Cf. *International Economic Report of the President*, Washington 1976.

75. Cf. for a recent overview: *Der Spiegel*, 46, 1977, pp. 196ff.

76. Cf. the case study: R. Heller and E. Heller, *Japanese Investment in the United States*, New York 1975.

77. Cf. the works cited in note 38, and K. Kojima, *Japan and a New World Economic Order*, Tokyo 1977, especially Chapters 3 and 4.

78. Only very indirectly this problem is investigated by K. Henkner, *Wettbewerbsrelationen im Außenhandel westlicher Industrieländer 1959-1973*, Berlin/München 1976. Official investigations often reach rather divergent results. Cf., i.e. the conclusions in: *International Economic Report of the President*, Washington 1976; and by the National Science Foundation, referred to in: *Der Spiegel*, 14, 1976, p. 216.

79. Cf. C. Deubner, *Die Atompolitik der westdeutschen Industrie und die Gründung von Euratom*, Frankfurt 1977, Vorwort: 'Das Brasiliengeschäft und die Krise der internationalen Atompolitik der Bundesrepublik Deutschland'.

80. Own calculations based on the Commerzbank,' *Lists of the Largest West German Industrial Enterprises*. Cf. also note 61.

81. Cf. the selective sample data contained in the HWWA studies (note 58). According to this data base, intra-MNC trade in several West German industries reaches an even higher percentage-share than in the corresponding US cases.

82. Based on presence in the *Fortune* (and other) lists of the largest corporations outside the US.

83. Cf. 'Spiegel Report über die Siemens AG', in: *Der Spiegel*, 42, 1977, pp. 199ff; F. Schlupp and R. Steinweg, 'Die Rüstungsproduktion westdeutscher Konzerne II: Der Siemens-Konzern', in: *Friedensanalysen*, No. 5, 1977, pp. 195ff.

84. Cf. H. D. Jacobsen, *Die wirtschaftlichen Beziehungen zwischen West und Ost*, Reinbek 1975.

85. Cf. Commerzbank, *Aussenhandelsblätter*, 4, 1977.

86. Especially Brazil, Iran, Nigeria, Indonesia, and similar cases.

87. Interview, in: *Europe-Bulletin*, No. 2085, 2 November 1976, p. 13.

88. 'The Industrial Structure Council's long-term vision seems implicitly to set up the composition of West Germany's industry and trade as a model for Japan', K. Kojima, op. cit. note 77, p. 145.

89. Cf. U. Steuber, *Internationale Banken*, Hamburg 1977.

90. Cf. the contributions cited in note 12.

91. Cf. N. Poulantzas, 'Die Internationalisierung der kapitalistischen Produktionsverhältnisse und der Nationalstaat', in: O. Kreye (ed.), *Multinationale Konzerne*, München 1974, pp. 81ff.

92. Cf. W. Link, 'Zum Problem der Kontinuität der amerikanischen Deutschlandpolitik im zwanzigsten Jahrhundert', in: M. Knapp (ed.), *Die deutsch-amerikanischen Beziehungen nach 1945*, Frankfurt 1975, pp. 86ff.

93. Cf. P. J. Katzenstein, 'West Germany's Place in American Foreign Policy: Pivot, Anchor, or Broker?' in: R. Rosecrance (ed.), *America as an Ordinary Country: US Foreign Policy and the Future*, Ithaca 1976; abridged German translation in: *Europa-Archiv*, 11, 1976, pp. 347ff.

94. Cf. the very divergent evaluations and analyses by H. Elsenhans, *Akkumulationsprobleme in der Bundesrepublik*. Paper presented at the DVPW congress, Bonn, October 1977; F. Haenschke, *Modell Deutschland? Die Bundesrepublik in der technologischen Krise*, Reinbek 1977; H. Baisch, J. Berger, C. Brockhaus et al., 'Die Wirtschaftskrise in der BRD', in: *Leviathan*, 2, 1977, pp. 163ff; R. Dahrendorf, 'Wanken die Fundamente unseres Staates?', in: *Die Zeit*, 34, 1977, p. 3. A short overview over West Germany's development until the early 1970s is contained in G. Minnerup, 'West Germany since the War', in: *New Left Review*, No. 88, 1976, pp. 3ff.

95. Cf. the differing approaches and results of the following long-term projections: H. Vögele, *Die Auswirkungen des gesamtwirtschaftlichen Strukturwandels auf die Nachfrage nach Arbeitskräften in den Bundesländern. Eine Prognose der Wirtschaftsstruktur und des Arbeitsplätzeangebots bis 1985*, Kiel 1975; G. Butler and B. Hof, *Bevölkerung und Arbeitsmarkt bis zum Jahr 2000*, Köln 1977; 'US-Prognose für die Bundesrepublik' (projection of the Chase Econometric Associates Inc), cited in: *Handelsblatt*, 12 December, 1977; E. Pestel et al., 'Das Deutschland-Modell', in: *bild der wissenschaft*, 1, 1978, pp. 22ff.

96. Cf. Rehfeldt Zwei, 'Offizielle' Strategien...', op. cit. note 1. Historical parallels in terms of social and economic orientations prevailing between 1929/33 and 1973/75 are investigated by H. Abromeit, 'Interessendurchsetzung in der Krise', in: *aus politik und zeitgeschichte*, No. 11, 1977, pp. 15ff.

97. Cf. Hauff and Scharpf, op. cit. note 70 and the recent SPD paper, *Vorausschauende Strukturpolitik fur Vollbeschäftigung und humanes Wachstum*, Bonn, June 1977.

98. An elaboration of this problem will be found in G. Junne, F. Schlupp et al., *Technischer Fortschritt und Rationalisierung in der Krise als wirtschaftspolitisches Problem* (in preparation). Cf. also the contributions to *Leviathan*, 1, 1979; 'Internationalisierung und Krise in der BRD'.

99. Cf. H. von Henninges and M. Tessaring, *Entwicklungstendenzen des Facharbeitereinsatzes in der BRD*, Bonn 1977; M. Tessaring, 'Qualifikationsspezifische Arbeitslosigkeit in der Bundesrepublik Deutschland', in: *Mitteilungen aus der Arbeitsmarkt- und Berufsforschung*, 2, 1977, pp. 229ff.

100. Cf. H. Dicke et al., *Beschäftigungswirkungen einer verstärkten Arbeitsteilung zwischen der Bundesrepublik und den Entwicklungsländern,* Tübingen 1976; U. Hiemenz and K. W. Schatz, *Transfer of Employment Opportunities as an Alternative to International Migration of Workers: The Case of the Federal Republic of Germany*, ILO (WEP 2-26/WP.7), Geneva, August 1976. Quite different results are contained in recent studies by the Deutsches Institut für Wirtschaftsforschung (DIW) — Cf. D. Schumacher, 'Verstärkter Handel mit der Dritten Welt: Eher Umsetzung als Freisetzung deutscher Arbeitskräfte', in: *DIW-Wochenbericht*, 5, 1977; and: 'Beschäftigungswirkungen von Importen aus Entwicklungsländern nicht dramatisieren', in: *DIW-Wochenbericht*, 1, 1978; and: '800 000 Erwerbstätige für den Export in Entwicklungsländer beschäftigt', in: *DIW-Wochenbericht*, 5, 1978.

101. Cf. J. Hirsch, 'Krise der Massenintegration. Zur Entwicklung der politischen Repression in der BRD', in: *links*, No. 81, October 1976, pp. 10ff.

102. Cf. above all the innovative and comprehensive French study: GRESI, *La division internationale du travail*, Paris 1976, containing three main scenarios; O. Kallscheuer, 'Völker und Fronten. Modelle für die Zukunft Europas', in: *Kursbuch*, 46, December 1976, pp. 33ff; also C. Lutz, *Von der Wirtschaftsgemeinschaft zur Europäischen Union*, Bonn 1977, and: 'Blick nach vorn voll Unsicherheit', in: *eg-magazin*, 7-8, 1977, pp. 28f.

103. Even quasi-official evaluations are increasingly marked by a rising uneasiness with respect to German-American bilateralism. Cf. i.e. U. Nerlich, 'Washington und Bonn: Entwicklungsstrukturen im deutsch-amerikanischen Verhältnis', in: K. Kaiser and H. P. Schwartz (eds.), *Amerika und Westeuropa*, Stuttgart/Zürich 1977, pp. 330ff.

3

WHATEVER HAPPENED TO GERMANY?

Gebhard Schweigler

I. STATE AND NATION IN GERMANY

WHATEVER HAPPENED TO GERMANY? Does the German nation still exist today or has it disappeared? In an attempt at answering this, for Germany existential, question, scholars and propagandists in both parts of Germany have produced a literature too voluminous to even survey.[1] And they have not reached any firm conclusions.

The easiest question to ask would seem to be: does the German *state* still exist today? For there is very little concrete evidence that it does. There now exist on German soil two states, a fact officially recognized by West Germany only in 1969, when then Chancellor Willy Brandt coined the term 'two states in one nation'. Still, when Brandt attempted to translate this belated recognition of post-war realities into concrete political gains, he was confronted once again with the incredibly complex intricacies inherent in German law and further developed by German legal scholars who had sought to prove all along that the German state, the Reich, still existed and had, in fact, never vanished. (The necessity to do so derived from many sources, not the least important of which was to define West Germany's responsibilities as a successor state to the Reich; politically, such efforts were motivated by the desire to prove that the GDR was, in legal fiction at least, an international outlaw, and thus to retain the political conditions for eventual reunification. The results of these efforts remained contradictory and were never very convincing.)[2]

When, in 1972, the West German Government concluded a 'Treaty on the Basis of Relations' with the GDR, in which West Germany extended recognition of sorts in exchange for East German and Russian concessions on Berlin, cross-border travel, and other relaxations of restrictions, one of the opposition parties, Bavaria's Christian-Social Union (CSU) under the leadership of Franz Josef Strauß, challenged the constitutionality of the treaty,[3] arguing that full recognition of the GDR as a separate state was against various provisions of West Germany's constitution, the Basic Law. The Constitutional Court ruled that the treaty was, in fact, constitutional, but in the process insisted that the German Reich is not extinguished, and that relations between the GDR and the Federal Republic are of a very special nature. The ruling, termed 'unpalatable conceptual mush' by one of West Germany's foremost legal scholars,[4] reaffirmed that the West German Government must seek the reunification of Germany, but it left the methods to be employed to the discretion of the government. The government, in turn, argued that a normalization of relations with the GDR was in the interest of reunification, since it would keep alive the Germans' sense of belonging together, and that it had, in any case, not extended full recognition to the GDR (it could point to a number of fine distinctions, such as that only 'representatives' and not ambassadors were exchanged, or even that President Heinemann wore only street clothes, and not the formal attire required by diplomatic protocol, when he received the GDR's 'representative').

Almost everybody outside of Germany, and indeed an overwhelming majority of public opinion within West Germany,[5] believed that with the conclusion of the 'Basic Treaty' the dissolution of the German Reich had become recognized in fact, if not yet in legal fiction. Certainly the membership of both German states in international organizations such as the United Nations would speak to that fact. However unsettled legally the question about the continued existence of the German *state* might still be (after the Constitutional Court's ruling only a change of the Basic Law would permanently settle the legal issues), there can be little doubt that, for all practical purposes, Germany as a state no longer exists.

That leaves the question about Germany's existence as a *nation*. In German scholarly tradition, reflecting in part Germany's historical experiences, the distinction has always been made between the state, defined by the limits of political power of its institutions, and the nation, defined by the limits of its cultural characteristics. The phrase 'two states in one nation' reflects that distinction between *Staatsnation* and *Kulturnation*. Particularly in the German case, however, this seems hardly a useful distinction, even though German intellectuals especially have time and again suggested that the Germans concentrate on the *Kulturnation* and forget about the *Staatsnation*.[6] For one, there is the difficulty of limits: the German language, the most important distinguishing cultural characteristic, is also spoken in Austria and in parts of Switzerland, neither belonging to, nor wanting to be part of, Germany.

It could of course be argued that the concept of *Kulturnation* is non-political, that it does not contain any notion of re-creating a German Reich even larger than that to be reunited in its borders of 1937. This seems an unpolitical argument. History, not the least German history, has shown that a *Kulturnation* will invariably strive not only for cultural but also for political unity and self-determination. Precisely in such a development lies the danger of the concept of *Kulturnation*. If, on the other hand, a German *Kulturnation* is to be devoid of any such political ambitions (and most supporters of the concept argue that it should be), then the German nation so defined could hardly serve as a focal point for the national loyalities and ambitions of the German people, not in a world that is made up of nation-states and seemingly ruled by nationalism. If, as is argued, the allegedly dangerous demands for institutional reunification are to be pre-empted by focusing instead on the 'spiritual unity of the nation' (so argues Mommsen), then such a policy is unlikely to be successful, but fraught with dangers of a different kind. In any case, for the time being the West German Government is obligated by the Constitutional Court not to pursue a policy of reducing the German nation to the concept of *Kulturnation*, since such a policy would, in the Court's opinion, lead the Federal Government away from the constitutionally mandated goal of seeking the reunification of Germany in institutional terms.

Kulturnation, as defined by German intellectuals, is an essentially elitist concept, since it refers to culture in its meaning of 'high culture'. For that reason alone it is unlikely to appeal to the population at large. But there is another, anthropological definition of culture as the distinctive way of life of a group of people, which enables such people to live together, to exclude 'outsiders', and to develop and maintain a sense of uniqueness — of being a nation. Does the German *Kulturnation* so defined still exist today? The answer is already difficult. Certainly the driving motive behind the new *Ostpolitik* pursued since 1969 derived precisely from fears that the Germans in East and West were becoming estranged from each other (for which there is considerable evidence). It was in order to overcome this process of estrangement — or, in other words, of increasing cultural alienation — that the Brandt Government sought to gain the means for increased contacts. As he put it: 'Nation means seeing each other again'.

But it is hardly enough to define nation in those terms, not in an age where increased communication across all borders contributes to a general levelling of cultural differences. (Innumerably more West Germans visit Austria each year than East Germany, yet from such contacts, and from the unquestioned similarity in cultural patterns, derive no demands for another *Anschluß*, or beliefs that Austria is or should be part of the German nation.) In the final analysis, it is the national consciousness of a people that defines a nation: 'a body of people who feel that they are a nation'.[7] That concept of a nation, which seems particularly applicable to the German case, might be termed, in untranslatable German, *Bewußtseinsnation*.[8] Only a people that believe that they form a nation do so; and only if they *want* the nation will they, unless external obstacles prevent them, achieve national unity. The German question, therefore, is a question about the Germans' national consciousness: do they still believe they are a nation? and do they really want the reunification of their nation? We will examine this question, first for the German Democratic Republic, then for the Federal Republic of Germany, developing categories and concepts for an analysis of national consciousness, and presenting empirical evidence as we go along.

II STATE AND NATION IN THE GERMAN DEMOCRATIC REPUBLIC

Can anything definite be said about national consciousness in the GDR? Researchers on East Germany are not agreed. There are those, particularly non-German observers, who in recent years have noted the development of a GDR-focused national conciousness and the decline of an all-German national consciousness.[9] Their observations are contradicted by prominent West German researchers, who tend to view such reports as faddish and argue that no definitive statements can be made, since proper empirical research within the GDR has not been conducted and cannot be conducted. As it was put in the *Materialien zum Bericht zur Lage der Nation 1974*:[10]

> There is a tendency to assume the existence of an increasing state-consciousness within the GDR, which is said to be the natural expression of the importance of communication and orientation, which the institutions of the state have assumed for the daily lives of the people. To what extent this state-consciousness coincides with normative elements of national concepts as proclaimed by the SED leadership must remain open.

A footnote to this statement explained that so far there has been no empirical work done on the question of national consciousness in the GDR.[11]

Despite this acknowledged lack of empirical data, many West German scholars do not hesitate to make assertions about the continued existence of an all-German national consciousness in the GDR. Thus the *Materialien 1974* claimed that, even though it could not really be proven empirically, Germans in East and West were still mutually relating to each other and that this constituted 'an essential part of the reality of the German nation'.[12] Peter C. Ludz, chief investigator for the *Materialien*, argued elsewhere that 'the continual insistence on *one* German nation and the very rejection of this insistence by the SED proves beyond all doubt that some sort of "one Germany" notion must exist in the minds of the Germans'.[13] Specifically for the GDR, Ludz claimed that the SED's propaganda line on the non-existence of the German nation 'remains unacceptable to large segments of the population, because it contradicts the still existing sense of national belonging-together and because it seems to put a final stamp on the division of Germany'.[14]

The confidence for such statements, based as they are on non-empirical evidence, derives from an interpretation of political events within the GDR. Such events may, however, well be of limited relevance. To take one prominent example: when Willy Brandt, during his first visit to East Germany, in March 1970, was called to the window by a surging crowd outside his hotel, many observers viewed this outburst of emotions as clear evidence for an all-German national consciousness among the East German population. It may well have been, but how can we be sure? Did those present at the time really reflect the emotional make-up of the GDR population at large? And did they, perhaps, react merely to the presence of a prominent statesman, with an emotion similar to that displayed by West German crowds when de Gaulle and Kennedy visited the Federal Republic? We cannot be certain, and therefore any interpretation of this and similar events must remain questionable.

More recent events that led to speculations about the state of East German attitudes had to do with attempts by the East German leadership to redefine its official position on the national question. According to one account, such efforts 'met with a lack of understanding and disagreement in broad strata of the population of the GDR'.[15] A West German journalist stationed in East Berlin claimed that 'a majority of the people could not muster any understanding for the denial of the nation. The national reality proved to be stronger than the will of the Party'.[16]

These are strong assertions, and they undoubtedly reflect the majority opinion of the West German scholarly and political community. Still, one may wonder on the basis of what evidence these statements about 'broad strata' or even 'a majority' of the East German population were made. And a different interpretation of the SED's actions and public reactions might well challenge the conclusion that the East German population still shares a strong all-German national consciousness.

As far as its treatment of the national question is concerned, the SED leadership's basic dilemma has always been that it announced changes in its position, often in reaction to developments in West Germany, without being certain beforehand where such changes were going to lead it. In its early years, the SED vigorously pursued a policy of national reunification, albeit under Communist rule (and thus not acceptable to the West). The border remained more or less open until 1952, when, in reaction to West Germany's signature under the so-called 'Germany Treaty' (the instrument of West Germany's integration into the Western military alliance), the border was closed. After the projected European Defense Community suffered an early death in the French Parliament, the SED saw a renewed chance to influence events in West Germany. Thereafter, it announced a policy of 'Germans at one table', which saw a deliberate effort to bring East and West Germans together (but representatives from both governments did not sit down at one table, as the SED had hoped). After 1955, however, when the Federal Republic became a member of NATO, the realization gradually grew in the SED that this early variant of a policy of 'change through rapprochment'[17] did not produce the desired results. Only then did the East German leadership announce the existence of two states in one nation and begin to submit plans for a confederation of the two states. The wall in Berlin, erected in August 1961, symbolized rather concretely the attempt by the SED to gain that external and internal freedom of manoeuvre required for a successful development of its own state.

Two years later, the SED once again tried to induce in West Germany a 'change through rapprochment'. It concluded a pass agreement in Berlin (allowing West Berliners to visit East Berlin during holidays), relaxed travel restrictions in general, and finally called for an ideological competition with the SPD (in which the SED placed particular hopes as the party representing the West German working classes). These hopes were dashed when an exchange of speakers, scheduled for the summer of 1966, failed. In Fall 1966, the SPD entered into a Grand Coalition with the CDU/CSU, thus proving her ideological unreliability — or so the

SED interpreted it. Thereafter the SED viewed the Federal Republic as neither capable nor worthy of a federation with the GDR. Consequently, the SED, in Spring 1967, announced a law providing for a separate East German citizenship; in 1968, it also produced a new constitution, in which the GDR was termed a 'socialist state of the German nation' — a nation which, as the new constitution put it, could be united, not reunited.

The SED's attempt to establish the GDR as a state in its own right proved more or less successful internally because of the domestic consolidation achieved after the building of the Wall.[18] It was also successful externally, though bought at considerable cost. West Germany's new *Ostpolitik* after 1969 brought international recognition to the GDR, but in the process also opened the GDR to new influences from the West, not the least through personal contacts which had previously been very much restricted. The SED felt compelled to combat these influences not only politically (for instance, by requiring party members and government employees not to have contacts with West Germans), but also ideologically. It began to cut all ties to the German nation, in an effort at solidifying its claims to separate nationhood (and thus denying all claims by West Germany about the continued existence of the German nation). To prove the point, it eliminated the word 'German' wherever it could; it also presented, to everyone's surprise, yet another revised constitution (in October 1974), in which all references to the German nation were deleted.

It is quite likely that many East Germans reacted to these efforts with disbelief and unrest. But their reaction need not necessarily have been based on an all-German national consciousness; it could just as well have been due to the SED's lack of a convincing answer to the question: what are we, if not German?

Apparently the SED leadership never bothered to ask itself that question; or, once it was confronted by it, could not answer it satisfactorily. Thus it had to halt its campaign before it had gone all the way (many had expected elimination of the word 'German' from 'German Democratic Republic' and *Sozialistische Einheitspartei Deutschlands*); this, in turn, created new unrest.

What could have been the answer? The 1974 constitution stated only that the GDR is a 'socialist state of workers and peasants', which hardly suffices to delineate national boundaries (after all, all East European countries are supposedly just that). Are there alternatives? None that are realistic at the moment. The SED is facing a real dilemma: German it does not want to be, something else — like People's Republic of Prussia? — it cannot be. For the time being, the SED is maintaining the position that the GDR is a socialist nation and thus in no way comparable with the capitalist nation West Germany, though both are admittedly of 'German nationality'.

But this cannot be the final resolution of the dilemma. To define the nation in terms of class characteristics is not convincing, either at home or abroad (nor does it conform to standard interpretations of nationhood in East and West). At best this definition can serve to describe an intermediate stage of development and thus to keep open certain options: either toward further integration with other 'socialist nations' (an option followed with some vehemence since 1970), or toward eventual reunification, once the other part of the nation has realized the dictatorship of the proletariat (an option currently eliminated from official propaganda, but of course always available because of Marxist interpretations of history). Nor does the distinction between 'socialist nation' and 'German nationality' free the SED from its definitional dilemma. If the GDR is still of German nationality, then it is by common definition part of the German *Kulturnation*, which it does not want to be. It therefore claims that the GDR represents elements of German culture different from those in West Germany (only the best, in other words).[19] And it also argues, since culture can be defined in other terms, that to the extent that a socialist way of life will take root in the minds of the people, certain ethnic characteristics will also change; 'thus the term "German" will gain, in the reality of the developing socialist nation, a richer and modified content, which reflects incipient changes in the ethnic area'.[20] This may well be the case (although more likely the result of life behind a wall rather than of life in a classless society); but once that process is completed, or even before then, the question will be asked anew: if no longer German, what then?

As can be seen, the SED's ideological dilemmas in and of themselves are sufficient cause for disbelief and unrest. The official positions can be challenged even from a non-all-German point of view. Indeed, if the argument is correct that the East Germans have already begun to develop a national consciousness of their own, then the SED's explanations on the national question — socialist integration vs. German nationality — are bound to create confusion, if not unrest, for they fail to address the central problem of separate East German nationhood: the lack of a term of national identification.

The importance of such a term was stressed theoretically by Karl W.

Deutsch, who in his seminal work on *Nationalism and Social Communication* defined national consciousness operationally as 'the attachment of secondary symbols of nationality to primary items of information moving through channels of social communication or through the mind of an individual'.[21] Its practical importance was proved throughout the history of German-German relations, with its often seemingly absurd battles over precisely such national terms.[22] In part, this battle reflected attempts by each side to portray itself as the legitimate heir to Germany (and to deny similar claims to sole representation by the other side), but it was also a struggle over the minds of the Germans themselves. The fact that the East Germans have gradually ceased to refer to themselves as 'German'[23] reflects at least the propaganda attempts to instil a separate national consciousness; at most, its very development.

Such a development would be more obvious, and more convincing, if the East Germans had been able to adopt a term of national self-identification of their own. So far they have only 'GDR' (as an abbreviation), which means little (if not the wrong thing, namely 'German') and does not lend itself to forming an adjective in German — a decisive disadvantage in every-day life. Nor will the SED be able to go back to 'German' (except under unforeseeable circumstances), particularly since the West Germans claimed that label for themselves (and use it to refer only to themselves). The battle for national labels was won by the West Germans, leaving the East Germans (who, incidentally, do not call themselves 'East Germans') with more than just a definitional dilemma.

What evidence is there that the East Germans no longer share an all-German national consciousness, that they have developed a national consciousness of their own, based on the GDR as a political, social and economic system? Since national consciousness is made up of a set of attitudes towards the state and the nation, however defined, it seems appropriate to investigate it in social-psychological terms, making use of analytical categories developed by Herbert Kelman and associates in a series of theoretical and empirical studies.[24]

Kelman distinguishes between a person's source of attachment to the national system and his manner of integration into it. The source of attachment can be either instrumental or sentimental orientations; the manner of integration is said to be either ideological or role-participant. Combining the two sources of attachment with the two manners of integration into the national system yields four analytically distinct dimensions of national consciousness:

1. Instrumental/ideological involvement in the national system represents essentially a commitment to the *Staatsnation*; that is, to the ideology that underlies the particular social, economic, and political institutions through which the society is organized.
2. Sentimental/ideological involvement finds its expression in a commitment to cultural values, in the belief that the cultural values of the people and its characteristic way of life fulfil one's emotional needs; it is a commitment to the *Kulturnation*.
3. Instrumental/role-participant involvement results in a functional commitment, which is based on the belief that only the continued functioning of the national system will make possible the continued and successful enactment of a variety of social roles important to an individual.
4. Sentimental/role-participant involvement leads to a symbolic commitment, marking an individual who is attached to the system because his role as system member provides him with a satisfying and important part of his personal identity.

Before this scheme can be applied to the German case, one important preliminary point must be made clear, and that concerns the question: what does 'German' or 'all-German' mean in concrete terms? More precisely: what does an 'all-German national consciousness' refer to? To a common history, and if so, which (Hitler?, Weimar?, Empire?)? Or to current realities, that is, from the West German point of view, to the Federal Republic in all its manifestations today?

The effectiveness, and this is the point to be made, of an all-German national consciousness that is to reflect more than just a vague desire for reunification, depends to a large degree on current realities. As long as the Federal Republic itself is no longer oriented towards a common past and has, in fact, become something completely new in its own right — which, as will be argued later, is the case — then an effective all-German national consciousness within the GDR can only be one that is oriented towards the Federal Republic. Or, to put it differently: an East German national consciousness that is oriented only towards a common past, would no longer be an all-German national consciousness, but rather an East German one, however much outdated. Only a national consciousness focused on West Germany would, in the GDR, be an all-German one. (The reverse argument could, of course, be made in the GDR. But since the West Germans were at no time willing to trade their own free development for reunification — which might theoretically have been possible — a strong case can be made for our argument that an effective all-German national consciousness, that could, as it were, keep the German nation alive, can, in the GDR, only be one that is focused on the Federal Republic of today.)

Does such an all-German national consciousness exist in the GDR? The argument is, in fact, frequently made in precisely those terms: that the East Germans are focused, if not fixated, on developments in West Germany, which is something of a model for them (not the least because more than two-thirds of the East German population can — and does — watch West German television). Therefore, so the argument runs, something like a 'German' national consciousness still must exist.

But the answer cannot be that simple. A different picture emerges when one looks at the four dimensions of national consciousness separately. Is there a 'state consciousness' focused on West Germany's political, economic, and social institutions? Apparently not. To be sure, there are many East Germans who are not satisfied with their state and even less with their regime (which is not the same, though often presumed!). But not all aspects of current-day reality in West Germany are appreciated by the East Germans today, as is very much evident in the personal experiences of refugees (who presumably are those most likely to support the West German model).[25] Apparently many East Germans are appalled by the competitive nature of life in West German society and have come to prefer the relatively secure, though perhaps dull, life afforded them by the East German system. As the *Materialien 1974* put it: 'When they compare their own conditions with those in the Federal Republic, many in the GDR do recognize positive aspects of their own system'.[26] There is, in other words, cause to doubt the existence of an all-German state consciousness in the GDR today.

The same doubts apply to the existence of an all-German cultural consciousness. As pointed out previously, fears of an ever-increasing process of estrangement led to the new *Ostpolitik*. That estrangement was, often painfully, evident in the all too infrequent personal contacts, where it seemed at times that people were not only no longer speaking the same language,[27] but also no longer communicating on the same wavelengths. Germans appeared to have become strangers to each other, mostly because life in separate societies means a life marked by separate experiences. East and West Germany have become culturally separated because of the dominant influence of each controlling superpower. West Germany is largely Americanized, with a great deal of personal responsibility. East Germany, on the other hand, seems to have undergone a marriage of socialism with traditional German petit-bourgeois values, with little personal liberty and responsibility. Thus the East Germans often react with discomfort, if not outright displeasure, at the seemingly boundless life-style in West Germany, whereas the West Germans turn up their noses at an East German way of life that strikes them as 'typically German' — something they themselves no longer want to be. The battles fought on the official level about who is the rightful heir to German culture, with the GDR emphasizing socialist traditions and claiming only the best (Beethoven, Goethe), and the Federal Republic being blamed for everything else (but in fact often giving the appearance of being disinterested in its cultural heritage) — these battles probably had little influence on the public's mind. Thirty years of separation, however, would appear to have shaped different ways of life, and — what is more important — an awareness of that fact. A consciousness of *Kulturnation* seems already waning.

What about the East Germans' commitment to the symbols of Germany? In its attempt to gain legitimacy internally and support externally, the East German regime had initially made deliberate efforts to retain national symbols of Germany, from the shape of its soldiers' uniforms and their goose-steps to the name of its railroad system. In some respects such efforts were duplicated in West Germany, so that in some instances the symbols were the same (the flags have the same colours, though they now contain different markings), while in others the West Germans were able to claim a traditional national symbol for themselves (the West German national anthem is the old *Deutschland über alles*, though only the third verse is sung; the East Germans adopted a national anthem of their own, which includes a reference to the 'one united fatherland' — it is no longer sung, only played).

The battle of national symbols was, as were the other battles, ardently fought. It only came to an end in 1972, when the West German Government, after much deliberation, was forced to allow the East German flag to be shown during the Munich Olympics. It also had to permit the playing of the East German national anthem, and the West Germans — and the world — heard more of that than they would have liked to. For the East German regime had, from early on, sought to gain national and international recognition through a display of athletic prowess. It seems to have largely succeeded. The successes of East German athletes, very much in evidence during recent Olympic Games, helped instil a GDR-focused national consciousness at home, particularly among the GDR's youth, while, at the same time, enforcing a consciousness of separateness in West Germany and elsewhere. (West German sports reporters can no longer refer to East Germans as Germans, not when they are competing against West Germans. In this case the practice has evolved of referring to the West Germans as 'the Germans' and excluding the East Germans from the definition, which is precisely the effect the Eastern regime had been seeking. Occasional attempts to claim East German successes as 'German' are no longer credible, because so blatantly out of touch with reality.) While there is little empirical evidence to show that most East Germans are today no longer symbolically committed to all-German symbols — that they derive emotional satisfaction from a display of such symbols — it would seem a fair assumption to make that they are not. They are, in any case, not committed to West German national symbols, and that would be the only kind of symbolic commitment of importance.

The same applies to the fourth and possibly least important dimension of national consciousness: functional commitment to the national system. It is doubtful that many East Germans are functionally committed to the Federal Republic, almost by definition: they do not believe that its continued functioning makes possible the successful enactment of a variety of social roles. The question remains whether many of them are functionally committed to their own system. It is difficult, if not impossible, to answer, though the supposition is that after thirty years of existence, the growth of a new generation, and the flight of more than three million (who must have been the least satisified and committed), functional commitment in the GDR has grown as well.[28]

With these assumptions, suppositions, and scanty evidence, the question about national consciousness in the GDR is hardly answered. But they offer clues. Thus it would seem that an effective all-German national consciousness, one that could keep alive aspirations and possibilities for eventual reunification, can no longer be assumed to exist. The alternatives are an outmoded national consciousness focused on the Germany of old, most likely shared by older generations, or a national consciousness oriented towards the German Democratic Republic, shared increasingly by the younger generations. Many East Germans may still harbour some hopes for reunification, but far fewer really expect it.[29] This discrepancy between hopes and expectations forces an accommodation with existing realities — with life in the GDR. Such accommodation, often noted by outside observers, would have been easier if official propaganda during the past thirty years had not boxed itself into a corner out of which it cannot escape at other than great costs. This dilemma makes it difficult for many East Germans to find a proper focus for their national consciousness, as the state of their own nation-state remains somewhat out of focus. But it is doubtful that the current state of uncertainty, which may in part explain domestic difficulties in the GDR, will serve to keep an all-German national consciousness alive. Much more likely will be the continued development of 'GDR-consciousness', not necessarily along the lines pursued by the SED, but effective nevertheless.

III STATE AND NATION IN THE FEDERAL REPUBLIC OF GERMANY

Even if present appearances were to prove false and the East Germans should continue to hold on, in their minds, to the one German nation, however defined, it would still cease to exist if the Germans living in West Germany were to lose their all-German national consciousness. In that case the East Germans might still want reunification, but if the West Germans do not want it, it would not come about. And, once the East Germans were to realize that they have been excluded by the West Germans from their national consciousness, they would, in turn, be forced to re-think their own situation. Such a dynamic process has long been feared by West German policymakers, and they have tried to combat it: first through massive propaganda campaigns designed to maintain an all-German consciousness, then through a policy of easier German-German contacts. Yet all these efforts appear to have been for naught: all evidence available today points to the conclusion that the West Germans have indeed begun to substitute their all-German national consciousness with a national consciousness focused exclusively on the Federal Republic — which, however, they call 'Germany' (meaning only West Germany), a fact which introduces considerable difficulties for an analysis of national consciousness in West Germany.

The decline of an all-German national consciousness in West Germany is most evident in the way West Germans have given up reunification as a political goal. For many years touted as the Federal Republic's most important goal, it has recently all but disappeared from public discussion and from the public's mind; it no longer plays a prominent role in official pronouncements and it no longer appears on the polling organizations' lists of the most important questions.[30] For the West German public, and to a large extent for West German politics, although it has not yet been able to adjust fully to the public mood, the reunification of Germany is a dead issue.

Or could it be only a sleeping issue, ready to be reawakened when external and internal conditions are right? This argument is frequently advanced, often with reference to the historical inevitability of reunification, because of the historical impossibility of keeping a nation divided. But the historical case for the indivisibility of nations is by no means clear-cut, and if it were, Germany could well become the first case to the contrary, for all available evidence points in that direction.

Figure 1
Willingness to Recognize the German Democratic Republic as Independent State

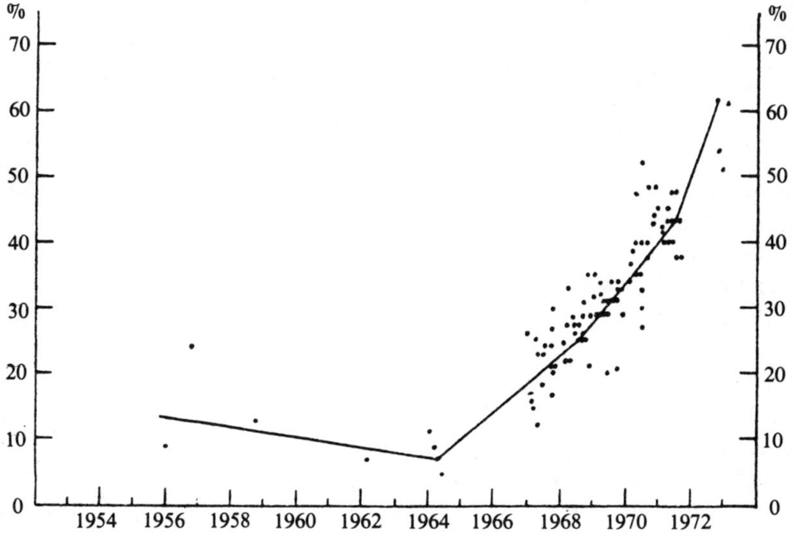

Sources: DIVO, EMNID, IFAK, IfD, IFM, INFAS, INFRATEST, MARPLAN

From: Schweigler, *National Consciousness*, p. 156.

For the West German case, the data are overwhelming.[31] Public opinion polls show that an ever-increasing majority of West Germans does not believe in reunification and has, in fact, got quite used to the division. A consistently increasing number approved of West German recognition of East Germany as a separate state (see Figure 1, which contains the results of ninety-eight polls taken on this question until 1973: after that, the question was no longer asked), being quite aware that recognition would mean the permanent division of Germany. In part, such recognition may have been the political expression of many West Germans' estrangement from everything East German (in general, knowledge of East Germany is minimal), for a large majority admits, when asked, that East and West Germans are becoming ever more estranged from each other. Not only that: most West Germans today fully expect that Germany will not remain one nation or, indeed, one people (*Volk*), but rather will grow apart in the course of history, just as Germany and Austria did fifty years earlier. With no expectation of continued unity, the permanent division of Germany may well become a self-fulfilling prophecy. Having given up all hopes for eventual reunification, the West Germans have also ceased to insist on reunification or to strive for it (the data also show that this process of dissolution of national will was a gradual one, taking place throughout the post-war period despite many attempts by the West German Government to arrest or even reverse it). But where there is no will for a nation, there can be no nation.

The historical irony of the thirty-year struggle over the modalities of eventual reunification (would it be along the Western or the Eastern model?) is that it unleashed a dynamic that now seems to have endangered the very existence of the nation. Both sides attempted to develop and to depict their own system as a model to be emulated by the other side, which in turn was described in the blackest of terms. In the process, people on both sides began to develop a supportive attitude toward their own system, particularly as it proved to be wondrously successful (as in *Wirtschaftswunder*), while excluding the other side from their consciousness. In the end, reunification, the original goal, had dropped from sight, while the maintenance of one's own model-country assumed utmost importance. In the West German case this development was symptomatically evident in the evolution of the SPD, which originally had fought Adenauer's policy of establishing the Federal Republic as a separate state closely allied with the West, arguing that such a policy would only help to cement the divsion of Germany, but which in the early seventies ran election campaigns under the slogans 'Germans, we can be proud of our country' (meaning West Germany), and *Modell Deutschland* (again meaning only West Germany).

The SPD's election campaign slogans reflect the growth of a West German national consciousness that has replaced an all-German one. Along all four dimensions of national consciousness, a majority of West Germans can today be said to share a West German national consciousness. Over the years they have come to be committed to their political institutions, to the cultural values prevalent in West Germany, to the symbols of the West German state, and to the functional roles they play within it.[32] The poll data reveal that this was a continuous development, shaped in part by generational changes, in part by increased prosperity. But the very fact that it was a continuous development goes to show that certain changes took place within the German public's mind and that they are unlikely to be reversed through internal propaganda efforts or even external events. On the one side, the West Germans are now preferring their own political, social, and economic system to any other kind of system that might be offered to them; on the other side, they are no longer intent on extending that system to their, as they used to be called, 'brothers and sisters' in the GDR.[33] For the West Germans, the German nation has shrunk to the Federal Republic; for them, the German Question has been answered.

IV THE GERMAN QUESTION ANSWERED

Public opinion in West Germany has always been ahead of governmental policies in regard to the German Question. So it is today. While the Federal Government is still committed to a policy of trying to create those conditions in Europe that would permit the exercise of the Germans' right of self-determination (with the implication that they would, of course, choose reunification), the public no longer gives more than verbal support to that policy, if that. For the policymakers, it appears to have become a pat phrase, used whenever the situation seems to demand it, and put away at all other times.[34] This state of affairs will continue as long as the Constitutional Court's ruling, which is likely to remain on the books as long as the Basic Law remains unchanged.

For years the Federal Republic had considered itself to be a provisional state, to be maintained only until the reunification of Germany. The very term 'Basic Law' was meant to express the provisional nature of the Federal Republic — a constitution is to be adopted only once reunification has been achieved. The Federal Government, for a long time, attempted to give expression to this provisional state of affairs, for instance by not pushing very hard the national symbols of the Federal Republic. In part the moderate tone of the West Germans' West German national consciousness may be due to such efforts. Still, such efforts could not prevent the provisional from becoming permanent. Time and success created realities of their own.

Now that these realities have been recognized, this process is likely to accelerate. Already the Federal Republic has begun to cement its no longer provisional status, literally: Bonn, the provisional capital, is finally to be built into a capital representative of the Federal Republic. New government office buildings and the new construction of the West German parliament are all designed to somehow express the democratic nature of the West German state (demands by some lone CDU voices that the plans also should express Berlin's continued status as Germany's future capital were coolly turned down by government spokesmen who argued that no way could be found to achieve this). Yet the construction of Bonn as a definite capital will offer a new symbol for West Germany's separate nation-statehood and serve to direct the focus of the West Germans' national aspirations on Bonn. In the political arena this process began some years ago, when the government finally initiated a long overdue reform of West Germany's laws (many of which were based on old German laws and had been retained with a view toward eventual reunification). In the meantime, Bonn is, as some would argue, almost overburdened with demands for changes and reforms, while it does not yet give the appearance of being a proper focus of national demands and aspirations. Some have argued that this gap between demands on the one side and the lack of national definition has contributed significantly to current difficulties, inasmuch as it has left many, particularly the young, without a focus for their energies and thus misdirected (into terrorism, for instance). There may be some truth to this argument, but if so, there is hope: conditions are in fact rapidly changing.

What, then, will happen to Germany? Not much, if our analysis is correct. The West Germans will develop an ever stronger national consciousness of their own; the East Germans will have to follow suit, though with more difficulties and somewhat less certainty as to the eventual outcome. Relations between the two German states should become based less on those special ties that the West German Government still claims and the East German regime occasionally accepts (as in the case of intra-German trade). Once, as seems inevitable, the West German Constitution is changed to express the non-provisional nature of the Federal Republic, those problems still open today, like the issue of a separate East German citizenship, will fade away. In the end, the Federal Republic and the GDR could become just neighbours. If they were to become good neighbours, such as Austria and Germany are today, an optimal answer to the German Question would have been found.

NOTES

1. For a select bibliography see Gebhard Schweigler, *Nationalbewußtsein in der BRD und der DDR* (Düsseldorf, 1973).

2. For summary reviews of the various legal doctrines concerning Germany as a state see Rudolf Schuster, *Deutschlands staatliche Existenz im Widerstreit politischer und rechtlicher Gesichtspunkte 1945-1963* (München, 1963) and Antje Mattfeld, *Modelle einer Normalisierung zwischen beiden deutschen Staaten. Eine rechtliche Betrachtung* (Düsseldorf, 1973).

3. For a more general discussion of the opposition's policy on *Ostpolitik* see Christian Hacke, *Die Ost- und Deutschlandpolitik der CDU/CSU. Wege und Irrwege der Opposition seit 1969* (Köln, 1975). On the controversies surrounding the *Grundlagenvertrag* see Karlheinz Niclauss, *Kontroverse Deutschlandpolitik. Die politische Auseinandersetzung in der Bundesrepublik Deutschland über den Grundlagenvertrag mit der DDR* (Frankfurt, 1977).

4. Quoted in Kay-Michael Wilke, *Bundesrepublik Deutschland und Deutsche Demokratische Republik. Grundlagen und ausgewählte Probleme des gegenseitigen Verhältnisses der beiden deutschen Staaten* (Berlin, 1976), p. 156, a very thorough analysis of the Constitutional Court's ruling in the light of legal doctrines and political practice.

5. Asked in February 1973 whether they thought reunification was still possible after the Basic Treaty, 57% said no, only 22% yes. (EMNID poll, quoted according to *Frankfurter Allgemeine Zeitung*, 27 March 1973).

6. For a representative recent statement along those lines see Wolfgang J. Mommsen, 'Die deutsche Frage als nationales und als europäisches Problem', *Politik und Kultur*, 1, 1977. For a representative critique of this notion see 'Der Mythus von der Kulturnation', in: Emerich K. Francis, *Ethos und Demos* (Berlin, 1965).

7. Rupert Emerson, *From Empire to Nation* (Boston, 1960). Emerson called this the 'simplest' and the 'ultimate' statement that can be made about a nation.

8. I have developed that concept more extensively in *Nationalbewußtsein,* op. cit. An expanded and up-dated English version appeared as *National Consciousness in Divided*

Germany (London/Beverly Hills, 1975).

9. For a survey of such observations see Schweigler, *National Consciousness*, op. cit., p. 107.

10. Each year, since 1967, the West German Government must report to parliament about the state of the nation. Originally conceived as a report on the state of Germany as a whole, the tendency in recent years has been to report on the state of the West German nation. Between 1970 and 1974, additional 'materials' were made available (prepared by a team of outside experts), which offered background information of a comparative kind. The 1974 *Materialien* focused on the national question.

11. *Materialien 1974*, p. 71. This is not quite correct, since the West German Ministry for Inter-German Relations has, for many years, conducted surveys among visitors to the GDR on precisely those questions. Most of the results have never been published. For some representative samples see Schweigler, *National Consciousness*, op. cit., pp. 123ff.

12. *Materialien 1974*, op. cit., p. 71.

13. Peter Christian Ludz, *Two Germanys in one World* (Paris, 1973), p. 30.

14. Peter C. Ludx, *Die DDR zwischen Ost und West. Politische Analysen von 1961 bis 1976* (München, 1977), p. 289.

15. Bundesministerium für Innerdeutsche Beziehungen (ed.), *DDR Handbuch* (Köln, 1975), p. 584.

16. *Süddeutsche Zeitung*, 19 February 1975.

17. The term was coined by Egon Bahr, close advisor to Willy Brandt, in 1963, when he called for a new *Ostpolitik* that should overcome the rigidities of the Adenauer era. Bahr later was to become the chief negotiator for the treaties with Moscow, Warsaw, and East Berlin.

18. On this point West German GDR-researchers are agreed, although they differ on just how stable the system is today.

19. See Hermann Axen, 'Die Herausbildung der sozialistischen Nation in der Deutschen Demokratischen Republik', *Probleme des Friedens und des Sozialismus*, March 1976.

20. Alfred Kosing and Walter Schmidt, 'Nation und Nationalität in der DDR', *Neues Deutschland*, 1975, p. 10.

21. Karl W. Deutsch, *Nationalism and Social Communication: An Inquiry into the Foundations of Nationality* (Cambridge, Mass., 1966, 2nd ed.), p. 172.

22. Until the late 1960s West Germany refused officially to use the term GDR without a qualifying 'so-called' (initially preferred were labels such as 'East Zone' or 'Soviet Occupied Zone', which denied East German claims to statehood). The battle is not quite over, as the Federal Government, in part under pressure from the CDU/CSU, is attempting to rule out usage of the term 'BRD' — for 'Bundesrepublik Deutschland' — as an alleged East German attempt to make West Germans use that term rather than the term 'Germany'.

23. This is particularly evident in the area of sports. See Gebhard Schweigler, 'Sport und Staatsbewusstsein im geteilten Deutschland', *Politische Studien*, 205, 1972.

24. See Herbert C. Kelman, 'Patterns of Personal Involvement in the National System. A Social-Psychological Analysis of Political Legitimacy', in James N. Rosenau (ed.), *International Politics and Foreign Policy* (New York, 1969, 2nd ed.), pp. 276-288.

25. See the interviews collected by Barbara Grunert-Bronnen, *Ich bin Bürger der DDR und lebe in der Bundesrepublik* (München, 1970).

26. *Materialien 1974*, op. cit., p. 75.

27. The possibility that the German language might be developing along separate lines in both parts of Germany has long exercised much fascination in East and West Germany. For

a review of the arguments and the evidence see Schweigler, *National Consciousness*, op. cit., pp. 44-47.

28. For a fascinating discussion of this issue and some evidence derived from refugee data see William Russell Hardin, 'Emigration, Occupational Mobility, and Institutionalization: The German Democratic Republic', unpublished PhD Dissertation, MIT, August 1971.

29. The polls among West German travellers to the GDR taken in the late 1960s (see note 11), however questionable they may be methodologically, revealed significant age differences among those who thought that the GDR is an independent state and ought to be recognized by West Germany (a majority appeared to have felt that way); they also showed that far more East Germans hoped for reunification than expected it.

30. See the *Jahrbücher für Demoskopie* of the Institut für Demoskopie, Allensbach, the most detailed compilation of public opinion data available in published form.

31. I have presented these data in *National Consciousness*, op. cit.; the following discussion draws on this presentation.

32. For the most thorough recent treatment of the West Germans' relationship with their new nation-state see Martin and Sylvia Greiffenhagen, *Ein schwieriges Vaterland. Zur Politischen Kultur Deutschlands* (München, 1979).

33. In fact, less than 5% of the West German population ever claimed to have close relatives in the GDR.

34. Only most recently (in Spring 1979) have some high-ranking politicians, though not members of the government, begun to argue publicly that reunification could no longer be achieved and should, therefore, no longer be sought.

4

OSTPOLITIK RECONSIDERED

Michael Kreile

MORE THAN HALF A DECADE HAS ELAPSED since the conclusion of the Basic Treaty between the Federal Republic and the GDR in December 1972 brought an end to one of the most dramatic phases in the history of West German foreign policy. Following three years of difficult and complex negotiations and passionate domestic debate, the SPD-FDP coalition government which had emerged from the elections of September 1969 had put West Germany's relations with its Eastern neighbours up on new foundations. Looking at Ostpolitik today, one is tempted to ask: *Mais où sont les neiges d'antan*? The accomplishments of the Brandt-Scheel government already seem to belong to history. The drama of high politics has been replaced by the routine of business transactions, periodic haggling over the interpretation of the Berlin Agreement and inter-German negotiations on transit fees or telephone lines. The passions have subsided and Ostpolitik is no longer an issue to win elections. This apparent loss of momentum is not so much a matter of pragmatists having replaced visionaries but rather stems from the very achievements of Ostpolitik. As a result of Ostpolitik, West Germany has ceased to be a revisionist power. By eliminating its special conflict with the East, the FRG freed its Western allies from the dilemma to either conduct a détente policy bypassing the Federal Republic or to underwrite West German revisionism. By cutting its losses West German foreign policy not only joined the mainstream of Western détente diplomacy but also gained considerably in freedom of manoeuver. The phase of policy-innovation initiated under Brandt's chancellorship has been followed by a phase of 'routinization' and implementation. In fact, Ostpolitik is actually characterized by three dominant tendencies:[1]

1. Economic relations with Eastern Europe and the Soviet Union have experienced a spectacular upswing as the *Ostverträge* (Eastern treaties) created a favorable climate for the expansion of trade and economic cooperation and enabled West German export industry to consolidate its lead in Eastern markets.
2. The process of normalization in the FRG's relations with Eastern Europe and the GDR is slow and laborious. The obstacles that have arisen so far are due to the legacies of the past (as in the case of Poland), to divergent interpretations of the Four Power Berlin Agreement and to the preoccupation with *Abgrenzung* (demarcation) that haunts the GDR leadership.
3. When the Berlin Agreement and the ratification of the Moscow and Warsaw treaties gave the green light for the opening of the CSCE preparatory talks at Helsinki, this was the beginning of an era of multilateral East-West diplomacy which supplements, overarches and partly even replaces the network of bilateral relations (CSCE, MBFR, EEC-COMECON contacts). The EEC's common commercial policy towards state-trading countries (which entered formally into effect in January 1973) deprives the member countries of a traditional instrument of foreign policy, and thus, in a sense, represents the most advanced form of multilateralization of Ostpolitik.

Research on the origins, development and consequences of Ostpolitik has been closely related to the course of events. Journalists, historians and political scientists first focused on the process of détente diplomacy, the interpretation of the Eastern treaties and their implications for European security. They thereby contributed to clarification of the domestic debate over Ostpolitik.[2] On the other hand, the development of research was also shaped by the emergence of new paradigms. The renaissance of 'political economy' under the auspices of the Frankfurt School (which provided intellectual leadership and ideological guidance to the student movement of the late sixties) spilled over into the study of foreign policy. It called for an analysis of the socio-economic determinants of foreign policy. The rising new discipline of peace research produced studies on hostility perceptions and the dynamics of conflict and cooperation in East-West relations.[3] These developments were part of a more general process of change in West German political culture which created the domestic conditions of large-scale policy innovation. Anti-communism had lost much of its ideological appeal and the public reacted favorably to a program of domestic reforms and a new course in foreign policy. The institutionalization of peace research was intimately connected with this process. It was President Heinemann (elected in 1969 by the votes of the SPD and FDP) who called for a German foundation of peace research and it was the Brandt government which established it in 1970.[4] The activities of the *Deutsche Gesellschaft für Friedens- und Konfliktforschung* (German Society for Peace and Conflict Research) have led to a significant expansion of research on problems of East-West relations.

The purpose of this paper is to sketch roughly the main directions of Ostpolitik research and to present some relevant findings in a condensed form. We will not retrace in detail the development of Ostpolitik itself, as some good accounts are available in English.[5] Separating the wheat from the chaff necessarily involves some subjective judgement and, hence, possibly injustice toward some contributions to the field.

CONCEPTS OF OSTPOLITIK: CONTINUITY AND CHANGE

When the SPD-FDP coalition government took power in October 1969, West German Ostpolitik had clearly reached an impasse. From its inception until the middle 1960s it had been dominated by the endeavor to achieve reunification of the German nation within the framework of a free and democratic constitution. The Federal Republic claimed sole responsibility for the representation of Germany as a whole (*Alleinvertretungsanspruch*) and continually exhorted the Soviet Union to grant the East German population the right to self-determination and to free elections. The 'Hallstein Doctrine' was designed to prevent other states from diplomatic recognition of the GDR. Moreover, the Oder-Neiße question, i.e. the problem of Germany's eastern borders, was to be kept open until a definitive peace settlement occurred. Adenauer's historical achievement, 'the restoration of bourgeois society in the Federal Republic' (Schwarz)[6] and the integration of the FRG into the economic and military alliances of the West had created a fundamental conflict of goals: As 'Westintegration' progressed, reunification receded into an ever more distant future. In a reappraisal of *Adenauer's Deutschland- und Ostpolitik*,[7] the historian Klaus Gotto has recently defended Adenauer against the accusation that he was not really interested in reunification and that his policies were plagued by immobilism. According to Gotto, the idea of a rigid and unimaginative *Deutschlandpolitik*, fixated on legal claims and limited to negation, represents a distorted picture.[8] Although, in contrast to his *Westpolitik*, Adenauer's Ostpolitik was basically defensive, it was much more flexible than is usually assumed. This is brought out, as Gotto argues, by the Adenauer proposal of an Austria status for the GDR as an interim solution to the problem of reunification which was presented to the Soviet Union in Spring 1958; by the so-called Globke Plan of 1959/60, an internal policy planning paper in the form of a draft treaty providing for the establishment of formal relations with the GDR and a referendum on reunification to be organized in both German states five years after the coming into force of the treaty; and by the offer of a ten-year *Burgfrieden* (political truce) made to the Soviet ambassador in June 1962. These and similar considerations were always present in Adenauer's Ostpolitik conception as a second line running parallel to official policy.[9] It should be noted, however, that these proposals never left the realm of secret diplomacy or the stage of planning exercises and, in the last analysis, did not bear fruit.[10]

When the Kennedy administration embarked on an active détente policy, West German diplomacy was confronted with a dilemma: détente implied a stabilization of the status quo, whereas the FRG sought to overcome it. Yet, Bonn could not afford to isolate itself from its Western partners and had to come up with its own contribution to détente policy. Foreign minister Schröder's (1961-1966) 'policy of movement' attempted to reconcile these conflicting requirements. It relied on the apparent evolution toward 'polycentrism' in Eastern Europe and economic diplomacy (in 1963, trade missions were set up in Poland, Hungary, and Rumania; in 1964 in Bulgaria) to improve the FRG's image in Eastern Europe and to gain sympathy for the vital objective of reunification. This approach failed, because the 'policy of movement', as Windsor put it, 'amounted to little more than a decision to direct the cold war against East Germany alone, and an unjustified hope that this would not affect the Federal Republic's relations with other East European countries'.[11] The Grand Coalition of CDU/CSU and SPD formed in Autumn 1966 to combat an economic recession made new overtures towards Eastern Europe and relaxed the Hallstein Doctrine, but shied away from a formal recognition of the GDR. Given the fragility of the consensus between the two governing parties, it was hardly surprising that the Kiesinger-Brandt government did not carry out the radical shift in West German Ostpolitik which growing forces within the SPD and FDP, the media and the churches advocated.[12] The Soviet crushing of the Prague Spring in 1968 heightened the tensions between the coalition parties. The CDU/CSU fell back on time-honored positions; the SPD leadership stressed the necessity of advance on the road to détente. This meant that an arrangement with Moscow and East Berlin could no longer be avoided.[13]

The turning away from positions that had become untenable, the acceptance of the European status quo and the readiness to take up formal relations with the GDR as expressed in Brandt's inaugural address as chancellor in 1969 undoubtedly reflected the insights gained and the frustrations experienced under the Grand Coalition (Chancellor Kiesinger had sometimes used his constitutional *Richtlinienkompetenz* [policy guidance authority] to block initiatives coming from Brandt's Foreign Office). But the origins of Brandt's concept of Ostpolitik can be traced back to the early sixties. The point of departure commonly referred to is Egon Bahr's Tutzing speech of July 1963. Then press secretary to Berlin mayor Willy Brandt, Bahr pleaded for an adaptation of West German foreign policy to the new international situation resulting from the Kennedy administration's 'peace strategy'. He argued that 'the only realistic prospect for an improvement of conditions in Germany was by way of a gradual change through rapprochement' (*Wandel durch Annäherung*) between the Federal Republic and the GDR. This required a 'policy of small steps' taking into account 'the instability of the East German regime and the fundamental interest of the USSR in forestaling upheavals in East Germany'.[14] According to Brandt's own testimony, the decisive event that led him to re-examine the traditional assumptions of West German foreign policy was the Berlin Crisis of 1961. The erection of the Berlin Wall symbolized in a dramatic way the failure of Adenauer's reunification policy. As Brandt puts it in his memoirs: 'In August 1961, a curtain was pulled aside and the stage was empty. . . What has been called my Ostpolitik, was formed before this background'.[15]

In a recent study, Diethelm Prowe has analyzed in detail Brandt's policy as mayor of West Berlin during the critical years 1961-1963, stressing the pragmatism of Brandt's approach to negotiating with the East German authorities.[16] Even then Brandt's strategy was to trade the renunciation of unrealistic legal positions for agreements with the East on humanitarian and technical questions.[17] Given the specific situation in divided Berlin, Brandt and his brains trust (Bahr, Albertz, Schütz) accorded high priority to negotiations with the GDR on visiting permits allowing West Berliners to go to see their relatives in East Berlin. In December 1963, the first Wall pass agreement was concluded for an extended Christmas period. The GDR could claim de facto recognition, whereas the West Berlin Senate pointed out that only non-consular technical personnel — East German post office clerks — handled applications for permits.

In line with his advocacy of a more elastic Ostpolitik, Brandt, in early 1963, was ready to accept an invitation by Khrushchev, but had to decline when the CDU of West Berlin which formed a local grand coalition with the Social Democrats opposed this move. This episode was crucial in Brandt's decision to break with the post-war tradition of grand coalition city government and to form a new coalition with the FDP after the elections of Spring 1963.[18] Brandt's memorandum to US Secretary Dean Rusk written in 1964 shows that his conception of détente at first included elements of functionalist thought. He suggested that the development of industrial societies as well as technological imperatives created needs and opportunities for cooperation transcending ideological cleavages.[19]

It has been suggested that there is a 'profound continuity'[20] between Adenauer's and Brandt's foreign policies. Although this thesis may appear paradoxical, if one bears in mind the embittered resistance Brandt's Ostpolitik met in the CDU/CSU camp, there is some merit to it. According to Roger Morgan, 'the continuity lies in the fact that both Adenauer and Brandt saw the Federal Republic as *the* political unit, *the* actor in the international system, whose interests they were concerned to promote'.[21] Both statesmen — Joffe argues — 'had sought to defuse the dangerous potential of revisionism, and both were haunted by the perils of Germany's position in the European center'.[22] It may also be useful to recall that Brandt was one of those SPD leaders who, towards the end of the fifties, persuaded the party to rally to Adenauer's security policy and to accept the Federal Republic's membership in NATO.[23] However, these considerations should not obscure the fact that in some respects Brandt's Ostpolitik meant a radical break with past policies.

The question of continuity has also been raised with regard to earlier periods of German history: is there a tradition of German post-war revisionism common to Weimar and the Bonn Republic? Is there a hidden thread running from Rapallo (1922) to the Moscow Treaty (1970)?[24] Is Brandt's Ostpolitik the latest — and sublimated — stage of a tradition of continental expansionism, the export offensive following the Eastern treaties representing a modern version of the Kaiser's or the Third Reich's *Drang nach Osten*?[25] Although such notions may appeal to the historical imagination a point of method is in order here: those who rush to premature conclusions on the basis of superficial similarities or formal analogies easily fall into the 'traps of continuity stereotypes' (Geyer).[26] Jacobsen has stressed the necessity of taking into account the overall configuration of the international system in which Eastern policies took place at different times, such as great power relationships, alliance constellations, economic interdependencies, the quality of weapons systems and ideological factors.[27]

The revisionist policy of the Weimar Republic was designed to revise the Versailles Treaty resented as a humiliating *Diktat* and to restore Germany's great power status.[28] In the pursuit of these aims, Stresemann and his successors primarily relied on diplomacy, economic cooperation and the League of Nations. The policy of revision was mainly directed against Poland and thus against the French security pact system in Eastern Europe. By 1933, the Weimar Republic had succeeded in regaining international confidence, thereby improving the climate for future negotiations concerning revision. This process was abruptly reversed when Hitler took power and embarked on an increasingly aggressive policy. For the Nazi regime the revision of the Versailles Treaty was only an intermediate goal in a far-reaching program of territorial expansion to be realized through war and annihilation. The Federal Republic's claim to reunification within the borders of 1937 certainly represented some sort of revisionism. But, as Jacobsen has pointed out, the Federal Republic had assumed the solemn obligation laid down in its constitution to use only peaceful means in order to achieve its national objectives. Yet the accusation of revanchism which the Eastern propaganda machines leveled against the FRG for years and years was not always totally unfounded. At least, the militant rhetoric of expellee organizations and the equipping of the Bundeswehr with nuclear devices could raise legitimate concerns in Eastern Europe. It was, after all, the entanglement of the 'German question' with the global contest of two antagonistic systems which rendered the FRG's revisionist claims potentially explosive.

For this very reason, however, the concept of an independent German foreign policy reviving the tradition of Rapallo or Bismarck's Russia policy, as contemplated by conservative writers and diplomats, led astray. The revolutionary transformation of the European system after World War II precluded any such option.[29]

THE DOMESTIC POLITICS OF OSTPOLITIK

The domestic debate over Ostpolitik led to a polarization of political forces which can only be compared to the battles fought over *Westintegration* and German rearmament. Yet this conflict not only involved the principles and procedure of foreign policy but also represented a struggle for political power. Its intensity derived from the fact that the SPD-FDP coalition formed in 1969 disposed only of a slender majority in the Bundestag (254 deputies out of 496). Relegated to the benches of the opposition for the first time since 1949, the CDU/CSU, which remained the strongest parliamentary group, experienced difficulties in adjusting to its new role and sometimes tended to behave like royalty in exile. The prevalent feeling in the opposition camp was well expressed by CSU chairman Franz-Josef Strauss when he said 'that the *Machtwechsel* (change of power) was "not a simple change of government according to the rules of parliamentary democracy, for it aims at introducing a fundamental and long-term reorientation in German politics both internally and externally".'[30]

The CDU/CSU's 'fundamentalist opposition' (Pridham) was inspired by a militant anti-communism coupled with an uncompromising adherence to the goal of reunification and a deep-seated distaste for 'socialist' tendencies in domestic politics. Brandt's commitment to the normalization of West Germany's relations with the East was stigmatized as a 'national sell-out' and perceived as an encouragement to socialist forces at home which threatened the system of *freie Marktwirtschaft* (free market economy).[31]

CDU/CSU spokesmen charged that the Moscow and Warsaw treaties sacrificed the German people's right to self-determination and claimed that real détente could only be achieved when the sources of tension were eliminated, namely the 'denial of human rights in Eastern Europe'.[32] Baron von Guttenberg warned of a 'penetration' of the Federal Republic from the East and Karl Carstens pointed to the risk that 'revolutionary groups' at home might ally themselves with communist parties in the East; democracy in the Federal Republic would thus be threatened simultaneously 'by a sort of a pincer movement from within and without'.[33] The legitimation of the totalitarian regime in the GDR — it was argued — was likely to undermine democratic consciousness in the Federal Republic.

In spite of this rhetoric, however, the parliamentary tactics of the CDU were somewhat more flexible. As a party that sought to regain power, the CDU could hardly afford an image of purely sterile opposition. Moreover, it was subject to intense American pressure as the time for ratification of the treaties approached.

In the most detailed study of the domestic and international developments of Ostpolitik between 1969-1973 published to date, Reinhold Roth provides an excellent analysis of the relationship between foreign policy innovation and *Herrschaftssicherung* (the strategy of power preservation), respectively the interaction between the conflict over Ostpolitik and the struggle for tenureship. Roth stresses the contradiction which existed between the confrontation strategy the CDU-CSU followed during the 1969 election campaign with regard to foreign policy and the requirements of power preservation. The SPD waged its campaign on the issue of *Ost- und Deutschlandpolitik* to advance its claim for political leadership. For the FDP this foreign policy issue proved a vehicle of intra-party change which opened up the possibility of switching coalitions. According to Roth, it was precisely the narrow parliamentary majority which pushed the new government to take bold foreign policy initiatives. To concentrate on domestic reforms was likely to produce clashes with powerful domestic interests.[34] Moving swiftly on the Ostpolitik front was facilitated by the traditional government prerogatives in the conduct of foreign relations. Decision-making was highly centralized. Policy-planning was in the hands of a small group of key advisers in the Chancellor's Office who operated in relative independence from established institutional channels.[35] This was bound to create some friction with Scheel's Foreign Office, and Helmut Allardt, the ambassador to Moscow, was later to deplore in his memoirs that he had been bypassed by Brandt's special envoy Egon Bahr.[36]

Ostpolitik became an important factor in the dynamics of intra-party politics. In an early stage Rainer Barzel, the chairman of the CDU/CSU's parliamentary group, became the opposition's main contact man for confidential consultations with the government. This in turn contributed to confirm his leadership position.[37] In the course of events, however, Ostpolitik created differences within the opposition which again were related to leadership ambitions. As Pridham aptly put it,

> Barzel's authority within the party as a whole was limited, and his position was frequently undermined by the machinations of Strauss. His steps as party leader were dogged by the Ostpolitik factor, for the issue was centrally related to the major internal problems he encountered: first, how to keep the party united when Ostpolitik proved so divisive; and secondly, how to prevent his party rivals and opponents from exploiting the issue to weaken his leadership.[38]

On the SPD side, a deputy representing the expellee organizations, Herbert Hupka, opposed Brandt's policy and joined the CDU. The Young Socialists, the party's youth organization, advocated a policy of 'system-transcending reforms' (*systemüberwindende Reformen*). Their pronouncements received much unfavorable publicity and were exploited by the opposition as a confirmation of their suspicions about the domestic repercussions of Ostpolitik. According to the CSU paper *Bayernkurier*, the SPD was changing into a 'Popular Front party which obediently acceded to communist demands'.[39] The party leadership therefore took steps to discipline its left wing and underlined its unrelenting opposition to communist objectives and practices. In the FDP, the conservative wing, the National Liberals, who from the very beginning had only reluctantly accepted the coalition with the SPD, advanced scruples about Ostpolitik to motivate their more general aversion to the coalition. When several FDP deputies went over to the CDU or withdrew their support from the government Brandt no longer disposed of a majority in the Bundestag. The opposition seized the occasion and, for the first time in the history of the Federal Republic, resorted to the 'constructive vote of no-confidence' to oust Brandt as Chancellor. This move failed by a (still unexplained) margin of two votes.[40]

The resulting parliamentary deadlock required a minimum of cooperation from the opposition if the Eastern treaties were to pass the Bundestag. As Roth has rightly emphasized, the ultimate guarantee of ratification resided in the international ramifications of Ostpolitik, namely its link to Western détente diplomacy. The US government brought heavy pressure to bear on the CDU by making it clear that a CDU government could not count on American support if a failure of the treaties led to a deterioration of German relations with the East, that international recognition of the GDR was irresistible, that the Berlin agreement could not come into effect...[41] In order to get the treaties through the Bundestag and to save the opposition's face, a joint resolution was worked out which stated that the treaties engaged only the Federal Republic and did not anticipate a peace settlement for Germany. Due to internal dissensions in the CDU/CSU camp — a minority in the CDU recommended acceptance of the treaties, whereas the CSU opted for rejection — the opposition finally ended up with an abstention vote preserving at least an appearance of cohesion (May 1972).[42]

In the absence of a viable government majority, new elections were scheduled for November 1972. The election campaign brought about an unprecedented degree of political mobilization which resulted in a record vote of 91%. The coalition parties benefited from the widespread approval that Brandt's Ostpolitik had met even among CDU voters. According to Werner Kaltefleiter, then head of the Adenauer Foundation's think tank, the CDU/CSU made a grave mistake when it practiced a strategy of confrontation with regard to foreign policy which perplexed part of its own electorate.[43] The initialing of the Basic Treaty between the Federal Republic and the GDR eleven days before the election deflected attention from economic issues (the CDU/CSU fared better in the polls on the inflation issue) and may have stabilized the voting intentions of potential coalition voters.[44] With 45.8% of the vote, the SPD for the first time became the strongest party, the CDU/CSU coming second with 44.9%. The FDP received 8.4%. This outcome secured the renewal of the existing government coalition and thereby the continuity of foreign policy. With splinter parties receiving only 0.9% (1969: 5.4%) of the vote, the concentration process in the West German party system had further advanced.

The outcome of the election also demonstrated that anti-communism was no longer potent enough to discredit political overtures toward the East. During the Cold War, anti-communism functioned as a pervasive ideology of integration which legitimized Adenauer's policy of *Westintegration* and served to isolate domestic critics of capitalist development.[45] Advocates of socialism were easily denounced as agents of Moscow. The particular intensity of anti-communism in the Federal Republic derived from its connection with the 'German question'. Communism was held responsible for the division of the nation, and the repressive nature of SED socialism was all too obvious. The process of détente and domestic developments during the second half of the sixties, such as the end of the period of reconstruction and the decline of CDU/CSU hegemony, were accompanied by a certain erosion of anti-communism. The student rebellion represented a fundamental challenge to political and ideological orthodoxy. The population at large favored an expansion of the welfare state. Foreign policy innovation and domestic reforms were intimately linked. Dirk Gerdes has argued that détente devalued a foreign policy conducted under the auspices of anti-communism as an instrument of 'normative control' (Etzioni) at the societal level. This resulted in an increase in unconventional political behavior and set free aspirations for an enlargement of subsystem autonomy. The securing of mass loyalty now required redistributive policies plus an increase in opportunities for political participation.[46] Yet anti-communism did not simply fade away. What took place was rather a process of differentiation. Whereas the ideological restrictions affecting foreign policy were largely removed, anti-communism remained vigorous on the domestic scene.[47] The student movement which finally disintegrated into a number of leftist sects even provided it with new targets. To disarm the opposition, the architects of Ostpolitik felt compelled to emphasize over and over again that international cooperation with communist regimes did in no way imply a weakening of the resistance offered to communist groups at home. That is how Ostpolitik rhymes with *Berufsverbot*.

THE POLITICAL ECONOMY OF OSTPOLITIK

Impressed by soaring West German exports to the Soviet Union (1971: 1.6 billion DM; 1974: 4.8 billion DM) some observers were tempted to interpret Ostpolitik as a strategy of market expansion dictated by the interests of West German industry. According to this view, Ostpolitik renewed the *Drang nach Osten* that had always characterized German imperialism. This sort of perception was in vogue in the French press[48] and reflected the fear that the Federal Republic might replace France as the Soviet Union's privileged partner in Western Europe. Claudia von Braunmühl has attempted to analyze Brandt's Ostpolitik in the framework of a theory of imperialism. Brandt's conception — she argues — could only be realized when it expressed the dominant interests of the West German economic system. Besides international and political factors, it was the export interests of the iron and steel industry which triggered the revision of Eastern policy because the traditional political claims were no longer compatible with the dynamics of capital.[49]

To put the economic dimension of Ostpolitik into perspective, it is useful to review briefly the history of the FRG's Eastern trade policy. It is common knowledge that the West German economy is highly dependent on exports. In 1974, the ratio of exports to GNP was 23.1% and one out of five jobs depended on exports. In 1975, the aggregate (direct plus indirect) export dependence of the investment goods industries which accounted for more than 55% of all industrial exports amounted to 47.4%. In the machine-building industry, it came to 56%, in the automobile industry to 52% and in the iron-producing industry to 67%.[50] By virtue of its size, the export sector has considerable clout in the process of foreign economic policy-making. Its structural economic importance is converted into political influence through a network of well-organized and articulate business associations.[51] However, the case of Eastern trade policy presents some complexities as trade was subject to the changing conditions of 'high politics'. At first sight, West German trade policy towards Eastern Europe and the Soviet Union seems to be a showcase for the subordination of economic motives and private interests to the primacy of foreign policy. Yet, a closer analysis reveals that the export sector was relatively successful, as the process of détente gained momentum, in overcoming government resistance to the removal of politically motivated restrictions on trade.

From its inception, Eastern trade policy was to serve as an instrument in the pursuit of reunification policy.[52] Consequently, trade with the East developed in a climate of political and psychological tension from the very beginning. Export interests and foreign policy objectives often clashed, and business was suspected of putting profits above patriotism. Under the Adenauer administration, trade relations with the Soviet bloc were consciously neglected. The inertia which then characterized Ostpolitik, in general, and trade policy, in particular, not only symbolized the refusal to deal with the enemies of German unity but also served to demonstrate Bonn's unfailing loyalty to the West. The Federal Republic had no diplomatic relations with communist countries until 1955 when Adenauer negotiated the establishment of diplomatic relations with the Soviet Union in exchange for the release of German prisoners of war. Consequently, prior to 1955, formal trade agreements could not be concluded. Industry stepped in to fill the vacuum. With government approval, the Eastern Committee of the German Economy (*Ostausschuß der deutschen Wirtschaft*) was set up in 1952 as the sole representative organ of the peak associations of industry, trade and banking. Its tasks were to advise the government on questions of East-West trade and to prepare documents for official trade negotiations. In the absence of diplomatic relations, it was authorized to conduct trade talks on its own. Its executive office was established at BDI headquarters in Cologne. The *Ostausschuß* was not an institutional innovation. It rather appears as a successor to the Russia Committee which, from the late 1920s on, coordinated trade relations with the Soviet Union.

De facto, on behalf of the German government, the *Ostausschuß* concluded the first commercial agreements with Rumania in 1953 and with the People's Republic of China in 1957. While the *Ostausschuß* leadership sought to improve trade relations with the East, the BDI leadership did not display much enthusiasm for *Osthandel*. BDI President Berg unconditionally supported Adenauer's foreign policy and did not object to the restrictive policy followed by the government with respect to import liberalization and the granting of government-guaranteed long-term export credits to Comecon countries. Criticism from industry mounted, however, when the government, in December 1962, denied export licenses to three of the largest steel producers for steel pipes ordered by the Soviet Union. This decision was taken on the grounds of a secret NATO Council resolution calling for a ban on the export of large-diameter steel pipes to the Soviet bloc. German compliance with the resolution was considered a test case for alliance solidarity and the Bundestag members representing the steel industry (Birrenbach of Thyssen and Dichgans, the deputy chairman of the Iron and Steel Industry Association) conformed to the government line. The embargo decision almost provoked a coalition crisis. The Free Democrats, junior partner of the Bonn coalition, rallied to the SPD in its opposition to the government. A government defeat in the Bundestag was only avoided because the CDU/CSU decided to boycott the vote and thus prevented the necessary quorum.[53]

The steel industry was outraged and viewed the embargo as causing enormous damage to trade relations with the Soviet Union. Moreover, the export sector became increasingly concerned about its 'terms of competition' when Great Britain and Italy started a credit race by granting long-term credits covered by government insurance for the export of capital equipment to the Soviet Union. This violated the terms of the Berne Union agreement which prohibited credit terms for deliveries of capital equipment exceeding five years. Italy, Britain, and France had adopted a more pragmatic approach to East-West trade in general and were eager to reap the commercial benefits of détente. The efforts undertaken by the Federal Government to achieve coordination of credit terms under NATO or EEC auspices met with failure as West-Germany's partner-rivals could pointedly refer to the West German lead in Eastern markets. The restrictive trade and credit policy had not prevented an almost continuous expansion of West German trade with Eastern Europe up to then. This was due to a long-standing tradition of commercial relations and the critical importance of imports of capital equipment for the industrialization process of the Comecon countries. Nonetheless, industrialists became alarmed at the prospect of losing Eastern markets to Western competitors. Spokesmen for the *Ostausschuß* therefore advocated a 'de-politicization' of Eastern trade. The gradual relaxation of credit restrictions was finally brought about by insistent pressure from the export sector in 1964/65. This was a time when, in political circles, it was increasingly recognized that the manipulation of trade was unlikely to yield significant concessions from the Soviet Union. The export sector was also the driving force behind the liberalization of imports from state-trading nations which became a necessity as Eastern trade deficits grew.

Once the strategic decisions regarding the course of trade policy had been taken by the government, the *Ostausschuß* proved to be influential in shaping the content of this policy. Its striking effectiveness stems from several factors. Having the monopoly over representation at the level of national peak associations, it functions as a clearing-house, seeking to reach 'quasi-unanimity' by in-house negotiations. It is thereby enabled to confront the government bureaucracy with a carefully hammered out common position. It is doubtful, however, whether the export sector would have succeeded, as it did, in bringing the government to reverse its trade policy had this not been in line with the change to the more flexible 'policy of movement' initiated by Foreign Minister Schröder.

When the Soviet Union — probably some time in early 1969 — decided to normalize relations with West Germany, economic motives undoubtedly influenced this decision. This is indicated by the huge compensation deal concluded in February 1970. The Soviet Union ordered 1.2 million tons of large-diameter steel pipes from Mannesmann. Payment was to be made through deliveries of Soviet natural gas to the Ruhrgas AG starting in 1973. The deal required a long-term credit of 1.2 billion DM which was granted to the USSR by a consortium of four banks led by the Deutsche Bank. The interest rate of 6.25% was called a preferential rate at the time, market rates being 1.5 to 2% above this level. But it is widely assumed that the banks, which owned a substantial part of Mannesmann shares, recovered their 'concession' through Mannesmann's selling price. Interestingly enough, the negotiations regarding this project coincided with a general step-up of diplomatic contacts between the USSR and the FRG. There is some evidence that in the winter 1969/70, a debate over economic policy took place among the Soviet leadership which resulted in a policy decision to rely on increased imports of investment goods and turn-key plants from the West in order to achieve higher levels of productivity and a modernization of industry.[54] It was only logical then that the Federal Republic's economic potential made it an attractive or even privileged partner for the Soviet Union.

West German industry favored a policy of normalization with the East. The Moscow Treaty of 1970 was greeted with discreet applause in the business press.[55] Yet, in general, industrial associations and business leaders were reserved in their pronouncements or adopted a position of 'benevolent neutrality'. The *Ostausschuß* cautioned against exaggerated expectations and pointed to the structural impediments to trade expansion with the East. During the ratification debate, Economics Minister Karl Schiller appealed to the business community to speak out publicly in favor of the treaties.[56] But only a few industrialists left their reserve. The economy was booming, and a failure of the treaties, though undesirable, was not considered an economic catastrophe.

Public advocacy of ratification would have inevitably supported a coalition which business mistrusted for ideological reasons. In the last analysis, it appears that, since the early fifties, Eastern trade policy, though closely related to the overall strategy of Ostpolitik, has been much more open to interest group influence than foreign policy in general. Ostpolitik stands out as an area of high politics par excellence in which business hardly ever dared to intervene.

By eliminating political and psychological barriers to trade expansion and long-term economic cooperation with the East, Brandt's Ostpolitik opened a new phase in foreign economic policy towards Comecon countries. To promote trade and industrial cooperation, the government deployed a wide range of instruments. It took further measures of import liberalization, set up joint commissions for economic and technical cooperation composed of government officials and businessmen, and raised significantly the ceiling for export credit guarantees. The Federal Republic's trade surplus in Eastern trade rose from 0.7 billion DM in 1970 to almost 8 billion DM in 1975. Exports tripled between 1971 and 1975. Cumulative indebtedness of East European countries (including the USSR) vis-à-vis the FRG amounted to 20 billion DM in 1975.[57] The main economic goals sought by the Federal Republic can be summarized as follows: diversification of export markets, development of new sources of raw materials and energy, and, if possible, the relocation of raw material and labor-intensive production lines.[58] In political terms, closer economic cooperation with the East is intended to create links of functional interdependence generating vested interests in the development of détente. Despite the temporary dynamism of West Germany's Eastern trade, its overall significance is relatively modest. In 1975, exports towards Eastern Europe (including the USSR) accounted for 7.2% of total exports; Eastern imports came to 4.3%. Due to the Eastern side's efforts to reduce its trade deficits with the West, the share of Comecon countries in West German exports went down to 5.6% by 1977 (with imports at 4.5%). The expansionary phase of West Germany's Eastern trade is being replaced by a period of consolidation.[58a]

THE FUTURE OF OSTPOLITIK

As normalization in the Federal Republic's relations with the East proceeds, Ostpolitik is likely to become part of a wider network of pan-European cooperation and détente diplomacy. Yet, it is safe to predict that inter-German relations will still constitute for many years a specific dimension of East-West relations. Although the 'German question' was removed from the agenda of world politics when the two German states were admitted to the United Nations, as Curt Gasteyger argues in his penetrating and thoughtful analysis,[59] relations between the FRG and the GDR are still a far cry from the 'good-neighborly relations' postulated by the Basic Treaty. They remain a source of tensions that may affect West Germany's overall relations with the East. These tensions arise from two sets of circumstances: (1) The 'national question' has not yet completely come to rest and there still exist some remnants of reunification policy; (2) the German case dramatizes general problems of East-West relations in the era of détente, such as the dialectics of rapprochement and demarcation (*Annäherung und Abgrenzung*),[60] the human rights issue or the problem of régime instability in Eastern Europe.

For the GDR leadership the conclusion of the Basic Treaty was the end of a 'nightmare' as it opened the road to international recognition.[61] For the Federal Republic, it was a reconciliation with reality. It was also the necessary precondition for a series of agreements which facilitated contacts and communication between the citizens of the two states. The constitutionality of the treaty was challenged by the State Government of Bavaria. The Constitutional Court ruled that the Basic Treaty was constitutional, but it reaffirmed an earlier decision stating that reunification was a constitutional imperative. According to the court, no government or legislative body was authorized to renounce the restoration of German unity as a political goal. It also referred to Article 7 of the *Deutschland-Vertrag* of 1954 in which the FRG, the US, the United Kingdom and France had assumed the obligation 'to work together in order to realize their common objective, namely a reunified Germany having a free and democratic constitution similar to that of the Federal Republic and integrated into the European Community'.[62]

The court also stated that the border between the two Germanies has the same legal quality as the borders between the *Länder* of the FRG, given the fact that the Reich still exists (the FRG being identical with the Reich as a state, though not in territorial terms). The court's ruling has come under devastating criticism from legal scholars[63] but it continues to be a favorite point of reference for the CDU/CSU's foreign policy establishment. Not surprisingly, the GDR considered the court's ruling a provocation. Although the court's decision is definitely at variance with the principle of 'judicial self-restraint', it only marginally restricts the Federal Government's freedom of action. Eventually, no court will be able to decide whether a policy will or will not lead to reunification. On the other hand, it invests the illusions some politicians may still harbor with the title of a constitutional imperative. Reunification is no more than a mirage on the horizon of West German foreign policy and the FRG's Western partners are unlikely to support a policy that carries a flavor of irredentism.[64] A 're-ideologization' of the German question[65] would only add to the strains that currently beset inter-German relations.

Normalization poses difficult problems to the SED regime. Eager to reap the benefits of increased economic cooperation with the FRG the GDR leadership had to make concessions with regard to travel regulations and other humanitarian questions. At the same time the SED has stressed the necessity of *Abgrenzung* in order to ward off the risks of ideological 'subversion'. The SED leadership continuously faces a dilemma: how to satisfy the population's aspirations for improved living conditions in the largest sense without provoking a revolution of rising expectations and a loss of political control. Millions of West German tourists and West German TV stations reporting on East German dissidents undoubtedly represent a challenge for the GDR leadership. These channels of communication provide standards of comparison in the peaceful contest of social systems which the SED could well dispense with. Yet, it would be shortsighted of the FRG government to try to exploit this weakness. Domestic liberalization can hardly be forced on the GDR leadership from outside lest it provoke Soviet intervention in one form or another. Only a consolidation of the GDR offers a promise for easing and overcoming the gruesome realities of barbed wire and death-strips at the inter-German frontier.

To minimize the *querelles allemandes* also seems to be the appropriate prescription for an active participation of the Federal Republic in multilateral détente diplomacy.[66] The overriding objective of West German foreign policy, the creation of a structure of peace in Europe (*europäische Friedensordnung*) can hardly be attained by means of an autonomous West German diplomacy. What does *europäische Friedensordnung* mean altogether? If one tries to translate this slogan into political objectives one must obviously avoid the temptation to reach for millenium. It may be useful to break it down into three essential components formulated as process-goals:

— the de-militarization of antagonistic competition;
— the enlargement of economic and technological cooperation with Eastern Europe and the Soviet Union;
— and the improvement of opportunities for contacts and communication between Eastern and Western Europe.

The pursuit of these goals clearly requires extensive coordination and concerted action with other West European countries and the United States. This is particularly true for the efforts aiming at troop reductions, the limitation of nuclear stock-piles and the control of innovation in arms technology. This is also true for the preservation of the actual status of West Berlin.[67]

The future of Ostpolitik therefore depends on the future of détente. The Federal Republic's Ostpolitik would hardly be left unscathed by a dramatic deterioration in US-Soviet relations.

On the other hand, it should not be assumed that there is a mechanical link between the superpower relationship and West Germany's Eastern policies. As Kissinger once observed, 'the interests of America and Europe are not identical everywhere'.[68] It is hard to see, for instance, why the Federal Republic or other West European nations should endorse ill-advised American policies, such as attempts to use economic and technological dealings as a lever to influence Soviet policy in Africa or to 'enforce' human rights in the USSR. Nor would it be in the European interest to support exercises in elementary Machiavelism like playing the 'Chinese card'. The Federal Republic may disagree with the US over the proper conduct of a concerted Western strategy. This has nothing to do with 'Finlandization', however.

Western efforts towards the promotion of human rights in Eastern Europe can easily be justified as an application of the Soviet principle that peaceful coexistence does not exclude ideological competition. However, private organizations may turn out to be more successful in this area than governments resorting to 'Jackson amendment' strategies. There is a risk that attempts to influence the dynamics of change in Eastern Europe from outside impede the desired evolution rather than promote it. During the years ahead, economic relations between Eastern and Western Europe will probably be conducted under the proviso formulated by an Hungarian economist: 'Mutual economic interests must be sufficient in quantity and quality to offer a counterweight to possible political tensions, but they must not be of a nature likely to weaken or loosen the inner forces of cohesion of either system'.[69] Yet it seems that 'the inner forces of cohesion' have weakened already under the impact of détente — in the East possibly more than in the West. Witness the emergence of organized protest movements in Poland and Czechoslovakia (Workers' Defense Committee, Charter '77) and the rise of Eurocommunism. As the Rumanian case shows, even Warsaw Pact defense spending is no longer unquestioned. However, this is not to obscure the fact that in the military field the record of détente is most disappointing. Unless a military balance can be achieved at lower force levels and the race to develop and deploy new weapons systems be stopped, peace and security in Europe will remain precarious.

NOTES

1. For a more elaborate treatment see my contribution 'Nationale Besonderheiten — Bundesrepublik Deutschland', in: Eberhard Schulz (ed.), *Die Ostbeziehungen der Europäischen Gemeinschaft* (München, Wien: 1977), 153-169, 161ff.

2. See e.g. Claus Arndt, *Die Verträge von Moskau und Warschau. Politische, verfassungsrechtliche und völkerrechtliche Aspekte* (Bonn: 1973); Peter Bender, *Die Ostpolitik Willy Brandt's oder die Kunst des Selbstverständlichen* (Reinbek: 1972); Dettmar Cramer, *Deutschland nach dem Grundvertrag* (Stuttgart: 1973); Josef Joffe, 'Westverträge, Ostverträge und die Kontinuität der deutschen Außenpolitik', in: *Europa-Archiv*, 4, 1973, 111-124; Volkmar Kellermann, *Brücken nach Polen. Die deutsch-polnischen Beziehungen und die Weltmächte 1939-1973* (Stuttgart: 1973); R. Löwenthal, *Vom Kalten Krieg zur Ostpolitik* (Stuttgart: 1974); G. Wettig, *Europäische Sicherheit. Das europäische Staatensystem in der sowjetischen Außenpolitik 1966-1972* (Düsseldorf: 1972).

3. Cf. *Friedensanalysen Vol. 1 (Feindbilder)* (Frankfurt: 1975); Ulrich Albrecht et al., *Durch Kooperation zum Frieden?* (München: 1974); Gerda Zellentin (ed.), *Annäherung, Abgrenzung und friedlicher Wandel in Europa* (Boppard: 1976).

4. Cf. Gebhard Schweigler, *Contemporary International Studies in the Federal Republic of Germany* (Bonn: 1975), 13.

5. See e.g. Karl E. Birnbaum, *East and West Germany. A Modus Vivendi* (Westmead, Farnborough, Hants.: 1973); Josef Korbel, *Détente in Europe. Real or Imaginary?*

(Princeton, NJ: 1972); Roger Tilford (ed.), *The Ostpolitik and Political Change in Germany* (Westmead, Farnborough, Hants.: 1975); Lawrence L. Whetten, *Germany's Ostpolitik. Relations between the Federal Republic and the Warsaw Pact Countries* (London: 1971); Josef Joffe, 'The Foreign Policy of the German Federal Republic', in: Roy C. Macridis (ed.), *Foreign Policy in World Politics* (Englewood Cliffs, NJ: 1976), 117-151.

6. Cf. Hans-Peter Schwarz, 'Der unbekannte Adenauer. Einige Aufgaben künftiger Forschung', in: Dieter Blumenwitz et al. (eds.), *Konrad Adenauer und seine Zeit. Bd. II: Beiträge der Wissenschaft* (Stuttgart: 1976), 589-609, 593.

7. Klaus Gotto, 'Adenauers Deutschland- und Ostpolitik 1954-1963', in: Rudolf Morsey and Konrad Repgen (eds.), *Adenauer-Studien Bd. III. Untersuchungen und Dokumente zur Ostpolitik und Biographie* (Mainz: 1974), 3-91.

8. Ibid., 90.

9. Ibid., 55. For the text of the Globke Plan see ibid., 202-209.

10. On Adenauer's Ostpolitik see also the contributions by Hillgruber, Salzmann, Blumenwitz, Meissner to the Adenauer Centennial volume: Blumenwitz et al., op. cit. note 6.

11. Philip Windsor, *Germany and the Management of Détente* (London: 1971), 67f. Cf. Ernst Kuper, *Frieden durch Konfrontation und Kooperation. Die Einstellung von Gerhard Schröder und Willy Brandt zur Entspannungspolitik* (Stuttgart: 1974), 306f.

12. Cf. e.g. Theo Sommer, *Denken an Deutschland* (Hamburg: 1966). For the Grand Coalition's Ostpolitik see Claudia von Braunmühl, *Kalter Krieg und friedliche Koexistenz. Die Außenpolitik der SPD in der Großen Koalition* (Frankfurt: 1973); Henning Storz, *Außenpolitik als Gesellschaftspolitik*, Phil. Diss. (Berlin: 1973).

13. Cf. v. Braunmühl, op. cit. note 12, 146ff; Löwenthal, op. cit. note 2, 76f.

14. Birnbaum, op. cit. note 5, 31. Birnbaum stresses the 'striking continuity' in Bahr's thinking.

15. Willy Brandt, *Begegnungen und Einsichten. Die Jahre 1960-1975* (Hamburg: 1976), 17.

16. Diethelm Prowe, 'Die Anfänge der Brandtschen Ostpolitik in Berlin 1961-1963', in: Wolfgang Benz and Hermann Graml (eds.), *Aspekte der deutschen Außenpolitik im 20. Jahrhundert (Festschrift Hans Rothfels)* (Stuttgart: 1976), 249-286.

17. Ibid., 256.

18. Ibid., 271.

19. Cf. 'Memorandum des Regierenden Bürgermeisters von Berlin Brandt an den amerikanischen Außenminister Rusk v. August 1964', in: Boris Meissner (ed.), *Die deutsche Ostpolitik 1961-1970* (Köln: 1970), 85-90.

20. Joffe, op. cit. note 5, 147.

21. Roger Morgan, 'The Ostpolitik and West Germany's External Relations', in: Tilford, op. cit. note 5, 95-108, 98.

22. Joffe, op. cit. note 5, 147.

23. Cf. Abraham Ashkenasi, *Reformpartei und Außenpolitik. Die Aussenpolitik der SPD Berlin- Bonn* (Köln, Opladen: 1968), 162ff; Joachim Hütter, *SPD und nationale Sicherheit. Internationale und innenpolitische Determinanten des Wandels der sozialdemokratischen Sicherheitspolitik 1959-1961* (Meisenheim: 1975), 78ff.

24. For the 'Rapallo complex' in the French press see Gerhard Kiersch, 'Frankreichs Reaktion auf die deutsche Ostpolitik', in: Egbert Jahn and Volker Rittberger (eds.), *Die Ostpolitik der BRD* (Opladen: 1974), 181-206, 182f.

25. Cf. ibid., 190ff.

26. Dietrich Geyer, 'Voraussetzungen sowjetischer Außenpolitik in der Zwischenkriegszeit', in: Dietrich Geyer (ed.), *Osteuropa-Handbuch, Sowjetunion, Außenpolitik I* (Köln, Wien: 1972), 1-85, 5; Cf. Hans-Adolf Jacobsen, 'Zur Kontinuität und Diskontinuität in der deutschen Außenpolitik im 20. Jhrdt.', in: H. A. Jacobsen, *Von der Strategie der Gewalt zur Politik der Friedenssicherung. Beiträge zur deutschen Geschichte im 20. Jahrhundert* (Düsseldorf: 1977), 9-32, 12.

27. Ibid.

28. This paragraph follows closely Jacobsen, op. cit. note 26, 20ff.

29. Cf. Morgan, op. cit. note 21, 95-108, 103ff.

30. Geoffrey Pridham, 'The Ostpolitik and the Oppostion in West Germany', in: Tilford, op. cit. note 21, 45-58, 46.

31. Cf. Roland A. Höhne, 'Die Motive der ostpolitischen Opposition seit 1969', in: Jahn and Rittberger, op. cit. note 24, 53-70; Karlheinz Niclauß, *Kontroverse Deutschlandpolitik. Die politische Auseinandersetzung in der Bundesrepublik Deutschland über den Grundlagenvertrag mit der DDR* (Frankfurt/M: 1977), 85ff. For a critical but sympathetic analysis see Christian Hacke, *Die Ost- und Deutschlandpolitik der CDU/CSU. Wege und Irrwege der Opposition seit 1969* (Köln: 1975).

32. Cf. Niclauß, op. cit. note 31, 54.

33. Ibid, 86, 88.

34. Reinhold Roth, *Außenpolitische Innovation und politische Herrschaftssicherung. Eine Analyse von Struktur und Systemfunktion des außenpolitischen Entscheidungsprozesses am Beispiel der sozialliberalen Koalition 1969 bis 1973* (Meisenheim: 1976), 41f.

35. Ibid., 59ff, 90.

36. Helmut Allardt, *Moskauer Tagebuch* (Düsseldorf, Wien: 1973).

37. Roth, op. cit. note 34, 61ff.

38. Pridham, op. cit. note 30, 54.

39. Roth, op. cit. note 34, 167.

40. Ibid., 196ff.

41. Ibid., 186. Cf. Manfred Knapp, 'Zusammenhänge zwischen der Ostpolitik der BRD und den deutsch-amerikanischen Beziehungen', in: Jahn and Rittberger, op. cit. note 24, 157-180, 168ff.

42. For the different groups in the opposition camp see Hacke, op. cit. note 31, 75f; Pridham, op. cit. note 30, 49f.

43. Werner Kaltefleiter, 'Zwischen Konsens und Krise. Eine Analyse der Bundestagswahl 1972' (*Jahrbuch Verfassung und Verfassungswirklichkeit 1973, Teil I*) (Köln: 1973), 33.

44. Cf. Max Kaase, 'Die Bundestagswahl 1972: Probleme und Analysen', in: *Politische Vierteljahresschrift*, 14, 2, 1973, 145-190.

45. Cf. Wilfried v. Bredow, *Vom Antagonismus zur Konvergenz? Studien zum Ost-West-Problem* (Frankfurt/M: 1972), 166ff; Waldemar Besson, *Die Außenpolitik der Bundesrepublik* (München: 1970), 61; Claudia Wörmann, 'Die Ostpolitik und die Wandlung des nach innen und außen gerichteten antikommunistischen Feindbildes', in: Jahn and Rittberger, op. cit. note 24, 123-134.

46. Dirk Gerdes, *Abschreckung und Entspannung. Legitimatorische Folgeprobleme bundesrepublikanischer Entspannungspolitik* (Meisenheim: 1976).

47. Cf. Wörmann, op. cit. note 45, 130.

48. See Kiersch, op. cit. note 24.

49. Claudia v. Braunmühl, op. cit. note 12; id., 'Ist die "Ostpolitik" Ostpolitik?', in: Jahn and Rittberger, op. cit. note 24, 13-28, 22.

50. Cf. DIW (Deutsches Institut für Wirtschaftsforschung), *Wochenbericht*, 22, 1976, 221, 224; Kurzmitteilung, 'Zur Internationalisierung der westdeutschen Wirtschaft', in: *WSI-Mitteilungen*, 4, 1976, 230-234.

51. Cf. Michael Kreile, 'West Germany: the Dynamics of Expansion', in: Peter J. Katzenstein (ed.), 'Between Power and Plenty: Foreign Economic Policies of Advanced Industrial States', *International Organization*, 31, 4, Autumn 1977 (Special Issue), 775-808, 785.

52. The following paragraphs draw heavily on section IV of my article in: Katzenstein, op. cit. note 51, 788ff and on chapters 2 and 3 of my study *Osthandel und Ostpolitik* (Baden-Baden: 1978).

53. Cf. Robert W. Dean, *West German Trade with the East: The Political Dimension* (New York: 1974), 127-40.

54. Cf. Wolfgang Leonhard, 'Sowjetische Innenpolitik seit Chruschtschows Sturz', in: R. Löwenthal and H. Vogel (eds.), *Sowjetpolitik der 7oer Jahre* (Stuttgart: 1972), 55-97, 76f.

55. Cf. Hans-Jobst Krautheim, 'Ostpolitik und Osthandel: Das Problem von auswärtiger Politik und Außenhandel in den Publikationen der Wirtschaftspresse und des BDI (1963-1972)', in: Jahn and Rittberger, op. cit. note 24, 96-124, 109ff.

56. Cf. Kreile, op. cit. note 52, 140ff.

57. Figures from Alex Möller, 'Probleme und Perspektiven der wirtschaftlichen Verflechtung zwischen der Bundesrepublik Deutschland und den Staatshandelsländern', in: *WSI-Mitteilungen*, 5, 1976, 288; *Monatsberichte der Deutschen Bundesbank*, July 1976, 14.

58. For a discussion of these goals see M. Kreile, 'Bundesrepublik Deutschland', in: E. Schulz (ed.) op. cit. note 1, 162ff.

59. Curt Gasteyger, *Die beiden deutschen Staaten in der Weltpolitik* (München: 1976), 130.

60. See Zellentin, op. cit. note 3.

61. Cf. Gasteyger, op. cit. note 59, 16.

62. Cf. *Entscheidungen des Bundesverfassungsgerichts, 36. Bd.* (Tübingen: 1974), 1-27.

63. For a thorough and perceptive analysis see Kay-Michael Wilke, *Bundesrepublik Deutschland und Deutsche Demokratische Republik. Grundlagen und ausgewählte Probleme des gegenseitigen Verhältnisses der beiden deutschen Staaten* (Berlin: 1976); see also Niclauß, op. cit. note 31, Ch. 6; Günther Schmid, *Politik des Ausverkaufs? Die Deutschlandpolitik der Regierung Brandt/Scheel* (München: 1975), 228ff; Roger Tilford, 'Introduction', in: Tilford, op. cit. note 5, 1-22, 14ff.

64. Cf. Gasteyger, op. cit. note 59, 151ff; Ernst Nolte, *Deutschland und der Kalte Krieg* (München: 1974), 597ff. For the problem of the German 'nation' see Gebhard Schweigler's contribution to this volume.

65. Cf. Peter C. Ludz, *Deutschlands doppelte Zukunft* (München: 1974), 102ff.

66. This paragraph draws on my contribution to Schulz, op. cit. note 58, 166ff.

67. For an analysis of the legal intricacies of the Berlin status see Ottfried Hennig, *Die Bundespräsenz in West-Berlin* (Köln: 1976).

68. Henry A. Kissinger, *The Troubled Partnership* (New York: 1975), 230; quoted from Simon Serfaty, 'The Still-troubled Partnership', in: George Ginsburgs and Alvin Z.

Rubinstein (eds.), *Soviet Foreign Policy toward Western Europe* (New York: 1978), 259-281, 271.

69. Josef Bognar, 'All-European Economic Cooperation', in: *New Hungarian Quarterly*, 47, 1972, 176-184, 181.

5

BUREAUCRACY AND FOREIGN POLICY IN THE FEDERAL REPUBLIC OF GERMANY

Joachim Krause and Lothar Wilker

FOREIGN POLICY — LIKE ANY OTHER POLICY AREA — is largely determined today by the activities of highly differentiated and highly specialized bureaucracies. Under these auspices the traditional notion of the distinction between politics and bureaucracy is being eroded by two factors: for one thing, a separation between 'political' government and 'unpolitical' executive can hardly be maintained any longer. The diversity of responsibilities and the abundance of ways to make important pre-decisions, have turned bureaucracy into a significant decision-making factor, i.e. into a political rather than purely executive parameter. For another, this affects possibilities and chances of policy-makers as well as parties to shape and implement policies in an active manner. More often than not bureaucracies play a preserving role in this process, i.e. by impeding political changes and preventing the development of comprehensive concepts. At times, however, they surprise by innovative approaches. In other cases they seem to resemble independent political coalitions which do not shrink from opposing their political leadership.

The implications of this bureaucractic element for the process of foreign-policy-making have at best been examined marginally to date. However, during the past few years a group of predominantly American scholars has published studies on the phenomenon of the so-called bureaucratic politics in US national-security policy.[1] Although the

Authors' note: This paper was translated from German by Frauke Jensen.

studies made by this group have meanwhile become an indispensable element of the analysis of American foreign and national-security policy, their application to German conditions appears to be a problematic undertaking for two reasons.

— the differences in size, organization and tradition of the bureaucratic machineries are considerable. Moreover, the fact that the Federal Republic of Germany has a parliamentary system with extensive competition between the parties, creates a different situation. This becomes obvious, for example, when looking at the role played by the cabinet within the German federal government. It is no advisory, preparatory and excutive body like the US federal government, but largely a decision-making body, and the position of the Chancellor cannot be compared with that of the American President as regards decision-making authority and power base.

— in addition, the bureaucratic-politics approach puts undue emphasis on the aspect of a bureaucracy in the process of becoming an independent entity. This fact has been criticized by a number of authors who, by the same token, pointed to corresponding shortcomings in the analyses.

In the following the authors attempt to develop some ideas of their own concerning the role of bureaucracy in the foreign policy of the Federal Republic of Germany. The paper is based on study of the West German planning and bureaucratic literature as well as on studies contributed by the authors on the foreign policy decision-making process in the Federal Republic of Germany.[2] The first section describes setup, structure, and function of the foreign-policy administration in Bonn. For an assessment of the working of this bureaucracy the second section will outline formal procedures and processes, while the third will study its implications for processes of policy-making.

I THE FOREIGN-POLICY BUREAUCRACY IN BONN — SETUP, STRUCTURE, FUNCTIONS

Generally speaking, the bureaucratization of foreign policy is a consequence of the extension of the area of government activities as well as of a complication of the classical foreign-policy matters. A characteristic feature is its 'functionalization', which means that 'the socio-economic sector increasingly coins the foreign-political problem-handling structure of the state'.[3] Foreign and domestic policies are not longer clearly separable in functional as well as organizational terms. Public responsibilities — e.g. job-securing measures — can be solved domestically (by controlling the economic cycle) or by foreign-policy actions (by concluding export- or trade agreements). In addition, the foreign-policy bureaucracy is no longer limited to the Foreign Office (*Auswärtiges Amt*) which has become confronted with competitors endowed in part with considerable authority.

According to Article 11 of the GOBReg,[4] the Foreign Office does have the central authority in the conduct of foreign affairs: 'Negotiations with foreign countries or in foreign countries may be conducted only upon approval of the Foreign Office, upon its demand they may even be conducted solely with its participation'. This steering competence has, however, been undermined in actual terms. For one thing, the constitutional law according to Article 65 GG[5] gives the Chancellor the right to engage or instruct his staff to engage in foreign policy matters. Above all at the beginning of the first social-liberal coalition, for example, the *Ostpolitik* was conceived and implemented by State Secretary Egon Bahr in the Chancellory, while the Foreign Office remained in a passive position. For another, other ministries are competent for issue areas which have meanwhile become core areas of foreign policy. Thus the Ministries of Defense, Economics, Economic Cooperation, Research and Technology as well as Finance are becoming important political actors acting independently in part on the international plane or else dominating a subject in organizational as well as substantive terms in such a way as to reduce the co-signing competence. The ways and means of the Foreign Office of channeling and steering this diversity of activities are hence restricted.

The activities of the foreign-policy bureaucracies in Bonn are primarily of a non-executive kind. It is a peculiarity of the federative system of the FRG that the federal ministerial bureaucracy, with the exception of a few cases, has no executive function, but instead primarily supports the federal government. This support activity ranges from the preparation of political concepts, the drafting of bills, regulations, treaties, etc. to the drafting of speech manuscripts for the political leadership. The ministerial bureaucracy is thus more of a huge secretariat for the ministers than an executive body. Although the area of foreign and security policies is one of the fields involving a federal-administration activity (diplomatic service, maintenance of armed forces, carrying out of development projects abroad), the executive-bureaucratic activity will be ignored below. Thus an action profile of the foreign affairs bureaucracy reveals that — like the federal bureaucracy in general — it deviates from that of other countries.[6] There are, above all, four types of activities that can be distinguished.[7]

- *Elaboration of conceptions, programming and planning.* This refers to the formulation and preparation of long-term conceptions on foreign policy as such or individual areas like military security, foreign-trade, and foreign-aid policy or *Deutschlandpolitik*. This is a political activity by definition which — if implemented — is mostly pursued in close contact with leaders of the political parties or the government (e.g. the Ostpolitik by Willy Brandt and Egon Bahr).
- *Secondary process activities.* These include above all the preparation of international negotiations and the drafting of action strategies. They further involve the development of conceptions on specific areas of foreign policy (like arms-transfer policy), replies to important diplomatic notes or the planning of setting regional or sectoral priorities.
- *Instrumental activities.* This category includes the drafting of texts for treaties and agreements; the conduct of international negotiations; preparation of summit meetings and conferences; activities in international boards and organizations; compilation of information; preparation of guidelines, regulations, etc.
- *Routine activities.* These refer to a number of different activity areas like replies to questions by members of parliament and parties; other PR activities (e.g. white papers, etc.); problems of business management.

All four — but above all the first three activity areas — contain various possibilities of influencing the type, direction and consequences of political outcomes. To better assess the implication of the bureaucratic factor for the policy-making process, the special conditions which govern internal bureaucratic processes have to be examined.

II FORMAL PROCEDURES AND OPERATING PATTERNS

The influence of bureaucracy in the political decision-making process is dependent on the existing organizational conditions. If the task of the foreign-policy bureaucracy is to consist in 'pursuing all activities relevant for foreign policy in a uniform process of political analysis, planning, decision and progress control'[8] the formal operating patterns have to be shaped correspondingly in functional terms.

The foreign-policy bureaucracy — like all other German bureaucracies — is organized hierarchically according to a line principle. A distinction is made between upper level (minister and state secretaries), intermediate level (division head and sub-division heads) and the level of the basic operating units (section chiefs). This organizational structure favors a vertical communication (*Dienstweg*). By the same token responsibilities and competences to issue directives are established.

The assumption that the upper level — in particular the minister who is responsible for the actions of his 'house' — can fulfill all politically relevant functions, ranging from conceiving the foreign-policy guidelines to controlling their bureaucratic execution, is a fallacy. The constantly increasing complexity of foreign afairs, which requires the maintenance of numerous external contacts by the upper level, prevents this. Even with the aid of a staff the upper level cannot guarantee sufficient information-processing and problem-solving capacity. Moreover, the staff has to fulfill a number of other functions.[9] Thus the function of the political leadership is reduced, in the final analysis, to drafting guidelines, controlling their bureaucratic translation and acting in many cases as crisis-manager.

Within the framework of the political directives issued by the political leadership it is up to the intermediate level to guarantee their implementation. In addition, it has to give substance to the foreign-policy guidelines conceived by the political leadership. This presupposes a flow of communication between the leadership level and the divisions. Furthermore, the continuity of the horizontal communication is secured by daily meetings of the division heads. The effectiveness of the work of the intermediate level suffers from the lack of staff. This limits their mediating function between leadership and basic operating units, and the division chiefs often act merely as 'spokesmen for the leadership'.[10] The most effective tool of the division heads to fulfill this role are the weekly conferences of the section chiefs.

Given the structural restrictions at the two levels mentioned, the basic units take on an especially crucial role in the foreign-policy decision-making process. It is here, at the working level that 'the information and background knowledge, the knowledge of the issues and their solutions and those differentiated environmental contacts can be found which enable the ministerial organization as such to fulfill its functions in the problem-solving process in their present proportions'.[11] As 'supporting units in the organizational setup of the ministry' (GGO I, Article 4, section 2),[12] the specialist sections prepare the political decisions. Within the confines of the areas assigned to them, they enjoy a relatively great autonomy of action.

Whereas, for the vertical communication within the ministerial bureaucracy, formal operating patterns are ruled by GGO I, such regulations do not exist for the horizontal communication. In view of the manifold complex terms of references in the area of foreign policy, however, cooperation at the working level is highly intensive.

Whether and to what extent a responsible section draws on the assistance of other working units within the same or other ministries involved, is thus largely up to the section chief unless a co-signature is mandatory. These interactions at the working level mostly take place in a non-formalized manner. Essential tools are unofficial meetings of the section chiefs involved and above all the telephone.

Suggestions and instructions of the upper level are channeled via the intermediate level down to the working units. Proposals by a section chief take the reverse route. Depending upon their political rank these instructions or proposals are initiated at various hierarchical levels. One purpose of this lengthy formal process is to identify those persons involved in possible changes of substance of texts. This formalization stipulates even that the individual persons in charge use certain colors for their initials (GGO I, Article 18). The manifold informal contacts mentioned, however — above all at the working level — undermine this formal operational plan.

These structures as outlined above are essential for an understanding of bureaucratic behavior. However, they present but a very general idea of the possible implications of the administrative handling of political problems. A more detailed analysis would have to throw more light on the administrative practice and would have to look for specific factors conducive to consequences of political substance. This can be done theoretically in two ways: by case studies which identify the phases of the political process where bureaucratic action has an impact on political substance; or by means of a systematic search for the causes which make conceptions and objectives get stuck in the bureaucratic apparatus. The following section will concentrate on the second approach even though the authors are well aware of its deficiencies. On the other hand, attempts at a systematic analysis of the capacity of today's governments to act with regard to their bureaucratic machinery have been scarce to date.

III RESTRICTIONS ON FORMULATION OF FOREIGN POLICY

A restriction analysis of West German foreign policy suggests itself for two eminently political reasons. It is obvious, for one thing, that following the conceptional 'thrust' on the occasion of the change of government in 1969 not only a decline of these conceptions set in, but, in addition, goals that had been considered essential for a new foreign policy were either not realized or were reversed in the course of their realization.[13] For another, it cannot be ignored that many of the foreign-policy innovations promised by the social-liberal government in 1969 and 1972 have not been realized. This development resembles that experienced in the field of social policy, thus suggesting parallels.

The planning literature within the political-science community has taken up this subject increasingly during the past few years. Many scholars asked the question why it is that despite, 'or because' of, the existence of comprehensive administrative machineries and resources the western industrialized nations have such great difficulty playing an active role in shaping social life. This literature developed a number of assumptions and substantiated some aspects by empirical means. It forms the basis of the subsequent remarks. By means of case studies within the above-mentioned research project on the foreign-policy decision-making process in the Federal Republic of Germany it was possible to subject some of these assumptions to empirical tests.

According to a rough systematization the planning literature proceeds from two types of restrictions: *internal* restrictions which can be derived solely from the working methods and structure of bureaucratic organizations and the *external* restrictions which merely become effective in the working methods and structure of bureaucratic organizations.

III.1 Internal Restrictions

Bureaucratic decision-making processes take place — as shown above — within the framework of formalized and non-formalized operating patterns. These have manifold effects and may also have the effect of restrictive factors. Four of the issues quoted most often will be addressed here.

III.1.1 Routine Procedures

For bureaucratic action on political problems — which generally implies a great number of working and cooperation processes — the development of routine procedures is indispensable. They serve to simplify decision-making processes. Routine decisions are the rule in the bureaucratic decision-making process. They are adequate as long as the routine program is adequate to the actual political situation and provides correct foundations for a specific objective being pursued. However, the easy application of this routine tends to lead to a certain bureaucratic inertia. Problems requiring innovative approaches are often treated as routine cases. Once the programs have been established, they are considered almost irreversible and are revised only with the greatest reluctance even under changed political circumstances (e.g. the Hallstein doctrine). This bureaucratic persistence proves to be a burden on an administration pursuing conception-oriented planning. It is felt the harder the more the organizational units are prevented through excessive workloads and time pressures from producing a conceptional input not subjected to routine procedures.

In the literature, however, bureaucratic routine is often accorded an important role which corresponds only partially to reality. Thus it should not be forgotten that the significance of routine is much lower in a non-executive bureaucracy than it is in a purely executive administration. Moreover, educational background, personnel turnover and, last but not least, the political self-perception of many ministerial civil servants imply a further de-emphasis of the 'routine' factor. The routine hence does not appear to be the most significant restrictive factor in the formulation of foreign policy.

III.1.2 Hierarchical Structure

The inner-organizational restriction factors quoted relatively often include the hierarchical structure of the administration. The preparations for the decision-making process performed at the section level must, in order to become politically relevant, pass through the official channels. Because of this formalized vertical communication the content of the orientations worked out by these section heads is always subjected to examination by higher-up ranks. The authors need not even be informed of possible substantive modifications of their proposals.[14] This procedure may, on the one hand, impede motivation at the working level; on the other hand, it may also result in the sections — knowledgable of this bureaucratic process — conceiving the decision-making preparations in such a way that these — deliberately foregoing specific substance-related statements — pass smoothly through the next upper hierarchical grade. This approach, which follows from motives of political opportunism, must also be regarded under the aspect of a career-promoting behavior.

In what manner are these restriction mechanisms, which are deduced in theoretical terms for the purpose of this paper, perceived as an actual obstacle by the persons involved? Interviews with civil servants of the ministries in Bonn revealed the surprising fact that — at least for processes of political planning — hierarchy is hardly felt to be a barrier. Rather, 'open decision-making systems' can be made out which 'are no longer based on hierarchically determined patterns of participation and non-participation, but run through all the grades of hierarchy'.[15]

The conclusion to be drawn from these observations is that the type of bureaucratic organization need not be an obstacle to the execution of conceptional and planning processes. To the extent that decision-making processes were observed in the ministerial bureaucracy in Bonn deserving to be qualified as 'elaboration of conceptions, program establishment and planning' or as 'secondary process activities', practices in inner-bureaucratic decision-making have evolved which are relatively 'open' both with regard to hierarchy and the inclusion of external persons. These assumptions — based above all on case studies on domestic policy — may also be considered as valid for the foreign-policy area.[16]

III.1.3 Negative and Positive Coordination

As outlined above, the importance of the various sections in the ministerial bureaucracy implies a primarily segmented problem-solving. The necessary cooperation regarding overlapping issues encounters considerable difficulties: the sectoral structure favors the emergence of 'restricted' viewpoints as well as 'truths' claimed by the individual sections. 'Every specialist unit tends to confine its attention to its own scope of responsibility and to pay less attention to problems beyond its limits considering them less important by the same token.'[17] Coordination of tasks with other organizational units, therefore, takes place in defensive rather than cooperative terms. Not 'positive coordination' — understood in terms of joint problem-solving — but 'negative coordination' is the rule. Negative coordination describes a process in which the responsible organizational unit requests positions from other units concerned either directly or indirectly. The content of these comments is usually restricted to information and data that are to prevent a negative effect on one's own subject of occupation.

Within specialist divisions positive coordination may be encountered at times; among the various ministries it hardly ever occurs, unless jurisdictions have been divided,[18] e.g. on issues of disarmament and arms control[19] or European policy. In these areas a fruitful positive coordination between two or three sections based on several years of collaboration is indeed feasible.[20]

As illustrated by Scharpf, negative coordination is a necessary consequence of the decentralized problem-handling process. Due to the addition of new organizational units this problem is being constantly aggravated with the complexity of the internal structure tending to become a planning barrier.[21]

The drawback of the negative coordination system consists in a twofold loss of alternatives: for one thing, those technically possible alternatives not represented by the competent organizational unit hardly ever have a chance of being considered. For another, this negative delimitation may profoundly alter the conception of the responsible section, since — depending upon the case on hand — various concessions towards the justified interests of other organizational units are required. 'For the overall system this results in a trend toward incrementalism, a policy of small steps and half-measures inherent in its structure.'[22] These assumptions must not, however, be taken to imply a regular automatism. On the condition that, firstly, not only one section is instrumental in a problem-solving process utilizing considerable manpower and technical resources, secondly, the responsible section is active in a field actually constituting 'new territory' and, thirdly, the conception-forming process is taking place within a relatively 'open' system (i.e. by neglecting hierarchical barriers, including scientific advice and synchronizing with international staffs and boards at the working level, such as EPC),[23] alternative methods and active policy-making are indeed conceivable within a bureaucracy.[24]

III.1.4 The Problem of the Political Leadership

As a consequence of the negative coordination the sections generally supply the political leadership merely with one proposal for a certain decision to be made. Theoretically, the political leadership is then left with the choice to either reject or accept it. A skilfull section head may thus succeed in 'guiding' his minister; on the other hand, proposals with a good conception may remain practically irrelevant if the political leadership does not agree with some aspects of the proposal or if it is displeased by the procedure.

This selective submission and acceptance of proposals, this blocking of alternatives, has already been pointed out by the political-science community. In the American literature on bureaucratic politics the proposition was put forward, for example, that this was more or less a deliberate strategy of organizational units pursuing their own policies. Studies on the behavior of the ministerial bureaucracy in Bonn, however, revealed a different result: on the part of civil servants the 'self-perception of a principal dependence — which can be activated at any time — of their actions upon the will of the political leadership prevails. . .' The herewith signaled preparedness to act according to the political guidelines, however, is frequently not rewarded, because the political leadership often fails to exercise comprehensive control and to present a clear objective.

> The political leadership interferes in the program-developing process merely by selective control. The selection criteria are, e.g. the political urgency of a program, its publicity appeal, its conflict potential or a personal commitment of the leadership in a certain field. For the everyday business of the basic operating unit thus the attention of the leadership and hence also the availability of directive substantive statements are some of the particularly scarce goods.[25]

A seemingly paradigmatic confirmation of these findings is provided by the example of the development of an MBFR conception within the ministerial bureaucracy in Bonn at the beginning of the seventies when political leadership and bureaucracy worked at cross-purposes because the leadership level had failed to present clear political guidelines.[26]

The question of controlling bureaucracy has moved to the center of efforts during the past few years. Various organizational endeavors were undertaken in order to resolve these problems.

— By means of establishing *cabinet committees* a substantive coordination at the highest level was to be achieved. Committees relevant for foreign-policy matters in this context are the Interministerial Coordination Committee for Economic Questions, the Federal Security Council (*Bundessicherheitsrat*), the Cabinet Committee for German-German Relations, the so-called Finance Cabinet, the Cabinet Committee for European Policy and the Cabinet Committee for Agriculture and Food Policy.[27] Although the Federal Security Council, e.g., has proved successful as an important foreign- and national-security-policy decision-making board, its function as an instrument of the political leadership is another matter. To date it has served primarily as a 'pre-checking center' in connection with approving white papers and national-security-policy guidelines.[28] Its conceptional influence, however, has proved to be rather limited. The high conceptional irrelevance of the cabinet committees is illustrated, for instance, by the Cabinet Committee for European Issues. From its establishment in the late fifties until 1975 it met just once. The actual coordination of European policy took place, as a rule, in the State Secretaries Committee, in the Committee of the European Experts within the individual ministries or in the preparatory committee meetings for the conferences of the ministerial councils in Brussels. Any substantive issues dealt with by a cabinet committee are generally issues on which no consensus has been achieved at the lower bureaucratic level.

In 1969 a *planning system* was introduced under the leadership of then Minister at the Chancellory, Horst Ehmke, which comprised the entire ministerial organization and had the following instruments at its disposal: by means of planning managers tasks and intentions of the government were to be coordinated and directed at an early point. A project monitoring system was to yield information at any time as to which organizational unit was acting on which issue with which implications. A working program to be set up was to permit long-term planning of goals and responsibilities of the federal government's policies. Apart from the fact that this planning concept did not materialize, this system also grossly neglected any foreign- or national-security-policy dimensions. The planning managers were directed to exclusively discuss domestic-policy steps.[29] Also, the work program was geared to 'internal reforms' only. The simultaneous extension of the Federal Chancellory and the concentration of the foreign-policy responsibilities on its division II were more of a by-product of the planning wave and did not prove appropriate for providing new ideas for foreign policy. Only during the tenure of Egon Bahr as State Secretary in the Chancellory did this division gain influence in this political area. At present it has a mandate conducive to conceptional purposes only with regard to the *Deutschlandpolitik*.

The institutions described above thus proved to be unsuitable to provide the required political guidelines for the internal administrative decision- and conception-making processes. It appears that purely organizational measures do not suffice in this context.

III.2 External Restrictions

It was this very misgiving regarding the relative ineffectiveness of internal organizational reforms which led 'planners' and scholars to the search for other restrictive factors originating from outside of the bureaucratic apparatus. The scientific literature assumes essentially two types of such restrictions: (1) restrictions resulting from the federal and pluralistic character of the political system, and (2) those pointing to a systemic incompatibility between a society with a capitalistic outlook and a planning state. To these two restrictions — defined exclusively in terms of domestic politics — is added a third one, the restriction of international incompatibility.[30]

III.2.1 Pluralism as a Restrictive Factor

The question whether the state is at all capable of a long-term, well deliberated policy in a pluralistic society, is by no means a new one. It has been the subject of various theoretical discussions.[31] Experiences gained in several years of planning trials in the Federal Republic of Germany raise this qeustion to a new level with a better empirical basis. It was primarily Fritz W. Scharpf who pointed to this interconnection in a series of publications. In his opinion the two guarantors of freedom, 'federalism' and 'pluralism', are barriers to a well-designed active policy.[32]

As far as the federalism issue is concerned, it can be ignored for the area of foreign and security policy, since — apart from a residual jurisdiction of the *Bundesländer* — the management of foreign affairs is the prerogative of the federal government. The formal involvement of the *Bundesländer* in areas of external cultural policy as laid down in the Agreement of Lindau of 1957, may be largely neglected in this connection. The situation is different, however, with regard to the restrictive implications of pluralism.

In his analysis Scharpf assumes that the organizational structure of the ministerial bureaucracy is the expression of a political distribution of attention. Every department, every operational division and sub-division as well as every operational section hence develops a special sensitivity to its own special sector. It is irrelevant, in principle, whether a ministry has a clearly outlined special field to act on (Federal Ministry of Labour, Federal Ministry of Food, Agriculture and Forestry) or whether it has to cover a great number of areas (Federal Ministry of the Interior or the Foreign Office). The organizational units always see fit to devote their special attention to groups, institutions or principles which they 'represent'. In part, genuine clientele relations arose, above all if an interest group recommended the creation of administrative units itself.[33]

The literature on bureaucratic politics also underlines this fact by mentioning the 'truths' claimed, and perspectives adopted by divisions and sections.[34] These analyses, however, do not go beyond pointing to the existence of an internal bureaucratic pluralism and are easily prone to resorting to truisms to explain it; for it is a platitude to state that the military thinks and decides differently from diplomats, financial experts or civil servants of the Ministry of Economics. The question not answered convincingly by the bureaucratic-politics literature, however, is why many organizational units intervene so vehemently in favor of the interests looked after by them and why they are even able to block and to play off each other. To explain this phenomenon, external factors have to be taken into consideration. If a resumé is in order, based on the German literature, it must be assumed that those organizational units are best off whose clientele or corresponding interest groups are both organized and capable of causing conflicts.[35]

Interests are organized whenever they act as pressure groups or if they are vested within political parties. They are considered capable of causing conflicts if they have the means to exert pressure, either by mobilizing masses or voters, by a collective denial of necessary services,[36] or by generating political and social instability.

Bureaucratic activities thus often assume the nature of consensus-procurement processes. Civil servants from the ministerial bureaucracy in Bonn stated in interviews that they spent a substantial part of their activities on the adjustment with interest groups.[37] However, to the extent that government activities expand and political claims rise, the internal bureaucratic problems of conflict increase. Disputes among organizational units on political issues are aggravated by tying them to external interests capable of pursuing conflict strategies and often end in a minimum consensus. The extension of the tasks and responsibilities of the state thus tends to lead to an increasing immobilism of politics and even to its self-blockade.[38]

Did the expansion of state activities in foreign policy correspond with a loss of control, a conceptional gap? The answer to this question must be a qualified yes. Although the extension of foreign-policy activities to include almost all departments of the federal government meant attention to a broader range of problems and more interests to be taken into account, there is but a very narrow scope for organized interests pursuing a conflict strategy to influence foreign policy. They include, above all, export-oriented industry and foreign trade. Other interests are either not or are no longer capable of exerting such pressures — like the associations of expellees which had a ministry of their own in the fifties and sixties — or are too vague to be organized (*Deutsche Frage*). Other economic interests (trade unions, professional organizations) have generally no foreign-policy motivations. Next to the economic interests only the churches — and above all the protestant church — have a limited area of influence through public relations and international contacts (World Council of Churches) which is, however, hardly ever addressed to the bureaucracy and which is not limited to individual areas of interest either.

Pluralism — in this context it means the influence of organized interests in politics capable of pursuing conflict strategies — takes on the shape of a veto system rather than that of a self-paralyzing antagonism which is reflected in bureaucracy. This means that concepts and measures of a non-economic nature have to assert themselves against this power or bypass it. Changes and innovations to date have been initiated exclusively by parties, as in the case of the appointment of an arms control commissioner of the federal government.[39] Some were recommended by foreign governments or resulted from international changes (accession to the UN). The influence exercised by economic interests is especially strong for the following reasons: the relationship between organizations of industry and trade, on the one hand, and of the foreign-political and foreign-economic administration, on the other, is of an almost symbiotic nature. An almost classical 'government by committee' prevails here[40] which is strengthened by the fact that industry is, or can be, a foreign-policy tool of the federal government. This does not only include the taking over of sovereign activities abroad by the organizations of industry. Frequently the promotion of private investments in other countries is a negotiating subject of the federal government. This close interaction and mutual dependence between foreign economic interests and the administration, though not to be qualified as a 'conspiracy',[41] constitutes a blocking factor whenever political notions and concepts are at variance with the interests of organized industry, which are articulated either within the administration (in particular through the influence of the Ministry of Economics on foreign policy) or via party or parliamentary channels.

III.2.2 Systemic Restrictions

The statement that economic interests form an important veto block does not suffice, however, to explain when and to what degree this influence is actually exercised. As the example of the tube embargo has indicated, there may be cases where strong economic interests are not taken into consideration by the federal government.

If it is possible to formulate principles for this phenomenon, it is that the importance of economic interests in comparison with those of a 'political' nature will increase to the extent that the management of internal economic crisis (unemployment, inflation, etc.) — threatening the legitimacy of the government — has become a problem. Economic concerns which, though contradicting political notions of value, promise, e.g., short-term or long-term relief in the labor market, are often preferred. This trend is especially obvious, e.g. in the arms-transfer policy of the Federal Republic toward the Third World. Loopholes in the cabinet resolution of 1971 with its restrictive provision have been increasingly exploited ever since 1973 — the beginning of the excessive unemployment rate in the Federal Republic.[42]

This permits the conclusion that, e.g., a peace- and arms-control-policy will reach its limit when a 'fine-weather period' in terms of internal socio-economic development ends. The degree to which the foreign policy pursued by the federal government may appear contradictory in this context is illustrated by the present policy toward Africa, which is, on the one hand, directed conceptionally and verbally against the South African policy of apartheid and in support of the interests of the black Africans, while, on the other hand—insensitive to the implications—promoting economic relations with South Africa and endorsing them by government credits.

This example of a 'two-faced' attitude indicates the limits of a conceptional foreign policy. These restrictions are to be characterized as 'systemic' in the sense that the dependence of countries with a market-oriented economy upon the economic cycle is a constitutive element. The longer-lasting and the more persistent economic crises are, the narrower is the margin of action for conceptional, planned politics. The restriction becomes effective also in disputes within the ministerial bureaucracy: those organizational units presenting the most convincing proposals for short-term crisis management actions tend to come out ahead of the others.

III.2.3 International Compatibility

The foreign policy of the Federal Republic has to take into account the legally fixed and actual dependencies arising from the international framework.[43] This refers primarily to the area of 'West integration', i.e. its close ties with the European Community and NATO. This fact is reflected in the bureaucratic handling of foreign and security policies and turns into a concept-barrier where, at the level of the special divisions and operational units, a synchronization takes place with the corresponding organizational units of allied states. This happens within the NATO bureaucracy, in the framework of EC and EPC[44] and is also a component of bilateral relations, e.g. between the United States and the Federal Republic.[45]

This 'early coordination' of foreign policy at a relatively low bureaucratic level results in a restriction of political alternatives — at least as regards the freedom of action of a *national* bureaucracy. In fact this cooperation more often than not contributes to a conceptional gain rather than a loss. On the one hand, the close collaboration of several civil servants involved in a special issue may augment the problem-handling potential without the risk of a segmentation. On the other hand, the conceptions attained in this way can be presented more strongly within the ministerial bureaucracy in Bonn, since the reference to the consensus already achieved with the alliance or Community partners constitutes, of course, a forceful argument.

Under the aspect of political responsibility, this development must, however, be viewed with skepticism, for the legitimacy of political action is sought through international (bureaucratic) consensus rather than through the translation of political demands and objectives into feasible concepts.

IV THE POLITICAL ROLE OF BUREAUCRACY

The role played by bureaucracy in foreign policy — to sum up — is of a highly political nature. It is by no means confined to the preparation of different proposals of a neutral substance for the political leadership, but is an essential catalyst in the preselection of political alternatives. 'The preparation of decisions always constitutes a selection from a variety of possibilities, including the possibility not to act.'[46] This position goes hand in hand with a largely political self-image of the civil servants within the ministerial bureaucracy[47] which is, however, only partially determined by the interests of the bureaucratic actors claimed by the special sections and depending upon the individual positions. This statement does not correspond with the views of bureaucratic-politics authors.[48] The success of 'his' policy within the bureaucracy is an essential factor for each section chief[49] but party adherence and political attitudes as well as the classical loyalty perception of some civil servants are equally important parameters to explain the behavior of the apparatus.

The political significance of bureaucracy grows with the increase of government activities and with the complexity of the problems to be acted on. The latter, above all, results in the management and control of government activities becoming more and more problematic. The immobilism of politics is largely determined by internal bureaucratic factors and factors which become visible in bureaucratic problem-solving. On this premise routine procedures and hierarchical structures do not appear to have a major impact upon the persistence of administrative organizations.

By far the greatest problem seems to be the segmented handling of complex issues as well as the difficulty of obtaining a comprehensive view of problems in the face of a constantly rising amount of demands, information and recommendations. What applies to the planning debate also applies to foreign policy, that the complexity of the political subject matter constitutes an inherent, omnipresent barrier to the drafting and development of conceptional, planned foreign policy.[50] Moreover, the management of foreign policy turns out to be problematic for a government which is held responsible for economic stability by the electorate whenever inflation and unemployment urgently require a crisis management which either circumvents existing concepts or dilutes the concepts while they are still in the development phase.

A bureaucratic — administered — foreign policy, therefore, implies a considerable, indispensable element of immobilism, inertia and incrementalism in a welfare state of the 20th century. The leverage for politically-motivated changes is but small. Although there are examples of violations of this rule — e.g. the preparation of the West German

CSCE-conception which proceeded under favorable organizational conditions with very little external influence — they underline that it is important to utilize 'marginal conditions' of the political process for the development and implementation of a well-designed foreign policy.[51] These marginal conditions include not only the increased application of the personnel turnover within the ministries (as well as among them), they also include the possibility of bureaucratic careers for outsiders or the reform of the recruitment procedures. A decisive influence may also come from a crisis management. 'The topical danger generally activates the political leadership thus leading to greater factual centralization of decision-making processes at the expense of the influence exercised by institutional subsystems.'[52] This is the way resistance against thorough going changes can best be eliminated. Crisis management thus becomes the most important tool for innovative and conceptional elements even in the foreign policy field.

For the political leadership the control of the foreign-policy machinery thus becomes a task which is in no way inferior to the 'diplomatic art' in terms of negotiating skill, problem awareness, toughness and willingness to compromise. In part, it seems to be more difficult to commit one's own administration to a policy than to wrest concessions from a foreign negotiating partner. The capacity of a chancellor, cabinet and minister to exploit the few possibilities and opportunities to implement conceptional elements in foreign policy, apparently dominates their political success to a greater extent than any programmatic statement made at the outset and during their tenure. The preparation, concretization, and translation of political goals does not only become a problem of the management of one's own bureaucracy in foreign policy (similar to the domestic policy). Rather, the political environment within which the administration acts and, indeed, to which it belongs has to be taken into consideration, too. Although the leverage for a clear-cut conceptional policy in foreign affairs is indeed small, something could be gained from a better utilization of the existing possibilities.

NOTES

1. Graham T. Allison, 'Conceptual Models and the Cuban Missile Crisis', in: *American Political Science Review*, Vol. LXIII, 1969, pp. 689-718; Graham T. Allison, *Essence of Decision, Explaining the Cuban Missile Crisis* (Boston 1971); Graham T. Allison and Morton H. Halperin, 'Bureaucratic Politics: A Paradigm and some Policy Implications', in: Richard A. Ullmann and Raymond Tanter (eds.), *Theory and Policy in International Relations* (Princeton 1972), pp. 40-79; Morton H. Halperin, *Bureaucratic Politics and Foreign Policy* (Washington DC 1974); I. M. Destler, *Presidents, Bureaucrats and Foreign Policy* (Princeton 1972).

2. Helga Haftendorn, Wolf-Dieter Karl, Joachim Krause and Lothar Wilker (eds.), *Verwaltete Außenpolitik. Sicherheits- und entspannungspolitische Entscheidungsprozesse in Bonn* (Köln 1978).

3. Wolf-Dieter Eberwein, *Auswärtiges Amt und Strukturwandel der Außenpolitik 1956-1973*, Diss. Phil. (Bielefeld 1975), p. 27.

4. *Geschäftsordnung der Bundesregierung* = rules of procedure of the federal government.

5. *Grundgesetz* = basic law.

6. Cf. Renate Mayntz and Fritz W. Scharpf, *Policy-Making in the German Federal Bureaucracy* (Amsterdam/Oxford 1975), p. 65.

7. Cf. Axel Murswieck, *Regierungsreform durch Planungsorganisation — Eine empirische Untersuchung im Bereich der Bundesregierung* (Opladen 1975), p. 54.

8. Paul Frank, 'Probleme der Reform des Auswärtigen Dienstes', in: *Außenpolitik*, Vol. 23, 1972, p. 42.

9. Günther Schmid and Hubert Treiber, *Bürokratie und Politik* (München 1975), p. 122.

10. Schmid and Treiber, op. cit., p. 120.

11. Fritz W. Scharpf, 'Komplexität als Schranke politischer Planung', in: 'Gesellschaftlicher Wandel und Politische Innovation' (Special issue No. 4 of the *Politische Vierteljahresschrift*) (Opladen 1972), p. 170.

12. *Gemeinsame Geschäftsordnung der Bundesministerien, Teil 1* = joint rules of procedure of the federal ministries, part one.

13. Cf. Ernst Kuper, 'Der Wandel der westdeutschen Entspannungskonzeption während der sozialliberalen Koalition', in: Haftendorn, Karl, Krause and Wilker, op. cit., pp. 241-262; Christian Loeck, 'Die Politik des Transfers konventioneller Rüstung — Strukturen und Einflußfaktoren im Entscheidungsprozeß', in: Haftendorn, Karl, Krause and Wilker, op. cit., pp. 209-224; Lothar Wilker, 'Das Brasilien-Geschäft — Ein "diplomatischer Betriebsunfall"?', in: Haftendorn, Karl, Krause and Wilker, op. cit., pp. 191-208.

14. Cf. E. Moths and M. Wulf-Mathies, *Des Bürgers teure Diener. Bürokratie ohne Leistungszwang* (Karlsruhe 1973), p. 17.

15. Peter Grottian, *Strukturprobleme staatlicher Planung* (Hamburg 1974), p. 111.

16. Cf. Rüdiger Lentz, 'Die Entwicklung der deutschen Position zur KSZE — multilaterale Problemstellung und innerorganisatorische Innovation', in: Haftendorn, Karl, Krause and Wilker, op. cit., pp. 151-165; Martin Müller, 'Konzeption und Akteur. Die Entwicklung der MBFR- Politik der Bundesregierung zwischen 1968 und 1971', in: Haftendorn, Karl,

Krause and Wilker, op. cit., pp. 167-189.

17. Scharpf, op. cit., 1972, p. 171.

18. Renate Mayntz and Fritz W. Scharpf, *Programmentwicklung in der Ministerialorganisation. Projektbericht erstellt im Auftrag der Projektgruppe für Regierungs- und Verwaltungsreform beim Bundesministerium des Innern* (Speyer/Konstanz 1972), p. 132.

19. Cf. Helga Haftendorn, 'West Germany and the Management of Security Relations: Security Policy Under the Conditions of International Interdependence,' in this volume, pp. 7-31.

20. Mayntz and Scharpf, op. cit., 1972, p. 306.

21. Scharpf, op. cit., 1972.

22. Ibid., p. 175.

23. EPC = European Political Cooperation.

24. Cf. Lentz, op. cit.; Müller, op. cit.

25. Mayntz and Scharpf, op. cit., 1972, p. 305.

26. Cf. Müller, op. cit.

27. Cf. Hans-Peter Schwarz, 'Die Bundesregierung und die auswärtigen Beziehungen', in: Hans-Peter Schwarz (ed.), *Handbuch der deutschen Außenpolitik* (München 1975), p. 71.

28. Haftendorn, in: Schwarz, op. cit., 1977, p. 344.

29. Hartmut Bebermeyer, *Regieren ohne Management? Planung als Führungsinstrument moderner Regierungsarbeit* (Stuttgart 1974), p. 50.

30. Cf. Wolfram Hanrieder, 'Compatibility and Consensus: A Proposal for the Conceptual Linkage of External and Internal Dimensions of Foreign Policy', in: *American Political Science Review*, Vol. LXI, 1967, pp. 971-982.

31. Cf. Charles E. Lindblom, 'The Science of "Muddling Through"', in: *Public Administration Review*, Vol. 29, 1959, pp. 79-88.

32. Fritz W. Scharpf, 'Planung als politischer Prozeß', in: Frieder Naschold and Werner Väth (eds.), *Politische Planungssysteme* (Opladen 1973), pp. 167-202; Fritz W. Scharpf, Bernd Reissert and Fritz Schnabel, *Politikverflechtung: Theorie und Empirie des kooperativen Föderalismus in der Bundesrepublik* (Kronberg 1976); Fritz W. Scharpf, *Politischer Immobilismus und ökonomische Krise — Aufsätze zu den politischen Restriktionen der Wirtschaftspolitik in der Bundesrepublik* (Kronberg 1977).

33. Cf. Klaus von Beyme, *Interessengruppen in der Demokratie* (München 1971), p. 113.

34. Allison and Halperin, op. cit.

35. Cf. Hermann Adam, 'Pluralismus oder Herrschaft des Kapitals? Überlegungen zu Theorien gesellschaftlicher Machtverteilung in der Bundesreplublik', in: *Aus Politik und Zeitgeschichte* B14/74, April 1974; Claus Offe, 'Politische Herrschaft und Klassenstrukturen. Zur Analyse spätkapitalistischer Gesellschaftssysteme', in: Gisela Kress and Dieter Senghaas (eds.), *Politikwissenschaft — Eine Einführung in ihre Probleme* (Frankfurt 1972), pp. 135-164; Scharpf, op. cit. 1973.

36. Adam, op. cit., p. 36.

37. Mayntz and Scharpf, op. cit., 1972, p. 308.

38. Scharpf, op. cit., 1973, p. 187; ibid., 1977, p. 104.

39. Helga Haftendorn, 'Der Abrüstungsbeauftragte — Zur Organisation der Abrüstungspolitik in der Bundesrepublik', in: *Politische Vierteljahresschrift*, Vol. 13, 1972, pp. 2-38.

40. Cf. also von Beyme, op. cit., p. 171.

41. See Arno Burzig, 'Ostpolitik und Osthandel — Das Zusammenwirken von Regierung und Wirtschaftsverbänden in der Ost-West-Wirtschaftspolitik', in: Haftendorn, Karl, Krause and Wilker, op. cit., pp. 225-237.

42. Cf. Loeck, op. cit.

43. Cf. Helga Haftendorn, 'Verflechtung und Interdependenz als Strukturbedingungen westdeutscher Außenpolitik', in: Haftendorn, Karl, Krause and Wilker, op. cit., pp. 15-38.

44. Cf. Johannes Altmeppen, 'Das MBFR-Entscheidungssystem der NATO — organisatorische Strukturen und Verfahren einer integrierten Bürokratie', in: Haftendorn, Karl, Krause and Wilker, op. cit., pp. 99-113; Müller, op. cit.; Hanns-Jürgen Küsters, 'Die außenpolitische Zusammenarbeit der Neun und die KSZE', in: Haftendorn, Karl, Krause and Wilker, op. cit., pp. 85-98.

45. Cf. Heinrich Buch, 'Die Rolle der Bundesrepublik bei SALT — Mitspieler oder Zuschauer?', in: Haftendorn, Karl, Krause and Wilker, op. cit., pp. 115-134.

46. Schmid and Treiber, op. cit., p. 181.

47. Bärbel Steinkemper, *Klassische und politische Bürokraten in der Ministerialverwaltung der Bundesrepublik Deutschland* (Köln 1974); Robert D. Putnam, 'Die politischen Einstellungen der Ministerialbeamten in Westeuropa', in: *Politische Vierteljahresschrift*, Vol. 17, 1976, pp. 23-61.

48. Allison, op. cit., 1969; Allison and Halperin, op. cit.; Cf. Franz Caspar, 'Einstellungs- und Verhaltensmuster in innerorganisatorischen Entscheidungsprozessen', in: Haftendorn, Karl, Krause and Wilker, op. cit., pp. 137-150.

49. Schmid and Trebier, op. cit., p. 181.

50. Cf. Scharpf, op. cit., 1972.

51. Scharpf, op. cit., 1973, p. 187.

52. Ibid., p. 187.

BIBLIOGRAPHY

Adam, Hermann (1974): 'Pluralismus oder Herrschaft des Kapitals? Überlegungen zu Theorien gesellschaftlicher Machtverteilung in der Bundesrepublik', in: *Aus Politik und Zeitgeschichte*, B 14/74, 6 April 1974.

Allison, Graham T. (1969): 'Conceptual Models and the Cuban Missile Crisis', in: *American Political Science Review*, Vol. LXIII, pp. 689-718.

Allison, Graham T. (1971): *Essence of Decision, Explaining the Cuban Missile Crisis*, Boston.

Allison, Graham T. and Morton H. Halperin (1972): 'Bureaucratic Politics: A Paradigm and some Policy Implications', in: Richard A. Ullmann and Raymond Tanter (eds.), *Theory and Policy in International Relations*, Princeton, pp. 40-79.

Altmeppen, Johannes (1978): 'Das MBFR-Entscheidungssystem der NATO — organisatorische Strukturen und Verfahren einer integrierten Bürokratie', in: Haftendorn, Karl, Krause and Wilker, 1978, pp. 99-113.

Bebermeyer, Hartmut (1974): *Regieren ohne Management? Planung als Führungsinstrument moderner Regierungsarbeit*. Stuttgart.

Beyme, Klaus von (1971): *Interessengruppen in der Demokratie*. München.

Buch, Heinrich (1978): 'Die Rolle der Bundesrepublik bei SALT — Mitspieler oder Zuschauer?' in: Haftendorn, Karl, Krause and Wilker, 1978, pp. 115-134.

Burzig, Arno (1978): 'Ostpolitik und Osthandel — Das Zusammenwirken von Regierung und Wirtschaftsverbänden in der Ost-West-Wirtschaftspolitik', in: Haftendorn, Karl, Krause and Wilker, 1978, pp. 225-237.

Caspar, Franz (1978): 'Einstellungs- und Verhaltensmuster in innerorganisatorischen Entscheidungsprozessen', in: Haftendorn, Karl, Krause and Wilker, 1978, pp. 137-150.

Destler, I. M. (1972): *Presidents, Bureaucrats and Foreign Policy*. Princeton.

Eberwein, Wolf-Dieter (1975): *Auswärtiges Amt und Strukturwandel der Außenpolitik 1956-1973*, Diss. Phil., University of Bielefeld.

Frank, Paul (1972): 'Probleme der Reform des Auswärtigen Dienstes', in: *Außenpolitik*, Vol. 23, pp. 40-47.

Grottian, Peter (1974): *Strukturprobleme staatlicher Planung*. Hamburg.

Haftendorn, Helga (1972): 'Der Abrüstungsbeauftragte — Zur Organisation der Abrüstungspolitik in der Bundesrepublik', in: *Politische Vierteljahresschrift*, Vol. 13, pp. 2-38.

Haftendorn, Helga (1978): 'Verflechtung und Interdependenz als Strukturbedingungen westdeutscher Außenpolitik', in: Haftendorn, Karl, Krause and Wilker, 1978, pp. 15-38.

Haftendorn, Helga, Wolf-Dieter Karl, Joachim Krause and Lothar Wilker (1978) (eds.): *Verwaltete Außenpolitik Sicherheits- und entspannungspolitische Entscheidungsprozesse in Bonn*. Köln.

Halperin, Morton (1974): *Bureaucratic Politics and Foreign Policy*. Washington DC.

Hanrieder, Wolfram (1967): 'Compatibility and Consensus: A Proposal for the Conceptual Linkage of External and Internal Dimensions of Foreign Policy', in: *American Political Science Review*, Vol. LXI, pp. 971-982.

Kuper, Ernst (1978): 'Der Wandel der westdeutschen Entspannungskonzeption während der sozialliberalen Koalition', in: Haftendorn, Karl, Krause and Wilker, 1978, pp. 241-262.

Küsters, Hanns-Jürgen (1978): 'Die Außenpolitische Zusammenarbeit der Neun und die KSZE', in: Haftendorn, Karl, Krause and Wilker, 1978, pp. 85-98.

Lentz, Rüdiger (1978): 'Die Entwicklung der deutschen Position zur KSZE — multilaterale Problemstellung und innerorganisatorische Innovation', in: Haftendorn, Karl, Krause and Wilker, 1978, pp. 151-165.

Lindblom, Charles E. (1959): 'The Science of "Muddling Through"', in: *Public Administration Review*, Vol. 29, pp. 79-88.

Loeck, Christian (1978): 'Die Politik des Transfers konventioneller Rüstung — Strukturen und Einflußfaktoren im Entscheidungsprozeß', in: Haftendorn, Karl, Krause and Wilker, 1978, pp. 209-224.

Mayntz, Renate and Fritz W. Scharpf (1972): *Programmentwicklung in der Ministerialorganisation. Projektbericht erstellt im Auftrag der Projektgruppe für Regierungs- und Verwaltungsreform beim Bundesministerium des Inneren.* Speyer/Konstanz.

Mayntz, Renate and Fritz W. Scharpf (1975): *Policy-Making in the German Federal Bureaucracy.* Amsterdam/Oxford.

Moths E. and M. Wulf-Mathies (1973): *Des Bürgers teure Diener. Bürokratie ohne Leistungszwang.* Karlsruhe.

Murswieck, Axel (1975): *Regierungsreform durch Planungsorganisation — Eine empirische Untersuchung im Bereich der Bundesregierung.* Opladen.

Müller, Martin (1978): 'Konzeption und Akteur. Die Entwicklung der MBFR-Politik der Bundesrepublik zwischen 1968 und 1971', in: Haftendorn, Karl, Krause and Wilker, 1978, pp. 167-189.

Offe, Claus (1972): 'Politische Herrschaft und Klassenstrukturen. Zur Analyse spätkapitalistischer Gesellschaftssysteme', in: Gisela Kress and Dieter Senghaas (eds.), *Politikwissenschaft — eine Einführung in ihre Probleme,* Frankfurt, pp. 135-164.

Putnam, Robert D. (1976): 'Die politischen Einstellungen der Ministerialbeamten in Westeuropa', in: *Politische Vierteljahresschrift,* Vol. 17, pp. 23-61.

Scharpf, Fritz W. (1972): 'Komplexität als Schranke politischer Planung', in: 'Gesellschaftlicher Wandel und Politische Innovation' (Special issue No. 4 of the *Politische Vierteljahresschrift*). Opladen, pp. 168-192.

Scharpf, Fritz W. (1973): 'Planung als politischer Prozeß', in: Frieder Naschold and Werner Väth (eds.), *Politische Planungssysteme.* Opladen, pp. 167-202.

Scharpf, Fritz W. (1977): *Politischer Immobilismus und ökonomische Krise — Aufsätze zu den politischen Restriktionen der Wirtschaftspolitik in der Bundesrepublik.* Kronberg (Ts.).

Scharpf, Fritz W., Bernd Reissert and Fritz Schnabel (1976): *Politikverflechtung: Theorie und Empirie des kooperativen Föderalismus in der Bundesrepublik.* Kronberg (Ts.).

Schmid, Günther and Hubert Treiber (1975): *Bürokratie und Politik,* Munich.

Schwarz, Hans-Peter (1975): 'Die Bundesregierung und die auswärtigen Beziehungen', in: Hans-Peter Schwarz, *Handbuch der deutschen Außenpolitik,* Munich, pp. 43-112.

Schwarz, Klaus-Dieter (1977): *Sicherheitspolitik — Analysen zur politischen und militärischen Sicherheit.* Bad Honnef.

Steinkemper, Bärbel (1974): *Klassische und politische Bürokraten in der Ministerialverwaltung der Bundesrepublik Deutschland.* Cologne.

Wilker, Lothar (1978): 'Das Brasilien-Geschäft — Ein "diplomatischer Betriebsunfall"?' in: Hafterndorn, Karl, Krause and Wilker, 1978, pp. 191-208.

6

THE POLICY OF THE FEDERAL REPUBLIC OF GERMANY TOWARDS 'THE SOUTH'[1]

Ulrich Albrecht

COMMENTATORS GENERALLY AGREE that 'it is only during the past few years that West Germany has made its true weight felt in international relations'.[2] At least in the seventies, Germany is regarded as bound 'to develop an autonomous foreign policy'.[3] The major reason for this is the relative economic strength of the West German economy, which has been said recently to contribute much more than in earlier times to rank order in international relations ('At a time when economic efficiency and power count increasingly in relations among nations', as Livingston puts it).[4] This recent economic strength by now compares favourably even with the long-time foremost economic power, the US. The West Germans are second to the US in international trade, but they keep the largest monetary reserves in the world, at $35 billion in 1976, twice as much as the US. Additionally, they can afford to be the second biggest spender on the military in the capitalist world — also a well-established yardstick for rank order in the international system. Little wonder that the Germans are valued 'as an economic "superpower",'[5] and that analysts start speculating about an 'activist' German role in world affairs. The level of expectations may be indicated by the statement that 'the United States, in particular, sees Germany as likely recipient of some US international responsibilities'. The author of this assessment foresees three regimes for a 'selective international role' to get into some kind of 'bigemony': first, 'an explicit bilateralism reflecting the two countries' predominance in the world economy'.[6] Secondly, as to US-

German divisions of labour in reflating the world business cycle, he suggests:

> Welcoming and encouraging German political and economic involvement in countries such as Spain, Portugal, Italy, and Turkey, where we [Americans, UA], are handicapped by past policy mistakes or failures.[7]

Thirdly, consultative procedures shall be expanded 'beyond Berlin and GDR-Federal Republic subjects to other political and economic issues'.[8]

The thrust of this argument clearly points to the US role in the Southern spheres of the globe — for in the relations between the military superpowers, or in the leadership of the Western alliance, the US are hardly seeking a replacement. It is understandable that one has to take non-German sources to delineate the new perspective of West Germany's role in international relations, and of her policy towards 'the South' in particular. Such frank wording will be found neither in official statements, which are still preoccupied with fears that an active German role may trigger off unpleasant remarks about Germany's search for *Weltmacht*, nor in the texts of the established analysts of foreign relations, who consider proximity to the stage as a prerequisite of paramount importance for their daily work. It may be that they are aware of the actual strength of the German position in international affairs — but there is a taboo involved, which is traditional in German elite circles. Hence only writers on the left of the political spectrum openly discuss German 'pre-eminence' in world affairs. The few writers on this side who have elaborated their views certainly make strong references to the at least implicit effects of the stark international role that the Federal Republic is going to acquire, but they also challenge the view that this is an independent decision. Thielen was the first to articulate this assessment in 1973:

> First, existence and domestic structure of the Federal Republic are in itself a product of Western allied, specifically Northern American, interests and strategies of foreign policies...From this result structurally equal domestic and foreign policy interests as well as power elites...Secondly, specific foreign policy goals of this dependent West German power elite...can only be converted into a foreign policy strategy if based upon the external policies of the NATO Alliance and upon those of the various members, according to the rank order of their power potential.[9]

A global specification of such assessments is, however, still missing. It also appears that the left critique is following the conventional vein that the Southern policy has a rather low priority in West German foreign policy and diplomacy.

In his widely-read textbook on West German foreign policy, the late Professor Besson goes so far as to place policies towards the South as only the fifth priority in his 'system of West German foreign policy'.[10] US-German relations, NATO, policies towards the USSR and the German Democratic Republic are judged to be more important and to receive more attention by German politicians than the Southern half of the globe. Furthermore, development policies for the Third World are evaluated as mere instruments for the pursuit of other, more high ranking priorities:

> Hence development policies certainly are more than a humanitarian demand. It shall dampen the uprising of the poor, shall channel revolution into the bed of evolution. Similarly as public social policy overcame class struggles in western European industrialised states in this century, and made a reformist force out of socialist protest, development aid must strive to balance the violent demand of former colonies for emancipation with the requirements of international stability.[11]

In contrast to political designs of the Federal Republic aimed at the North, there is no Third World voice heard which specifically rejects such notions. In Northern Europe, the West German view that Scandinavia forms the 'Northern flank' of continental defence measures, which implies far-reaching German interests in the region, is usually rebutted. The North is regularly considered as politically and militarily stabilized in itself; West German invitations for co-operation are perceived as disturbing, to say the least. A Finnish analyst goes as far as to recommend to the West Germans to abstain from any active policy in the Baltic region.[12]

The policies of West Germany towards the South are to be assessed in a much more complicated setting. There is a colonial heritage to some Third World countries, and there are, above all, the overwhelming economic interests of Germany as an industrial power in the raw material-rich countries of the Southern half of the globe. Generally, the policies of the Federal Government towards the Third World have for long been embedded in the more general framework of external relations as patterned by the East-West confrontation. It is the central hypothesis of this contribution that the emergence of the Federal Republic as a major actor in international affairs is not to be attributed just to sheer economic might. Rather, the international system and its development set the conditions for West Germany's rise to global status, and there was also always a countervailing trend at work which sometimes managed to challenge the course of developments. The paper is hence organized in three main sections: first, a general hypothesis on the interdependencies of global currents and the West German search for an autonomous policy is established. The latter usually caused controversy when military overtones were involved. Hence this element shall be considered with special attention. Second, the domestic set-up of foreign policy-making is analyzed, in order to demonstrate the unique combination of economic and political interest in West German foreign policy issues — which is assumed to provide for the specific thrust of this national entry into international politics in general. The relative autonomy of the Federal Government is defining foreign policy goals is checked by few and influential non-governmental actors, as will be shown. This set-up is needed for the presentation of the third section, which shows how German political and economic interests were over time brought more into line, and how the preoccupation of West German foreign policies shifted into a more balanced situation, characterized by a higher priority for Third World problems. Finally, with a view to future developments, the question of appropriate self-perception and analysis of this development is taken into consideration.

COLD WAR AND DÉTENTE AND WEST GERMAN POLITICS — A GENERAL HYPOTHESIS

The basic features of early global West German foreign policy moves were dictated by the rise of the Cold War and its aftermath. The causes of the Cold War appear as not too well understood by the West German foreign policy actors of the period. The peak of Cold War tensions (1956, with the uprisings in Hungary and Poland; the protracted crisis from autumn 1958 until autumn 1962, in which Berlin played a particular role; the second half of 1968)[13] regularly came across to them and were perceived as an unexpected accident, and policies on a wide range of issues were hastily rechecked and adapted to the last crisis scenario. Tensions were experienced as a complex set of contradictions and specific conflicts, mixed up with fears and uncertainties about the next step of the Federal Republic's principal opponents in the East, but also with suspicions about the reaction on Western side. Cold War attitudes were characterized on all sides by little inclination to arrive at partial compromises on the issues at stake, and by resort to high levels of military preparedness.

The countervailing elements to the build-up of Cold War tensions were intermittent periods of global detente (credited to the years from 1953 to 1956, the change from 1957 to 1958, the phase from 1962 to 1968, and the development since 1970).[14] With the exception of developments in the second half of the sixties, the West German Government never took an active role in promoting detente — also the lessening of tensions came across to the policy planners as some kind of surprise to which they had to react rather than engineering it.

This major setting, the experience of surprise about global developments towards both increased tensions and detente, opened ways for two basic patterns in policy orientation. The government could seek to be as close as possible to the leading Western power, the US, in order to gain both maximum insurance against all fallacies which should occur as well as a maximum of information and interpretation of global currents. The other choice would have been to strive for a gradual leeway of action in international politics, to bring West German national interests in economic affairs more into line with official foreign policies. The consequence would necessarily have been a certain amount of rivalry with Western allies, not only in the economic sphere, where German competition was always considered to be tough, but also in diplomatic endeavours.

Both strands may be identified in German foreign policy, also in the Third World policies of the successive Federal Governments. It appears that the phases of detente correlate with the 'active' phases in German global policies, when the domestic debate and decision process perceived more freedom of manoeuvre and placed a political safeguarding at higher rating than in periods of high tensions. This proposition may be easily checked: the first move towards the Third World can be seen in the provision of some money for what was later called 'development assistance'. In 1956, the Federal Diet accepted a Social Democratic motion and voted DM 50 million for 'underdeveloped countries', within the budget of the Foreign Office. It may be characteristic of the West German approach that the 'Handelspolitische Grundsatzreferat' (section on basic trade policy issues) in the Foreign Office was assigned the task to define '. . . first time whatsoever the principles, methods and objectives for cooperation with underdeveloped countries.'[15] In the following phase of increased Cold War tensions after the uprisings in Poland and Hungary, the Germans favoured channelling funds budgeted for Third

World countries into multilateral efforts. The brief relaxation of Cold War tensions during 1957/58, combined with the first experience of an economic recession in the brief history of postwar Germany, led to the decision to invest predominantly in heavy industries, providing the break-through for the Rourkela Project of a steel plant in India, which German industrial leaders had been advertising for some time.[16]

The 1957/58 Indian affair remained but an episode for the West German Government as well as for foreign relations detente and the Cold War reached new heights in the following few years. The German Government experienced heavy pressures, particularly from the US, to 'share' the 'burden' of defence of the 'Free World', and to contribute financially to efforts tying the emerging Third World to this Free West. From 1957 to 1959, the Germans paid more multilateral aid than any other Western government except the US. The Federal Reserve Bank acquired shares and obligations amounting to DM 1.7 billion from 1957 to 1960.[17] The development fund of the European Common Market received another DM 0.8 billion multilateral German aid from 1958 to 1962.

The change in general political attitudes which commenced in late 1962, most clearly indicated by the increasing detente between the major powers, also had direct implications for West German policies towards the Third World. From the beginning of the sixties, 'the significance of multilateral aid was downgraded', as some writers have observed.[18] The Federal Government embarked upon several initiatives which were felt to be beyond the reach of Germans in earlier years. A military aid programme was conceived and carried out with considerable vigour, involving the government in severe international problems, particularly in the Middle East, but also in Black Africa. Initiatives for the rebuilding of traditional trade relations were launched coinciding with redefined tasks of the 'Kreditanstalt für Wiederaufbau', the German Reconstruction and Development Bank formerly engaged in domestic credit work, and with the establishment of a special Ministry for Economic Cooperation.[19] Because this phase is still continuing, with minor disturbances after the invasion of Czechoslovakia by the USSR and other Warsaw Pact member states in 1968, these features shall be delineated in some more detail.

Military aid is one means for safeguarding economic as well as political interests by non-economic measures, and the German programme is no exception in this respect. Military aid supplements economic aid; while the latter, at least in theory, is aimed at the enhancement of the economy, the former is directed towards the development of political institutions, and its objectives exceed by far the simple establishment of a European-type army. The then Minister of Defence, Herr von Hassell, stated in 1966:

> Without certain means of coercion, those governments will fail to establish the vital domestic stability in their countries and maintain it... [military aid] hence supplements economic and technical aid, which cannot be brought to bear without domestic stability. I am of the opinion that civilian development aid and military aid supplement each other. Both are directed towards the same aim.[20]

A similar view had been expressed by a government spokesman as early as 1963: '[Those measures] mean technical aid in the military sector for friendly states being in the process of build-up'.[21] The West German Government, was however, annoyed by claims, particularly in Eastern Europe, that her military aid had solely economic functions. A fair balance of the contradicting views is given by the American writers Holbik and Myers:

> As part of their unqualified denunciation of West German foreign aid, Eastern sources also regularly charge that military aid is really part of the West German program, in spite of Bonn's assurances to the contrary. Once again, there is some truth in this allegation: but here, too, it is necessary to look closely at the West German position on this subject... As long as it remains reasonably clear that military aid, let alone an alliance, is no prerequisite for capital or technical assistance, the Ministry for Economic Cooperation has no objection to a discussion of economic and military aid to the same country.[22]

THE DOMESTIC SET-UP OF FOREIGN POLICY-MAKING

The foreign economic policy of the Federal Republic is the result of the action of a complex network of interest groups, institutions and global currents. Despite this complicating setting, the policy produced has 'been consistent in its design to develop and expand export markets for West German industry (during the last 25 years)', as one analyst observes.[23] The cause may be that structural and social factors rather than the relative power of individual pressure groups formed the basis for German economic policies abroad. Kreile gives 'a synthetic perspective' of the features of policy-making in foreign economic policies, which identifies (in rank order)

1. a close cooperation between...government and well-organized, articulate and powerful interest groups, namely a dominant export sector...
2. a central bank (Bundesbank), ...a kind of 'counter government'...
3. a pervasive free trade ideology...
4. the supranational regulation of certain policy sectors and instruments under the Treaty of Rome.[24]

The active German element is covered under the first two notions, the cooperation between government and interest groups, and the role of the Bundesbank. The latter is at least in part to be considered as but another representation of the interest groups mentioned under (1); hence any assessment of German foreign economic policies has to take this actor into account. Kreile stresses that this is by no means a homogeneous actor:

> The configuration of interest groups resembles an oligopolistic structure that is clearly dominated by export industry. The high degree of interest aggregation within the Federation of German Industry (BDI) involves sometimes a lengthy and laborious internal bargaining process to overcome conflicts of interest between different industrial branches. Oligopolistic competition between interest groups occasionally confers a broker function to the ministerial bureaucracy.[25]

Capital finds in the Federal Republic a peculiar organization in the banking system (in contrast to the situation in other comparable states, German banks are 'universal' in the sense that they engage in all kinds of banking business). Foreign operations were, according to one observer, 'up to the middle of the sixties nearly completely carried out through banks of correspondence (*Korrespondenzbankverbindungen*) and local agents'.[26] Today, affiliates and other means of direct local presence are heavily preferred, establishing a network of correspondence and information which matches the diplomatic representation of the Federal Government at least in quantitative terms. It is hard to arrive at specific figures, because a lot of banking investment is done by acquiring shares of local banks, participation in multinational banks, national development banking corporations, etc.

The banks exert influence on foreign economic policy predominantly through three channels: via submissions to the government (*Eingaben*) put forward by their associations (*Verbände*); via their participation in public corporations both in production and banking; and via direct personal contact with political leaders.

Submissions to the government appear to be the most important means of exerting influence on the Federal Government. The articulation of national interest is in self-perception seen as the foremost task of the responsible politicians in the Foreign Ministry — these interests are, after all, not self-explanatory, and need to be articulated and advertised in order to be understood by others. While the banks and other groups are careful to avoid overt violations of the principle that it is up to the government to define the German national interest on the international scene, they keep a close eye on the government, and intervene massively when they feel that their interpretation of the 'national interest' is misread by the bureaucracy. For the mode of interaction is not simply that the government gives its view and that then — invited or not — comments are offered to correct those views — it is rather a process where the bureaucracies make every effort to read from the lips of the most influential speakers of the business world what the message about German foreign economic policies is. This task can certainly be eased by approaching interest groups, e.g. banks, at an early date to learn about their views on certain new issues. Moreover this task is eased by a specific lack of interference from other sides:

> The technical and often esoteric nature of foreign economic policy questions shields these activities to a large extent from public scrutiny and reduces the role of parliament to that of a 'quantité negligible'.[27]

The civil servants engaged in formulating the principles and actual decisions in German Third World policies certainly cannot be characterized as being mere lackeys of capital. But what makes their task so hardly distinguishable from such roles is the failure of other interest groups to intervene as specifically and precisely as spokesmen of capital are able to do. Milbrath tries to generalize the phenomenon on a formal level: 'Those issues that attract the attention of special publics, but that attract little general public attention are more open to group influence than issues that attract wide and/or intense public scrutiny'.[28] This observation may be true, but the wording does not help to provide for analytic inroads into the whys of this phenomenon. In order to avoid any misunderstanding about moral claims, it should be stressed that those civil servants who write the texts of the declarations about German Third World policies complete their daily work with the somewhat pathetic conviction that they really cover all pluralistic aspects of the German national interest, and that anybody challenging their conclusions out of the views lying on their desks should themselves address them.

Lying on their table are predominantly bankers' and industrialists' views. These are critical comments on current government policies, and — more specifically —

> Hints to develop or innovate new initiatives and declarations regarding planned [foreign] economic policy measures (including pending legislation). The intervention may be exerted by direct, often confidential exchange with the Bundesbank, the respective ministries and committees of the Federal Diet, or by cooperation in consulting bodies or public statements.[29]

There is an array of fora offering platforms for the articulation of foreign economic policy objectives by capital. It includes the Arbeitsgemeinschaft Entwicklungsländer (working group on developing countries), and the Ostausschuß der Deutschen Wirtschaft (Committee of German Industry for Relations with Eastern Countries). The two most important public institutions providing financial assistance to developing countries, the Kreditanstalt für Wiederaufbau and the Deutsche Entwicklungsgesellschaft, have not only representatives of private business banks as members of their boards; even their supervising bodies are chaired by representatives from private capital. Additionally, the Kreditanstalt adopted the policy of handling export credits indirectly via private banks, offering additional inroads to development policies which are often considered as vital on the recipient end.

Direct personal involvement of leading bankers appears to have diminished since the days when the most respected banker in the Federal Republic, Hermann Josef Abs, Chairman of the Boards of the Deutsche Bank, was appointed head of the German delegation to the London debt renegotiations from 1951 to 1953, or when business banks contributed significantly to the preparations for the ill-fated tube deal for Russian gas in 1970. In recent years, the parallel interest of banking and exporting industries and their concerted influence upon foreign policy decision-making in a systematic way, exceeding any influence by senior bankers, appears to form the pattern for the day-to-day execution of foreign policies. Tax laws arranging for development aid (*Entwicklungshilfe-Steuergesetz*) of 1963 and legislation on foreign investment (*Auslandsinvestitionsgesetz*) of 1969 can be mentioned as appropriate examples to study the performance of this coalition of interests in distorting planned courses of action into ways and means more commensurate with financial interests.

Besides the banks, industrial federations (*Wirtschaftsverbände*) should be mentioned as another forceful means of exerting influence on foreign (economic) policies for West German capital. According to a categorization by Hartmut Weisert, the action from this side may be classified as diplomacy by delegation, by treaty, and by investment.[30]

Diplomacy by delegation can be observed when large industrial delegations fly to Third World capitals to decide about real business. Comparing the respective roles of (formally competent) government delegations and the (formally incompetent) business delegations, one analyst observes:

> Not the Federal Minister for Economics, but they [the business delegation] were in the end the competent discussion partners of their Iranian State hosts; they themselves recognised this by the earlier visit of their Prime Minister to the Federation of German Industries [BDI].[31]

Diplomacy by delegation is also used by the associations of German banks and industry. They receive foreign delegations, governmental or private, and send their own delegations around the globe. There appears to be frequent interaction with officials of other powers — the sole discrepancy between the official representatives of the Federal Government and the business delegations obviously being the fact that the latter carry out their negotiations with less public attention, but at comparable levels of commitment.

Diplomacy by treaty, usually regarded by conservative diplomats as the ultimate sanctuary for officialdom in diplomacy, is also carried out on an impressive scale by private business organizations of the Federal Republic. The Ostausschuß of German industry originally profited from the reluctance of the Federal Government to extend at least some diplomatic recognition towards the East European states. The Cabinet formally ratified treaties concluded by this private organization, certainly sensational for the historian of diplomacy. Moreover, the Ostausschuß was able to conclude formal trade treaties with Rumania in 1953 and China in 1957 when there were no official diplomatic contacts, with the subsequent approval of the West German Cabinet. The perception of those affairs by diplomats as *Nebenher-Diplomatie* (Wilhelm Grewe) or *Ersatz-Diplomatie* is certainly inappropriate and tells more about the reservations on the side of civil servants than about the real nature of the transactions.

Diplomacy by investment gives a role to private business hardly challenged by any other social force in the Federal Republic. The decision to invest, e.g. in the Cabora Bassa dam project (Mozambique) was certainly a major foreign policy event, even though the government stood formally silent and only private business was involved. This is not to repeat the truism that any major foreign investment decision has potentially severe political consequences. On the contrary, the essence of this qualification is that private business often takes the political repercussions of its decisions into consideration, and tries to use investment decisions also for political ends. Another aspect of this is that one must assume that capital seeks to learn about government views regarding its decisions well in advance, and that diplomacy by investment tends to be a concerted action involving official diplomacy.

All three levels of diplomatic action are also well reflected in institutional arrangements set up to integrate official and private diplomacy. The Außenwirtschaftsbeirat (Council on Foreign Economic Affairs) attached to the Ministry of Economics can be compared in its role and impact to the 'Concerted Action' for domestic economic policies; it is jointly staffed by civil servants and representatives of capital, the chairperson always coming from the latter. Inter-governmental agreements about economic cooperation usually make provisions for the participation of business representatives; the commissions set up for co-operation with the various CMEA countries or with China have in common a strong participation from this side.[32] Finally, foreign chambers of commerce integrate diplomatic and business efforts to represent capital interests abroad. 'In the course of reorganising the Foreign Service, the Federal Government found it appropriate to invite representatives of [business federations] into the commission', notes one observer.[33] These are only the *direct* involvements of capital in the foreign policies, particularly Third World policies, of West Germany. A grey area which is much harder to investigate is the indirect means — intermediate influence via parliamentary representatives, bribes, etc., or implicit consequences like the orientation of civil servants towards business attitudes. It may be argued that, in this respect, business federations form the most formidable veto groups, i.e. exert a kind of negative influence against which hardly any group would be willing to object.[34]

THE ACTUAL POLICIES OF THE FEDERAL REPUBLIC TOWARDS THE SOUTH

An empirical inspection of actual policies pursued with respect to the Southern half of the globe reveals quite persistent patterns. In his first message as head of government, Konrad Adenauer set the tone with the first phrase which addressed non East-West problems: 'The development and the freedom of international trade is subject of our special attention.'[35] An independent foreign policy, at least in the formal sense of the word, did not start before the mid-fifties, when the FRG became a sovereign state. The inception of foreign policy took place in a rapidly expanding field of actors: the number of formally independent governments in Africa, Asia and Latin America rose slowly from 48 in the year 1949 (when the FRG was founded) to 53 in 1955; there was a sharp increase in the second half of the fifties, leading to 76 governments in these regions and to 105 Third World governments in 1970.

It must be stated that Bonn reacted slowly and with considerable delay to this change in the international environment. Following a motion from the Social Democrats, the Federal Diet budgeted a limited amount for 'development aid' as early as 1956. The first piece of legislation setting guidelines for development policies was not enacted before 1960, however, and the first comprehensive debate about Third World politics was launched in Parliament in May 1961 — when the so-called 'development decade' of the UN was already in full flux. The head of the trade policy section in the Foreign Ministry (then in charge of development affairs) defined as the motives of the German 'Third World Politics' in 1965:

- humanitarian motives, in order to mitigate the misery in many countries;
- economic motives, because only economically strong countries would provide for meaningful markets, sufficient supplies and investment opportunities;
- finally, motives of national policy.[36]

Despite the first rank given to the humanitarian motive, the second motive soon began to dominate relations with the Third World. A priority humanitarian aid programme would have focussed West German policies on the poverty-stricken belt of countries which later became labelled 'the least developed countries', and would have extensively supported food aid and disaster relief. None of these priorities can be found to be predominant in actual West German aid patterns.

Some humanitarian aid can indeed be identified, but the commitment of Bonn was strongest to those regions where a clear cut economic interest could also be served. The third issue, namely the open question of German reunification, played a certain role in the first decade of German 'Third World Politics', but it is hard to find cases where this priority contradicted the second one of economic interest. In the international structure of production and trade, the FRG had long-standing priorities, inherited from former political systems — economic priorities apparently transcend the persistence of the legal system, which changed, in the case of Germany, three times during this century. Among the global regions under consideration, Africa played a particular role. Latin America was largely considered as the backyard of the US and, despite all engagements on the side of industry, received little political attention, indicated by the absence of e.g. military aid programmes. The penetration of Latin America was left to commercial endeavours, and it was not until the late sixties that Bonn undertook large aid programmes and political experiments like the training of union officials in this hemisphere.

Asia was also a secondary option for policy planners in Bonn. They felt much more comfortable concentrating on the traditional focus of German colonial policies, i.e. Africa. The *Afrika-Handbuch* of the semi-official *Afrika-Verein* maintains that

> the comparatively low share of Africa in international trade (between 5 to 6 percent of imports and exports at this time, UA) does not reflect the actual importance which the continent enjoys today, and will enjoy even more so in the future. Also today Africa plays an important role with a variety of crops in production and export. . . in another area, Africa is about to become one of the most important partners of the world: in the production of minerals. Numerous stocks, partially rich in potential, are known.[37]

The *Afrika-Verein* quotes known reserves as

> being very vast in chromium, bauxite, diamonds, iron ore, gold, cobalt, copper, mangan, phosphatus, platin;
> being vast in asbestos, beryllium, lead, columbite, natural gas, petrol, glimmer, graphite, uranium, vanadium, vermiculite;
> being average in antimonium, barite, cadmium, fluorite, silver, titanium, tin;
> being small in coal, molybdenum, nickel, sulphur, tungsten, zinc.[38]

When the FRG became a sovereign international actor in the mid-fifties, the paramount pre-occupation was with so-called Deutschlandpolitik, i.e. the relation with Eastern Germany or the German Democratic Republic. In the view of the Bonn Government (and, as the stream of refugees indicates, of a significant part of the East German population itself), the current government of the Sozialistische Einheitspartei (SED) was not legitimate, and every effort was propagated which would have revised the division of Germany. Both states were seeking international recognition (the GDR becoming sovereign after a unilateral Soviet declaration in 1954), and because the Northern hemisphere was divided between the adherents of the respective legitimacy claims (NATO countries supported the FRG, and the Warsaw Pact the GDR), the Third World quite naturally became a meeting ground for specific teutonic rivalry for recognition of legitimacy claims. The desires of the Bonn Government went much further than the respective claims of the East Berlin regime: the FRG wanted to be treated as the sole legal successor of the Reich, while the GDR asked for the recognition of the two Germanies which succeeded the Third Reich.

The discriminatory instrument of non-recognition was apparently not popular among Third World governments. The United States has repeatedly used this tool to oppose regimes which came to power after liberation wars, most notably in China.[39] The GDR was, at least in the views of the more Moscow-oriented Third World governments, a state which emerged from a social revolution, and the withholding of recognition as a measure of discrimination, punishment and isolation was easily compared with cases when the Western powers treated some revolutionary Third World governments in exactly the same manner. When Yugoslavia formally recognized the East German Government in October 1957, there was no wave of other recognitions on the side of non-aligned countries.[40] At the 1961 Belgrade conference of the non-aligned countries, the leaders of this group of states, Nehru, Sukarno and Nkrumah, accepted the existence of two Germanies — but the overwhelming economic weight of the FRG apparently prevented these governments from acting against the explicit will of the Bonn Government.[41] Hence the so-called Hallstein Doctrine, which declared the recognition of the GDR as an unfriendly act to the FRG, remained a forceful weapon until the mid-sixties. Unfortunately, no exact figures are available to indicate how much money was invested into this pet goal on Bonn's side (and what monies on the side of the GDR to counteract it), but it can be assumed that a number of Third World countries benefited by hundreds of millions of marks from this teutonic struggle.

The Hallstein Doctrine collapsed in the Third World in 1965/66 when Tanganyika (a supporter of the West) and Zanzibar (with a Consulate General of the GDR) united to form Tanzania, and the Head of State, Nyerere, could not see why he should annoy the East Germans by closing the consulate. Bonn stopped all military and some economic aid. Developments in the Middle East were more significant, where relations of Arab nations with Bonn turned sour when the support of Israel by military deliveries from the West German Government became known, and Ulbricht, GDR Head of State, toured Egypt on a state visit. The Arab governments quickly copied Bonn's strategy and threatened to apply a reversed Hallstein Doctrine, i.e. to sever diplomatic relations with the FRG if there was an exchange of ambassadors between West Germany and Israel. The following years saw protracted efforts on the side of Bonn to contain the recognition of East Germany, but after the reorientation of Ostpolitik in 1969, there was a 'wave' of diplomatic recognitions, and since then this troublesome, exotic problem has vanished. One may ask what the participation (since the 'Great Coalition' of 1966), and later the leading position of the Social Democrats in Cabinet (1969) meant for this setting. The SPD was, after all, the most formidable force in the domestic politics of the FRG which had been advocating alternatives, particularly in the field of foreign policy, and it was, among all the factions in the Federal Diet, the group which worked at the greatest distance to the powerful economic interest groups which had been so skilful in masterminding past 'Third World Politics' of CDU governments.

The rise of Ostpolitik, as well as a fresh approach towards the quarrels among the Western alliance, gave the new SPD/FDP Cabinet considerable credit, and one could also expect some significant change in the 'Third World Politics' of the governments after 1969. In the beginning, there indeed developed some kind of confrontation between the established forces, which so overwhelmingly exerted influence in foreign policy-making, and the newcomers of the SPD. This confrontation was particularly sharp in the question of future arms sales to Third World countries. As an opposition force, the SPD had repeatedly asked for strict limitations on German arms shipments, i.e. to NATO countries. In April 1966, the SPD faction introduced a motion:

> The Federal Government is asked to limit in principle future arms sales and military aid as well as the transfer of excess military weapons to the members of the North Atlantic treaty.[42]

Two months later, the SPD renewed their efforts, this time asking for a law to prohibit the involvement of Germans in the manufacture of arms abroad:

> Germans according to the Basic Law are prohibited from developing in foreign countries arms of war, producing them, contributing to their manufacture, or transferring them.[43]

The then Defence Minister (and later Chancellor) Schmidt frankly engaged in a direct exchange with industry. He declared:

> With respect to the export of arms and weapon systems, I arrived as a member of parliament, together with friends, at a fundamental position in the 'fifties, which has not changed in the sixties, and also not since I became minister of defence. There are no new insights which could have led me to change my views. . . the present defence minister is not willing to act as the substitute of the salesmanagers of German arms industries.[44]

Another statement in this vein was issued by the Secretary of State in the Defence Ministry, Berkhan, in 1974:

> It would be irresponsible to let the arms industry of the Federal Republic grow into the role of a foreign exchange earning export industry. Not only for good political reasons, but also because of moral judgements, this governemnt has decided that as a matter of principle arms of war may be exported to NATO countries only.[45]

The waves of the soon permanent economic depression, and the rise in the price of crude oil in 1973 in particular, led to second thoughts within the ranks of the Social Democratic-Liberal Cabinet. There was a general fear that the electorate, despite all the successes in Ostpolitik, would blame the Socialists for the slowdown of the economy — under Christian Democratic rule, the economy generally had been flourishing. Opposition from both the established power groups and the electorate would be insurmountable for any government, and gradually, as well as secretly, the government stepped away from former major decisions, repeatedly creating tensions with the faction of the SPD in Parliament — which rapidly became annoyed about the repeated invitations to defend a government course of action for which at least a minority in the faction felt no enthusiasm whatsoever. Industry did their utmost to push the issue and brought immense pressures to bear on the arms export question particularly. The Federation of German Aerospace Industry (BDLI) declared:

> The restrictive course of the Federal Government with respect to the export of military planes has cost the aerospace industry sales worth billions of marks in the past. The chances for the export of military goods are extraordinary. With respect to the repeatedly hinted economic shifts on world markets and the pressures to sell high-technology products in order to maintain the economic position of the Federal Republic on world markets, a review of this restrictive policy is urgently required. In this context it is worth mentioning that now France and Britain undertake the greatest effort to export military hardware, neglecting any reservation of a foreign policy nature.[46]

Commercial sales of German weapons developed from a meagre niveau of around 100 million dollars, when the Social Democrats took over in 1969, to 1 billion dollars in 1977.[47] According to figures from the US Arms Control and Disarmament Agency, the export contents destined for Third World countries rose to some 150 million dollars in the same time periods, and was in full swing recently (when the Shah of Iran left his country in early 1979, orders placed with the German armament industry were valued at DM 1 billion — small, if compared with the 20 billion dollars spent on arms deals with the United States, but an amount comparable with French and British figures).[48] Government spokesmen lamely commented upon this drastic change of attitude: 'Provided the case that the business cycle does not alter, one may become more flexible. . . but only to safeguard jobs.'[49]

The redirection of government policies was most dramatic in the field of arms exports; other sectors of production, which are much more relevant for the reproduction of the German economic system, quickly followed suit. The fate of the nuclear industry, another prime example of sophisticated technology, fits well into the picture. The commercial interest involved in the transfer of nuclear power stations is even more formidable than in the case of arms sales: at a unit cost of DM 5 billion, each individual sale creates six thousand jobs for six years.[50] The German nuclear industry paid, for twenty years, a fairly high entry cost into this technology, lacking the huge military orders for nuclear facilities which their main competitors enjoyed. In the mid-seventies, the nuclear industry seemed to have passed the threshold of profitability:

> In order to use existing capacities economically, under given contract volumes the sale of six power station units per annum is mandatory, KWU export sales manager Hildenbrand recently revealed to a confidential circle of experts.[51]

After orders from Brazil and Iran, the German industry foresaw orders for eight power stations annually, four of them for export. When environmentalists brought construction work for nearly all nuclear power stations to a halt in the FRG (the facilities at Grohnde, Wyhl and Brokdorf, small places nowadays widely known, were blocked by court decisions), and the biggest firm in the business, Kraftwerksunion (KWU) failed to secure a single domestic order for four years, pressures to go into exports mounted sharply. In 1979, with eight nuclear power stations contracted to the Germans (out of a total of twenty), the Shah left Iran, leaving behind uncompleted facilities which had cost DM 5 billion.[52]

This meant another shock for the German nuclear industry, which was unable to secure other nuclear power station export orders during the late seventies: even though there was a demand in the Soviet Union, as well as in South Africa. Fighting for survival, the nuclear industry of the FRG is in no position to weather another storm of international criticism such as it had to ride out in the case of the nuclear deal with Brazil. The Social Democrat-Liberal coalition also sees no flexibility in this respect — in Bonn, nobody is willing to write off for good the DM 9 billion which the establishment of a nuclear capability has cost the taxpayer in the past twenty years.

This picture could be delineated in nearly the same dramatic fashion for other strongholds of German industrial competence: steel, shipbuilding, computers, heavy engineering equipment, to name just a few which have suffered most from the combined impact of a shrinking home market and the high cost of the mark (which battled with dollar prices on increasingly disadvantageous terms). For foreign economic policies, the room for purely political considerations was also dramatically reduced, and diplomats hardly had a choice other than underwriting the claims of German firms who fought for survival on world markets.

THE PROPER ANALYTICAL APPROACH

In the diplomatic machinery, observers note an increased tendency to a bureaucratic course of German foreign policy. While Anglo-Saxon analysts express the belief that there is an increased possibility to instrumentalize economic potential for foreign policy goals in a world of detente and the advent of new international actors like the OPEC group or the various groupings in the Third World,[53] German writers conventionally disregard Third World politics in a manner similar to Besson's assessment ten years ago. Haftendorn and her co-authors, in a recent assessment of poltical decision-making in Bonn in foreign affairs matters, address Third World problems in two aspects: they analyze the legal status of the arms transfer business, and they attempt an in-depth study of the Brazilian nuclear deal.[54] In their study, which focusses upon decision-making procedures, these authors note that 'political leaders — Chancellor, Cabinet, the ministers — usually are concerned with a selection of political decisions — mainly international, domestic or interministerial crisis decisions — while the bureaucracy in Bonn and their counterparts in international staffs and secretariats tend to become the real foreign policy actors'.[55]

Because German policies are entangled and interdependent in their structure with other policies of other powers, there is little room for innovation.

Entanglement means

> a pattern of interaction processes, which entails a considerable amount of continuity and formalisation...Entanglement implies...dependency processes. In this respect, it is not decisive that dependency is really existing, but how it is perceived...For political actors, this means a reduction of room for manoeuvre, i.e. there is barely a problem which can be solved without taking notice of external condition factors.[56]

This view can be characterized as representative of the mainstream of foreign policy analysis in the FRG; Karl Kaiser should be quoted as the most prominent author in this vein.[57] If their hypothesis holds, it is hard to see how such innovations as Ostpolitik or the Brazilian nuclear deal came into being at all. If analysts like Haftendorn and Kaiser, with their conclusions about 'administered foreign policy' are correct, is one justified to assume that industrial interests (which by and large are considered as secondary in those studies) play a decisive role in recent German foreign policy moves, and that in the era of the Social Democrat-Liberal Government the established guardians of foreign policy goals, i.e. the diplomats, barely did more than to take stock and to [illegible] such moves?

On the analytical level, a number of writers also assess the West German political decision-making process in a contradictory way. David Rudnick, in a case study about the sale of West German *Leopard* tanks to Spain, goes so far as to maintain that 'in the German case...the bureaucratic politics model is less applicable than elsewhere'.[58] Byrd and Paterson, in their systematic comparison of actual decision-making processes in Britain and the FRG, arrive at the same conclusion.[59] The assessment of a more passive role of the policy-making bureaucracy is on the other hand also challenged at least in part by case studies, particularly the one about the Brazilian deal in Haftendorn et al. Wilker writes about 'field work' in Brazil carried out by the Ministry for Research and Technology, which led to research work contracted for DM 100 million, based on an agreement stemming from 1963.[60] After the then Foreign Minister Willy Brandt had declared 'the interest of the Federal Republic in joint projects with Brazil in the field of nuclear technology' in 1968, an agreement on 'scientific cooperation' was signed a year later, placing strong emphasis upon nuclear activities.

Given these preparatory efforts, the deal of 30 April 1975 with Brazil appears as hardly more than the culmination of a long-standing, concerted effort by both the Bonn administration and industry. It is hardly convincing that the Foreign Ministry was ignorant all the time; the relatively low level at which this case was dealt with can be interpreted as an example of 'business as usual' procedures in the Bonn administration — which accepts huge commercial transfers of a sensitive nature, e.g. for arms or nuclear power stations, as an ordinary implication of day-to-day politics rather than as an extraordinary moral or political challenge.

The view of an overwhelming interdependence in international relations and the loss of actual decision-making power within national foreign policy-making bodies is also challenged by differentiated empirical studies. Strongly competitive decision-making has been observed by Hernes, who specifies under which conditions market situations are dominant.[61] One study of international shipping and the implications for specific UN policies also shows significant interest domination based on national industrial priorities.[62] A study of the World Food Conference, which used 'national food economy profiles', revealed that such patterns were usable with good results to predict the negotiating behaviour of national policy-makers.[63] Even such remote subjects as fishery and whaling suggest more that large international conferences are dominated by the variety of national interests than by pressures as described by the 'interdependencionists'.[64]

It appears as more appropriate to accept that both developments, the increase of structural international determination as well as the higher pressures form vital economic interests, shape the actual outcome of Bonn's Third World policies, interplaying not necessarily on an equal footing. There are, of course, also efforts to bring a more normative orientation into actual German concepts.

The consequences for a Southern policy instrumented according to UNCTAD goals are summarised for the theoretical organ of the SPD, *Die Neue Gesellschaft*, as follows:

> Enterprises and branches using extensively raw materials (e.g. metal-working industries) may feel such a drastic rise in production cost that they hardly will remain competitive with firms from raw material-rich industrialised states (the US, Canada, Australia, the USSR). The industrial structure of the Federal Republic must be altered for this sole reason — with all its consequences for the labour market. . . Products from developing countries ought to reach indeed the Federal Republic. In consequence, this will lead to

> closures with some firms, e.g. of the textiles, fashion, and/or shoe making industries in view of the import pressures from developing countries. In this area hence an alteration of economic structures is also due.[65]

The goals for foreign economic relations can be easily derived from such statements. Because of the vulnerability of West German exports to deliveries of raw materials, the government must strive both for a strong controlling influence in multilateral bodies like UNCTAD, as well as to build up bilateral client relations with important suppliers outside the industrialized world, which are likely to be politically dependent from Bonn's desires. Quite naturally, Africa with its rich resources becomes a focus of interest, and it is no wonder that Africa receives the largest amount of German development aid. On the other hand, policy planners are fully aware of the fact that the Federal Republic is in no position to significantly change the tide of global division of labour developments. She wants, however, to exert some controlling influence, to slow down the pace, in order to have sufficient leeway for dealing with the domestic economic consequences. Policy recommendations in this respect appear as rather vague. The SPD theoretical organ quoted above summarises in most general terms:

> Generally, in future discussions about development policies one should think in a larger context, recognise mutual dependencies, and take care of the consequences of the various measures.[66]

The scenario as described leaves the diplomatic machinery which executes Bonn's Third World policies in a persistent dilemma. The self-perception can be described as one of hard grinding work, sometimes meticulous, even pedantic, to take stock of all concerns which might reasonably interfere with one's decisions about how to implement high level priorities for the foreign policy of the FRG. On the side of the recipients of such efforts, there are charges about bureaucratic inertia, little sensitivity or even flexibility as regards the problems of the Southern half of the globe. If Third World concerns have found their way into international negotiations, let alone international treaties, they tend to be observed in Bonn with legalistic scrutiny, adding by this to the slow movement of the bureaucracy. The foreign policy of the Federal Republic, as numerous observers increasingly imply, as it is articulated and executed by the diplomatic services, is under Social Democratic-Liberal rule in 'South Politics' more or less equivalent to earlier patterns, i.e. a most formidable amalgamation of industrial interests, Western-style tutelage, based on a penetrating effort to lure Third World powers into connivant continuation of former colonial relations which contributed so much to the rise of Western Europe in earlier times.

NOTES

1. For conceptual clarification, the meaning of the term 'politics' needs to be circumscribed. I adhere to a definition by the Norwegian analyst Knudsen, who found

> . . . it convenient to distinguish between three elements which together may be said to make up what in daily usage is called foreign policy: I. at the most general level, a basic *orientation* or posture towards the external world: open/closed, cooperative/isolationist; II. at a more specific level, a set of *action programms* ('undertakings' in Rosenau's terminology) which covers specific, concrete goals and plans for achieving them: a new SALT agreement for the US, membership in the European Communities for Spain or Portugal; and III. at the most specific level, the day-to-day actions and pronouncements of the government: offering a proposal for international agreement, delivering a protest note, giving comment on a current international problem (Olav Knudsen, *National Economic Interests in Foreign Policy: Sketch of a Model*, Paper presented to the Nordic Political Science Convention, Bergen, 27-30 August 1978, p. 1).

2. F. S. Northedge, *The Foreign Policies of the Powers*, London 1975, p. 237. Cf. also Waldemar Besson, *Die Außenpolitik der Bundesrepublik. Erfahrungen und Maßstäbe*, München 1970, pp. 448, 454 ('The complicated play with five lines [of principal foreign policy concerns, UA] started in full only in the sixties').

3. Robert Gerald Livingston, 'Germany Steps Up', in: *Foreign Policy* No. 22 (Spring 1976), p. 114.

4. Ibid, p. 116.

5. Ibid, p. 118.

6. C. Fred Bergsten, 'The United States and Germany, The Imperative of Economic Bigemony', in: *Towards a New International Economic Order*, Lexington, Mass. 1975, p. 180. Cf. also Richard Löwenthal's rejoinder to Livingston's article about 'a diplomatic division of labour that would leave judgements on West European internal problems to reliable allies both closer to the scene' (in: *Foreign Policy* No. 22 [Spring 1976], p. 181).

7. Livingston, op. cit., p. 179.

8. Ibid.

9. Helmut Thielen, *Thesen zur machtpolitischen Stellung der BRD im kapitalistischen Bündnissystem — Rüstung als Machtopotential von Außenpolitik*, Paper for the International Conference 'Arms Race Dynamics and the MICs', Frankfurt-Main, 5-7 April 1973, p. 1 (mimeo). All translations in the text by the author.

10. Besson, op. cit., p. 453.

11. Ibid.

12. Osmo Apunen, 'Pohjolan Tasapainon teoriat — osa Lännen strategia', in: *Ydin* (Helsinki) 4/1977, pp. 11-13.

13. Hans-Peter Schwarz, 'Die Ost-West-Spannungen als Orientierungsrahmen westdeutscher Außenpolitik', in: Hans-Peter Schwarz (ed.), *Handbuch der deutschen Außenpolitik*, Munich 1975, p. 466, referring to 'a widespread understanding' about these dates. This author also deals with 'Tensions in East-West-relations' instead of speaking about 'War'.

14. Cf. Schwarz, op. cit., p. 446.

15. A. Kruse-Rodenacker, H. Dumke and N. von Götz, *Kapitalhilfe*, Berlin 1970, p. 96. The authors, closely linked with German development aid policy (Kruse-Rodenacker acting then as the Chairman of the Board of Advisors to the Ministry for Economic Cooperation, Dumke being a civil servant at this department), maintain this has nothing to do with export promotion, and that no political strings were attached. One wonders why they do not ponder the fact that the trade policy section was asked to define the purpose of those DM 50 million.

16. India experienced at this time a heavy crisis in her balance of payments, making investment hardly attractive to anybody else than the German late-comers. The Indian Government found itself unable to honour debts amounting to DM 1.2 billions, while the financial burden incurred by the Rourkela project was estimated at DM 2 billion, including local costs. The 'go ahead' decision by the Federal Government was to offer to India in this situation credits for refinancing amounting to DM 660 million — a step never taken before by the Germans towards any Third World government (two years earlier, the total volume for this kind of refinancing amounted to a mere DM 1 million).

17. J. White, *German Aid*, London 1965, p. 21.

18. Kruse-Rodenacker et al., op. cit., p. 96.

19. In 1961 the Kreditanstalt was given the task of implementing financial aid projects, after the political decision-making process within the government was more or less completed. The establishment of a special ministry for Third World problems is often explained with reference to Chancellor Adenauer's problems to arrive at a cabinet formula which would compromise the new coalition with the Liberals after the loss of one-party majority in the 1961 general elections; the reference to the need for co-ordinated measures as well as the requirement of basic principles for Third World relations appears as a more convincing cause.

20. Quoted from *Afrika heute*, No. 7, 1 April 1966, p. 93.

21. Bundespressekonferenz, 7 June 1963 (Quoted from the unpublished protocol).

22. Karel Holbik and Henry Allen Myers, *West German Foreign Aid 1956-1966. Its Economic and Political Aspect*, Boston 1968, p. 125.

23. Michael Kreile, *West Germany: The Dynamics of Expansion*. Paper prepared for the Conference on Foreign Economic Policy of Advanced Industrial States, 1-2 June 1976, Cornell University, Ithaca, New York, 1978, p. 1. Cf. also the version of this paper in: *International Organization*, Vol. 31, No. 4 (autumn 1977).

24. Ibid.

25. Ibid, p. 2.
26. Hans-Eckart Scharrer, 'Die Rolle der Banken', in: Schwarz (ed.), op. cit., p. 220.
27. Kreile, op. cit., p. 2.
28. L. W. Milbrath, 'Interest Groups and Foreign Policy', in: James N. Rosenau (ed.), *Domestic Sources of Foreign Policy*, New York, 1967, p. 249.
29. Hans-Eckart Scharrer, 'Die Rolle der Banken', in: Schwarz (ed.), op. cit., p. 223.
30. Cf. Hartmut Weisert, *Die Ausübung von auswärtiger Gewalt durch Privatpersonen*, Tübingen 1973 (Diss.).
31. Dieter Piel, 'Die außenpolitische Rolle der Wirtschaftsverbände', in: Schwarz (ed.), op. cit., p. 207.
32. Ibid., p. 211.
33. Ibid.
34. The veto group concept has been candidly applied to West German politics by Gerhard Brandt (*Rüstung und Wirtschaft in der Bundesrepublik*, Witten and Berlin 1966, p. 77), who analyzed the role of entrepreneurs in the German rearmament question.
35. Erste Regierungserklärung des Bundeskanzlers Dr Konrad Adenauer vor dem Deutschen Bundestag vom 20. September 1949, quoted from: Auswärtiges Amt (ed.), *Die Auswärtige Politik der Bundesrepublik Deutschland*, Cologne, n.d., p. 148.
36. Quoted in ibid., p. 83.
37. Afrika-Verein e.V., Hamburg (ed.), *Afrika-Handbuch für Wirtschaft und Reise*, Vol. II, *Afrika als Wirtschaftspartner*, Hamburg 1968, p. 21.
38. Hance, *Geography of modern Africa*, New York 1964, quoted from : Afrika-Verein, op. cit., p. 24.
39. As a standard reference, cf. Hersh Lauterpacht, *Recognition and International Law*, Cambridge 1947. The American practice has been extensively researched by Knud Krakau, *Missionsbewußtsein und Völkerrechtsdoktrin in den Vereinigten Staaten von Amerika*, Frankfurt/Berlin 1967.
40. Cf. Heinrich End, *Zweimal deutsche Außenpolitik. Internationale Dimensionen des innerdeutschen Konflikts 1949-1972*, Cologne 1973, p. 48.
41. Cf. End, ibid.
42. *Antrag der Fraktion der SPD*, Deutscher Bundestag, 5. Wahlperiode, Drucksache V/535 v. 20.4.1966, paragr. 1.
43. Antrag der Fraktion der SPD, *Entwurf eines Zweiten Ausführungsgesetzes zu Artikel 26 Abs. 2 des Grundgesetzes*, Deutscher Bundestag, 5. Wahlperiode, Drucksache V/601 v. 15.6.1966, paragr. 1.
44. Interview, quoted from: *Bulletin*, No. 110, 19 August 1970, p. 1167.
45. K.-W. Berkhan, 'Rüstungspolitik: Verpflichtung auf das Gemeinwohl', in: *Die Neue Gesellschaft* Vol. 21, No. 6 (June 1974), p. 471.
46. Statement by Drs Benecke and Baumeister, BDLI, hearing on aerospace, Bonn, 24 September 1975 (quoted from *Wehrdienst*, 4 August 1975). There are numerous parallel statements by other industry spokesmen at this hearing, cf. the Philips GmbH Hamburg variety: 'In the interest of German industry, whose export orders have been shrinking enormously during the past months, and in the interest of retaining jobs, it is recommended that the Federal Government should ease its heretofore restrictive policy in the export of armaments' (ibid).
47. Figures taken from: *Zwischenbericht der Arbeitspruppe Waffenexport* (of the SPD faction in the Bundestag), Bonn, 16 March 1978, p. 73.

48. The Iran figures are discussed in detail in my preface in: Fred Halliday, *Iran*, Berlin 1979.

49. Secretary of State Bölling, quoted from: *Industriemagazin*, No. 4, April 1976, p. 22.

50. Wolfgang Hoffmann, 'Fehlstart in die Zukunft', in: *Die Zeit*, 2 February 1979.

51. Quoted from ibid.

52. Ibid.

53. Cf. S. Brown, *New Forces in World Politics*, Washington 1974; E. L. Morse, *Modernisation and the Transformation of the International Relations*, New York, 1976.

54. H. Haftendorn, W.-D. Karl, J. Krause and L. Wilker (eds.), *Verwaltete Außenpolitik, Sicherheits- und entspannungspolitische Entscheidungsprozesse in Bonn*, Cologne 1978, pp. 191-224.

55. Ibid., p. 7.

56. Ibid., p. 16.

57. Karl Kaiser, 'Das internationale System der Gegenwart als Faktor der Beeinträchtigung demokratischer Außenpolitik', in: *Probleme der Demokratie heute* (PVS-Sonderheft 2), Opladen 1971, pp. 340-358; Karl Kaiser and Beate Lindemann, *Kernenergie und internationale Politik*, Munich-Vienna 1975.

58. David Rudnick, 'Atlantic Relations: Policy Co-ordination and Conflict. The Case of the Leopard Tank', in: *International Affairs* (London), Vol. LII, No. 2, 1976, p. 205.

59. H. Byrd and W. E. Paterson, *Foreign Policy-Making in Britain and West Germany*, University of Warwick (mimeo), 1974.

60. Cf. Lothar Wilker in Haftendorn et al., op. cit., p. 197.

61. G. Hernes, *Makt og avmakt. En begrepsanalyse*, Oslo 1975, p. 33.

62. Tor Chr. Hildan, *Koalisjonsdannelser i multilaterale konferanser. En studie av UNCTAD-forhandlingene om en atferdskode for linjekonferanser*, MA thesis, University of Oslo 1976, mimeo.

63. H. O. Bergesen, *When Interdependence Doesn't Work: A Study in World Food Politics*, MA thesis, University of Oslo, 1977.

64. A. Underdal, *The Politics of International Management: The Case of Northwest Atlantic Fisheries*, University of Oslo 1978.

65. Hans-Georg Kiera, 'Entwicklungspolitik: Ziele, Mittel, Konsequenzen', in: *Die Neue Gesellschaft*, 6/1977, p. 493.

66. Ibid.

7

THE DEVELOPMENT OF INTERNATIONAL RELATIONS STUDIES IN WEST GERMANY

Gisela Gantzel-Kress and Klaus Juergen Gantzel

I INTRODUCTION

THE STUDY OF INTERNATIONAL RELATIONS as an accademic discipline is relatively new. But it is at the same time based on a tradition of thought rooted in the emergence of international relations themselves. The inability to reflect this circumstance, along with its theoretical and practical consequences, explains a large portion of the difficulties, contradictions and deficits of the discipline. The history of the development of international relations in Germany is a case illustrating this point.

The conceptual point of the departure of this thesis is that a social theory cannot be constructed arbitrarily but that it is part of the social reality it attempts to explain. Theory exposes the laws of movement which constitute and change social reality as well as the working mechanisms which transform these laws into concrete structures, actions and interrelations. We also view each epochal formation of society in history as following characteristic, specific laws of its own. Thus the development of the European system of absolutist states and of the bourgeois society in its womb preconditioned the present reality. That is why international relations discipline begins with the real history of these relationships in the total context of modern history, namely the un-

Authors' note: This paper is dedicated to Eugen Kogon, to whom Political Science in Germany has much to be grateful for, on the occasion of his 75th birthday.

folding of the capitalist mode of production out of the crises of feudalism and the accompanying world-wide expansion of dominance (*Herrschaft*) of the European state-system committed to this mode of production.[1] The laws of movement underlying this history, a self perpetuating dynamics embedded in and dialectically driven by social contradictions, also govern the scientific reflection of this epoch. This reflection, in its development and its analytical categories, can thus be seen as being a part of this international system — simultaneously its reflex, its product and its intellectual driving force.

To illustrate this let us at the outset present some of the basic concepts of our discipline. International relations only began to become a problem with the rise of contradictions between the claims to sovereignty of the absolute states on the one hand and the economic need for expansion of their material pillar, namely bourgeois society (which, in turn, could only develop under the protective shield of these sovereignty claims), on the other. The ideological constructions trying to explain and to solve these problems in theoretical as well as practical terms emerged out of bourgeois exchange relations: in the crystallization of the competition and contract models.[2] Both models, along with their conceptual and historical contradictions arising out of static and dynamic tendencies of social organization, established themselves as the cornerstones of international politics. In the course of the capitalist history of the international system, the substance of these models increasingly shifted from their initially progressive to their tendentially conservative side. The idea of a calculable exchange between free and equal partners, which emerged in the emancipation process of bourgeois society and the rational state from feudal forces, became reduced to an ideological concealment of relations between unequal and asymmetrically dependent powers. Just as the specific bourgeois interests inherent in the competition and contract models transformed themselves into independent, absolute and seemingly generally valid political principles legitimizing these models as instruments of political rule, so also the concept of the nation state[3] as the basic unit of the international system came, in the course of history, to be formulated in such a way that all differences between various social interests, their chances of articulation and their possibilities to affect change, were subsumed within the complex of raison d'etat. The international system within which the world society of today is organized carries the metropolitan perspective of its history within itself.[4]

Where the influence of social history in its total context is not present in formalized concepts any more, there arises on the one hand a wide variety of analytical approaches allowing detailed analyses of aspects of international politics (as in the neopositivistic approaches of the 1960s). On the other hand it offers a seemingly direct way to political practice (as suggested in the normative approaches designed to serve as guidelines for practical action). However, these approaches at the same time imply the loss of substantial analytical power in their capacity to explain reality in its totality and thereby also to categorize single aspects in a meaningful way. This is one of our conclusions after studying the conceptual and institutional development of the discipline of international relations in Germany.

The less a social science remains conscious of its own social history the more it tends to become instrumentalized for the interests of ruling classes only. For political science, which, from its very beginnings developed closely to governmental politics, this danger seems to be specially acute.[5] This is particularly so in Germany, where the social sciences in general followed a tradition of subservience to state authority[6] and where international relations began as a subdiscipline of international law and diplomatic history or was at least decisively influenced by such an orientation.[7] If the attempt to develop a science of international relations in itself constitutes social activity, then the description of its institutionalization and its main research subjects should simultaneously consider the political and social background through which it has been conditioned.[8]

II THE BEGINNINGS OF THE DISCIPLINE 1919-1933

It is even possible to ascertain the exact date of birth of the academic discipline, i.e. of the institutionalization of research and teaching of international relations: 30 May 1919, when the British and American delegations to the Paris Peace Conference agreed upon the foundation of institutes for research on international relations.[9] The British Institute of International Affairs and the American Institute of International Affairs owe their existence to this initiative. One member of the German delegation, Albrecht Mendelssohn-Bartholdy, professor of international law at the newly founded University of Hamburg, urged the establishment of a similar research institute in Germany — supported especially by Max Weber, Hans Delbrück, Count Montgelas, and Count Brockdorff-Rantzau. A 'Research Centre for War Causes' was founded in Hamburg in 1921, and in 1923 the follow-up organization, the 'Institute for

Foreign Policy' (Institut für Auswaertige Politik) came to be established.[10] It was financed by the city-state of Hamburg, the German Foreign and Home ministries, a society of promoters from Hamburg's trade and industry, and the Rockefeller Foundation. Its political basis was centered in the support for the liberal-democratic Weimar government coalitions, mainly by the numerous public activities of its founder and his influence as a political adviser in appropriate circles at home and abroad. The actual work of the institute consisted of information collection and documentation, especially relating to the First World War, and, above all, in stimulating the academic-journalistic discussions taking place in the magazine *Europäische Gespräche* and the publication series *Politische Wissenschaft*.[11]

The second move towards the institutionalization of international relations in Germany, promoted more by teaching than by research considerations, was made in 1920 at the Deutsche Hochschule für Politik (DHfP) in Berlin, which was outside the university and about 80% privately financed.[12] Here the desire to deal with international problems formed one of the two key constitutive elements shaping the development of the institution. One of its main purposes was to educate democratic elites by functioning as a 'school for citizenship' (*Staatsbürgerschule*, as it was called by Friedrich Naumann). The other prevailing concept was an education scheme especially appropriate for future foreign policy decision-makers, modeled on the Paris Ecole Libre des Sciences Politiques. Last but not least, this concept was supported by the later Prussian minister for cultural affairs, Carl Heinrich Becker, to whom a number of teaching and research institutes about the knowledge of foreign countries at Prussian higher educational institutions owe their existence.[13] Among the five departments of the DHfP at least one was devoted to 'Foreign Policy and Foreign Countries'.[14] A Carnegie-Chair for International Relations was established in 1927,[15] and in 1929 the research center of a peace academy was founded.[16]

After the Nazi seizure of power in 1933 the Hamburg Institute and the DHfP in Berlin were both totally restructured and the founding fathers were nearly all forced into emigration. Among the scholars of these institutions who entered into the service of German fascism were some international relations experts. We cannot view this independently of the fact that the research on international politics in both these institutions in the 1920s had not been able to achieve a theoretically coherent profile. The first systematic approach to foreign relations of capitalist societies, the theory of imperialism with its variants, had been formulated before and during the First World War, but outside the academic field, and was taken up seriously by the discipline of international relations only half a century later.[17] Indeed, the attempts to institutionalize political science were explicitly directed against a materialistic social theory, which derived from historical dialectics and threatened the legitimacy of the very existence of a capitalist society in Germany. The liberal-democratic founders and promoters of the discipline were concerned, on the contrary, with the consolidation of the bourgeois system, with the resolution of the social crisis after the First World War, with help for decision-making of governmental policies of the young Republic, and with making Germans more 'skilfull' in their handling of politics.[18] If, in spite of this, the political science of that time to begin with perceived itself as an 'opposition science', then to that extent it corresponded to, and reflected, Weimar democracy, which sought to establish itself and prevail against reactionary social classes. It was a mainly political protest against the reduction of the social sciences to an apolitical affirmation of the existing state of affairs and against the conservative tradition of scientists.[19] However, this did not give rise to any alternative rooted in scientific thinking. In fact, the demonstrative pluralistic balance displaying partisan neutrality at the DHfP and its 'scientific' development from an evening school to an institution with university character mirrored its special need to legitimize itself vis-à-vis the conservative establishment by seeming to be 'above party lines' and 'objective', which, in turn, merely expressed the absence of a clearly defined political conception. The international relations discipline of the 1920s did not develop a new approach in the context of its institutionalization. It largely remained preoccupied with the legal historiographic, geopolitical, and pragmatic patterns of foreign policy analysis which were rooted in the 19th century. At best some isolated attempts to develop the studies bearing on institutions and customs of foreign nations (*außenpolitische Realienkunde*) into a systematic teaching of facts (*Tatsachenlehre*)[20] of world political connections can be regarded as a vague precursor of research perspectives of the reestablished discipline of the 1950s and early 1960s.

III THE INSTITUTIONAL ESTABLISHMENT 1949-1977

The stimuli for the political sciences in Germany after the First and the Second World Wars were similar. The impetus after 1945 was again the intention to educate the people in democratic thinking and to legitimize the new republic against the traditions of subservience to state authority.

In contrast to the 1920s, West German political science managed to establish itself, slowly and against much opposition, at the universities themselves, primarily in the various faculties of philosophy, law, economics, or *Staatswissenschaft*. Although it thereby received the academic legitimation regarded as so important in Germany, political science has, till today, been unable to command the status of the traditional sciences, from among whose students the political elites (even of today) are almost entirely recruited.[21] Furthermore, political science paid the price of its integration into the traditional German university system with a far-reaching depoliticization of its educational ideal, which could have only been fulfilled by a comprehensive social approach, i.e. an approach directed against the segmentalization of the German academic system into more or less isolated sciences.

A further difference from the 1920s lay in the changed perception of international politics. The Federal Republic of Germany, 'an artificial product of an international system newly coming into being, saw. . . its passage during the heyday of the Cold War bound to firm and deep tracks. . . Being a pure function of the East-West-conflict was the law of its beginning'.[22]

What is more, it obtained its state sovereignty, internal as well external, through an active foreign policy (however narrowed from the outside) and through its political and — above all — military and economic integration into the West; even the reunification of Germany was to be achieved in this way. Contradiction enough: it is a fact, that, up to the 1960s, international politics was, for the West German comprehension of world affairs, perceived in terms of the so-called 'German question', which, to an extent, explains the backwardness and the long incubation period of the science of international relations. The partition of Germany appeared as a microcosm of the central problem of world politics, the conflict between East and West, and even this was reduced to the Berlin problem.[23] The immense significance of foreign policy and of the international system for the Federal Republic from its inception notwithstanding, the science of international relations, as the last offshoot of the political sciences, was built up only after all political-practical consolidation, and began to grow mainly from the mid-1960s.[24] As late as 1965 only four of the interviewed candidates responding to an inquiry regarding 'The Situation of Political Science in Germany' named international politics as an important polito-logical research field;[25] and even today one cannot deduce the existence of an established discipline of international relations from the job descriptions of teaching personnel at the institutions of higher learning in the FRG alone[26] — this in spite of the fact that isolated lectures or seminars in the field of international relations are documented as far back as the winter semester of 1945/46.[27]

1. The Exception: West Berlin

The institutional rebuilding of political science in Germany began in West Berlin with the renewed foundation of the DHfP in 1948/49,[28] once again outside the university and, as before, with a very practice-oriented conception of basic and supplementary education and training.[29] The renewed academization of the DHfP set in even during the year of its reopening (under the pressure of the high percentage of full-time students) and led to its complete integration with the Free University (FU) of Berlin in 1959.[30]

The newly refounded DHfP, in contrast to its predecessor, which was initiated by liberals, received its support from the very beginning from social democrats, who looked at it as an explicitly anti-communist institution like the FU founded at the same time. They, however, envisaged a non-capitalist re-formation of West Germany, and were, moreover, aware of the connection between the failure of social democratic political aims and the absence of a scientifically stringent political theory — at least in the circles close to Otto Suhr, the first director.[31] The political hopes of the founders, that the DHfP could play a theoretically founded guiding role in the process of reshaping of post-war Germany, did not materialize because of unforseen early political consolidations. Nevertheless, it produced a more successful model for the scientific analysis of organizational and theoretical aspects of politics (developed further at the FU) than could be the case at the other largely traditional universities of the Federal Republic.

This circumstance is, to an extent, also reflected in the institutionalization of research and teaching in international politics. Because it was newly founded it was possible to build up a scientific organization at the FU less encumbered by traditional German conceptions of science as a number of separate disciplines — that is, with the social sciences as its nucleus. Whereas individual political scientists at the universities of the Federal Republic, isolated from one another and within their faculties, taught and researched what interested them most, the quantitatively massive institutionalization in Berlin was much less influenced by similar personal idiosyncracies.[32]

During the beginning of the 1960s two of the eleven chairs in political science at the FU were already devoted to international politics; in contrast, none of the chairs in political science in the Federal Republic specialized in international politics before 1966.[33] During the winter semester of 1977/78 approximately eight among the thirty-seven permanent teaching posts in the FU political science department, which had absorbed the Otto-Suhr Institute in 1970, were at the disposal of the field of international politics, as against between one and two permanent posts (in normal cases) at the universities in the Federal Republic. Frankfurt was the exception with five or six out of eighteen political science teaching posts devoted to that field; however, there remain some universities where the teaching of international politics is not institutionalized at all.[34] In comparison with the universities in the Federal Republic, the FU Berlin offers a sum of lectures, courses and seminars corresponding to the numerical strength of their teaching personnel. Calculations on the basis of university lecture registers show that between 1950 and 1975 nearly 23% of all academic courses in the field of international politics in the FRG and Berlin were given at the FU; the University of Frankfurt ranked second with 9.2%.[35]

A differentiated qualitative evaluation of the academic courses up to 1968 does not only show that all aspects of international politics were represented in Berlin better than elsewhere. It also indicates that, in addition to focusing on those aspects of international politics relating to history, international law and single-country foreign policy typical for the period up to the beginning of the 1960s, Berlin was among the first German universities to become involved in studies related more to the theory of international relations, economic problems and problems of the Third World,[36] which are all looked on today as being particularly relevant for the understanding of international structures and dependencies. Since the beginning of the 1970s and especially while preparing the establishment of a special research division, which was to concentrate its efforts on the analysis of 'The Determining Factors of Foreign Policy in the Second Half of the Twentieth Century', there emerged in the FU a degree of cooperation unique for German conditions and which led to results whose subtle differentiation and complexity elevated the academic discussion of the discipline in Germany to a new qualitative level.[36a] This was in no small degree due to the interdisciplinary nature of the organization of teaching and research in Berlin. Problems of the political economy of the international system, of international dependency structures, of armaments, of restraints on the freedom of action in the foreign policies of Western European societies, of the foreign policies of socialist countries as well as of peripheral societies, were and are being taken up in Berlin. Permanent working units for discussion and the coordination of dissertations aimed at counteracting the mostly distorting effects of traditional research work conducted in isolation, were established in Berlin, e.g. 'Politics in China and East Asia' established in 1967 (under Domes, up to 1977), and 'Politics in Africa' (headed by Ansprenger).

A number of prominent centers also devoted to research on international politics have sprung up outside the political science department of the FU — within as well as outside the university: the German Institute for Economic Research (Deutsches Institut fuer Wirtschaftsforschung), the German Institute for Development Policies (Deutsches Institut fuer Entwicklungspolitik) and the Berlin Science Center (Wissenschaftszentrum Berlin).[37]

2. The Foundations of Institutionalization

The development of political science and, within its framework, of international relations as a university discipline in the Federal Republic, proceeded at a very slow pace as long as it aimed at 'the claim to the institutionalization of the scientific self-reflection of the social order'.[38] It thereby simultaneously questioned the institutional structure of German universities, which was characterized by a disciplinary approach encouraging the restoration of authoritarian tendencies. However, the claim of German political science to be a science in the service of democracy was largely unsupported by any relevant conceptual framework, and it allowed itself to be absorbed by the traditional academic structures without protest. Ultimately it was the inability of the discipline to critically reflect democratic theory which facilitated its easy absorption. The first generation political scientists had a primarily moral commitment to democracy, strongly colored by their personal experiences which corresponded to the opposition to fascism and Soviet communism and led to the idealization of the liberal model of democracy without a sufficiently critical approach to its capitalist implications. Thus, because the democratic concept postulated, which involved a comprehensive social approach critical of domination, was not pursued — they favored merely a more 'humane' model of dominance — the newly reborn discipline of political science slipped 'unforseen — hardly anybody noticed it — into the creaking machinations of the general restoration taking place within and without the zealously renovated academic precincts'.[39]

In 1949 the institutional build-up was commenced at the Conference of Waldleiningen, organized by the Hessian state government in response to an American initiative. Its final resolution strongly recommended that the universities establish 'chairs in political science, especially in *World Politics*, political sociology, comparative government, contemporary universal history, and political theory'.[40] These 'subjects' — initially conceived as general courses for students of all sciences — contained the now customary division of political science at most universities; except that the order institutionalized later literally put international politics at the tail end of the program.

The Berlin Conference organized by the DHfP was more concrete in its statements. Its participants noted that 'there exists an independent science of politics' and referred to the 'comprehensive societal and historical conditions in their political perspective' as its object of inquiry. They further declared that 'this science is concerned especially with the acquisition, use and loss of power, with civilization and its decay. This includes the examination of the decisive problems of our age of the masses, of intrasocietal political structures, of *International Politics* and the application of the results to daily political practice'.[41]

The Conference of Koenigstein in July 1950 went a step further and approached the Conference of the State Ministers of Culture (institutions of higher education came under their jurisdiction) with a view to introducing and developing 'the science of politics' at West German universities. They moreover paved the way for the establishment of a professional association. This was the German Political Science Association (Deutsche Vereinigung fuer Politische Wissenschaft — DVPW), founded in February 1951 by forty university teachers.[42]

However, the Conference of West German University Rectors warned against a too rapid establishment of political science and recommended the creation of appropriate chairs as late as 1954 — and only then with reservations.

Following the conferences of 1949/50, political science was introduced at most of the West German universities and at a few of the Technical High Schools. A decade later, in 1960, a basis of twenty-four ordinary and extraordinary chairs (ten of which were in Berlin alone) had been created and a further four were in the process of being established. Furthermore, three honorary professors, a number of lecturers and about forty assistants with teaching assignments were devoting themselves to political science. Thirteen university institutes had been built up, composed of one full professor, to which were usually attached one or two assistants, one part-time post for a famulus, one secretary, a budget of DM 2,500-8,000 for ancillary expenses, and a library with 3,500 volumes on average. (The exceptions to this modest framework were the two institutes in West Berlin — the Otto Suhr Institute and the Institute for Political Science, which was purely a research establishment.)[43] Only in Berlin were the political science chairs thematically specified according to distinct areas.

This was the point of departure for the recommendations of the West German Science Council (Wissenschaftsrat) in the autumn of 1960.[44] As a rule it demanded one chair in political science per university and two for larger universities; it named Berlin, Frankfurt and Cologne as the universities where the teaching of political science ought to be concentrated and demanded ten further chairs for the discipline, whose areas, however, remained unspecified except in one case: the chair for the 'Foreign Policy of Eastern Countries', which was to be established in Berlin.[45]

At the same time — in the summer of 1960 — Mario Rainer Lepsius prepared a 'Memorandum on the Situation of Sociology and Political Science' on behalf of the German Research Foundation (Deutsche Forschungsgemeinschaft), in which he demanded a sufficient degree of institutional expansion as a precondition for the vigorous development[46] of these disciplines. He viewed the proportion of one-chair-per-university (along with assistants, etc.) as a temporary measure for the beginning, at best, and recommended the adoption of an interdisciplinary departmental structure, which has till today, eighteen years later, been realized at only very few newly founded universities.[47] Lepsius also described the substantive achievements of political science as being unsatisfactory, he criticized the 'lack of planned research', especially in the whole area of foreign policy and international politics,[48] and he drew attention to the fact that political science had been unable to extend recognition of the discipline and political consideration beyond its own boundaries, as had been intended at the end of the first phase of its institutionalization.

3. The Three-Phased Process of Institutionalization

In his memorandum, Lepsius envisaged a three-phased development of political science. Looking back, one might say that (1) the phase of reconstitution in Germany took place in the 1950s; that (2) the consolidation phase extended from the 1960s to the mid-1970s; and (3) the phase of its full unfolding has, by and large, not even begun.[49] Further, institutional development is, for the time being, stagnating.

The institutionalization of the study of international relations developed roughly as shown in the following table. Our categorization is based on actual work done and not on the official job descriptions attached to academic positions.

For the first and second phases our detailed raw data are incomplete and we therefore have to limit ourselves largely to the counting of full professorships, whereas the data for the third phase, during which the traditional academic hierarchy was changed as a consequence of the university reforms, also encompasses other permanent teaching posts. Actually, the majority of new entries in the data of the 1970s represent professorships below the H- or C-4 level of full professor; this should be kept in mind while interpreting the data. In the third phase many middle-rank positions were transformed into professorships, which, however, should not be interpreted as a general increase in teaching capacity, or as a change in the traditional staff hierarchy.

The institutionalization of political science at the teachers' colleges should not be mentioned without going into details. On the one hand, no specialization in the field of international relations has, as a rule, taken place here. On the other hand, we were forced, for reasons of comparability, to disregard those parts of university political science departments which had absorbed former teachers' colleges (as, for example, with four posts in Munich, one of which is a post in international politics; and six posts in Frankfurt, one of them again being in the field of international politics).

In North-Rhine Westphalia and Lower Saxony teachers' colleges in some cases formed the basis for newly founded universities; our counting in these cases begins with the founding dates (e.g. the Universities of Oldenburg and Osnabrueck, and the Integrated High Schools (*Gesamthochschulen*) of Wuppertal, Duisburg, Essen, Paderborn, and Siegen).

The first steps in the research and teaching of the study of international relations were taken in the 1950s — at first in Southern Germany where they were promoted mainly by Arnold Bergstraesser, who, after

TABLE 1
The Three-Phased Process of Institutionalization of Political Science in West Germany

Federal State/Institution	First phase approx. since 1950	Second phase approx. since 1961	Third phase approx. since 1969
BADEN-WÜRTTEMBERG			
Heidelberg			
University	2 PS (approx. 1950, 1960)	(1 IR 1967), 1 PS (1968)	1 IR (approx. 1974), 2 PS
Research	Research Centre (Protestant Study Association, 1958)	South Asia Institute (1962) Res. Cen. for Int. Agricult. Dev. (1965)	
Tübingen			
University	1 PS (1952)	1 PS (1967)	1 PS, 1 IR (1972), 1 IR-Reader (1974)
Freiburg			
University	1 PS (1954)	1 PS (1967)	1 PS (approx. 1974)
Research	Arnold Bergstraesser Institute		
Stuttgart			
Tech. Uni. Col./Uni.		1 PS (1965)	
Stuttgart-Hohenheim			
Agr. U.C./University		1 PS (1966)	
Mannheim			
Eco. U.C./University		2 PS (1964, 1965)	(1 IR app. 1972), approx. 3 PS

TABLE 1 (continued)

Konstanz University		1 IR (1966), 2 PS (1968, 1970)	approx. 3 PS (about 1974)
BAVARIA			
Munich University	1 PS (1946)	3 PS (1962, 1967, 1969), 1 IR (1967)	2 PS (approx. 1974)
Tech. University		1 PS (1967)	2 PS (approx. 1974, 1977)
Armed Forces Col.			6 PS (1974), 1 IR (1976)
Ebenhausen Research		Research Center for Int. Politics and Security of Foundation for Science and Politics (1965)	
Starnberg Research			Max Planck Inst. for Research of the Conditions of Life in the Scientific-Technological Age (1970)
Würzburg University	1/2 PS 1951	1 PS (1968)	1 PS (approx. 1974)
Regensburg		1 IR (1963), 1 PS (1967)	2 PS (approx. 1970, 1977)
Erlangen-Nürnberg University		1 IR (1961), 1 PS (1964)	2 PS (approx. 1972, 1977)
BREMEN University			approx. 9 PS (1972-74) 3 IR (1972, approx. 1976, 1978)

TABLE 1 (continued)

HAMBURG			
University	1 PS (1951)	1 PS (1962 ⟶ IR (1966)	5 PS, 1 IR (1972/73)
Armed Forces Col.			3 PS, 1 IR (1974)
Research	Inst. for Int. Affairs (former Inst. for Foreign Pol. (1923-47)	Foundation German Over-sees Institute	
	Hamburg Archives for World Economics	VDW-Research Group ⟶	Study Group on Armaments and Underdevelopment
HESSE			
Marburg			
University	1 PS (1948)	1 IR (1966)	approx. 7 PS (1972-77), 4 IR
Darmstadt			
University	1 PS (1951)	1 PS (1962)	approx. 4 PS (1972-77), 1-2 IR
Frankfurt/Main			
University	1 PS (approx. 1952) ⟶ IR (1970)	1 PS (1963)	approx. 5 PS (1972-77), 4 IR
Research			Peace Research Institute Frankfurt (1970)
Giessen			
University	1 PS (1952)	1 PS (1966)	approx. 7-8 PS (1973-77), 2 IR
Kassel			
Integrated U. Colleges			approx. 8 PS (1972-77), 1 IR (1972)

TABLE 1 (continued)

LOWER SAXONY			
Göttingen			
University	1 PS (1947) → IR approx. 1974	1 PS (1962)	approx. 7 PS (approx. 1972-77), 1 IR
Hannover			
Tech. University		1 PS (1963)	approx. 13 PS (approx. 1972-77)
Braunschweig			
Tech. Uni. Col.		1 PS (1965)	approx. 7 PS (approx. 1974-77), 2 IR
Osnabrück			
University			1-2 PS, 2-3 IR (1974-77)
Oldenburg			
University			approx. 10 PS (1974-77)
NORTH-RHINE WESTPHALIA			
Cologne			
University	1 PS/IR (1948)		2 PS (approx. 1972-77), 1-2 IR
Research	R. Inst. for Pol. Science and European Questions		
Bonn			
University	1 PS (1954)		1 IR (1970), 5 PS (approx. 1972-77)
Research	Res. Inst. for the German Soc. for Foreign Policy (1955)	Soc. Scien. Inst. of the Konrad Adenauer Foundat. Res. Inst. of the Friedrich Ebert Foundation. German Foundation for Int. Development	

TABLE 1 (continued)

Aachen			
Tech. Uni. Col.		1 IR (1961)	
Research		Res. Inst. for Int. Tech.-Economic Cooperation	
Münster			
University		1 PS	1 PS (approx. 1974)
Bochum			
University		2 PS, 1 IR (1966)	3 PS (approx. 1972-77), 1 IR (approx, 1974)
Research		Institute for Dev. Res. and Development Policy (1966)	Special Research Section
Bielefeld			
University			3 PS (1970-74)
Research			Center for Interdisciplinary Research
Duisburg			
Integrated U. Colleges			1 IR (1974), 5 PS (1974-77)
Essen			
Integrated U.C.			3 PS (1974-77), 1 IR (1977)
Wuppertal			
Integrated U.C.			1 IR (1974)
Paderborn			
Integrated U.C.			2 PS (1974-77)
Siegen			
Integrated U.C.			3 PS (1974-77)

TABLE 1 (continued)

RI NELAND-PALATINATE			
Mainz			
University		2 PS (1963, 1968)	2 PS, 2 IR (1974-77)
Trier-Kaiserslautern			
University			3 PS, 2 IR (1972-77)
SAAR			
Saarbruecken			
University		1 PS (1964)⟶IR (1969)	1 PS (approx. 1977)
SCHLESWIG-HOLSTEIN			
Kiel			
University	1 PS (1956)		1 PS (approx. 1972)
Research	Institute for World Economy (since 1911)		

PS = Permanent post for political science
IR = Permanent post for International Relations
PS ⟶ IR = Redefinition of a post through a new filling

This tabular summary was compiled from the lists of teaching personnel of the German Political Science Association. Regarding reliability see note 26.

returning from American exile, held the first chair in political science in Freiburg from 1954 until his death in 1964. He was primarily responsible for two research areas. Through the Research Institute of the German Society for Foreign Policy[50] (Forschungsinstitut der Deutschen Gesellschaft fuer Auswaertige Politik) founded in 1955, the concept of a scientific tradition of advisory services for practical politics was resuscitated (as had been intended in the 1920s at the Hamburg Institute for Foreign Policy). The Arnold Bergstraesser Institute,[51] founded in 1960, introduced research on developing countries to the Federal Republic. Right into the 1960s much academic discussion was dominated by the normative-ontological, politically rather conservative orientation of the 'Freiburg school'. The reception and further development of ideas from modern American research in international relations began during the mid-1960s in Freiburg too, at first in a rather imitative manner — a seemingly radical departure of the third generation of political scientists from Bergstraesser's comprehensive cultural-philosophical perspective. Both variants of the 'Freiburg School' receded into the background when the increasing awareness of the importance of economic, social-historical and structural — and hence also intra-societal — factors shaping international politics came into the academic discussion.

The geographical centers of the discussion shifted to Frankfurt, Berlin and Marburg, where the theoretical and organizational aspects of the reform movement of the 1960s brought into discussion the marxist traditions of thinking in dialectical terms, which had been neglected in the traditional West German universities. It is no coincidence that these centers became focuses of the student movement in the second half of the 1960s.

On the academic front private communications between political scientists and the migration of some led to the creation of certain kinds of 'enclaves', as, for example in Constance, where, from the time Ziebura was appointed to a chair for IR, an extraordinarily productive group of young students from Berlin have been working, or in Hamburg, where research interests, which had developed in Berlin and Frankfurt, were drawn into the field of international political studies and combined with local research traditions of the study of the world economy.

As in other disciplines, so also in the field of international relations, one can observe an increasing division of labor between teaching and research since the beginning of the 1970s. From the late 1960s the sudden influx of students became totally disproportionate to existing teaching capacities. Moreover, the laws governing the reform of the system of higher education did not lead to the intended improvements, but instead to an excessive bureaucratization of the universities. Thus, the net result was an extension of the educational tasks of the universities at the expense of research.

In some cases research activities moved out of the university, examples of which are the establishment of the Peace Research Institute in Frankfurt[52] (Hessische Stiftung fuer Friedens- und Konfliktforschung-HSFK; although this institute remains closely connected with the university through personnel links), the Institute for Peace Research and Security Policy[53] in Hamburg (Institut fuer Friedensforschung und Sicherheitspolitik) and the Max Planck Institute for Research of the Conditions of Life in the Scientific-Technological Age[54] in Starnberg (Max-Planck-Institut zur Erforschung der Lebensbedingungen der Wissenschaftlich-technischen Welt).

Besides these independent research institutes, the Research Institute for International Politics and Security of the Foundation for Science and Politics[55] (Forschungsinstitut fuer Internationale Politik und Sicherheit der Stiftung Wissenschaft und Politik), a government institute employing about forty scientists and with a yearly budget of more than DM 5 million, was established in 1965 in Ebenhausen near Munich. (The preparations for its establishment derive from a Bergstraesser initiative.) Analyses, conceived as advice in the decision-making process for the foreign and security policies of the Federal Republic, are carried out here, and can be grouped as follows: (1) structural problems of international politics and of the international system; (2) problems of arms policy and arms control on all international levels; (3) international economic problems; and (4) problems of conflict-prone areas in the Third World relevant for West German and Western European politics.

IV THE DEVELOPMENT OF THEORETICAL FOUNDATIONS AND DIRECTIONS OF RESEARCH SINCE 1950

Although the world political constellation after the Second World War and the foreign policies of the allies — especially those of the USA and the USSR, as well as the West German policy of integration into the West — were decisive for the timing of the founding of the Federal Republic of Germany, its shape and its international role; although political science became established academically during the 1950s and although the study of world politics was especially stressed during this period, conceptual approaches to the science of international relations began only towards the end of the decade and then aimed in a direction prejudiced by the past development of politics in West Germany. The time lag and the preconditions had both positive and negative consequences for the specialized discipline of international relations in the 1960s. It is therefore necessary to first view the conceptual directions of political science in the FRG in the 1950s.[56]

West German political science at first concentrated on two associated areas: democratic theory and research on totalitarianism. While the latter expressed, on the one hand, the endeavor to come to grips with the past and, on the other, the simultaneous ideological search for a new identity by equating national socialism with Soviet communism, the aim of the former was to indicate the practice of democracy as a form of government and a way of life. Just as, on the one hand, the identification of 'brown' with 'red' diverted attention from the fact that fascism was a specific form of capitalism and that, in this context, national socialism was a particular German variation, so, on the other, the history of capitalist democracy and its endangering by capitalist structures, was ignored. Consequently, the critical attitude towards capitalism initially present in parts of the social democratic movement was conveniently sublimated and converted into anti-communism, whereby the original intention to develop a theory of politics as an integral part of a theory of society was abandoned. Not only the political economy approach in the tradition of Karl Marx, but also the categories of a political and historical sociology in the tradition of Max Weber were again buried.

The narrowing of the concept of politics resulted in the exclusion of its substantive contents and reduced their understanding to a question of form — and that mostly with abstract ontological premises and postulates. Even the central problem of the analysis of power was reduced to a formalistic analysis of the expression of power, whereby the democracy model was robbed of its substance and formalized into a set of rules of the game. West German political science, even before it really became established, thus transformed itself into a legitimating science which, with its didactic services, became identified with the system instead of fulfilling its intention of being a critical instance of control in the democratic system with the aid of scientific examinations. Under the banner of de-ideologization political science turned de facto into an ideological, conservative apology; it integrated and was itself integrated with the existing political system.

We can here only briefly mention some of the causes of this development: (1) the academic acceptance of political science; (2) the personal experiences of suffering and emigration of its founders; (3) the traditions of German academic organization — which were taken for granted by this generation; (4) the political stability and economic achievements of the young republic; (5) the structural and ideological integration of the workers' movement within the restoration of the social system and within the Western alliance; (6) and last but not least, the belief in normative deductions in place of empirical analyses. All these facts taken together, in addition to the continuing resistance of conservative faculties to the new political science, produced a syndrome which, in one way or another, contributed to the integrative tendencies.

In this first decade of political science almost nothing was done for the study of international relations. This was for two reasons: firstly because so much study was devoted to the debate over the nature of totalitarianism, thus to be used in domestic politics as a paradigm of the cold war.[57] The second field of study looked to the past, and is exemplified by the first special encyclopaedia on foreign policy (*Aussenpolitik*) which was published in 1957.[58] A statistical evaluation of the main headings and the bibliography shows that a large majority of themes (over 50%) may be subsumed within the two following categories: 'Men (statesmen) make history' and 'the world as a collection of states'. In so far as the relations between states are approved as elements of a system at all, they are mentioned merely as regulations of foreign trade and commerce, and of economics, transport and international law. Historical and geopolitical accounts and studies of individual regions and countries constitute the vast majority of entries, followed by institutional and legal themes. The encyclopaedia thus expresses an orientation which Walther Schotte had as early as 1926 characterized as an important but insufficient 'science of facts' (*Realienkunde*).[59] 'Theory of international relations' is missing under the indexed headings[60] and only a few titles in the bibliography may be classified as fundamental theoretical works or comprehensive descriptions of international politics. About a quarter of the cited literature was produced before 1945 and goes back to the 19th century. Among the post-war literature included in the encyclopaedia only a very few titles are by German authors and practically no work of any major importance for the conceptual development of the discipline can be found at all.

The pioneering approach came from Arnold Bergstraesser. He directed the development of the discipline not in the direction of any valid analysis of international politics, but rather mirrored the syndrome sketched above. A guarantee for academic success appeared to lie precisely in the unplanned research interests, in the eclectic and theoretically unfounded application of traditional specialized research methods to the study of political science. At the same time it seemed to lie in the ontologically absolutized hypertrophy of common sense results which were passed off as 'synoptic science' and recommended as scientifically tested decision-making guides for practical politics — precisely because they reflected the general insecurity of political science and hence confirmed the premises of day-to-day politics. The aim of serious study was not so much the causal explanation of politics as the playing of an active, formative rôle through political education and advice.[61] The cultural-morphological review of all relevant aspects, whose criteria of relevance remained arbitrary because they were not bedded in a theory of society, was considered to be an adequate research method for political science.

Hence the conceptual approach in Bergstraesser's memorandum on 'International Politics as a Branch of Political Science'[62] was primarily an extrapolation of his ideas concerning domestic politics and internal order. Mindful of the post-First World War intentions to abolish war by institutional means, he characterized 'the prescriptive anticipation of foreign political actions' as the aim of the discipline. He called for the examination of (1) the states as the actors of international politics in the totality of their cultural-sociological dynamics; (2) the 'politically sensitive dimensions of life in the international sphere'; and (3) the procedures of international political dynamics. With the aid of these analyses international political events should be synoptically evaluated.

In an important radio broadcast in 1963 on 'The Hope for a Worldwide Political Order'[63] Bergstraesser articulated the normative aims more clearly: long-term creation of world peace on the basis of Western social conceptions making use of a détente policy reinforcing the loosening and dissolvent tendencies in the Soviet sphere of power and the modernization of the underdeveloped world on the occidental model. 'The concept of man as...homo faber and...homo sapiens, as the active master of his existence and the perceiving wise man is the core of the occidental cultural heritage...In this hour of world history it is up to the occident itself to remain true to the spiritual assumptions on which its culture and way of life rest...'

Bergstraesser's concept, however, did not have any consequences for the study of international relations in spite of the lasting influence that the 'Freiburg School' had on earlier debates within political science;[64] it had come too late. The reception of the modern theories and methods of the social sciences with which research on international relations in the USA was conducted started at nearly the same time. The development of the international relations discipline started off with this perspective in the mid-1960s, on the one hand unencumbered by the legacy of the 1950s, but on the other with such a leap into empiricism that neither was the synoptic quasi-theory of a Bergstraesser discussed or questioned nor were the imported empirical methods problematized with regard to their theoretical implications. We may even discern a hidden relationship between the theoretical deficits of both research directions and their consequences for political practice.

However, Bergstraesser's approach still contained a humanistic global horizon which was lost with the dominance of the piecemeal strategies and systems approaches of research. Their premises viewed their analytical methods as value neutral, equating the analyzed phenomena with reality, whose totality was considered as reconstructible by the compilation of part results. This, as well as their corresponding incapacity to 'place' the results of the analysis of specific subjects into a total social and historical context, resulted in a third research direction oriented on the social totality approach of the 'Critical Theory'[65] School. Based on a theory unfolding itself out of socio-economic and historically systematic analyses, the problem of contextual assessment was identified as being a central problem of theory, thus bringing to light the ideological elements immanent in the normative and the behaviorist approaches.

1. Theoretical and Methodological Developments Since 1965: a Review of Steps and Tendencies

Several signs of an upswing in the conceptual development of the discipline can be noted in the first half of the 1960s. Firstly, there was a rise in the percentage of articles on international politics in the *Politische Vierteljahresschrift* — the organ of the German Political Science Association (GPSA) after 1961.[66] Three innovative articles which especially influenced the course of further discussion appeared there in September 1963.[67] Czempiel and Krippendorff tackled the question of the interconnection between domestic and foreign policy. Krippendorff particularly, with his provocative question, 'Is foreign policy *foreign*?', attacked a basic premise of German political analysis and thereby took up a criticism of German historiography in the tradition of subservience to state authority begun by Eckart Kehr in the late 1920s. The third article was inspired from outside: Karl W. Deutsch formulated the first critical reflections on the principles of the deterrence system.

A second sign was the founding of the International Politics Section of the GPSA after a decision taken by its governing board in April 1964 (together with a section of 'Theory of Politics' and another on 'Domestic Politics', which assembled for the first time in March 1965).[68]

A third sign can be seen in the resonance which questions on international politics found during the conferences of the association.[69] They appeared for the first time at a GPSA conference in 1956, when Arnold Bergstraesser delivered a lecture on 'The World Political Situation and the Position of Individual Powers on the Question of Coexistence'.[70] In 1958 the association requested several of the board members to prepare a memorandum with concepts for the five main branches of political science: (1) political philosophy; (2) social and socio-psychological preconditions; (3) political communites; (4) international politics; and (5) political teaching. Bergstraesser formulated the paper on international politics. However, international politics first reappeared on the conference agenda in 1963 with Richard Loewenthal's lecture (along with Cornides) on 'Alliance Systems and National Interests'. The 1965 conference saw one full day reserved for themes on international politics for the first time; with papers by Czempiel and Krippendorff on the 'Contribution of Science towards the Formulation of American Foreign Policy', it was the first time that the section was publicly represented. Thenceforth contributions to international politics increased from conference to conference, and in 1969 they dominated three working groups: on systems theory, development theory and on foreign policy, thereby manifesting the different orientations within the discipline. In 1971 the analysis of foreign policy and of the international system from the perspective of global interdependence and structural dependencies constituted one of the main subjects of the conference.

It is not easy to summarize the development of the conceptual discussion and the various theoretical and methodological positions and to place them in their determining contexts with their relevant scientific, socio-economic, internal political and international problem areas. We here have to take into account the expansion of the discipline to its very boundaries and risk making seemingly inadequate or unsuitable assessments and categorizations. Reviewing the whole period since the mid-1960s, for an initial orientation one can observe the following developmental stages and trends:

— Whereas the beginnings were characterized by narrow and one-sided views we now have an extraordinarily broad and differentiated spectrum of methodological-theoretical orientations.
— While initially the discussion was primarily centered around abstract general approaches, it is today dominated by empirical research. Even fundamental theoretical questions are discussed with respect to concrete reality.
— Whereas the discipline at first boasted just a dozen or two specialized representatives and younger scientists, who despite their mutual differences would assemble for amicable discussions, it now presented the picture of a number of islands. A lot is discussed on some of the islands, less on others; above all, nearly no bridges of communication seem to exist among them.
— The levels of anlaysis were raised and enlarged step by step: from the level of 'foreign policies of individual states' to that of 'international politics', from there via the inclusion of the economic and social foundations of politics to the level of 'international relations' and ultimately to 'world society' inclusive of its history.

Most important is probably that series of steps by which the builders and representatives of each further step tried to transcend, or at least enlarge the scope of the preceding one: the methodologically traditional, mostly historically oriented foreign policy research including the research on eastern countries (the so-called *Ostforschung*) and studies on individual countries — the reception of approaches developed in the USA, initially those of the realist school and then the scientific approaches of the modern social sciences (behaviorism, systems theory, cybernetics) — the reception of US and Scandinavian peace research and at the same time the application of the insights of the 'Critical Theory'[71] to international relations — the reception of the Latin-American *Dependencia* theory as well as the resumption of the theoretical discussion on imperialism and on the *Critique of Political Economy*. These stages did not develop as successively as it here appears; some developed simultaneously. We merely suggest a logical reconstruction. Each of these steps is, by the way, 'occupied' till today.

The phases, shifts and debates outlined below were to a large extent born by, or within, the International Politics Section of the GPSA. Some of the research interests and theoretical orientations were located or arose outside the section (e.g. in the fields of security and arms politics or of the imperialism theories). Considering the importance of the International Politics Section for international relations studies in the FRG it seems to use to be useful to first outline its history.

2. *The History of the International Politics Section (IPS): the Learning Process of the Discipline*[72]

The first conference in March 1965 — like the two following ones organized from Freiburg — served as a review of the discipline and of its aim to propagate peace since the First World War with special reference to the USA, to the discussions of the realist school and to the reception of the political implications of strategic problems as described in the American literature. The conference had a dual objective: first, to review the discipline's historical and academic position and to examine its self-understanding in view of its practical social task, that of maintaining peace. This task was mainly seen in the light of international law and of Western cooperation and integrative conceptions as they were known from the time between the wars and it was viewed through the looking-glass of the deterrence system. Second, a step was taken towards the reception of American approaches, which, from the then prevailing point of view, represented some progress towards the modernization of ideas on international politics with respect to the necessity of theory building.

If the discipline wanted to contribute to securing peace then it also had to make itself felt in practice. Czempiel's lecture at the 1965 GPSA conference on the contribution of science towards the formulation of American foreign policy was thus not accidental. But the differing assessments of the practical role of the discipline became clear even in Krippendorff's following lecture.[73] During the second conference of IPS in October 1965 this subject was taken up again, this time with reference to the potential of the discipline to act in conjunction with the foreign policy decision-makers of the FRG to aid in a practical way the modernization of its foreign policy, especially in view of the fact that the Federal Republic was emerging out of its provinciality in foreign policy and steering towards its new *Ostpolitik*. This demonstrated not merely a 'governmental' type of thinking with respect to political practice but also exposed a limited and even distorted understanding of practice which overestimated the immediate possibilities of political science. Aspects of legitimation relevant for the young science also played a role. Efforts of this kind to come into contact with practical politics, were however, soon discontinued.

The third conference of IPS in July 1966 took up the themes of the first conference, this time with regard to theory building. The controversies regarding US research contributions[74] reflected to some extent the positivism dispute of the 1960s. At first, however, the affirmative attitude dominated. The debate heightened awareness of the necessity for theory building and countered some of the main arguments against ideographic views, while the contents and the specifically political elements of international politics began to recede into the background.

The fifth to seventh conferences (1968/69), presided over by Czempiel (Marburg), were notable in more ways than one and had long-term effects. First, the delegates chose to debate one general subject — the relationship between internal and external politics — over several sessions, enabling the contributions to be discussed intensively until they were ready for publication. As a result, the IPS was the only one among the three sections of the GPSA which was in a position to publish a separate report.[75] Second, the chosen subject encompassed a number of different fields of research; it was of fundamental importance and concrete as well as broad in scope. The methodological and theoretical discussions of former conferences were applied to one concrete object of examination, thus reducing the danger of a depoliticizing abstraction.

The third change in the activities of IPS lay in the fact that henceforth research and communication was primarily in the hands of younger scientists belonging to the third generation of political scientists in the FRG.[76] Not yet fully established in academic terms, they were stimulated by the student movement, were active against US policy in Vietnam and in internal politics, they were against the emergency laws of the federal government, all the more because the depression of 1966/67 had signaled the end of continuous economic growth and the birth of the interventionist state. They were politicized by the public discussion about the coalition between conservatives and social democrats in Bonn and the expected end of the conservative CDU-rule, which, after twenty years, had led to immobility and stagnation in all spheres of political life. A large majority sympathized with the political and social reformist ambitions of the leftist social democrats and the liberals.[77] The political scientists had not produced the politicization — nor even been able to accelerate it — because the discipline, on account of its legacy from the 1950s, was incapable of analyzing the political problems in the context of social contradictions and was therefore incapable of working out adequate solutions. With very few exceptions this was also true of the discipline of international relations. But the active IPS members were infected by the general politicization and influenced in their understanding of science in as much as they became increasingly conscious of the deficits of traditional research. Not yet being bound by definite alternatives, it was for the first time possible to maintain a basic political and scientific consensus in IPS. In this way a caucus could be formed, a core of inter-university cooperation and communication in the field of international relations, which then formally constituted itself with a democratic statute of its own — a fourth innovation.[78]

It was Ernst-Otto Czempiel, who, having clearly recognized the necessity of ensuring a solid base for the further establishment of the discipline of international relations, stimulated the active core group of IPS to draft an outline for the work of the coming years.[79] The reception of systems-theoretical conceptions, already begun, was to be continued and their analytical-heuristic value, as well as their empirical usefulness, tested under the heading 'Structure and Process of International Systems'. The endeavor, as in political science, was, on the one hand, to grasp the social totality and, on the other, to reduce its complexity to an analyzable level. However, the work proceeded sluggishly and the discussion was limited to a small group of experts. This was because a growing divergence in academic circles, against the background of heightened tensions in the arena of university politics, manifested itself in IPS in a de facto division — and partial slackening — of interest in the ongoing project (respectively of disinterestedness) and correspondingly also in its management.[80] Moreover, systems theory increasingly proved to be the wrong road to a general theory,[81] revealed itself as an apolitical, ahistoric, formalistic, sterile, and praxeologically unsuitable approach — which accounts for its lack of motivational strength.[82] Only the cybernetic version of Karl W. Deutsch, inspired by learning theory and communications theory, offered possibilities of critical and progressive interpretation.[83] To this extent the publication documenting this part of the IPS project[84] is a negative report, yet at the same time a new start.

The new start was stimulated from two directions: firstly, from the early reception of the Latin American *dependencia* discussion and that of Johan Galtung's 'structural theory of imperialism',[85] and secondly, from the rediscovery of the *Critique of Political Economy*.[86] The *dependencia* theories were formulated as a local reaction to the failure of the modernization strategies of the 'development decade' propagated by the UN; these development strategies were more or less based on the development history of the industrialized societies, without taking into account the specific social conditions of the developing countries and their role in the world division of labor as a consequence of their structural dependency on the industrialized metropoles. The resumption of the scientific marxistic discussion, on the other hand, was a reaction to the increased social and economic contradictions in these metropoles themselves, as well as to the inability of the theories and methods imported from the USA to explain and overcome these contradictions.

This new theoretical orientation was carried into the project work of IPS in 1971 mainly by a group of fourth generation political scientists which had come into being in the course of the preparations for the planned Special Research Unit in Berlin[87] under the direction of Gilbert Ziebura. In a highly regarded paper[88] Gerd Junne, Salua Nour and Frieder Schlupp — with numerous data regarding potentials and interactions — exposed the much cited international interdependence as an ideological veiling of onesided dependencies necessitating a critical examination with the analytical help of the concept of a 'synthesis of domination'. Thanks to this critical description of the rough structure of the international system a more substantive means of perception found its way into the work of IPS and characterized the second part of the IPS project. The first perspective for this second part of the project had been born in 1968 out of the observation that two general approaches, under which nearly all the theoretical treatises and empirical studies from the USA, England and the FRG could be subsumed, stood side by side and unrelated to each other: on the one hand, the analyses of international cooperation (integration research), on the other, the analyses of tendencies towards conflict (conflict research). The IPS wanted to examine these approaches with the aim of formulating new research categories with which integration and conflict could be made visible as dimensions of interstate relations in a definite process and evaluated with respect to their theoretical relevance. An approach was needed combining both concepts as parts of a real dialectics in international history. To give a concrete example: Western European integration, itself a conflict-rich process between national capital fractions owing to the historically uneven socio-economic and political development of individual states, could be grasped as a conflict strategy within the framework of intercapitalistic rivalry with US dominance, on the one hand, on the other as a conflict strategy — in cooperation with the USA and against the socialist block dominated by the USSR — in the framework of the rivalry between the capitalist and socialist systems.[89] In this sense integration implied pragmatic cooperation towards the improvement of chances of national accumulation of capital and towards the more effective securing of the capitalist system internally as well as externally. The multinational, or transnational corporations appeared to be one of the most important motors and bearers of international integration through the capitalization of world society.

The association of South European and African countries with the EEC could be seen as vertical integration in the sense of an absorption into the process of the international division of labor dominated and steered by metropolitan capital and supported by the native bourgeoisie of the developing countries, who had internalized metropolitan interests and views through colonial and post-colonial education, training, consumer interests, etc. From this viewpoint class struggles as well as proxy and civil wars in the less developed societies appear to be a result of social disintegration and deformation produced by the long structural dependence on the developed metropoles. Regional integration processes, resistance movements and regional 'socialism' movements ('Arabic', 'African' socialism, etc.) in the Third World were therefore to be examined as to whether they were cases of 'emancipative counter-integration'. Similar questions posed themselves with regard to the socialist bloc, its internal conditions and its relationship to its global capitalist environment. In this way conflict and integration were viewed as domination and freedom strategies in world society. These shaped and influenced each other and demanded socio-economic and political analysis in relevant historical dimensions, inclusive of interactions between structures and processes on macro and micro levels.[90] Thus the subject of the IPS project was more narrowly defined and the title was decided upon: 'Integration and Conflict: Penetration Processes, Dependency Structures and Counter-strategies in World Society'.

This comprehensive approach took up the earlier 'universal horizon', viewing international politics as world politics; it was not, however, based on conservative, apologetic philosophies but rather on a materialistic and critical theory of history and society. The phase of reception of American social sciences and the so-called positivism dispute had left a closer awareness of the necessity of and conditions for theory building and empirical research. But at the same time there was consciousness of the dangers accompanying narrowed views about science and empirical research. As in the theory of democracy, so also in the field of international relations, ideas turned from pure 'methodocracy', and from the corresponding restriction of scientific analysis and practical politics to mere forms and tactics to eliminate substantial social problems. From the discussions centering around systems theory and systems anlaysis the view had remained that the world is more than a sum of its states and their foreign policies, and that this totality ought to be reflected in the framework and in the individual categories of analyses and theories. Attempts were made to transcend the lack of substance, sterility and pure taxonomy of formal approaches of systems theories by resuscitating the social-historical, structural-sociological and politico-economic traditions of European thought. Cybernetics and communications theory had pointed to the importance of information streams and channels and their feed-back effects in the political process and in social change (e.g. with regard to the function of nationalism). At least indirectly, the cybernetic approach stimulated more dynamic views which were, however, then substantiated in the attempted reconstruction of social dialectics.

More restrictive government action became apparent in the political practice of the social-liberal coalition the more one retreated from the action-oriented euphoria for reform which had been present before. Correspondingly, 'Change through Enlightenment' seemed the only understanding of practice appropriate for an approach oriented on long-term and comprehensive world social structures and processes. This educative intention was articulated and given form in the 'Tutzing theses on a curriculum for the teaching of the science of international relations',[91] which where worked out by the participants at the 14th conference of the IPS in September 1972. The Tutzing theses wanted to provide a guideline for teaching at the universities, but they encountered massive resistance at the next conference from many colleagues who did not agree with the contents and the critical intentions of the curriculum draft. This debate showed that the basic consensus within the discipline had finally been broken.

IPS was not a research institute but a forum for communication and coordination. Its function — and that of its projects — was to stimulate and coordinate research studies at the different universities and institutes and to organize the exchange of information. In the course of the project work a number of IPS members not interested in it withdrew more and more, but at the same time the membership expanded because of the resonance that the new approach received.[92] In 1972 there were twenty-five studies by single researchers and study groups registered and another thirteen by the autumn of 1973.[93] The studies were to analyse the penetration processes, dependency structures and counterstrategies between capitalist industrial societies, between these and the socialist states, within the socialist states, between industrial societies and developing societies, and finally, within the Third World. The studies were to be based on selected cases and were to test, deepen or modify the conception of the project with the aid of empirical research and to work out further questions. Naturally, it could not be the aim of the IPS project group to develop one, all-embracing theory. But it did want to place analytical perspectives in an integrating framework which would be in a position to clarify connections, equivalances and similarities between phenomena in different regions and different social sectors and problematize them as expressions of world social development. Most studies of the project were finished in 1974;[94] IPS's work had reached its zenith.

In retrospect, the dedicated collaboration of so many young scientists in the second IPS project seems to be above all an expression of the political reality of the early 1970s. Several factors demanded new analytical orientations: world-wide inflationary tendencies and monetary crises; the ever deepening gulf between the development of the Third World and the rich industrial countries — notwithstanding the crisis susceptibility of the economic growth of the latter; the oil crisis; the pessimistic reports of the Club of Rome; the wars and struggles in Vietnam, in South Asia, in the Middle East, in Africa, and in Ireland; terrorist actions at the international level; the expansion of the military-industrial complexes in spite of détente between East and West, and its militarization effects on the developing countries etc. — crises and contradictions in world society whose consequences can be felt more and more by the individual.[95] This need, felt particularly by younger scientists and progressive students, was to an extent met by the project. An added stimulus to the IPS project was that similar communicative forms of work were hardly possible at West German universities; firstly, because there were hardly any professors of international politics and the few who did exist mostly had different perspectives; and secondly, because the universities were usually structured in a way not conducive to cooperation in teaching and research.

Finally, the second sectional project helped to identify two deficits. Firstly, there was a lacuna with respect to the political-economic analysis of world history, especially concerning the origins, forms and consequences of the European expansion since the 15th century. Secondly, in its consideration of the economic basis of politics the project had overemphasized the relevance of capital and neglected the factor of labor, its international migrations, its conditions of political consciousness and its forms of resistance. In 1973 the planning of a follow-up project was therefore begun — thanks specially to the initiative of Ekkehart Krippendorff (Bologna, now Berlin) and Hartmut Elsenhans

(Berlin, thereafter Marburg).[96] For the third IPS project, which was titled 'History and Structure of the International System, with Special Reference to the Development of the Labor Factor and its Political Conflict Manifestations', it was possible to obtain a two-year grant commencing in 1975 from the German Society of Peace and Conflict Research. However, from the beginning it was difficult to secure the collaboration of a sufficient number of qualified participants for the project or to achieve a consensus on the areas of concentration. Ultimately two study groups did manage to establish themselves. They worked without communicating with the section's chairmen and are currently preparing their studies for publication.

Similarly, the study group 'International Organization and Integration', formed under the aegis of IPS in 1972, is now independent; headed by Volker Rittberger (Tuebingen) it decided in 1974 to concentrate on two areas, 'External Relations of the European Community' and 'International Organizations as Instruments for the Revision of the International Division of Labor'. This study group today works in close collaboration with the 'Study Group on European Integration' (Arbeitskreis Europaeische Integration e.V.), which was founded in the 1960s by the Bonn office of the European Community and operates under the direction of Beate Kohler (Darmstadt) and Lothar Brock (Braunschweig, now Frankfurt) as an autonomous group of the GPSA. Besides problems of European integration it continues to handle some questions concerning global integration and organization.

In this context two study groups, which were also formed outside IPS in 1972 after an initiative by the board of GPSA, have to be mentioned: first, the study group 'Socialist Countries', which, directed at first by Egbert Jahn (Frankfurt) and then by W. Eichwede (Bremen), presented a number of studies on the Ostpolitik of the FRG at the GPSA Hamburg Conference in 1973,[97] but whose work has stagnated since 1976; second, the group 'Development Theory and Development Policy' (P.V. Dias, followed by F. W. Heimer, both Freiburg), which first discussed analyses of individual developing countries and diverse development problems in the tradition of the Arnold Bergstraesser Institute and which has recently — under the direction of P. Hanisch and R. Tetzlaff, both Hamburg — handled questions of under-development, dependency and social formation in the peripheral countries — subjects which were 'at home' in IPS earlier.[98] Another study group initiated within IPS, on the foreign policy of the FRG, did not get off the ground in spite of efforts over the years by H.-P. Schwarz (formerly Hamburg, presently Cologne), Seibt

(Bremen) and Link (Kassel, then Trier). The initiators wanted to start off a project comparable to 'Integration and Conflict' and in 1974 Werner Link proposed a project entitled 'Atlantic Industrial Society and Transatlantic Politics. Studies on the Function of State and Social Actors'. But this project draft encountered massive criticism, especially from the leftist group within IPS. However, the project failed to get off the ground not because of the criticism but because of lack of participation.

The IPS finally fell dormant in February 1974. Apparently there was no longer any demand for the cooperation offered there. During the GPSA conference in October 1977 in Bonn, the IPS members met for the last time to discuss the question of reactivation or dissolution of the association. Only very few of the active members from the years 1971-74 appeared; and the old opponents of this project group in matters scientific (and perhaps political too) did not want to keep IPS alive even as an information agency. Only a few more members than had founded it twelve years previously dissolved IPS, like an institution that had outlived itself.

How can this surprisingly rapid decline after such fruitful work, which can, for example, also be seen in the share of contributions on international politics in the *Politische Vierteljahresschrift*, be explained?

Several reasons may be suspected. First, IPS had expanded beyond its optimum size, as the fact that study groups became independent ('emigrated') and the creation of thematically related but more narrowly defined study circles show. Second, the development of the discipline of international relations, to which IPS had largely contributed, had led to research becoming highly differentiated (and specialized) so that not even a conception with a very broad scope could contain the differences any longer. After the new orientation had been discovered it was not so much the fundamental theory which remained, as parts of theory and detailed empirical studies. Such a consolidation is necessary but leads to individual scientists becoming overloaded with time-consuming empirical work, leaving only enough time for organizing themselves within informal and specialized circles. Third, the increased competition and performance pressure, as well as the lack of job availability at the universities for a new and larger number of young scientists, were not at all conducive to the type of work for which IPS had so successfully been a forum. Fourth, IPS became practically incapable of asserting its integrative power in the face of the division of the discipline into differing directions largely isolated from one another; in spite of all reservations about simple categorization, one can make out four main directions:

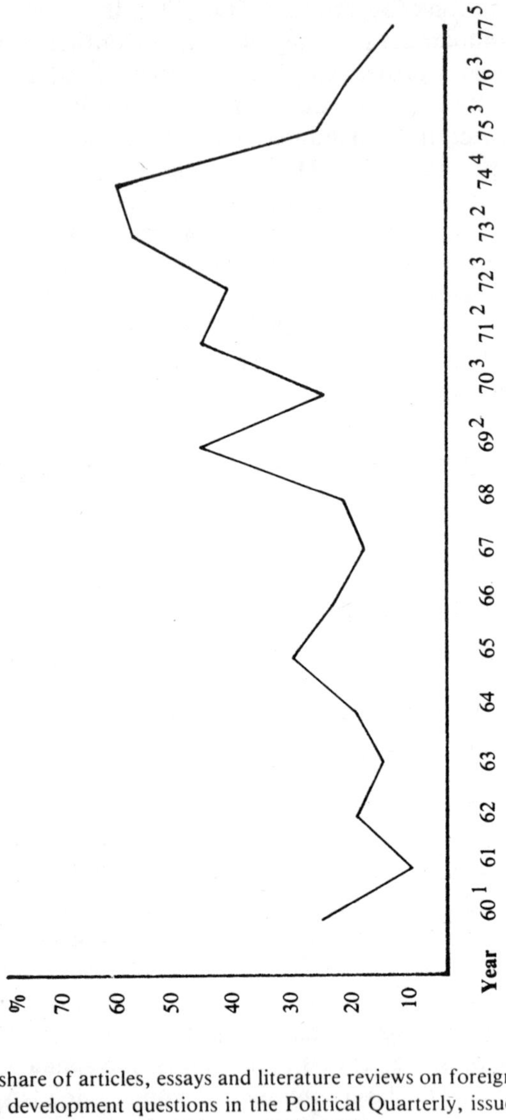

Development of the share of articles, essays and literature reviews on foreign policy, international politics and development questions in the Political Quarterly, issued by the German Political Science Association, 1st-18th year (1960-1977)
(Percentage of pages to total number of pages in the respective years, including special issues. 1: The 1st year had only two issues. 2: Including a special issue on international relations. 3: Including a general special issue. 4: One of the four regular issues was concentrated on international relations. 5: At the time of the survey just three issues had appeared (January 1978).)

traditional, formalistic, reformistic and approaches criticizing the dominant forms of social life. Although the intra-scientific declaration of war (observed by Kastendiek in other areas of political science)[99] can rarely be made out for the discipline of international relations, there is nevertheless no communication among the various directions; each is occupied with itself and does not see the others' views. The representatives of some of these different 'schools' either never took part in the work of IPS or else did so only intermittently. On the other hand, the radical direction of social criticism in international relations is today widespread and strong enough to be able to assert itself without needing a forum like IPS.

3. *The Main Directions Within the Discipline*

The history of IPS is to a large extent the history of the development of the discipline of international relations in the Federal Republic and in West Berlin. But it is not the whole history. That is why, in the following, we shall give a brief survey of the main directions of the discipline and their creation. Some of the authors we cite would perhaps categorize themselves differently; others have — with the passage of time — reoriented themselves or taken up an 'in between' position; yet others — perhaps wrongly — are not represented at all. It has therefore to be emphasized that we do not claim that the following examples are either exhaustive or sufficiently representative.

(a) Traditional Foreign Policy Research

This is the oldest research effort in the discipline and was present at the beginning of its history in the 1920s as well as in the 1950s, overshadowing all other orientations right into the 1960s. Only very few of its representatives were professional political scientists; its most important scholars were at home in history, especially in contemporary history, or in journalism. Others adhered to the traditions of Bergstraesser's school of thought. Their methods of work — source interpretation in the style of historiographic research — were based on a mostly unconscious theoretical framework, and thus foreign policy research refused to let its basic traditional orientation be confused by the 'theory and methods discussion' of the social sciences in the 1960s; at most some of the researchers used more or less marginal concepts to supplement systematization. Within foreign policy research, therefore, there exists a diversity of theoretical perspectives and methodological approaches not allowing a homogeneous categorization, largely because the analytical categories, systematizations, empirical selection criteria, causal explanations, and standards of judgement derive from a more or less informed, stimulating, intelligent and plausible 'common sense'. Their criteria are mostly deduced from a normatively determined framework which is not infrequently related to the political horizons of established political parties (with the exception of radical or extreme wings). It is certainly no coincidence that just these representatives of foreign policy research found 'advisory' access to practical politics; they have enormously enriched factual knowledge, particularly of German, American and Soviet foreign politics.[100]

(b) The Small 'Realistic School'

The reception of the approaches of Reinhold Niebuhr and Hans Morgenthau came at the beginning of the attempt to provide a theoretical basis for research on international politics in the FRG. Gottfried Karl Kindermann introduced the thoughts of the Realistic School into the German discussion[101] and combined their fundamental pillars of 'power', 'interest' and 'morals' with the basic ontological assumptions and the synoptic approach of Bergstraesser's Freiburg School. However, this approach did not find many supporters in West Germany; as far as we can see, Kindermann, along with his assistants in Munich, seems to be the only one who has explicitly continued using it.[102] Criticism was mainly directed against the anthropological premises of the approach, against its normativism and against Morgenthau's concept of interest.[103] At any rate his concept of power politics was not easily applicable to the powerless situation of the FRG, which perhaps also explains the poor response.

(c) The Scientific Approaches

The scientific orientation developed through the reception of modern methods of social science research in the USA after the middle of the 1960s; its representatives in the FRG nearly all belong to the third and fourth generations of political scientists. The causes of this modernization process and the role that the IPS played in it have already been described. Notwithstanding some overlaps, essentially two different groups can be discerned, but it must be remembered that the 'science' orientation also influenced the empirical work of some of the approaches to be described later.[104]

The first of these orientations is behavioristic. It seeks to put deductive statements about international behavior to the test and to unearth regularities in an inductive way by aid of quantitative methods and real data. It is used nearly exclusively in the research on arms races (stimulated by the work of Lewis Richardson and his followers) and the causes of war (stimulated above all by J. David Singer and his Correlates of War project).[105] In our opinion, however, the price of its applicability is paid with too far-reaching simplifications and with a statistical view leading to fatalistic conclusions and a justification of the global political status quo.

The other approach can be characterized as formalistic systems analysis. In connection with the systems theoretical revolution in political science in Freiburg, it was brought to bear on international politics by Klaus Faupel; he formalized it very extensively and worked out its logical determinants in detail.[106] As far as we can see the step to an empirical application in accordance with the deducted methodological postulates has not yet been taken.[107]

A number of studies on factor analysis and simulation methods[108] or using the methods of exact model building[109] and committed to the postulates of critical rationalism (Popper) can be seen as being science oriented. Notwithstanding all affirmation of such methods, these studies have retained a critical distance from them with regard to the political problems to be analyzed and also take recourse to more substantial sources.

Although game theory was discussed in West Germany, it was criticized because of its ideological premises[110] and hardly applied in the analysis of international politics.

On the whole, scientific methods in their strict sense did not achieve a breakthrough in the West German international relations discipline. The relevant experts have remained a small and largely isolated group. This is due firstly to the fact that at West German universities the training in methods necessary for the application of the scientific approaches is not, or is hardly, in existence; and secondly, because the historical-sociological and radical (i.e. *gesellschaftskritisch)* theories of the European tradition of thought do not allow themselves to be forced into the procrustean bed of the scientific approaches (or only in a distorted fashion).[111]

(d) Integration Research

Although the politics of integration of the FRG into the West was and remains of tremendous importance for the young republic, theoretical integration studies led a shadowy existence for a long time.[112] Inspired by functionalistic integration theory as, for example, laid out by David Mitrany and Ernest B. Haas, Gerda Zellentin worked on problems of Western European integration.[113] On a more global level, Volker Rittberger examined international organization and integration from the angle of the evolutionary growth of international interconnections.[114] His studies, which are increasingly problematizing the instrumental functions of international organization towards the maintenance of the structurally violent nature of the existing conditions of the capitalist division of labor and of liberal-bureaucratic domination,[115] indicate a change in direction which will divide integration researchers into two blocs. In contrast to the USA, however, integration research has on the whole remained an undeveloped area in West German political science.

(e) The 'Habitat' of Peace Research

As with all the other modern research orientations mentioned above, the development of peace research in the FRG owes much to foreign approaches. Above all, Scandinavian studies from the circle around Johan Galtung at the International Peace Research Institute in Oslo and American contributions from, among others, Karl W. Deutsch, J. David Singer, Kenneth Boulding, Amitai Etzioni and from those centered around the *Journal of Conflict Research*, influenced its beginnings. Organizationally well prepared for by the Association of German Scientists (Vereinigung Deutscher Wissenschaftler) and especially by the Association for Peace and Conflict Research (Arbeitsgemeinschaft fuer Friedens-und Konfliktforschung, AFK, founded in 1968),[116] its substantial and institutional possibilities outlined by the memorandums of Karl Kaiser and Claus Koch,[117] and then above all publicly supported by the then officiating Federal President Gustav Heinemann, peace research in the FRG found surprisingly quickly a social niche in which it could establish itself.[118] The causes and objective function of the rapid establishment of a new research area, as well as the reasons for resistance in the academic establishment and in politics in the light of the general reversal of West German social tendencies in the last few years, have not yet been analyzed. However, the fact that the social-liberal coalition in the Bonn government was setting off on its course of social reforms and towards a new 'Ostpolitik' was undoubtedly in favor of the breakthrough of peace research, whereas the motivation of the researchers derived from the fact that the social sciences in the FRG had until then contributed almost nothing towards solving the problem of securing peace.

We have here to refrain from going extensively into the development, structure, directions, and perspectives of peace research in the FRG. It pursues a political-scientific aim — the reduction of violence and the establishment of inter- and intra-national peace. Peace researchers are largely united regarding this aim but no consensus exists as to the causes of non-peace, the concrete shape of a future peace order and the means and strategies towards its realization. One can essentially differentiate between two main groups: whereas traditional peace research is primarily concerned with avoiding war and direct violence and consequently strives for the stabilization of deterrence, improvement of arms control, diplomatic détente, and interstate cooperation (favoring institutionally secured forms, e.g. integration), critical peace research[119] views the causes of non-peace as being mainly located in intrasocietal conditions and in the social and political domination structures of the international system and judges the chances of disarmament by means of arms control and similar diplomatic manoeuvers pessimistically. It strives to secure peace by the reduction of structural violence through social change. These two basic orientations and the positions in between are to be found in several of the special research areas within the discipline of international relations — partly simultaneously — so that the notion of 'peace research' is not suited to a structuring of the discipline into conceptual, methodological-theoretical directions. Critical peace research especially implies an approach viewing the societal totality and demands an integration of the social sciences in opposition to the traditional compartmentalization of the scientific disciplines — thus going far beyond the usual dimensions of international relations.

(f) The Arms Control School

In contrast to scientists engaged in critical peace research, the representatives of the arms control school do not basically question the system of deterrence but rather tend towards the official 'two pillar doctrine' on the principle of: Defence + Détente = Security. With technocratic criticism of this or the other measure of armament politics and military strategy, they above all examine the conditions preventing the further escalation of the arms race and a consequent destabilization of the deterrence system. The arms race is mainly viewed as a process of interstate action and reaction; correspondingly, countermeasures are located mainly at the military-strategic and diplomatic level (CSCE and cooperative arms control, e.g. SALT, MBFR, etc.). Measures of this kind aim at reducing the distrust between the main parties in the arms race (USSR and the Warsaw Pact countries on the one side and the USA and the NATO countries on the other), at helping prevent the accumulation of destructive potential and thus consolidating détente and the growing East-West exchange within a political security framework.[120]

A special branch of military-strategic research considering ideas of reform in this area has established itself in the Max Planck Institute in Starnberg and is especially associated with the names of Carl Friedrich von Weizsaecker and H. Afheldt. Exact methods of calculation were here used to simulate the catastrophic consequences of an atomic war on German territory and a defence concept, conceived as a countermeasure to prevent the employment of nuclear warheads including 'just' tactical strikes and based on small, scattered, independently operating 'technical commandoes', was developed. But the warnings and the proposal for an alternative defence concept have not yet influenced official policy (although v. Weizsaecker reckons with a Third World War on the basis of his probability models).[121]

(g) The Influence of Critical Theory: the Critique of Deterrence and of Armament Dynamics

Critical theory[122] has hardly occupied itself with international relations or with foreign policy. Although at an early stage Ludwig v. Friedeburg and Gerhard Brandt published social and economic studies on the West German military forces[123] under the auspices of the Protestant Study Association (Evangelische Studiengemeinschaft), which lay outside the affirmative 'mainstream', nevertheless it was Dieter Senghaas who, using the basic theoretical and methodological concepts of critical theory, took up the task of analyzing international relations and thereby decidedly influenced a whole direction of research. He was the first in West Germany to reflect American research approaches to international politics while placing them in a context of social theory,[124] and in his critique of the system of deterrence formulated in 1966/67[125] he juxtaposed the categories and perspectives of critical theory derived from the social-philosophical, socio-economic and historical-systematic analysis of bourgeois European society to the communications-theoretic concept of Karl Deutsch, which became well known in the FRG mainly through his efforts.[126] Senghaas' criticisms of deterrence triggered off a more thorough discussion of the policies necessary for the securing of peace; and, with few exceptions,[127] the West German arms control school of thought developed itself mainly in the wake of the scientific controversies over Senghaas' ideas.

Through his analysis of doctrines of deterrence, Senghaas attacked their basic premises, especially their understanding of the relationship between politics and violence. Whereas the invention of atomic weapons had to begin with made war as an instrument of politics seem absurd, the revision of the doctrine of massive retaliation through the doctrine of flexible response again placed military violence at the disposal of politics. This manifested itself in an enormous expansion and differentation of the armaments spectrum, ranging from intercontinental ballistic missiles to the all-round combatant for counter-insurgency. Senghaas studied how international relations in its current constellation of states wedded to the doctrine of deterrence is intertwined with the intrasocietal conditions prevailing in these countries. The vicious circle of deterrence cannot be immanently falsified: the inherent loss of reality perception makes it constitutionally immune from practical testing of the mutually ascribed aggressive intentions. Imprisoned within their respective autistic fences the elites of the deterrence societies exchange threats, but these threats do have as much impact on the societies on the other side of the fence as on their own. The function of deterrence is thus revealed: the prevention of any attempted emancipatory transformation of the status quo and the consolidation of a 'system of organized peacelessness'.[128]

From that point it was a logical step towards the analysis of the intrasocietal causes of the autistic character of armaments politics, i.e. of economic, technological, bureaucratic, and domestic political interests and influences as well as their ideological and institutional roots in the society. Senghaas also performed pioneering work in this area. In his evaluations of the studies made by American critics of armaments he compiled a set of theorems explaining the dynamics of armament and reconstructed an exemplary model of the American military-industrial complex.[129]

Senghaas' third step was consequently the critique of SALT and MBFR as a 'symbolic use of politics' and the substantiation of his view that arms control, i.e. the cooperative steering of armaments, contributes more to rearmament than to disarmament.[130] The conclusions for political practice seem obvious. Agreements like SALT, MBFR and CSCE can at best improve the mutual diplomatic atmosphere of trust, but essential measures towards disarmament have to start with the intrasocietal interests and conditions which promote rearmament.[131]

To a large extent, the contributions of Senghaas have been responsible for the stimulation of research being conducted in West Germany on the politics and economics of armaments production. An important such center has established itself at the Peace Research Institute in Frankfurt (Hessische Stiftung Friedens- und Konfliktforschung, HSFK).[132] Further, critical analyses of the politics, economics and technology of armaments have been formulated by Alfred Mechterscheimer (Munich), Manfred G. Schmidt (Tuebingen), Wilfried v. Bredow (Marburg), as well as by Ulrich Albrecht (Berlin), and Peter Lock and Herbert Wulf (both Hamburg),[133] who emphasized the retarding effects on the development of the Third World of its militarization through arms exports from the developed countries.

On the whole, it is possible to see strategic and armaments policy as one of the main areas in which research in international relations is focussed in the FRG — divided, however, into the two directions mentioned above. This concentration of research efforts is not a result of intellectual interests alone, but is also a reaction to the continually growing role of the FRG in NATO and in the international system under the government of the social-liberal coalition since 1969, and also to the growing problems and contradictions ensuing from this role within the country itself. The qualitatively and quantitatively very low levels of public discussion on the topic stand in strong contrast to the relative intensity and quality of the research work done in the field. The 'Arms Control School' still has a certain degree of contact with the political establishment because it does not question the premises of official policy, but the critical voices do not stand a chance of being heard against the military and ministerial bureaucracy and against the armaments industry, with its large resources, propaganda instruments and possibilities of political influence. Their theses and research results are officially almost completely ignored. An inter-university 'Study Group on Military Policy' tried to stimulate the defence establishment to take up the challenge of a public discussion by publishing 'anti-White Books' on the military and armaments policies in the FRG and the GDR based on their research findings, but they were rebuffed in a brusque and partly defamatory manner.[134] The armaments criticis have up to now at best been able to supply information and argument aids to a small section of the informed public, where they have achieved a limited degree of sensitization to the political and economic dimensions of the arms problem. This is the case with parts of the Churches, with a few journalists,[135] with not even a handful of left-wing social democrat members of parliament, with the youth organizations of the SPD and FDP,[136] and with a section of the students.

(h) The Renaissance of Marxian Theory

At this stage it becomes difficult to delineate the further discussion in the discipline of international relations because in many of the different research areas it is associated with the 'schools' which have arisen thanks to the *Critique of Political Economy* in the tradition of Marx, Engels, Lenin, Trotsky and Luxemburg, and of their epigones who studied and formulated imperialism, development and state theory. And as in critical theory, so also within the framework of political economy, the research fields 'internal politics' and 'international relations' are being fused in a growing symbiosis under a theory-horizon viewing the total society.

The renaissance of marxist theory was primarily carried into the universities by the extra-parliamentary opposition movement of the second half of the 1960s, the student movement and the New Left, and was facilitated by the introduction of the university reforms with their extension of participation to teaching assistants and students. It was a reaction to national and international social problems, crises of legitimation, and conflicts, for which the so-called bourgeois sciences, with their narrow, isolating object definitions and their ideologically tinged theories and methods, evidently had no satisfactory answers. Last but not least, it was also a reaction to critical theory, which had failed to supplement its analyses of bourgeois forms of consciousness with a corresponding analysis of its economic basis. Marxist approaches and questions were applied in research on inner-societal problems approximately from the mid-1960s but in international relations only from the beginning of the 1970s.

Today, teaching and research in the marxist tradition of thought have a firm (but neither dominant nor secure) place in the scientific pluralism of West German universities and research institutes[137] (irrespective of the number of their variants and the intensity of the controversies between one another).

(i) The Theory of State-Monopolistic Capitalism

This approach, for which the abbreviation 'stamocap' theory has established itself, was introduced to the West German discussion[138] from the socialist countries via the German Democratic Republic, mainly by the supporters of the (West) German Communist Party (Deutsche Kommunistische Partei — DKP). Although it does not have a commanding position in West German international relations studies, it nevertheless influenced the discussion with respect to, firstly, the development of the theory of imperialism and, secondly, with respect to the explanation of the military-industrial complex. In contrast to the position of the armaments critics sketched in the previous section, stamocap theory maintains that an already fully developed military-industrial complex exists in the highly armed FRG as a consequence of the direct or indirect instrumentalization of the political and military state apparatus in the interests of the monopolistic armaments industry.[139] This thesis met with resistance and some of the critics developed a variant which attempts to explain the armaments policy of the Federal Government from the perspective of 'state theory'.[140]

(j) Structural Dependency and Peripheral Capitalism

Early theoretical research on development was characterized by research on developing countries (modeled on modernization theory and its idealization of Western industrial society) of the type introduced in Freiburg and Hamburg.[141] The *dependencia* theories — the bourgeois-nationalist as well as the marxist versions — were created in Latin America as a reaction to the evident failure of the modernization strategies.[142] Their common denominator is the basic thesis that political domination and economic exploitation by the industrial societies resulted in such a disintegration and deformation of the social structures of the peripheral countries that specific social forms, heterogenous production structures and marginalizations were created, which, subjected to capitalist modernization through aid and capital inflows, increase underdevelopment and structurally consolidate dependency on the industrial metropoles. The *dependencia* theories were mainly introduced to the FRG through Dieter Senghaas[143] and they have decidedly influenced research on development problems (especially in Frankfurt, Berlin, Hamburg, Bremen, Goettingen and at the Max Planck Institute in Starnberg).[144] The implications of the diagnosis of the *dependencia* theoreticians culminate in the demand for a politically self-reliant development oriented towards internal economic needs and not towards those of the metropoles. (That is why questions of agrarian development play an increasingly important part in the discussion.) Correspondingly, Senghaas pleads for a strategy of at least selective dissociation.[145]

At any rate, two basic groups of problems are relevant for the transformation of peripheral societies. Firstly, there is the group of questions concerning the function of the state in developing societies, its relationship with the social classes and its margins of action. However, the discussions in this direction in West Germany are relatively new and have not yet ripened into a theory of the peripheral state.[146] Secondly, a precise examination of the structure and tendencies of the international division of labor, including the role of the multinational corporations and the conditions of the New International Economic order, is needed; in this field some research contributions have already been published.[147]

However, the concepts and premises of the *dependencia* theories have of late been under attack. The observation of certain trends in the socio-economic development of some Latin American countries, as for example Brazil or Columbia, have led to the thesis of the permanent nature of the 'development of underdevelopment' (Andre Gunder Frank), which would imply the impossibility of development under conditions of structural dependency (except for sectorally limited, 'distorted' forms), being seriously questioned. Ongoing conceptual debates and empirical studies are reviewing the history of the Western capitalist industrial societies (especially the presently highly developed ones peripheral to the 'giants') with the aim of eventually finding structural similarities with which the question can be answered as to whether there is anything inherently different in peripheral capitalism. The alternatives here seem to lie between the conceptualization of a theory of dependent development and the (re-)validation of the original marxian law of capitalization (i.e. the unavoidable historical tendency in bourgeois societies towards the subsumption of all social relations under capitalist relations of production and the consequent homogenization of economic and social structures in the whole world — including economically backward societies but excluding the socialist ones). At least at the descriptive level, elements of this discussion about adequate theory building seem to have a lot in common with the modernization concepts of the 1950s and early 1960s, though not at the level of theoretical categories, political judgements and practical conclusions. Considerations of this kind have stimulated research projects (e.g. of Dieter Senghaas, now at Bremen) on the conditions under which European countries like Denmark or Belgium, for example, developed in spite of strong dependencies.

(k) International Transfer of Value and the Movement of Capital in the World Market — Neo-Marxist Imperialism Theory

Approaches to the explanation of underdevelopment have also been influenced by French research contributions (Samir Amin, Arghiri Emmanuel, Pierre Jalée and Christian Palloix), which mainly trace back underdevelopment to open or concealed value transfer from the Third to the First World by way of the 'unequal exchange' between them. Whereas the *dependencia* theories concentrate on the internal consequences of dependency from the viewpoint of the periphery, the French school handles the intersocietal correlation from the viewpoint of the metropoles.

The scientific controversies with this 'school',[148] on the one hand, and with leninist imperialism theory respectively with stamocap theory, on the other,[149] have resulted in the crystallization of an imperialism-theoretic direction in West Germany which takes recourse to the original categories and methods of Marx' *Critique of Political Economy*. It postulates that the marxian law of value, his theory of accumulation of capital and of the tendential fall in the profit rate are generally valid and should therefore also apply to the capitalist world market (which Marx did not analyse). The representatives of this approach[150] are studying (to date more theoretically than empirically) the mechanisms of how the law of value operates in the world market; they maintain that it does operate, but with modifications which they locate in the mechanism of changes in the exchange rate and in administratively imposed tariff and trade restrictions. As these manipulations represent acts of state, the question of the function of the state in capitalism and its relation to multinational corporations and to modern and backward capital fractions again poses itself. Although this question has been raised, it has not yet been systematically analyzed. This approach remains very economistic and is closer to liberal national economics in the tradition of free trade philosophy or interventionism than, for example, to *dependencia* research. Specific social formations in the peripheries are not taken into account at all.

(l) Internationalization of Capital and Labor

This is less a definite theoretical-methodological approach than a field of research in which different orientations can be observed — systems-immanent as well as systems-critical. The former is mainly located in the sphere of liberal economics;[151] the latter we have already outlined in the context of the history of IPS and the reception of both *dependencia* and neo-marxist imperialism theories and their application in studies on multinational corporations.[152] The studies on the internationalization of labor and on the international migration of labor[153] as well as those on the international trade union movement[154] can be more or less viewed as belonging to the 'critical' category.

Little attention has up to now been paid to international capital markets and their political consequences as have been studied in the case of the Euromoney market and the financing of US investments in Europe.[155]

The noticeable lack of research work on European integration is even more obvious with regard to politico-economic studies. However, a research potential in the area of the internationalization of capital and labor within the Western European framework has started to develop around Frank Deppe (Marburg).[156]

An intermediate position between the kind of integration research mentioned above and the critical orientation being outlined here is taken up by the studies of Hanns-Dieter Jacobsen on the economic relations between East and West.[157]

(m) Beginnings of a Critical Theory of 'Real Socialism'

Societal studies of the socialist Soviet and East European societies with respect to their external relations are still very much in their early stages. Firstly, traditional East European history which, in the last few years, has adopted a more social-historical orientation, and the anti-communist 'East-research' (*Ostforschung*) rooted in the years of the cold war, as well as the above-mentioned totalitarianism research, at first predominated in West Germany. Secondly, as is well known, access to information on socialist societies is limited. Thirdly, a certain foundation of socially critical politico-economic approaches had first to develop in West Germany; these could then stimulate fresh questions for the assessment of socialist societies. Fourthly, appropriate analytical categories, problem formulations and hypotheses are necessary, which neither derive from the justificatory Western bourgeois or socialist doctrines, nor can directly and simply be transferred from the theories on the *Critique of Political Economy* for the analysis of socialist countries. First attempts in this direction have been formulated.[158]

(n) Politico-Economic Structural History of the World Society

As already mentioned, Krippendorff and Elsenhans have initiated an approach which grasps the international system as a product of its societal history and aspires towards a comprehensive macro-theory of world society.[159] It is no coincidence that one can observe such attempts being made simultaneously in different parts of the world independently of one another.[160] In contrast to the Popperian postulate for a piecemeal strategy of research and to the neo-positivist criticism of 'historicism', they are taking up the tradition of the social history of capitalism as developed especially in England (Dobb, Landes, Hobsbawm and others). The point of departure of this approach is that current international situations and tendencies like underdevelopment, military systems, war, world economic crises, integration processes, etc., cannot be grasped without taking into account the laws of the birth, development and the expansion of capitalism in its different phases, each determined by respective internal social crises and uneven international development — phases reaching as far back as the middle ages and the age of inventions. The broad scope of this approach makes possible the construction of a framework with the following characteristics:

1. It allows an integration of the different research areas of international relations, including the intranational determinants of foreign policy.

2. It avoids both one-sided politicism as well as economism and instead concentrates on the relations between different social dimensions.

3. It makes the historically determined relations and differences in development of the different states or societies and between constellations in different epochs visible. It hence allows a structuring of the very complex world with categories developed from the growth of the structures themselves instead of a straightjacketing into isolated 'external' and hence seemingly fitting categories, i.e. it prevents ahistoric theory building.

4. It is better suited to counteract short term technocratic frog-in-the-well policies.

In this direction no conception has yet been achieved which could be described as being sufficiently stringent (especially considering that the world of the socialist states has not been accorded the necessary attention up to now). There are more questions than there are answers — questions, however, which lead to the recognition of the outlines of a yet embryonic historical world society perspective.[161]

(o) Theory of State Functions

One of the wider gaps in the discussion in international relations is that the theory of the functions of the state in capitalism (hereinafter 'state theory') has hardly been concretized for external policies. The urgent need for such a theory, as has already been mentioned, arises out of its indispensability for various research areas and for problem-solving in different theoretical and methodological directions. Two questions which crystallized in the discussion of internal politics are important in this context:

1. How can the fact that it is possible for the state of a capitalist society to be a 'social state' (*Sozialstaat*), e.g. the Federal Republic of Germany, be explained?

2. What explains the reform aspirations and planning attempts of the social-liberal Federal Government in Germany and their partial failure?

These questions led to a lively, partly subtle and esoteric discussion[162] on an hitherto widely neglected aspect of marxian theory. It is difficult to find a common denominator among the different attempts to deduce the functions of the state from the principles of capitalist accumulation. However, there is wide agreement on the functions which the state of a capitalist society takes over or which are handed over to it, namely creating and securing

1. the framework of a legal and constitutional order;

2. the general conditions for production, also in specific branches (infrastructure, securing raw materials supply, etc.);

3. as far as possible, conditions for the accumulation of capital free of disturbances (policy relating to economic trends, subsidies, foreign aid, etc.);

4. the reproduction and qualification of labor (social insurance, the educational system, professional training, etc.);

5. mass loyalty (legitimation, elections, etc.); and

6. if necessary, the use of repressive measures to secure the system and its rule internally (police, etc.) and externally (defence forces).

One can argue about the details of classification but more important — apart from the problem of how these functions came historically to assert themselves — is the question of which contradictions between which different functions arise under which conditions? Which contradictions can arise between the capitalist necessity for such functions on the one hand and the capitalist endeavor to surrender as little as possible in taxes necessary for the realization of the functions? Which of the policies are multifunctional (e.g. armament policies for defence, employment and technology)? How does the state become aware of its functions, how does it institutionalize them and how does it master its structural information deficit? etc.

For the purposes of foreign and international politics this discussion has hardly made any advances to speak of, let alone with respect to a theory of the internationalization of the functions of the state corresponding to the internationalization of capital and labor. An important step in this direction can be expected from the forthcoming book on the World Bank by Rainer Tetzlaff (Hamburg). The construction of theory in this direction could also form the basis for the necessary attempt to overcome the senseless division between the political subdisciplines of 'international relations', 'internal politics', 'comparative government' and 'political philosophy'.

Further serious deficits in the West German discussion on international relations, among others, exist for:

— a comprehensive political-economic analysis of West German foreign policies;

— a social psychology of international relations related to the politico-economic perspective;[163]

— a social-historically and politico-economically oriented framework for the comparative analysis of the causes of war;

— a critical exposure of ideologies in the history of the theories of international relations[164] and international law; and

— operationalizations of concepts and statements in the framework of a critical societal theory which can also be used for exact empirical research.

NOTES

This paper was translated from the German by Sujon Chanda, Hamburg; the authors are thankful for the revision of the translation by G. Glenswick, London, and for the help of Ekkehart Krippendorff and Volker Rittberger. The manuscript was completed by the authors in October 1978.

1. For an example of this approach see Wolfgang Abendroth, 'International Relations und Aussenpolitik als Teildisziplinen der politischen Wissenschaft', in: J. Mueck (ed.), *Internationale Politik, Vol. 4, Bad Wildunger Beitraege zur Gemeinschaftskunde*, Wiesbaden 1970, pp. 357-363. A substantive exploration of this approach is attempted by Ekkehart Krippendorff, *Internationales System als Geschichte*, Frankfurt/New York 1975, and *Internationale Beziehungen als Wissenschaft*, Frankfurt/New York 1977; Hartmut Elsenhans, *Geschichte und Oekonomie der europaeischen Welteroberung*, Frankfurt/New York (in print).

2. Cf. Georg Simonis, *Aussenpolitik und Abschreckung. Ansaetze zu einer kritischen Theorie des internationalen Systems*, Frankfurt/New York 1977, pp. 267ff, further cf. Abendroth, op. cit. note 1 and Rainer Rotermundt, Ursula Schmiederer and Helmut Becker-Panitz: *Entspannung, Systemkonkurrenz und 'realer Sozialismus'*, Nuernberg/Osnabrueck 1977, pp. 11ff.

3. Cf. Krippendorff, op. cit. note 1 (1977), Ch. V., pp. 68ff and ibid, 'Staatliche Organisation und Krieg', in: Dieter Senghaas (ed.). *Friedensforschung und Gesellschaftskritik*, München 1970, pp. 23-38.

4. With respect to broadening metropolitan perspectives of the study of international relations cf. Arthouros-David Calamaros, *Internationale Beziehungen. Theorien — Kritik — Perspektiven*, Stuttgart 1974, pp. 18ff; Kurt P. Tudyka, *Internationale Beziehungen. Eine Einfuehrung*, Stuttgart 1971, pp. 7ff, stresses the North American character of the discipline in this context.

5. Wolf-Dieter Narr, 'Entwicklung der Politologie — Entwicklung der Gesellschaft', in: *Koelner Zeitschrift fuer Soziologie und Sozialpsychologie*, Vol. 22, 1970, pp. 98-120, hence speaks of a 'didactic "helping science" for political integration' (p. 99).

6. Cf. Hans Maier, *Die aeltere deutsche Staats- und Verwaltungslehre (Polizeiwissenschaft). Ein Beitrag zur Geschichte der politischen Wissenschaft in Deutschland*, Neuwied/Berlin 1966. Bernd Wunder, 'Die Entstehung des modernen Staates und des Berufsbeamtentums in Deutschland im fruehen 19. Jahrhundert', in: *Leviathan*, Vol. 2, 1974, pp. 459-478, develops a thesis, which is important in this context, that the reform of the state apparatus preceded socio-economic changes in Germany, thereby contributing to securing the absolutist state in the bourgeois society which was in the making. Hans Kastendiek, *Die Entwicklung der westdeutschen Politikwissenschaft*, Frankfurt/New York 1977, illustrates the affirmation of the authority of state rule with its tendencies of depoliticization with the example of the positivist theory of public law (pp. 76ff); see also Peter von Oertzen, *Die soziale Funktion des staatsrechtlichen Positivismus. Eine wissenssoziologische Studie ueber die Entstehung des formalistischen Positivismus in der deutschen Staatsrechtswissenschaft*, Frankfurt 1974.

7. Abendroth, op. cit. note 1, p. 14f. Otto Kimminich, 'Die Disziplin der Interna-

tionalen Beziehungen an den Hochschulen der Bundesrepublik Deutschland', in: *Voelkerrecht und Aussenpolitik*, Vol. 16, 1972, pp. 22-53, calculated (on the basis of the lecture registers between the winter semester 1945/46 and the summer semester 1968) that the discipline was dominated in this period mainly by historians, lawyers and economists and that only a third of the lectures on international politics in 1968 were formally conducted within the framework of the academic discipline of political science (p. 36f and the appendix tables).

8. The following report should *not* be understood as an attempt at redeeming the claims, which, to our mind, are necessary and briefly outlined in our introduction. It is nothing more than a not necessarily complete material collection. In the process of the collection we became aware of the important desideration of a politically, historically and theoretically reflected history of the international relations discipline of the kind formulated e.g. by Hans Kastendiek for the development of West German political science (op. cit. note 6). In this sense this report is a kind of methodological foreword and can be considered to anticipate a future, more thorough study.

9. On this point and on the subsequent development of the discipline, especially in the USA, cf. Ernst-Otto Czempiel, 'Die Entwicklung der Lehre von den Internationalen Beziehungen', in: *Politische Vierteljahresschrift*, Vol. 6, pp. 270-290 (here: p. 275f).

10. Cf. Albrecht Mendelssohn-Bartholdy, 'Institut fuer Auswaertige Politik, Hamburg', in: Ludolf Brauer et al. (eds.), *Forschungsinstitute, ihre Geschichte, Organisation und Ziele*, Vol. 1, Hamburg 1930, pp. 332-346. The Institute for Foreign Affairs functioned as described here until 1933. The Nazi reshuffle took place under the direction of Friedrich Berber, who, from a lecturer at the DHfP in Berlin rose to the rank of an adviser to Ribbentrop. Berber included the Hamburg Institute in his concentration of foreign policy 'research' in Berlin, to where it was transferred in 1937. It there became reduced to the status of an appendage of the German Foreign Ministry, its publications being used in the service of anti-English and anti-French propaganda. In 1946 the remnants of the library and the archive for newspaper cuttings (started in 1923) were brought back to Hamburg. In 1947 the Research Center for International Law and Foreign Public Law in Hamburg was delegated the responsibility of managing the affairs of the former Institute for Foreign Affairs. Cf. Carla Raabe, *Das Institut fuer Auswaertige Politik. Seine Geschichte und Bibliothek*, Koeln 1950 (cyclostyled manuscript). Within this new organizational framework the establishment of one permanent scientific post was granted in 1957. In 1973 both instititions were merged into the Institute for International Affairs and affiliated to the Faculties of Law and of Social Sciences of the University of Hamburg.

The choice of Hamburg as the geographical location for the former Institute for Foreign Affairs must itself be viewed in a certain context of practical interests. The local commercial capital was especially interested in research on external and world politics. In nearby Kiel the Institute for World Economy and Marine Transport had been in existence since 1911, the Colonial Institute in Hamburg, out of which the university developed (a circumstance which was by no means a coincidence), since 1908. Over and above, the founding of the Universities of Frankfurt (1914), Cologne (1919) and Hamburg (also 1919) is to be seen in connection with reform aspirations towards a more practical oriented research and education, especially for the natural, the economic and the social sciences as well for medicine. Cf. Hans Kastendiek, op. cit. note 6, pp. 95ff, 109f and Fritz K. Ringer, *The Decline of German Mandarins. The German Academic Community 1890-1933,* Cambridge, Mass. 1969.

11. For example the institute promoted multi-volume publication projects like the *Handbuch der Politik* (edited by Gerhard Anschuetz, Max Lenz and others), the *Handbuch des Abruestungsproblems* (edited by Th. Niemeyer on behalf of the German Research Committee for Questions of Securing Peace), the *Wirtschafts- und Sozialgeschichte des Weltkrieges* (edited by James T. Shotwell as a publication of the Carnegie Foundation), and the collection of documents 'Die Grosse Politik der Europaeischen Kabinette 1871-1914', Berlin 1926. A complete publication list may be found in Raabe, op. cit. note 10, appendix 3.

The journal *Europaeische Gespraeche* appeared between 1923 and 1934; the publication series *Politische Wissenschaft* was a joint venture together with the Deutsche Hochschule fuer Politik and appeared from 1927. Under Nazi rule these publications were replaced by the *Hamburger Monatshefte fuer Auswaertige Politik* and the *Schriften des Instituts fuer Aussenpolitische Forschung und des Hamburger Instituts fuer Auswaertige Politik*. The charter of foundation of the Institute for Foreign Affairs in Hamburg described its purpose as being 'the scientific observation and recording of the political and economic forces determining the foreign politics of states and — through the study of history — the finding out of the regularities governing interstate relations with a view to providing a training in foreign policy' (Raabe, op. cit., p. 4).

12. The foundation of the DHfP outside the university was not only the result of a specific educational 'school for citizenship' concept but was also due to the massive resistance of the universities to a 'political' science embodying the republican, liberal-democratic opposition against an outmoded educational ideal. Cf. Kastendiek, op. cit. note 6, pp. 107-116; on the importance of the DHfP for the subsequent establishment of political science in general cf. pp. 117-140.

The percentage figures for the financing of the DHfP: 20% from the government of the Reich and of Prussia and 80% 'from democratic friends and promoters' (the largest share coming from the South German liberal industrialist Robert Bosch), as well as from the Carnegie and Rockefeller Foundations, are cited by the founder of the DHfP, Ernst Jaeckh in: 'Die "alte" Hoschschule fuer Politik, 1920-1933', in: Ernst Jaeckh and Otto Suhr, *Geschichte der Deutschen Hochschule fuer Politik*, Berlin 1952, p. 15.

13. Thanks to Becker's initiative a memorandum on the promotion of foreign studies at Prussian universities and high schools was presented to the Prussian parliament as early as 1917. In this connection the Institute for World Economy and Marine Transport in Kiel experienced a rapid upswing. At the same time several new institutions came into being: the Institute for East German Economy (Koenigsberg), the Institute for Eastern Europe (Breslau), the Nordic Institute (Greifswald), the Institute for Germans Living in Border Areas and Abroad (Marburg), and the courses in languages and culture which were organized by the Advisory Council for Foreign Studies.

> Under the immediate influence of the First World War the principle came to be formulated that in a great, important society knowledge about external affairs and foreign countries not only represented the tools for diplomats and others occupied with German interests abroad but were also an indispensable part of national education. And the then Ministerial Director Becker certainly had the lack of political acumen of our people, who were taken by surprise by the outbreak of the war, in his mind when he described 'the raising of our educational standard in foreign matters', for which less had been done up to then for the natural sciences and for vocational training, as being one of the most urgent tasks of Prussian educational policy.

Cf. Becker's contemporary, Walther Schotte, *Weltpolitik als Wissenschaft. Die Weltpolitische Bildungsarbeit an Preussischen Hochschulen. Festschrift aus Anlass des 50. Geburtstages des Preussischen Ministers Prof. C. H. Becker*, Berlin 1926, pp. 182-240 (here p. 183). Creating a parallel to the Paris Ecole Libre had been considered since 1914 and was presented in the Prussian parliament by the national-liberals in 1917.

14. Thus described by Jaeckh, op. cit. note 12, p. 18, whereas Kastendiek, op. cit. note 6, p. 137, calls it 'Foreign Politics and International Law'; it was called 'Foreign Studies' from 1932, when Otto Hoetzsch took over the study group. Kastendiek names another department not mentioned by Jaeckh, which was dissolved in 1932: 'Political Psychology and Foreign Studies', which was directed by Wilhelm Haas. These institutional names are not irrelevant with respect to the derivation of a theory of international relations and to its own understanding.

15. Anong the lecturers were Charles Beard, G. P. Gooch, James Shotwell, Nicholas Murray, Henri Lichtenberger, William Rappard, André Siegfried, Ernst Robert Curtius, Francesco Ruffini, Thaddaeus Zielinski. Cf. Czempiel, op. cit. note 9, p. 276.

16. The term 'peace science' seems to have appeared for the first time in Germany in this particular context. The academy was to (1) publish international research findings 'on the possibilities of creating a just, peaceful order in international politics'; (2) 'work at educating' students and public officials; (3) propagate 'the different opinions on the concept of world peace among as large a public as possible', 'especially by conducting international conferences, in which farsighted participants with good will and creative energy would discuss thoroughly the important questions pertinent to the development of international peace and thus prepare and ease the tasks of "statesmen".' (Jaeckh, op. cit. note 12, p. 20.)

17. John Hobson, *Imperialism*, London 1902; Rudolf Hilferding, *Das Finanzkapital. Eine Studie ueber die juengste Entwicklung des Kapitalismus*, Berlin 1910. (As a lecturer of the DHfP as well as sometime finance minister of the Weimar Republic, Hilferding may have had a similarly pluralistic 'fig leaf' function as had, decades later, Wolfgang Abendroth in West German political science.) Rosa Luxemburg, *Die Akkumulation des Kapitals. Ein Beitrag zur oekonomischenErklaerung des Kapitalismus*, Berlin 1912; Karl Kautsky, *Nationalstaat, imperialistischer Staat und Staatenbund*, Nuernberg 1915; W. I. Lenin, *Der Imperialismus als hoechstes Stadium des Kapitalismus*, Berlin 1917. One of the early bourgeois scientists who took note of and criticized imperialism theory (from the viewpoint of the 'Geopolitical School') was Adolf Grabowsky, *Deutschland und das Weltbild der Gegenwart*, Berlin 1928. Grabowsky was co-editor of the *Zeitschrift fuer Politik*, which first appeared in 1907, lecturer at the DHfP and, in 1923, founder of the geopolitical seminar of the DHfP. A short review of the reaction of bourgeois science to the theories of imperialism is given by Ekkehart Krippendorff, 'Zum Imperialismus-Begriff', in ibid. (ed.), *Probleme der Internationalen Beziehungen*, Frankfurt 1972, pp. 177-203 (especially pp. 182ff).

18. So the first director of the DHfP, Theodor Heuss, 'Deutsche Hochschule fuer Politik', in: Schott, op. cit. note 13, pp. 155-164 (here p. 156). Cf. also the charter of foundation of the Institute for Foreign Affairs (note 11) and the quotation of Schotte (note 13).

Considering the naivety with which political science here started operating under practical circumstances, which were not at all reflected in its teaching, one must especially take the North American origins, which were a model for this discipline, into account. From the very beginnings of the existence of the United States of America, politics and the sciences were correlated to each other in a naturally positive process of give and take. From the times of the founding fathers of the federation right down to the advisers of present-day presidents, intellectuals cannot be thought of as divorced from the practical politics of the USA. Cf. Ekkehart Krippendorff, 'Profil einer Disziplin. Versuch ueber Herkunft und Stand der Politischen Wissenschaft in den Vereinigten Staaten', in: *Politische Vierteljahresschrift*, Vol. 6, 1965, pp. 184-204. This relationship cannot, of course, be compared to Germany, where the origins and development of the sciences — and specially the social sciences — were determined by their role in the shadow of political power. While, on the one hand, the belief in the instrumental nature of reason, evolved out of concrete historical experience, asserted itself in the USA (Man as the maker of his destiny!), on the other hand conceptions of social order politically legitimized by 'laws of God or nature' predominated in Germany: cf. Ralf Dahrendorf, *Die angewandte Aufklaerung. Gesellschaft und Soziologie in Amerika*, Muenchen 1963, pp. 24ff, and Hannah Arendt, *Vita activa oder vom taetigen Leben*, Stuttgart 1960, Ch. 4, pp. 124ff.

We have not dealt with the eminently practical impetus of the peace movement — again primarily American in origin. Although it provided important impulses for the founders and promoters of international relations in Germany, nevertheless its voice was at first not heard beyond some educated circles. Cf. Paul Noack, *Friedensforschung — ein Signal der Hoffnung?*, Freudenstadt 1970, pp. 45ff.

19. Cf. Kastendiek, op. cit. note 6, pp. 76-93; Herbert Doering, *Der Weimarer Kreis. Studien zum Bewusstsein verfassungstreuer Hochschullehrer in der Weimarer Republik*, Meisenheim 1975; as well as Franz Neumann, 'Die Wissenschaft der Politik in der Demokratie', in: Heinrich Schneider (ed.), *Aufgabe und Selbstverstaendnis der Politischen Wissenschaft*, Darmstadt 1967, pp. 20-40 (here: pp. 21ff).

20. Schotte, op. cit. note 13, pp. 184f, 187f.

21. In the German Federal Parliament (Bundestag) 55% of the 518 members between 1969-1972 held an academic degree: cf. Thomas Ellwein, *Das Regierungssystem der Bundesrepublik Deutschland*, Opladen 1973^3, p. 683. Nearly one-third of the present members elected in 1976 hold doctoral degrees. The distribution figures for the numbers of academics each party has in the Bundestag are as follows: CDU — 73%; CSU — 70%; FDP — 65%; and SPD — 52%. Sociologists and political scientists are a small minority within this group: CDU — 9%; CSU — 5%; FDP — 1.5%; and SPD — 11%. Members of the legal profession dominate numerically in all parties. Cf. Ulrich Lohmar, 'Die sechs Schlagseiten des neuen Bundestages', in: *Der Spiegel*, No. 43, October 1976, p. 52. The ranks of the higher civil service are in nearly all cases only open to university degree holders and the diplomatic and consular services have no exceptions to this rule.

22. Waldemar Besson, 'Bonn auf dem Pruefstand. Chancen westdeutscher Aussenpolitik', in: *Der Monat*, Vol. 21, 1969, pp. 453 and 48.

23. This aspect was brought to our attention by Ekkehart Krippendorff.

24. This is reflected in the institutionalized division of the discipline of political science in the FRG into the traditional fields of political theory (methods, history of political ideas, political philosophy), systems of public administration (internal politics, domestic politics of the FRG, comparative government) and international politics (including the politics of development). This division of political science — realized by the DHfP at an early date — was formally made a part of the academic 'language' by the Conference of Waldleiningen and it still dominates the universities in institutional terms, although it is continuously becoming less relevant for research. Cf. Kastendiek, op. cit. note 6, pp. 177.

25. Hans Maier, 'Zur Situation der Politischen Wissenschaft in Deutschland', in *Zeitschrift fuer Politik*, New Series, Supplement 12, 1965, pp. 201-223. Twenty-five per-

sonalities from the sciences, politics and journalism were interviewed; thirteen replied and only Iring Fetscher, Karl Loewenstein, Felix Messerschmid and Mohammed Rassem emphasized the importance of international politics. In 1963 O. H. von der Gablentz felt 'the knowledge and the presentation of foreign affairs and countries to be the weakest point of German political science' ('Politische Forschung in Deutschland', in: Otto Stammer (ed.), *Politische Forschung, Beitraege zum zehnjaehrigen Bestehen des Instituts fuer politische Wissenschaft,* Koeln/Opladen 1963, p. 171). Even in 1967 the assessment of Rudolf Wildenmann, that West German political science had not produced any research worth mentioning on problems of international relations and on problems of war and peace, was still valid ('Politologie in Deutschland', in: *Der Politologe,* No. 23, 1967, pp. 13-23).

26. Our data on the quantitative development of teaching personnel were collected from the material of the German Political Science Association (GPSA) by Barbara Sindermann. However, the figures are based mainly on voluntary information and not on systematically collected statistics. They are therefore neither complete nor fully reliable. However, at the moment better data are not available. According to the figures the total number of permanent teaching posts in political science in the winter semester of 1977/78 at the forty-three universities, integrated university colleges (*Gesamthochschule*) and polytechnics, two colleges of the armed forces (*Bundeswehrhochschule*) and at the nineteen otherwise not integrated teaching colleges of the FRG and West Berlin is 397. However, for the field of international politics only sixteen posts of H4 (full professor/ordinary chair) or equivalent status, eight H3 or equivalent posts (extraordinary or associate professor, scientific counsellor), and six H2 posts or their equivalent (academic counsellor, partly with a professor title; lecturer/reader) have been institutionalized up to now. The posts of scientific assistants and assistant professors, which are temporary posts running for a period of up to six-eight years maximum, have not been considered here. Looking at the figures solely from the institutionalized job descriptions one can compute a percentage of less than 7.6 among all permanent posts for political science devoted specifically to international politics. On the other hand the formal degree of institutionalization does not give a true picture of the position because, firstly, the filling of posts which have become vacant sometimes changes their thematic categorization, and secondly, because very many posts are still not specialized and their categorization is dependent on who holds the posts.

27. Lectures and seminars on international politics were at first held sporadically by historians, economists and lawyers and from the 1950s more by the holders of the newly established posts in political science (who, however, were not themselves trained political scientists in the first generation). Cf. Otto Kimminich, op. cit. note 7, p. 29 and the tables in the appendix.

28. The resolution on the reestablishment of the DHfP was passed by the West Berlin representative assembly in March 1948 in commemoration of the 1848 revolution, and the opening took place during the Berlin blockade in 1949. Cf. the report of the first director of the newly founded DHfP, Otto Suhr, 'Drei Jahre Deutsche Hochschule fuer Politik', in Jaeckh and Suhr, op. cit. note 12, pp. 33-48. For an analysis cf. Kastendiek, op. cit. note 6, pp. 167ff.

29. The DHfP hoped to attract, for example, functionaries of political parties and professional associations, trade unionists, civil servants, journalists, teachers; but also those who had been soldiers in the war and had therefore been unable to complete their higher education or professional training. The nearly simultaneous founding of the College for Labor, Politics and Economy (Hochschule fuer Arbeit, Politik und Wirtschaft) in Wilhelmshaven and the College for Political Science (Hochschule fuer Politische

Wissenschaft) in Munich are to be seen in a similar context. These academic courses concentrating on politics were perhaps initially considered to reinforce the College for Administrative Sciences (Hochschule fuer Verwaltungswissenschaften) founded in Speyer in 1947.

30. The DHfP was converted into the multi-faculty Otto Suhr Institute, whose organizational development is sketched by Gert von Eynern, 'Das Experiment des Otto-Suhr-Instituts', in: *Politische Vierteljahresschrift*, Vol. 9, 1968, pp. 644-650. Cf. also Kastendiek, op. cit. note 6, pp. 180ff.

31. These circles were associated with the periodical *Das sozialistische Jahrhundert*; cf. Kastendiek, op. cit. note 6, p. 168f. Cf., on the other hand, the more precise conceptualization in the political analysis of the social democrats, in which the development of a stringent theory of society is prevented by their retention of the division between state and society; ibid., pp. 195ff and 227ff. Cf. lastly the influence of the primarily Anglo-Saxon emigration experiences of many of the social scientists associated with the rebuilding of the DHfP and the Free University of Berlin, resulting in a divergence from their original historical-dialectical perspectives and socialist postulates; ibid., pp. 146ff, 220ff.

32. During the incorporation of the DHfP into the FU, ten chairs for political science were installed — divided among the faculties of philosophy, economics and law. The DHfP department of external politics and foreign studies (*Aussenpolitik und Auslandskunde*), in existence since 1949, was taken over by the Otto Suhr Institute as one of their seven departments and in 1953 integrated into the FU as the chair for the Theory and History of Foreign Politics (*Theorie und Geschichte der Auswaertigen Politik*), the first full professorship for international politics at any German university. The eleventh chair for political science, the second for international politics, was established in 1961. Until a few years ago both these chairs were decisively influenced by the work of their holders, Richard Loewenthal and Gilbert Ziebura.

33. The information on this point shows discrepancies. Czempiel counts four professorships for international relations in the FRG as early as 1964 (see his article 'Internationale Beziehungen', in: Goerres-Gesellschaft (ed.), *Staatslexicon, 1968*,[6] p. 366); apart from the two Berlin chairs he probably includes the two chairs for international law at the Universities of Wuerzburg and Regensburg, whose holders (von der Heydte, from 1951; and Kimminich, from 1963) were in addition entrusted with the teaching of international relations. Kimminich, op. cit. note 7, p. 24 quotes the 1968 universities register issued by the Association of Professors (Hochschulverband) in support of his statement that the chair established in 1967 in Munich (Kindermann) was the first for international relations in the federal territory of West Germany (excluding Berlin). On the basis of the GPSA lists which we have used we have come to the conclusion that the first political science chair in international relations in the *federal territory* of West Germany was installed in 1966 in Marburg and was held by Ernst-Otto Czempiel until 1970.

34. All figures on the basis of GPSA material (cf. note 26).

35. Berlin: 62 of 271 courses; Frankfurt: 25 of 271 courses. See Arno Mohr, 'Anfaenge einer materialen Analyse der (west)-deutschen Politikwissenschaft. Dargestellt an den Determinanten der Institutionalisierung und Lehre', MA thesis at the Phil.-Hist. Faculty of the University of Heidelberg, 1977 (mimeographed manuscript).

36. Otto Kimminich, op. cit. note 7, p. 27 differentiates the courses according to the following categories: (1) theory of international relations; (2) foreign policy; (3) European integration; (4) international cooperation; (5) development aid; and (6) sundries (international relations, etc.). However, we can only make limited use of Kimminich's data because

he firstly includes courses in the faculties of history, economics and law and does not limit himself to political science, and secondly, his study begins in 1946, at a time when political science was not even institutionalized, let alone international relations. One of his primary aims, of course, is to demonstrate how slowly political science started to 'take over' the teaching of international relations from the disciplines of law, history and economics. Thirdly, his report, and hence his data collection, follows theoretical criteria and perspectives different to ours.

36a. For more details Cf. section 4 below.

37. The organization and research work of these institutions is sketched by Gebhard Schweigler, 'Contemporary International Studies in the Federal Republic of Germany', Bonn 1975, pp. 1, 23ff, 27, 34, 31ff. One of the most wide-ranging projects (world model research) was started in 1977 by Karl W. Deutsch at the Institute for Comparative Social Research (Institut fuer Vergleichende Gesellschaftsforschung) of the Berlin Science Center (Wissenschaftszentrum Berlin).

38. Mario Rainer Lepsius, *Denkschrift zur Lage der Soziologie und der Politischen Wissenschaft*, Wiesbaden 1961, p. 19. For a comprehensive context cf. also Wunder, op. cit. note 6 and Kastendiek, op. cit. note 6, parts II, III, IV.

39. Eugen Kogon, 'Die Lage der Politischen Wissenschaft in der Bundesrepublik Deutschland', lecture opening the 1969 annual conference of GPSA, in: 'Problem der Demokratie heute', Special issue of the *Politische Vierteljahresschrift*, Opladen 1971, pp. vii-xx (here: p. viii).

40. The complete records of the conferences in Waldleiningen and Koenigstein were unfortunately not accessible during the preparation of this paper; we therefore quote from Kastendiek, op. cit. note 6, p. 177 (our italics).

41. Note here the first use of the singular instead of 'the political scienc*es*'. Quoted by Suhr, op. cit. note 29, p. 41.

42. For the history of the foundation of the GPSA in the international context see Konrad Kettig/Bloch, 'Vereinigungen fuer die Wissenschaft von der Politik', in: *Zeitschrift fuer Politik*, New Series, Vol. 1, 1954, pp. 184ff. The first governing board was composed of Alfred Weber (Heidelberg), Honorary Chairman; Alexander Ruestow (Heidelberg), Chairman; Otto Suhr (Berlin, Director of DHfP), Secretary; and the following members: Wolfgang Abendroth (Marburg), Adolf Grabowsky (Basel), Ernst Wilhelm Meyer (Wiesbaden), Erwin Stein (Offenbach, Minister of Culture of Hesse), and Georg Weippert (Erlangen). The Association for the Science of Politics, as it was called in the first years of its existence, conducted yearly and then two-yearly conferences from 1952 onwards, issued circulars on the situation in the discipline from March 1953 onwards, and issued the *Zeitschrift fuer Politik*, which was refounded by Grabowsky, between 1954 and 1959 and the *Politische Vierteljahresschrift* from 1960.

43. The figures are taken from Lepsius, op. cit. note 38, pp. 91ff.

44. The Council for the Sciences (Wissensschaftsrat) was formed in 1957 following an agreement between the federal and the state governments. Its function was to work out an overall plan for the development of the sciences, as well as yearly plans and recommendations for the distribution of finances and special grants. Cf. *Empfehlungen des Wissenschaftsrates zum Ausbau der wissenschaftlichen Einrichtungen. Part I: Wissenschaftliche Hochschulen*, Tuebingen 1960, pp. 83f, 96ff.

45. Ibid., p. 181. Cf. note 32 above for more details. With respect to the details of the

distribution of chairs in Berlin, cf. note 32 above.

46. Lepsius, op. cit. note 38, p. 25.

47. The restructuring of the classical faculties into coherent and yet more differentiated interdisciplinary departments was conceived with a view to enabling better cooperation and was pushed through more or less bureaucratically in the last few years. But this has unfortunately hardly broken down the tendency of the individual disciplines to persist in staying within their own boundaries.

48. Lepsius, op. cit. note 38, pp. 86 and 95.

49. Cf. Christian Graf von Krockow, 'Politik als praktische Wissenschaft', in: *Gesellschaft — Staat — Erziehung*, Vol. 11, pp. 84-98. Krockow speaks of 'waves' and 'thrusts' of foundings (p. 85). For an assessment of the all-round development cf. also Mohr, op. cit. note 35, pp. 43-52.

50. Located in Frankfurt, then in Bonn; Bergstraesser himself was the first institute director. Though it has close contact with government circles at the ministerial level, it is not a government institute like the Research Institute for International Politics and Security of the Foundation for Science and Politics in Ebenhausen, which was founded ten years later; rather, it understands itself to be an 'independent' mediator between theory and practice. However, a certain one-sidedness, which makes the lack of comprehensiveness of its understanding of 'practice' clear, can be observed; but we cannot go into its details here. In this connection two periodicals must also be mentioned: the *Europa-Archiv*, edited by Wilhelm Cornides, which has been the official organ of the German Society for Foreign Policy (GSFP) since its foundation in 1955 (date of first issue: 1946), and *Außenpolitik*, issued by an editorial board headed by Heinrich Bechtholdt since 1950. The GSFP Research Institute has also issued a yearly publication since 1958, *Die Internationale Politik*, which reflects the development of that particular part of the discipline which sought to combine world political interpretation with day-to-day advice on policy matters at quasi one and the same government level. Cf. also Schweigler, op. cit. note 37, p. 20.

51. Its work is concentrated on regional studies on political socialization and administration in the Third World. Cf. Schweigler, op. cit. note 37, p. 28; for a discussion of its approaches cf. Bassam Tibi, 'Die Entwicklungsländerforschung des Arnold-Bergstraesser-Instituts zu Freiburg/Br.', in: *Verfassung und Recht in Uebersee*, Vol. 5, 1972, pp. 347-351.

52. Cf. its *Mitteilungen* and the *Forschungsberichte*, issued by the PRIF since 1971, for details of the history of its foundation, of its structure and its work. Up to now PRIF has focussed on the analysis of armament dynamics in the East-West conflict and possibilities of problem solutions, including peaceful education.

53. Cf. Schweigler, op. cit. note 37, p. 21f and the institute's publications since 1977, *IFSH-Forschungsberichte* and *IFSH-Diskussionsbeiträge*. Up to now the institute's research has concentrated on European security policies.

54. Cf. Schweigler (op. cit. note 37), p. 22. Under the direction of Carl Friedrich v. Weizsaecker and Juergen Habermas projects on strategy analysis, underdevelopment and the world division of labor, crisis research, and further fundamental problems of the social and natural sciences were developed.

55. Cf. Schweigler, op. cit. note 37, p. 19f.

56. Cf. Kogon, op. cit. note 39. Regarding the social preconditions for this development in international relations cf. e.g. Wolfgang Abendroth, 'Die soziale Struktur der

Bundesrepublik und ihre politischen Entwicklungstendenzen', in: *Politische Vierteljahresschrift*, Vol. 4, 1963, pp. 150-167. For an assessment of the relevance of later developments cf. e.g., *Frankfurter Hefte, Zeitschrift für Kultur und Politik* (ed. by Walter Dirks and Eugen Kogon), Vol. 31, 1976, 4th issue: Special issue 'Bundesrepublik'.

57. This applies to many of the contributions of the time in the field of *Ostforschung* (research on socialist countries). A number of periodicals established themselves in this sector, e.g. the organ of the German Society for East European Studies, *Ostprobleme* (Bonn, since 1949, in 1969 integrated into the periodical *Osteuropa*), and *Osteuropaeische Wirtschaft* (since 1951); the journal *Hinter dem Eisernen Vorhang* (Behind the Iron Curtain) published by Free Europe Incorporated since 1955 was renamed *Osteuropaeische Rundschau* in 1965.

58. Golo Mann and Harry Pross (eds.), *Außenpolitik, Fischer-Lexicon*, Vol. 7, Frankfurt 1957. The title of the encyclopaedia is in itself revealing for the contents and the views expressed in it. The completely changed second edition, which appeared twelve years later, reflects in both title and contents the modernization the discipline underwent in this time: Karl Dieter Bracher and Ernst Fraenkel (eds.), *Internationale Beziehungen, Fischer-Lexicon*, Vol. 7, Frankfurt 1969.

59. Cf. note 13 above.

60. The new edition, however, includes 'theory' in its index; and the bibliography contains a large number of titles on the theory of international relations: cf. 'Internationale Beziehungen' (note 58).

61. The idea is aptly expressed in the term 'scientific politics'.

62. In: *Politische Vierteljahresschrift*, Vol. 1, 1960, pp. 106-119; reprinted in Heinrich Schneider (ed.), *Aufgabe und Selbstverstaendnis der Politischen Wissenschaft*, Darmstadt 1967, pp. 100-119.

63. Reprinted in Arnold Bergstraesser, *Weltpolitik als Wissenschaft*, posthumously edited by Dieter Oberndoerfer, Koeln/Opladen 1965, pp. 146-155. Another basic contribution in this collection is: 'Gedanken zu Verfahren und Aufgaben der kulturwissenschaftlichen Gegenwartsforschung' (1962), pp. 85-101.

64. Cf. Kastendiek, op. cit. note 6, pp. 252ff.

65. We cannot here attempt to give even a synopsis of the complex referred to by the term 'critical theory'. Some information on representatives and institutional history is given in note 122 below.

66. See figure 1 below.

67. Ernst-Otto Czempiel, 'Der Primat der auswaertigen Politik — Kritische Würdigung einer Staatsmaxime'; Ekkehart Krippendorff, 'Ist Außenpolitik AUßENpolitik? Ein Beitrag zur Theorie und der Versuch, eine unhaltbare Unterscheidung aufzugeben'; Karl W. Deutsch, 'Zur Theorie der Abschreckung', all three in *Politische Vierteljahresschrift*, Vol. 4, 1963, pp. 266ff, 243ff and 222ff.

68. For the foundation history of the IPS cf. GPSA circular No. 28, p. 3. The other two sections were at first also very active but they did not survive the end of the decade and dissolved into independent study groups which were bound to either limited themes or specific theoretical orientations.

69. These topics were compiled from conference programs and from circulars of the German Political Science Association.

70. Whereas the following is on record in the minutes of the conference proceedings: 'the liveliest and longest controversies were the ones on the genuineness of the Soviet-Russian wish for coexistence' (Circular of the GPSA, No. 12, November 1956, p. 11).

71. When we here and in the following use the attribute 'critical', then it is with reference to 'critical theory', Cf. notes 65 above and 122 below.

72. Cf. the reports on the 1st-4th general meetings of the IPS between 1965-1967 in Wiesneck near Freiburg: *Politische Vierteljahresschrift*, Vol. 8, 1967, pp. 162-166; on the 5th-6th meeting in Marburg 1968: ibid., Vol 9, 1968, p. 644; on the 7th meeting in Marburg 1969: ibid., Vol. 10, 1969, p. 168. The following conferences of the section were not reported in the *Politische Vierteljahresschrift*. For the 8th-18th conferences from October 1969 to October 1977 see the circulars of the GPSA as well as the prefaces to the following IPS publications:
Ernst-Otto Czempiel (ed.),
'Die anachronistische Souveraenität. Zum Verhaeltnis von Innen- und Außenpolitik', Special Issue No. 1 of the *Politische Vierteljahresschrift*, Opladen 1969.
Klaus Juergen Gantzel (ed.),
(1) 'Internationale Beziehungen als System', Special Issue No. 5 of the *Politische Vierteljahresschrift*, Opladen 1973.
(2) *Herrschaft und Befreiung in der Weltgesellschaft*, Frankfurt/New York 1975.
(3) *Kapitalistische Penetration In Europa*, Hamburg 1976.
(4) *Zur Multinationalisierung des Kapitals*, Hamburg 1976.
(5) *Afrika zwischen Kolonialismus und Neo-Kolonialismus*, Hamburg 1976.
(Nos. 3-5 appeared as independent publications of IPS.) 'Interaktionen im internationalen System', a topical issue of the *Politische Vierteljahresschrift*, Vol. 15, 1974, No. 3/4, edited under the supervision of Raimund Seidelmann.

73. Both lectures were published in: *Politische Vierteljahresschrift*, Vol. 6, 1965, pp. 465-496.

74. Cf. Dieter Senghaas, 'Horizonte einer Disziplin. Anmerkungen zur Theorie der internationalen Politik', in: *Politische Vierteljahresschrift*, Vol. 6, 1965, pp. 375-410 and 'Internationale Beziehungen: Amerikanische Beitraege zur Theorie, 1960-1966', in: *Zeitschrift fuer Politik*, Vol. 14, 1967, pp. 8-13; Klaus Juergen Gantzel, 'Eine Disziplin ohne "Disziplin"?' and Klaus Faupel, 'Die Internationale Politik im Rahmen der Sozialwissenschaften: Neuere Entwicklungen', both in: *Politische Vierteljahresschrift*, Vol. 8, 1967, pp. 167-211. Apart from these studies the collection in Ekkehart Krippendorff (ed.), *Political Science. Amerikanische Beitraege zur Politikwissenschaft*, Tuebingen 1966, also contributed to the critical reception of the 'scientific' approaches to a great extent.

75. Czempiel, op. cit. note 72.

76. During their tenure of study, research or teaching in the USA many of the young scientists had reached a critical assessment of the approaches dominating there in the social sciences.

77. For the connections between the modernization needs of the social sciences in Germany and the reform and planning aspirations of the political administration see Kastendiek, op. cit. note 6, pp. 248ff.

78. From then participation in the activities of the IPS was not dependent on membership in the GPSA; also, the office-bearers of the IPS were elected by the members instead of being appointed by the governing board of the GPSA. In 1965 some IPS members were elected to the governing and advisory boards of the GPSA and under the presidency of Eugen Kogon (1965-69) they helped to enlarge the participation in the decision-making of the GPSA organs and to make membership in the GPSA possible for younger scientists without doctoral degrees.

79. The Foundation of the Volkswagen Works granted DM 150,000 for the financing

of this project. Until then the individual conferences had been supported by the Thyssen Foundation.

80. Besides the contributions for the project, studies on German foreign policies and on European questions were also discussed. This provided the basis enabling the IPS to also form study groups for many of the GPSA conferences. See e.g., the published lectures in special issues 2 and 4 of the *Politische Vierteljahresschrift*, Opladen 1970 and 1972 respectively. These were the main research interests of a group around Hans-Peter Schwarz, who was elected to office in 1969 as the section's third director. A co-directorship was newly introduced and Klaus Juergen Gantzel, who supervised and coordinated the work of the project group, was elected to the post.

81. See Wolf Dieter Narr, 'David Easton's Systemanalyse. Ein Koenigs- oder Holzweg einer allgemeinen Theorie des politischen Verhaltens', in: *Politische Vierteljahresschrift*, Vol. 8, 1967, pp. 424-444.

82. Cf. Kastendiek, op. cit. note 6, pp. 274ff, 281ff, as well as the report on the publications of Klaus Juergen Gantzel, 'Zwischenbilanz der "International Relations",' in: *Neue Politische Literatur*, Vol. 19, 1974, pp. 281-295.

83. Karl W. Deutsch, *The Nerves of Government*, New York/London 1966[2] (German: *Politische Kybernetik*, Freiburg 1969). Cf. the reviews by Dieter Senghaas, 'Kybernetik und Politikwissenschaft. Ein Überblick', in: *Politische Vierteljahresschrift*, Vol. 7, 1966, pp. 252-276 and 'Sozialkybernetik und Herrschaft', in: *Atomzeitalter*, Nos. 7/8, 1967, pp. 386-399.

84. Klaus Juergen Gantzel, 'Internationale Beziehungen als System' (op. cit. note 72), with contributions from P. Pawelka (Tuebingen), G. Simonis (Konstanz), R. Seidelmann (at that time Frankfurt), K. Faupel (Freiburg, then Salzburg, Austria), H. Kammler (Cologne), H. Scheer (Stuttgart), F. Schlupp, S. Nour and G. Junne (at that time Berlin), Ursula Schmiederer (Marburg, then Erlangen-Nuernberg), and E. Jahn (Frankfurt). Problems of systems analysis were examined further under more methodological aspects by an IPS group led by Seidelmann: 'Interaktionen im internationalen System' (op. cit. note 72), with contributions from R. Seidelmann, S. Klaczko (Frankfurt), D. Ruloff (Zürich) and H. Rattinger (Freiburg).

85. These new ideas were introduced into the West German discussion mainly by Dieter Senghaas (ed.), *Imperialismus und strukturelle Gewalt. Analysen über abhängige Reproduktion*, Frankfurt 1972; and ibid (ed.), *Peripherer Kapitalismus. Analysen über Abhängigkeit und Unterentwicklung*, Frankfurt 1974.

86. Its dissemination, together with perspectives of critical theory, owes much to the student movement and the efforts of young social scientists from Berlin, Frankfurt and Marburg.

87. Cf. above, section 3.1; detailed expositions may be found in the memoranda and research programs issued in 1971 and 1974 by Ziebura et al.

88. 'Zur Theorie und Ideologie internationaler Interdependenz', in Gantzel (ed.), 'Internationale Beziehungen als System', op. cit. note 112, pp. 245-308; reprinted in shortened form under the title: 'Zur Grobstruktur des internationalen Systems', in: Ekkehart Krippendorff (ed.), *Internationale Beziehungen*, Köln 1973, pp. 217-241.

89. Cf. Ursula Schmiederer, 'Systemkonkurrenz als Strukturprinzip der internationalen Politik', in: Gantzel (ed.), *Internationale Beziehungen als System*, op. cit. note 72, pp. 309-346.

90. See Gantzel, 'Zu herrschaftssoziologischen Problembereichen von Abhängigkeitsbeziehungen in der gegenwärtigen Weltgesellschaft', in Senghaas (ed.), *Im-*

perialismus und strukturelle Gewalt, op. cit. note 85, pp. 105-120; in a slightly altered version and with a list of the individual project studies under the title: 'Dependency Sructures as the Dominant Pattern of World Society', in: *Journal of Peace Research*, Vol. 10, 1973 (No. 3), pp. 203-215. See also the prefaces in Gantzel, op. cit. note 72, Nos. 2-5. Important for the planning and conception of the project was above all a paper by Hartmut Elsenhans (at that time Berlin): 'Wellen der Penetration und die Mehrstufigkeit der internationalen Arbeitsteilung' (mimeo., December 1971), which the author has in the meantime expanded into an important book: *Geschichte und Oekonomie der europaeischen Welteroberung*, Frankfurt/New York (forthcoming). Important impulses also came from E. Krippendorff, 'Internationale Beziehungen. Versuch einer historisch-politoekonomischen Rahmenanalyse', in: *Politische Vierteljahresschrift*, Vol. 13, 1972, pp. 348-373.

91. Reprinted in Krippendorff, op. cit. note 88, pp. 364ff. Cf. also W. Hein and G. Simonis, 'Theoretische und methodische Probleme einer kritischen Theorie internationaler Politik', in: *Politische Vierteljahresschrift*, Vol. 14, 1973, pp. 85-106. The efforts to structure a critical course of study of international relations ran parallel to similar efforts for the whole of political science: Cf. Rolf Richard Grauhan and Wolf-Dieter Narr, 'Studium der Sozialwissenschaft — demonstriert an der Politikwissenschaft', in: *Leviathan*, Vol. 1, 1973 (No. 1), pp. 90-134.

92. In August 1972 the IPS had seventy-two ordinary and seventy-two guest members, in June 1973 the figures were eighty-two and seventy-nine respectively, including scientists from abroad and neighboring disciplines. Foreign experts such as Karl W. Deutsch (Harvard), Johan Galtung (Oslo), Armando Córdova, Hector Silva-Michelena, Heinz Rudolf Sonntag (all Caracas), André Gunder Frank (at that time Santiago), Alberto Martinelli (Milan), Bruno Fritsch (Zurich) followed the progress of the project work and offered their advice.

93. Cf. Gantzel, 'Dependency Structures...', op. cit. note 90. Not all the planned studies were finally realized, nor were all the studies which were discussed published.

94. The published studies are in Gantzel (ed.), op. cit. note 72, Nos. 2-5.

95. Cf. Gisela Gantzel-Kress and Klaus Juergen Gantzel, 'Individuum und internationales System', Preprint No. 10 of the studies by members of the Institute for Social Sciences, University of Mannheim, March 1974.

96. Cf. Krippendorff, op. cit. note 1; Hartmut Elsenhans, 'Geschichte und Struktur des internationalen Systems', in: Helga Haftendorn (ed.), *Theorie der internationalen Politik. Gegenstand und Methode der Internationalen Beziehungen*, Hamburg 1975, pp. 150-170; as well as his book (Notes 1 and 90).

97. Egbert Jahn and Volker Rittberger (eds.), *Die Ostpolitik der Bundesrepublik — Triebkräfte, Widerstände, Konsequenzen*, Opladen 1974. The work of the study group is also documented in: E. Jahn (ed.), *Sozioökonomische Bedingungen der sowjetischen Außenpolitik*, Frankfurt/New York 1975.

98. For details of the activities of all these study groups see the individual circulars of the GPSA. Incidentally, the study groups were more or less influenced by the discussion within the IPS due to various 'double memberships'.

99. Kastendiek, op. cit. note 6, pp. 305ff.

100. Some of the representatives of traditional foreign policy research are e.g. Waldemar Besson, *Die Außenpolitik der Bundesrepublik. Erfahrungen und Maßstaebe*, Muenchen 1970 (before his death in 1971 at the age of 41 Besson held a chair in Konstanz). Wilhelm Cornides, *Die Weltmächte und Deutschland. Geschichte der juengsten Vergangenheit — 1945-55*, Bonn 1957. Until his death in 1966 at the age of 45 Cornides was

the editor of the *Europa Archiv*, co-editor of the yearbook *Die Internationale Politik* of the Research Institute of the German Society for Foreign Policy and chairman of the research commission of the society. Heinrich End (Trier), *Zweimal deutsche Außenpolitik. Internationale Dimensionen des innerdeutschen Konflikts 1949-1972*, Koeln 1973 (End died in 1973 at the age of 38). Werner Link (Trier), *Die amerikanische Stabilisierungspolitik in Deutschland 1921-1932*, Duesseldorf 1970. Richard Loewenthal (Berlin), *Chruschtschow und der Weltkommunismus*, Stuttgart 1963; and (as co-author): *Der Zwang zur Partnerschaft (Außenpolitische Perspektiven des westdeutschen Staates, Vol. 3)*, Muenchen/Wien 1972. Paul Noack (Munich), *Deutsche Außenpolitik seit 1945*, Stuttgart 1972. Hans-Peter Schwarz (Cologne), *Vom Reich zur Bundesrepublik. Deutschland im Widerstreit der außenpolitischen Konzeptionen in den Jahren der Besatzungsherrschaft*, Neuwied/Berlin 1966; and (ed.), *Handbuch der deutschen Außenpolitik*, Muenchen 1975. Along with Loewenthal and Jacobsen (Bonn), Schwarz also belongs to the scientific board of directors of the German Society for Foreign Policy. Gerhard Wettig (Cologne), *Entmilitarisierung und Wiederbewaffnung in Deutschland 1943-1955*, Muenchen 1967; *Frieden und Sicherheit in Europa, Probleme bei der Konferenz fuer Sicherheit und Zusammenarbeit in Europa (KSZE) und bei der wechselseitigen Truppenreduzierung in Europa (MBFR)*, Stuttgart 1975; *Die Sowjetunion, die DDR und die Deutschlandfrage 1965-1976*, Stuttgart 1976; *Europaeische Sicherheit. Das europaeische Staatensystem in der sowjetischen Außenpolitik 1966-72*, Duesseldorf 1972. Gilbert Ziebura: *Die deutsch-franzoesischen Beziehungen seit 1945. Mythen und Realitäten*, Stuttgart 1970; (ed.), *Grundfragen der deutschen Außenpolitik seit 1871*, Darmstadt 1975. Originally Ernst-Otto Czempiel also belonged to the traditional school: *Das amerikanische Sicherheitssystem. Studie zur Außenpolitik der buergerlichen Gesellschaft*, Berlin 1966. He is one of the very few foreign policy researchers who were receptive to modern social scientific methods and approaches to theory and allowed himself to be decisively influenced by them; and, apart from Ziebura, he is probably the only 'traditionalist' who ventured to engage himself with the theoretical problems posed by a comprehensive social approach. Cf. his ideas on the analysis of foreign and international politics, but also his debate with Wolfgang Abendroth, in Mueck, op. cit. note 1, pp. 12-166 and 357-380. Such an open-mindedness certainly contributed to Czempiel's significant role in the building of the discipline of international relations and of peace research in West Germany.

101. Cf. Kindermann's preface ('Hans Morgenthau und die theoretischen Grundlagen des politischen Realismus') in the German edition of Hans Morgenthau, *Macht und Frieden. Grundlegung einer Theorie der internationalen Politik*, Guetersloh 1963, further 'Politische Theorie und internationale Politik in der Sicht der realistischen Schule Hans J. Morgenthaus und Reinhold Niebuhrs', in: *Politische Vierteljahresschrift*, Vol. 6, 1965, pp. 291-301.

102. His newest book is a first tentative presentation of the 'neo-realistic' research approach: Kindermann (ed.), *Grundelemente der Weltpolitik. Eine Einfuehrung, mit einem Geleitwort von H. J. Morgenthau*, Muenchen 1977. Cf. also the project report on the research work at the Seminar for International Politics of the University of Muenchen on the occasion of the conference of the German Society for Peace and Conflict Research, 27-28 January 1978 in Muenchen-Ebenhausen. Kindermann otherwise occupies himself mainly with politics in Asia.

103. Cf. e.g. W. Link, 'Die Allgegenwart des Machtkampfes. Ueber die Praemissen der Theorie Hans J. Morgenthaus', in: *Neue Politische Literatur*, Vol. 10, 1965, pp. 17-22.

104. Cf. e.g. Joerg Becker and Klaus Juergen Gantzel, 'Feindbilder in

Regierungserklaerungen und Bundestagsreden', in: *Friedensanalysen*, No. 1, Frankfurt 1975, pp. 63-86; Gert Krell, 'Falken und Tauben im amerikanischen Senat. Konfliktideologien und oekonomische Interessen als Bedingungsfaktoren der amerikanischen Ruestungspolitik', in: *Aus Politik und Zeitgeschichte*, No. N 44/75, 1 November 1975, pp. 15-31.

105. As the only representative of this branch in the West German field of international relations, Erich Weede (Mannheim), rigidly exploits this approach with all its consequences: *Weltpolitik und Kriegsursachen im 20. Jahrhundert. Eine quantitativ-empirische Studie*, Muenchen/Wien 1975. With certain reservations Johannes Rattinger (Freiburg, at present USA) can also be considered as belonging to this approach: *Ruestungsdynamik im internationalen System. Mathematische Reaktionsmodelle fuer Ruestungswettlaeufe und die Probleme ihrer Anwendung*, Muenchen/Wien 1975. At first Klaus Juergen Gantzel (1964-1970 Mannheim) also tended in this direction: 'Ruestungswettlaeufe und politische Entscheidungsbedingungen', in Czempiel, op. cit. note 72, pp. 1120-137; and *System und Akteur. Beitraege zur vergleichenden Kriegsursachenforschung*, Duesseldorf 1972; as well as *Konflikt — Eskalation — Krise. Sozialwissenschaftliche Studien zum Ausbruch des Ersten Weltkrieges* (co-edited by Gisela Kress and Volker Rittberger), Duesseldorf 1972.

106. Klaus Faupel (see note 74), 'Internationale Politik und Aussenpolitik', in Czempiel, op. cit. note 72, pp. 11-79; 'Quantitative Systemforschung in der Internationalen Politik: Die Forschungspraxis', in Gantzel, op. cit. note 72, No. 1, pp. 173-192; 'Meßkonzepte und Skalen: Einige erkenntnistheoretische, methodologische und terminologische Vorfragen zur allgemeinen Systemtheorie', in: Dieter Oberndoerfer (ed.), *Systemtheorie, Systemanalyse und Entwicklungslaederforschung*, Berlin 1971, pp. 135-150; 'Systemeinheiten und systemische Relationen: Eine partielle Reorganisation der allgemeinen Systemtheorie', ibid., pp. 151-197; in the same volume, lastly, two further contributions on Almond's and Easton's systems theory: pp. 317-408.

107. An exception is the second Club of Rome study of the world situation, which, although not a political science study, is relevant for the discipline and was prepared by Eduard Pestel together with Mihailo Mesarović: *Menschheit am Wendepunkt*, Stuttgart 1974. A new, very much improved world model is currently being developed at the Berlin Science Center under the supervision of Karl W. Deutsch.

108. Reimund Seidelmann (formerly Frankfurt, now Giessen), 'Systemische Interaktionen und die Lokalisierung ihrer nationalen Bedingungsfaktoren. Exemplarische Kritik der Studien von Rudolph J. Rummel im Rahmen des "Dimensionality-of-Nations Project",' in Gantzel, op. cit. note 72, No. 1, pp. 87-172. See also his 'Akteur und Interesse als analytische Konzepte zur Erfassung von Beziehungen am Beispiel der USA — Südafrikanische Republik', in the topical issue of the *Politische Vierteljahresschrift*, whose edition he supervised (op. cit. note 72, Vol. 15, 1974, No. 3/4), pp. 313-390; *Simulation in Internationaler und Auswaertiger Politik. Die Inter-Nation Simulation (INS) und ihre Verwertbarkeit für Analyse und Prognose*, Meisenheim 1973.

Lucian Kern and Horst-Dieter Roensch (eds.) also worked for some time in this field: 'Simulation internationaler Prozesse', Special issue No. 3 of the *Politische Vierteljahresschrift*, Opladen 1971.

109. Hans Kammler (Cologne), 'Formal Models vs. Real Models: Tools of Inquiry in International Relations', in: *General Systems*, Vol. 19, 1974, pp. 353ff; 'Zur Leistungsfaehigkeit des kybernetischen Modells in der Theorie der internationalen Politik', in: Special Issue No. 4 of the *Politische Vierteljahresschrift*, Opladen 1972, pp. 315-329; 'Nachbarschaftsrelationen und Buendnispolitik', in: *Zeitschrift fuer die gesamte*

Staatswissenschaft, Vol. 126, 1970, pp. 496ff; *Logik der Politikwissenschaft*, Wiesbaden 1976.

110. Klaus Juergen Gantzel, 'Anwendung der Spieltheorie in den Sozialwissenschaften', in: *Staatslexikon* (of Goerres-Gesellschaft), 3rd Supplementary Volume, Freiburg 1970, pp. 286-293; Gerd Junne, *Spieltheorie in der internationalen Politik. Die begrenzte Rationalitaet strategischen Denkens*, Duesseldorf 1972.

111. Systems theoretical studies in the field of international relations in the sense of, for example, a Kaplan, Rosencrance, Rosenau, or a McClelland, practically do not exist in the FRG. At best cf. Niklas Luhmann (Bielefeld), 'Die Weltgesellschaft' in: *Archiv fuer Rechts- und Sozialphilosophie*, Vol. 57, 1971, pp. 1-35; as well as — with concrete reference to the UN and combined with questions posed by critical peace research — Peter Pawelka (Tuebingen), *Vereinte Nationen und strukturelle Gewalt*, Muenchen 1974. Cf. also Pawelka's review of systems theoretical approaches with respect to their usefulness in analyzing behavior in international relations in Gantzel, op. cit. note 72, No. 1, pp. 17-60.

112. See Eva Senghaas-Knobloch, *Frieden durch Integration und Assoziation*, Stuttgart 1969.

113. Gerda Zellentin, *Der Wirtschafts- und Sozialausschuss der EWG und Euratom. Interessenrepraesentation auf uebernationaler Ebene*, Leiden 1962. The importance of international organizations for the governmental system and the constitutional reality of the FRG (e.g. EEC, EURATOM, NATO, etc.), had already been pointed out by Rudolf Wildenmann, *Macht und Konsens als Problem der Innen- und Aussenpolitik*, Frankfurt/Bonn 1963.

114. Volker Rittberger, *Evolution and International Organization. Toward a New Level of Socio-political Integration*, Den Haag 1973.

115. 'Friedensforschung und europaeische Integration', opening address on the 7th scientific colloquy of the AFK, Bonn 1976. For another thesis in this direction see Eva Senghaas-Knobloch, *Reproduktion von Arbeitskraft in der Weltgesellschaft. Zur Programmatik der Internationalen Arbeitsorganisation*, Frankfurt/New York 1979.

116. Cf. AFK (ed.), *Jahrbuch fuer Friedens- und Konfliktforschung*, Vol. 1, Duesseldorf 1971, in particular pp. 283ff (Helmut Rosenfeld). Seven volumes of this yearbook are published up to now. For West German peace research see as well the summary by Wolf-Dieter Eberwein and Peter Reichel, *Friedens- und Konfliktforschung. Eine Einfuehrung*, Muenchen 1976. There is also given a list of peace research institutions.

117. Karl Kaiser (by order of the Volkswagenwerk Foundation), *Friedensforschung in der Bundesrepublik*, Goettingen 1970, including a list of research institutes; Claus Koch (by order of the AFK and the Federal Department of Education and Sciences), *Friedensforschung. Forschungsvorhaben — Institutionen — Planungen*, Bonn 1970 (series 'Forschungsplanung' of BMBW).

118. In 1970 an organization for the promotion of peace research was formed: the German Society for Peace and Conflict Research (Deutsche Gesellschaft fuer Friedens- und Konfliktforschung — DGFK), followed by the founding of two research institutes, the Peace Research Institute in Frankfurt in 1971 (Hessische Stiftung Friedens- und Konfliktforschung — HSFK) and the Institute for Peace Research and Security Policy in 1971 in Hamburg (Institut fuer Friedensforschung und Sicherheitspolitik — IFSH).

119. Dieter Senghaas (ed.), *Kritische Friedensforschung*, Frankfurt 1971. A mediatory position between traditional and critical peace research is taken by Czempiel, *Schwerpunkte und Ziele der Friedensforschung*, Muenchen 1972.

120. The following two foundations and their research institutes can be seen as belonging to this approach: the German Society for Foreign Policy (Deutsche Gesellschaft fuer Auswaertige Politik) in Bonn (cf. note 50 above and section 3.3) and the Foundation for Science and Politics (Stiftung Wissenschaft und Politik) in Ebenhausen (cf. above note 55 and section 3.3), which is the Federal Government's brains-trust in this field, headed by Klaus Ritter and Uwe Nerlich. The authors to be named are e.g. Helga Haftendorn (Hamburg), *Abruestungs- und Entspannungspolitik zwischen Sicherheitsbefriedigung und Friedenssicherung. Zur Aussenpolitik der BRD 1955-73*, Duesseldorf 1974; K.-Peter Stratmann (Ebenhausen), 'Vom Autismus kritischer Friedensforschung. Zur Kritik der Kritik', in: *Aus Politik und Zeitgeschichte*, No. B 40/73 (6 October 1973); Wolf Graf von Baudissin (Hamburg; as a general of the armed forces he became famous through his concept of 'inner leadership' and through his example of the 'citizen in uniform'; presently director of IFSH, cf. above section 3.3 and note 53), *Soldat fuer den Frieden*, Muenchen 1969; for his studies on security policy see the IFSH publications *Diskussionsbeitraege* and *Forschungsberichte* and e.g. 'Vertrauensbildende Massnahmen als Instrument kooperativer Ruestungssteuerung', in: J. Delbrueck, N. Ropers and G. Zellentin (eds.), *Gruenbuch zu den Folgewirkungen der KSZE*, Koeln 1977, pp. 215-230; Otto Kimminich (Regensburg), *Ruestung und politische Spannung. Studien zum Problem der internationalen Sicherheit*, Guetersloh 1964; Gerhard Wettig (Koeln), op. cit. note 100; with reservations also Erhard Forndran (Braunschweig), *Ruestungskontrolle. Friedenssicherung zwischen Abschreckung und Abruestung*, Duesseldorf 1970; and: *Abruestung und Friedensforschung. Kritik an Krippendorff, Senghaas und Ebert*, Duesseldorf 1971.

121. Cf. v. Weizsaecker, *Die Verantwortung de Wissenschaft im Atomzeitalter*, Muenchen 1957; and (ed.), *Kriegsfolgen und Kriegsverhuetung*, Muenchen 1971; *Wege in der Gefahr. Eine Studie ueber Wirtschaft, Gesellschaft und Kriegsverhuetung*, Muenchen 1976; H. Afheldt et al., *Durch Kriegsverhuetung zum Krieg? Die politischen Aussagen der Weizsaecker-Studie 'Kriegsfolgen und Kriegsverhuetung'*, Muenchen 1972; Afheldt, *Verteidigung und Frieden. Politik mit militaerischen Mitteln*, Muenchen 1976.

122. The term 'critical theory' denotes that particular social scientific, philosophic approach which is associated with the Institute for Social Research in Frankfurt (Institut fuer Sozialforschung since 1924; in exile at first in Paris then in New York, there renamed New School of Social Research; refounded in Frankfurt in 1950), with the Zeitschrift fuer Sozialforschung (1932-1939) and with social scientists such as Max Horkheimer, Theodor W. Adorno, Herbert Marcuse, Erich Fromm, Henryk Grossmann, Franz Neumann, Friedrich Pollock, Karl August Wittfogel. Starting from the theory of Marx it combined a critical analysis of bourgeois society with humanistic protest. In the 1940s, 1950s and 1960s the 'Frankfurt School' around Horkheimer, Adorno and later Juergen Habermas worked out the forms of consciousness of bourgeois society. An exemplary work is: Horkheimer and Adorno, *Dialektik der Aufklaerung*, Amsterdam 1947.

123. Ludwig von Friedeburg, 'Zum Verhaeltnis von Militaer und Gesellschaft in der Bundesrepublik', in: G. Picht (ed.), *Studien zur politischen und gesellschaftlichen Situation der Bundeswehr*, Part II, Witten/Berlin, 1966, pp. 10-65; Gerhard Brandt, *Ruestung und Wirtschaft in der Bundesrepublik*, Witten/Berlin 1966.

124. Cf. note 74 above.

125. Dieter Senghaas, *Abschreckung und Frieden. Studien zur Kritik organisierter Friedlosigkeit*, Frankfurt 1969.

126. Cf. note 83 above.

127. H. Volle and C. J. Duisberg, *Probleme der internationalen Abruestung. Die*

Bemuehungen der Vereinten Nationen 1945-1961, 2 vols., Frankfurt/Berlin 1964; Uwe Nerlich (ed.), *Strategie der Abruestung. 28 Problemanalysen*, Guetersloh 1962 (enlarged edition of the 1961 Daedalus edition with D. G. Brennan [ed.]).

128. Cf. note 125. For criticism of Senghaas see Stratmann, op. cit. note 120, Forndran, op. cit. note 120, Josef Joffe, 'Abschreckung und Abschreckungspolitik. Kritische Bemerkungen zu Dieter Senghaas' Beitrag', in: *Jahrbuch fuer Friedens- und Konfliktforschung*, Vol. 1 (note 116), pp. 133-158.

129. Dieter Senghaas, *Ruestung und Militarismus*, Frankfurt 1972. Cf. also the somewhat more 'popularly' written study by Fritz Vilmar, *Ruestung und Abruestung im Spaetkapitalismus*, Frankfurt 1965, 1973.[4] For an application of the MIC approach on armaments policy for the time preceding the First World War see Volker Berghahn, *Ruestung und Machtpolitik. Zur Anatomie des 'Kalten Krieges' vor 1914*, Duesseldorf 1973. For a correspondingly modified view after the Second World War see K. J. Gantzel, 'The Armament Dynamics in the East-West Conflict: An Arms Race?', in: *Papers*, Peace Research Society (International), Vol. 20, 1973, pp. 1-24.

130. Dieter Senghaas, *Aufruestung durch Ruestungskontrolle. Ueber den symbolischen Gebrauch von Politik*, Stuttgart 1972; D. Senghaas, V. Rittberger and B. Luber, 'MBFR — Aufruestung durch Ruestungskontrolle?', in: *Aus Politik und Zeitgeschichte*, No. B 13/73 (31 March 1973), pp. 26-54.

131. Cf. Gantzel, 'Zur Analyse internationaler Ruestungsdynamik', in: *Mannheimer Berichte aus Forschung und Lehre an der Universitaet Mannheim*, No. 8, February 1974, pp. 227-233.

132. Cf. note 52 above. Further: Carola Bielfeldt, *Ruestungsausgaben und Staatsinterventionismus. Das Beispiel der Bundesrepublik Deutschland 1950-1971*, Frankfurt/New York 1977; Peter Schlotter, *Ruestungspolitik in der Bundesrepublik. Die Beispiele Starfighter und Phantom*, Frankfurt/New York 1975; Monika Medick, 'Das Konzept des "Military-Industrial Complex" und das Problem einer Theorie demokratischer Kontrolle' and Gert Krell, 'Die Kritik der amerikanischen Ruestung und die Debatte um die "National Priorities",' both in: *Politische Vierteljahresschrift*, Vol. 14, 1973, pp. 499-526 and 527-566; Francoise Sirjacques, *Determinanten der franzoesischen Aussenpolitik*, Frankfurt/Bern 1977; C. Bielfeldt et al., *Frieden in Europa? Zur Koexistenz von Ruestung und Entspannung*, Reinbek 1973; Egbert Jahn, *Kommunismus — und was dann? Zur Buerokratisierung und Militarisierung des Systems der Nationalstaaten*, Reinbek 1974; Jahn et al., 'Sozialstrukturelle Grundlagen der auswaertigen Beziehungen sozialistischer Gesellschaften am Beispiel der Planung der europaeischen Sicherheitskonferenz in der UdSSR und in der DDR', HSFK Research Report in several parts, Frankfurt (HSFK) 1977.

133. A. Mechtersheimer, *Ruestung und Politik in der Bundesrepublik. MRCA-Tornado: Geschichte und Funktion des groessten europaeischen Ruestunsprogramms*, Bad Honnef 1977; Manfred G. Schmidt, *Staatsapparat und Ruestungspolitik in der Bundesrepublik Deutschland (1966-1973), Schranken und Folgeprobleme der Staatsinterventionspolitik im Militaer- und Ruestungssektor*, Giessen (Lollar) 1975; Wilfried v. Bredow, 'Intersystemare Kooperation und Abruestung', in: Aboltin et al., *Oekonomische und soziale Folgen der Abruestung*, Koeln 1974, pp. 7-20; Ulrich Albrecht, *Der Handel mit Waffen*, Muenchen 1971; Albrecht, Ernst, Lock and Wulf, *Ruestung und Unterentwicklung. Iran, Indien, Griechenland/Tuerkei: Die verschaerfte Militarisierung*, Reinbek 1976; Albrecht, Lock and Wulf, *Arbeitsplaetze durch Ruestung? Warnung vor falschen*

Hoffnungen, Reinbek 1978. Cf. also Haftendorn, *Militaerhilfe und Ruestungsexporte der BRD*, Duesseldorf 1971.

134. Studiengruppe Militaerpolitik, *Ein Anti-Weissbuch. Materialien fuer eine alternative Militaerpolitik*, Reinbek 1974, and: *Die Nationale Volksarmee. Ein Anti-Weissbuch zum Militaer in der DDR*, Reinbek 1976.

135. For example, C. Potyka (*Sueddeutsche Zeitung*); Pierre Simonitsch (*Frankfurter Rundschau*); Anton-Andreas Guha (*Frankfurter Rundschau*), see also his book: *Die Neutronenbombe oder die Perversion menschlichen Denkens*, Frankfurt 1977; Ansgar Skriver (*Westdeutscher Rundfunk*); Karl-Heinz Harenberg (*Norddeutscher Rundfunk*).

136. Cf. *Friedensanalysen*, No. 7, Special Issue: 'Jungsozialisten und Jungdemokraten zur Friedens- und Sicherheitspolitik', Frankfurt 1977.

137. One tends to find marxists in North Germany rather than in the South, especially at the Universities of Berlin, Bremen, Frankfurt, Hamburg, Hannover, Marburg, and Osnabrueck.

138. Cf. Margret Wirth, *Kapitalismustheorie in der DDR*, Frankfurt 1973; cf. also Institut fuer Gesellschaftswissenschaften beim ZK der SED (ed.), *Der Imperialismus der BRD*, Frankfurt/Berlin (East), 1971.

139. K. Engelhardt and K.-H. Heise, *Der militaerisch-industrielle Komplex im heutigen Imperialismus*, Berlin (East)/Koeln 1974.

140. Cf. Peter Schlotter, op. cit. note 132; Manfred G. Schmidt, op. cit. note 133.

141. For a review of the modernization theories see M. Bohnet (ed.), *Das Nord-Sued Problem. Konflikte zwischen Industrie- und Entwicklungslaendern*, Muenchen 1971, pp. 49ff.

142. Cf. T. T. Evers and P. v. Wogau, 'Lateinamerikanische Theorien zur Unterentwicklung', in: *Das Argument*, Vol. 15, No. 79 (July 1973), pp. 404-452.

143. Cf. note 5.

144. Cf. Rainer Tetzlaff, 'Die Ursachen von Unterentwicklung in der Dritten Welt und das Problem ihrer Ueberwindung. Eine Einfuehrung', in: *Friedensanalysen*, No. 1, Frankfurt 1975, pp. 150-181; Alfred Schmidt (ed.), *Strategien gegen Unterentwicklung. Zwischen Weltmarkt und Eigenstaendigkeit*, Frankfurt/New York 1976; Bassam Tibi and Volker Brandes (eds.), *Handbuch 2: Unterentwicklung*, Frankfurt/Koeln 1975; Dieter Nohlen and Franz Nuscheler (eds.), *Handbuch der Dritten Welt, Vol. 1: Theorien und Indikatoren der Unterentwicklung und der Entwicklung, Vol. 2: Afrika, Vol. 3: Lateinamerika, Vol. 4: Asien*, Hamburg 1974-1976.

145. Dieter Senghaas, *Weltwirtschaftsordnung und Entwicklungspolitik. Plaedoyer fuer Dissoziation*, Frankfurt 1972. Cf. also his research project on the 'strategies for overcoming peripheral societal formations', which has up to now resulted in the publications by Ulrich Menzel, *Theorie und Praxis des chinesischen Entwicklungsmodells. Ein Beitrag zum Konzept autozentrierter Entwicklung*, Opladen 1978; Gerd Wontroba and Ulrich Menzel, *Stagnation und Unterentwicklung in Korea. Von der Yi-Dynastie zur Peripherisierung unter japanischer Kolonialherrschaft*, Meisenheim 1978; Rosemarie Juttka-Reisse, *Agrarpolitik und Kimilsungismus in der Volksrepublik Korea. Ein Beitrag zum Konzept autozentrierter Entwicklung*, Meisenheim (in print).

146. Cf. T. T. Evers, *Buergerliche Herrschaft in der Dritten Welt — Zur Theorie des Staates in unterentwickelten Gesellschaftsformationen*, Koeln/Frankfurt 1977.

147. F. Froebel and J. Heinrichs and O. Kreye, *Die neue internationale Arbeitsteilung*, Reinbek 1977; H. Elsenhans and G. Junne, 'Einige Aspekte des gegenwaertigen Wandels der internationalen Arbeitsteilung', in: Gantzel, op. cit. note 72, No. 2, pp. 234-281; D.

Senghaas and U. Menzel (eds.), *Multinationale Konzerne und Dritte Welt*, Opladen 1976; Senghaas-Knobloch, op. cit. note 115.

148. See, for example, Klaus Busch, 'Ungleicher Tausch — Zur Diskussion ueber internationale Durchschnittsprofitrate, ungleichen Tausch, komparative Kostentheorie, anhand der Thesen von Arghiri Emmanuel', in: *PROKLA*, Nos. 8/9, 1973, pp. 47-88.

149. One example for the Stamocap variant of the imperialism theory is Katja Nehls, *Kapitalexport und Kapitalverflechtung*, Frankfurt/Berlin (East) 1970.

150. Without taking individual differences into consideration; the following authors should be named: Christel Neusuess, *Imperialismus und Weltmarktbewegung des Kapitals*, Erlangen 1972; Klaus Busch, *Die multinationalen Konzerne. Zur Analyse der Weltmarktbewegung des Kapitals*, Frankfurt 1974; Wolfgang Schoeller, *Weltmarkt und Reproduktion des Kapitals*, Frankfurt/Koeln 1976; Claudia von Braunmuehl, 'Weltmarktbewegung des Kapitals. Imperialismus und Staat' in: Braunmuehl et al., *Probleme einer materialistischen Staatstheorie*, Frankfurt 1973, pp. 11-91.

151. For example D. Kebschull and O. G. Mayer (eds.), *Multinationale Unternehmen — Anfang oder Ende der Weltwirtschaft?*, Frankfurt 1974; M. Holthus (ed.), *Die deutschen multinationalen Unternehmen*, Frankfurt 1974.

152. Cf. also Otto Kreye (ed.), *Multinationale Konzerne*, Muenchen 1974; M. Behrning et al, *Die Regionalverteilung auslaendischer Investionen in der Bundesrepublik Deutschland*, Konstanz (mimeo), 1975; Folker Froebel, et al., op. cit. note 147.

153. M. Nikolinakos, *Politische Oekonomie der Gastarbeiterfrage. Migration und Kapitalismus*, Reinbek 1973.

154. K. P. Tudyka (ed.), *Multinationale Konzerne und Gewerkschaftsstrategie*, Hamburg 1974; E. Piehl, *Multinationale Konzerne und internationale Gewerkschaftsbewegung. Ein Beitrag zur Analyse und zur Strategie der Arbeiterbewegung insbesondere in West Europa*, Frankfurt 1974.

155. G. Junne, *Der Eurogeldmarkt. Seine Bedeutung fuer Inflation und Inflationsbekaempfung*, Frankfurt/New York 1976; V. Henke, 'Die Finanzierung der Investitionen US-amerikanischer Unternehmen in Europa über den internationalen Kapitalmarkt', in Gantzel, op. cit. note 72, No. 4, pp. 139-184.

156. F. Deppe (ed.), *Europaeische Wirtschaftsgemeinschaft (EWG). Zur politischen Oekonomie der westeuropaeischen Integration*, Reinbek 1975; ibid. (ed.), *Arbeiterbewegung und westeuropaeische Integration*, Koeln 1976. Cf. also K. P. Tudyka, *Marktplatz Europa. Zur politischen Oekonomie der EG*, Koeln 1975.

157. H.-D. Jacobsen, *Die wirtschaftlichen Beziehungen zwischen West und Ost — Strukturen, Formen, Interessen, Auswirkungen*, Reinbek 1975.

158. Jahn, op. cit. note 97; Rotermundt, Schmiederer and Becker-Panitz, op. cit note 2; U. Stehr, 'Unequal Development and Dependency Structures in COMECON', in: *Journal of Peace Research*, Vol. 14, 1977 (No. 2), pp. 115-128; P. W. Schulze, *Herrschaft und Klassen in der Sowjetgesellschaft. Die historischen Bedingungen des Stalinismus*, Frankfurt/New York 1977; ibid (ed.), *Uebergangsgesellschaft: Herrschaftsformen und Praxis am Beispiel der Sowjetunion*, Frankfurt 1974.

159. Cf. notes 1 and 96 above.

160. Cf. E. Krippendorff, 'Die Enstehung des internationalen Systems', in: *Neue Politische Literatur*, Vol. 22, 1977, pp. 36-48.

161. An attempt to use a non-marxist dialectical approach combining North-South and West-East conflict as well as state theory at a world political level is represented by Bernard Willms (Bochum), *Selbstbehauptung und Anerkennung. Grundriss einer politischen*

Dialektik, Opladen 1977; *Entwicklung und Revolution. Grundlagen einer dialektischen Theorie der Internationalen Politik*, Frankfurt 1972.

162. Joachim Hirsch, 'Bemerkungen zum theoretischen Ansatz einer Analyse des buergerlichen Staates', in: *Gesellschaft — Beitraege zur Marxischen Theorie*, Nos. 8/9, Frankfurt 1976, pp. 99-149, seems to us to be the most promising approach because it is the most political of those mentioned and is also empirically useful. Another study in this category but specifically bearing more on international relations is C. v. Braunmuehl, 'Kapitalakkumulation im Weltzusammenhang. Zum methodischen Ansatz einer Analyse des buergerlichen Staates', in: *Gesellschaft*, No. 1, 1974, pp. 30-51, and 'Die nationalstaatliche Organisiertheit der buergerlichen Gesellschaft', in: ibid, Nos. 8/9, 1976, pp. 273-334.

163. Cf. until now D. Danckwortt et al., 'Internationale Beziehungen. Ein Gegenstand der Sozialwissenschaften, Frankfurt', in: *Politische Psychologie*, Vol. 5, 1966; Klaus Horn, 'Menschliche Aggressivitaet und internationale Politik', in: D. Senghaas (ed.), *Friedensforschung und Gesellschaftskritik*, Muenchen 1970, pp. 133-179; A. Karsten (ed.), *Vorurteil*, Darmstadt 1978.

164. For the theories of the 20th century, cf. perhaps Calamaros, op. cit. note 4 and Simonis, op. cit. note 2.

8

BIBLIOGRAPHY OF WEST GERMAN POLITICAL SCIENCE LITERATURE 1977-1979

Volker Rittberger

LIST OF PERIODICALS AND ABBREVIATIONS

Das Argument	
Aus Politik und Zeitgeschichte (Beilage zur Wochenzeitung 'Das Parlament')	AP
Aussenpolitik	
Beiträge zur Konfliktforschung	
Blätter für deutsche und internationale Politik	Blätter
Deutschland-Archiv	DA
Europa Archiv	EA
Friedensanalysen	
Kölner Zeitschrift für Soziologie und Sozialpsychologie	KZfSS
Leviathan	Lev
Osteuropa	OE
Politische Vierteljahresschrift	PVS
Probleme des Klassenkampfes	Prokla
Sozialistische Politik	SoPo
Der Staat	
Sozialwissenschaftliches Jahrbuch für Politik	
Die Verwaltung	
Zeitschrift für Parlamentsfragen	ZParl
Zeitschrift für Politik	ZfP

MAIN SECTIONS

A Political Science
General Studies

Methods, Research Techniques
Congresses, Symposia, Associations, Curricula
Works of Reference, Bibliographies

B Political Thought
History of Political Ideas
General Works
Ancient Times and Middle Ages
Modern Times until 1789
19th Century
20th Century
Ideological Foundations of Political Systems
General Studies
Democracy
Socialism
Marxism, Communism
Nationalism, Fascism
Totalitarianism, Authoritarianism
Liberalism
Conservatism
Theories of Political Systems (State, Power, Legitimacy)
Political Development and Change (Crisis, Violence and Revolution)

C Government and Politics
The Political System (Theoretical and Comparative Studies)
The Political System of the FGR
Constitutional Problems
Federalism
The Powers
Executive
Legislative
Judiciary
Freedom and Civil Rights
Public Policy
Economic System and Economic Policy
Social Policy
Educational Policy and Science Policy
Environmental Policy
Infrastructural Policy
Developmental Policy
Public Administration
General and Comparative Studies
Planning
Civil Service
Local Government

D Political Process
Political Influences and Trends

Interest Groups
Trade Unions and Labour Movement
Rural Influences
Promotional Groups
Military Influences
National Minorities and Racial Factors
Political Parties
Political Socialization
Elite Recruitment
Mass Media and Political Communication
Representation and Elections
Area Studies
West European Countries
  France
  Great Britain
  Italy
  Spain
  Other Countries
The USA and Canada
Socialist Systems
Comparison of Capitalist and Socialist Systems and Theoretical Discussions of Research on Socialist Systems
Comparisons between the two German States
The Political System of the GDR
Berlin
The Soviet Union
Other Socialist Systems
  East European Socialist Countries
  Yugoslavia
  Cuba
  China
Developing Countries
Latin America
Africa
Arab Countries and the Middle East
Asia

E International Relations
General Studies on Theory and Methodology
State in International Affairs: Their Foreign Relations in
  General
  FRG
  GDR
  United States
  USSR
  China
  Other Countries
International Politics
General Studies

A. POLITICAL SCIENCE

General Studies

Albert, Hans: Traktat über rationale Praxis. Tübingen: Mohr 1978.

Arndt, Hans-Joachim: Die Besiegten von 1945. Versuch einer Politologie für Deutsche samt Würdigung der Politikwissenschaft in der Bundesrepublik Deutschland. Berlin: Duncker & Humblot 1978.

Bermbach, Udo (ed.): Politische Wissenschaft und politische Praxis. Opladen: Westdeutscher Verlag 1978, PVS special issue 9.

Böhr, Christoph: Zur politischen Philosophie des Kritischen Rationalismus, in: Aus Politik und Zeitgeschichte B 35/77, 1977, pp. 15-32.

Bracher, Karl Dietrich: Schlüsselwörter in der Geschichte. Mit einer Betrachtung zum Totalitarismusproblem. Düsseldorf: Droste 1978.

Braun, Karl-Heinz: Einführung in die politische Psychologie: Zum Verhältnis von gesellschaftlichem und idividuellem Subjekt. Cologne: Pahl-Rugenstein 1978.

Brenner, Michael/Strasser, Hermann (eds.): Die gesellschaftliche Konstruktion der Entfremdung. Frankfurt et al.: Campus 1977.

Bückner, Jutta: Staatswissenschaften, Kameralismus und Naturrecht. Ein Beitrag zur Geschichthe der Politischen Wissenschaft im Deutschland des späten 17. und frühen 18. Jh. Munich: Beck 1977.

Bühl, Walter L.: Theorie sozialer Konflikte. Darmstadt: Wissenschaftliche Buchgesellschaft 1976.

Buse, Michael/Pabst, Siegfried: Politische Wissenschaft und politische Praxis, in: Aus Politik und Zeitgeschichte, B 39/77, 1977, pp. 3-14.

Bußhoff, Heinrich: Methodologie der Politikwissenschaft. Stuttgart: Klettt-Cotta 1978.

Derschka, Peter/Stöber, Adolf: Grundlagen der anwendungsbezogenen Sozialwissenschaft. Opladen: Westdeutscher Verlag 1978.

Eberlein, Gerald/v. Kondratowitz, Hans-Joachim (eds.): Psychologie statt Soziologie? Zur Reduzierbarkeit sozialer Strukturen auf Verhalten. Frankfurt: Campus 1977.

Ellwein, Thomas: Über politische Verantwortung. Constance: Universitätsverlag 1978.

Frey, Bruno S.: Moderne Politische Ökonomie. Die Beziehungen zwischen Wirtschaft und Politik. Munich: Piper 1977.

Gabriel, Oscar W. (ed.): Grundkurs politische Theorie. Cologne, Vienna: Böhlau 1978.

Geulen, Dieter: Das vergesellschaftete Subjekt. Zur Grundlegung der Sozialisationstheorie. Frankfurt: Suhrkamp 1977.

Göhler, Gerhard (ed.): Politische Theorie. Begründungszusammenhänge in der Politikwissenschaft. Stuttgart: Klett-Cotta 1978.

Görlitz, Axel: Politische Funktionen des Rechts. Wiesbaden: Akademische Verlagsgesellschaft 1976.

Haarmann, Harald: Soziologie und Politik der Sprachen Europas. Munich: Deutscher Taschenbuch Verlag 1975.

Heimann, Horst: Theorie ohne Praxis. Sozialwissenschaft zwischen Gegenreform und Antireformismus. Cologne et al.: EVA 1977.

Hennis, Wilhelm: Politik und praktische Philosophie. Schriften zur politischen Theorie. Stuttgart: Klett-Cotta 1977.

Heyder, Ulrich: Der sozialwissenschaftliche Systemversuch Eduard Heimanns. Darstellung und Kritik der Möglichkeiten einer einheitlichen Theorie der modernen Wirtschafts- und Sozialsysteme. Frankfurt: Lang 1977.

Interaktion von Wissenschaft und Politik. Theoretische und praktische Probleme der anwendungsorientierten Sozialwissenschaften (ed.), Wissenschaftszentrum Berlin. Frankfurt et al.: Campus 1977.

Kastendiek, Hans: Die Entwicklung der westdeutschen Politikwissenschaft. Frankfurt et al.: Campus 1977.

Keuth, Herbert: Realität und Wahrheit: Zur Kritik des kritischen Rationalismus. Tübingen: Mohr 1978.

Lehner, Franz/Schneider, Friedrich: Einführung in die Neue Politische Ökonomie. Eine kritische Einführung. Königstein/Ts.: Athenäum 1978.

Lenk, Hans (ed.): Handlungstheorien interdisziplinär, vol. 4: Sozialwissenschaftliche Handlungstheorien und spezifische systemwissenschaftliche Ansätze. Munich: Fink 1977.

Lorenzen, Paul: Theorie der technischen und politischen Vernunft. Stuttgart: Reclam 1978.

Lührs, George et al. (eds.): Theorie und Politik aus kritisch-rationaler Sicht. Berlin et al.: Dietz 1978.

Meyer, Peter: Kriegs- und Militärsoziologie. Munich: Goldmann 1977.

Mück, Josef (ed.): Politische Ökonomie. Frankfurt et al.: Campus 1977.

Röhrich, Wilfried: Politik als Wissenschaft. Eine Einführung. Munich: Deutscher Taschenbuchverlag 1978.

Rohe, Karl: Politik. Begriffe und Wirklichkeiten. Eine Einführung in das politische Denken. Stuttgart et al.: Kohlhammer 1978.

Schmucker, Joseph F.: Adorno — Logik des Zerfalls. Stuttgart-Bad-Canstatt: Frommann-Holzboog 1977.

Spaemann, Robert: Zur Kritik der politischen Utopie. Zehn Kapitel politischer Philosophie. Stuttgart: Klett 1977.

Spinner, Helmut F.: Popper und die Politik. Rekonstruktion und Kritik der Sozial-, Polit- und Geschichtsphilosophie des kritischen Rationalismus. Berlin et al.: Dietz 1978.

Steinvorth, Ulrich: Eine analaytische Interpretation der Marxschen Dialektik. Meisenheim a. Gl.: Hain 1977.

Sternberger, Dolf: Drei Wurzeln der Politik. Frankfurt: Insel 1978, 2 vols.

Willms, Bernard: Selbstbehauptung und Anerkennung. Grundriß einer politischen Dialektik. Opladen: Westdeutscher. Verlag 1977.

Willms, Bernard: Offensives Denken. Philosophie und Politik. Wiesbaden: Westdeutscher. Verlag 1978.

Wittkämper, Gerhard W.: Grundkurs Politikwissenschaft. Königstein/Ts.: Athenäum et al. 1978.

Methods, Research Techniques

Deutsch, Karl W./Wildenmann, Rudolf (eds.): Mathematical Political Analysis: From Methods to Substance, in: Sozialwissenschaftliches Jahrbuch für Politik (special issue), 1976.

Günther, Klaus/Schmitz, Kurt Thomas: Parteien und Gewerkschaften als Forschungsfeld. Einführung in die Material- und Methodendiskussion an ausgewählten Beispielen. Düsseldorf: Droste 1977.

Haug, Frigga: Dialektische Theorie und empirische Methodik, in: Argument, 1978, pp. 644-656.

Hoffmann-Loerzer, Günter: Topik und Politikwissenschaft. Die Topik des Hugo Grotius: ein Modell moderner Problemlösungen ?, in: Archiv für Rechts- u. Sozialphilosophie, 1977, pp. 379-398.

Kammler, Hans: Logik der Politikwissenschaft. Wiesbaden: Akademische Verlagsgesellschaft 1976.

Kreppner, Kurt: Zur Problematik des Messens in den Sozialwissenschaften. Stuttgart: Klett 1975.

Krupp, Hans-Jürgen: Möglichkeiten der Verbesserung der Einkommens- und Vermögensstatistik. Göttingen: Schwartz 1975.

Mohn, Erich: Der logische Positivismus. Frankfurt: Campus 1978.

Müller, F. F./Schmidt, M. G.: Empirische Politikwissenschaft. Eine Einführung in die Methoden und Techniken. Stuttgart: Kohlhammer 1978.

Schneider, Friedrich: Politische-ökonomische Modelle. Königstein/Ts.: Athenäum 1978.

Weede, Erich: Hypothesen, Gleichungen und Daten. Spezifikations- und Meßprobleme bei Kausalmodellen für Daten aus einer und mehreren Beobachtungsperioden. Kronberg/Ts.: Athenäum 1977.

Congresses, Symposia, Associations, Curricula

Baier, Horst (ed.): Freiheit und Sachzwang. Beiträge zu Ehren Helmut Schelskys. Opladen: Westdeutscher Verlag 1977.

Böhret, Carl (ed.): Politik und Wirtschaft. Festschrift für Gert von Eynern. Opladen: Westdeutscher Verlag 1977.

Haungs, Peter (ed.): Res Publica. Studien zum Verfassungswesen. Dolf Sternberger zum 70. Geburtstag. Munich: Fink 1977.

Horn, Hannelore et al. (eds.): Sozialismus in Theorie und Praxis. Festschrift für Richard Löwenthal zum 70. Geb. Berlin: de Gruyter 1978.

Schulz, Karl-Ernst (ed.): Militär und Ökonomie. Beiträge zu einem Symposium. Göttingen: Vandenhoeck & Ruprecht 1977.

Wildenmann, Rudolf (ed.): Form und Erfahrung. Ein Leben für die Demokratie. Zum 70. Geburtstag von Ferdinand A. Hermens. Berlin: Duncker & Humblot 1976.

Works of Reference, Bibliographies

Beck, Reinhart: Sachwörterbuch der Politik. Stuttgart: Kröner 1977.

Bermbach, Udo et al. (eds.): Hamburger Bibliographie zum Parlamentarischen Regierungssystem der Bundesrepublik Deutschland. 3. Ergänzungslieferung 1975-76. Opladen: Westdeutscher Verlag 1978.

Lange, Gerhard (ed.): Vademecum der politischen Bildungsarbeit. personen, Institutionen, Materialien der politischen Bildung in der BRD. Bonn-Bad Godesberg: Hohwacht-Verlag 1977.

Politikwissenschaftliche Forschung 1977 (ed.): Leitstelle Politische Dokumentation. Munich: Vlg. Dokumentation 1977.

Ullmann, Hans-Peter: Bibliographie zur Geschichte der deutschen Parteien und Interessenverbände. Göttingen: Vandenhoeck & Ruprecht 1978.

B. POLITICAL THOUGHT

History of Political Ideas

General Works

Holz, Hans Heinz: Die abenteuerliche Rebellion. Bürgerliche Protestbewegungen in der Philosophie. Stirner, Nietzsche, Sartre, Marcuse, Neue Linke. Darmstadt et al.: Luchterhand 1976.

Ibrahim, Salim: Nichtkapitalistischer Entwicklungsweg. Ideengeschichte und Theoriekonzept. Cologne: Kiepenheuer & Witsch 1976.

Krämer-Badoni, Thomas: Zur Legitimität der bürgerlichen Gesellschaft. Eine Untersuchung des Arbeitsbegriffs in den Theorien von Locke, Smith, Ricardo, Hegel und Marx. Frankfurt: Campus 1978.

Neumann, Franz (ed.): Handbuch politischer Theorien und Ideologien. Reinbek: Rowohlt 1977.

Suhr, Dieter: Staat-Gesellschaft-Verfassung. Von Hegel bis heute, in: Staat, 1978, pp. 369-395.

Weber-Fas, Rudolf (ed.): Der Staat. Dokumente des Staatsdenkens von der Antike bis zur Gegenwart, 2 vols. Pfullingen: Neske 1977.

Ancient Times and Middle Ages

Meier, Christian: Entstehung und Besonderheit der griechischen Demokratie, in: ZfP, 1978, pp. 1-31.

Podlech, Adalbert: Die Herrschaftstheorie des Johannes von Paris, in: Staat, 1977, pp. 465-492.

Weber-Schäfter, Peter: Einführung in die antike politische Theorie, vol. 2: Von Platon bis Augustinus. Darmstadt: Wissenschaftliche Buchgesellschaft 1976.

Modern Times until 1789

Bachmann, Hans-Martin: Die naturrechtliche Staatslehre Christian Wolffs. Berlin: Duncker & Humblot 1977.

Becher, Ursula A. J.: Politische Gesellschaft. Studien zur Genese bürgerlicher Öffentlichkeit in Deutschland. Göttingen: Vandenhoeck & Ruprecht 1978.

Bender, Karl-Heinz: Revolutionen. Die Entstehung des politischen Revolutionsbegriffs in Frankreich zwischen Mittelalter und Aufklärung. Munich: Fink 1977.

Forschner, Maximilian: Rousseau. Freiburg: Alber 1977.

Hensmann, Folkert: Staat und Absolutismus im Denken der Physiokraten. Ein Beitrag zur physiokratischen Staatsauffassung von Quesnay bis Turgot. Frankfurt: Haag & Herchen 1976.

Krautheim, Ulrike: Die Souveränitätskonzeption in den englischen Verfassungskonflikten des 17. Jahrhunderts: Eine Studie zur Rezeption der Lehre Bodins in England von der Regierungszeit Elisabeths I. bis zur Restauration der Stuartherrschaft unter Karl II. Frankfurt: Lang 1977.

Luft, Gerhard: Freiheit und Gleichheit: Die Aktualität im politischen Denken Kants. Vienna: Springer 1978.

Nonnenmacher, Günther: Theorie und Geschichte. Studien zu den politischen Ideen von Jame Harrington. Meisenheim a. Gl.: Hain 1977.

Rohbeck, Johannes: Egoismus und Sympathie. David Humes Gesellschafts- und Erkenntnistheorie. Frankfurt: Campus 1978.

Siedschlag, Karl: Der Einfluß der niederländisch-neustoischen Ethik in der politischen Theorie zur Zeit Sullys und Richelieus. Berlin: Duncker & Humblot 1978.

Stolleis, Michael et al. (eds.): Staatsdenker im 17. und 18. Jahrhundert. Reichspublizistik, Politik, Naturrecht. Frankfurt: Metzner 1977.

Wember, Viktor: Verfassungsmischung und Verfassungsmitte. Moderne Formen gemischter Verfassung in der politischen Theorie des beginnenden Zeitalters der Gleichheit. Berlin: Duncker & Humblot 1977.

19th Century

Albrecht, Reinhardt: Hegel und die Demokratie. Bonn: Bouvier 1978.

Blasisu, Dirk/Pankoke, Eckart: Lorenz von Stein. Geschichts- und gesellschaftswissenschaftliche Perspektiven. Darmstadt: Wissenschaftliche Buchgesellschaft 1977.

von Borcke, Astrid: Die Ursprünge des Bolschewismus. Die jakobinische Tradition in Rußland und die Theorie der revolutionären Diktatur. Munich: J. Berchmans 1977.

Fenske, Hans: Lorenz Stein über Weltpolitik und Kolohein, in: Staat, 1977, pp. 539-556.

Hanschmidt, Alwin: Republikanisch-demokratischer Internationalismus im 19. Jahrhundert. Leben, Formen, Organisationsversuche. Husum: Matthiesen 1977.

Koch, Rainer: Demokratie und Staat bei Julius Fröbel: 1805-1893. Liberales Denken zwischen Naturrecht und Sozialdarwinismus. Wiesbaden: Steiner 1978.

Lademacher, Horst: Moses Heß in seiner Zeit. Bonn: Ludwig Röhrscheid 1977.

Schnur, Roman (ed.): Staat und Gesellschaft. Studien über Lorenz von Stein. Berlin: Duncker & Humblot 1978.

Uhde, Ute: Politik und Religion: Zum Verhältnis von Demokratie und Christentum bei Alexis de Tocqueville. Berlin: Duncker & Humblot 1978.

20th Century

Meinck, Jürgen: Weimarer Staatsrechtslehre und Nationalsozialismus: Eine Studie zur Problematik der Kontinuität im staatsrechtlichen Denken in Deutschland 1928-1936. Frankfurt: Campus 1978.

Menschik, Jutta: Feminismus. Geschichte, Theorie, Praxis. Cologne: Pahl-Rugenstein 1977.

Ideological Foundations of Political Systems

General Studies

Graf von Krockow, Christian: Herrschaft und Freiheit, Politische Grundpositionen der bürgerlichen Gesellschaft. Stuttgart: Metzler 1977.

Lichtblau, Klaus: Theorie der bürgerlichen Gesellschaft: Zum Verhältnis von Ökonomie, Recht und Politik. Lahn-Gießen: Focus 1978.

Meissner, Boris/Hacker, Jens: Die Nation in östlicher Sicht. Berlin: Duncker & Humblot 1977.

Michalski, Wolfgang (ed.): Industriegesellschaft im Wandel. Probleme. Lösungsmöglichkeiten, Perspektiven. Hamburg: Weltarchiv 1977.

Ritsert, Jürgen: Denken und gesellschaftliche Wirklichkeit. Arbeitsbuch zum klassischen Ideologiebegriff. Frankfurt: Campus 1977, vol. 1.

Schabert, Tilo: Gewalt und Humanität: Über philosophische und politische Manifestationen von Modernität. Freiburg: Alber 1978.

Schmitt, Carl: Die legale Weltrevolution. Politischer Mehrwert als Prämie auf juristische Legalität und Superlegalität, in: Staat, 1978, pp. 321-339.

Sorg, Richard: Ideologietheorien. Zum Verhältnis von gesellschaftlichem Bewußtsein und sozialer Realität. Cologne: Kiepenheuer & Witsch 1976.

Tuschling, Burkhard: Die 'offene' und die 'abstrakte' Gesellschaft. Habermas und die Konzeption von Vergesellschaftung der klassisch-bürgerlichen Rechts- und Staatsphilosophie. Berlin: Argument-Verlag 1978.

Democracy

Bayertz, Kurt: Der Streit um die geistigen Grundlagen der Demokratie, in: Blätter, 1978, pp. 804-821.

Bopp-Schmehl, Annemarie: Konflikt und Demokratie. Eine Auseinandersetzung mit Kompromiß- und Gleichgewichtsvorstellungen moderner Politiktheorien. Frankfurt et al.: Lang 1977.

Ebert, Theodor: Toleranz und Konfliktfähigkeit — Konkurrierende Tugenden in der pluralistischen Demokratie?, in: Aus Politik und Zeitgeschichte B 38/77, 1977, pp. 13-22.

Graf Kielmannsegg, Peter: Volkssouveränität. Eine Untersuchung der Bedingungen demokratischer Legitimität. Stuttgart: Klett 1977.

Haumann, Heiko (ed.): Vom Hotzenwald bis Wyhl. Demokratische Traditionen in Baden. Cologne: Pahl-Rugenstein 1977.

Kimminich, Otto: Die Grundwerte im demokratischen Rechtsstaat, in: ZfP, 1977, pp. 1-17.

Kremendahl, Hans: Pluralismustheorie in Deutschland. Entstehung, Kritik, Perspektiven. Leverkusen: Heggen-Verlag 1977.

Lameyer, Johannes: Streitbare Demokratie. Eine verfassungshermeneutische Untersuchung. Berlin: Duncker & Humblot 1978.

Maier, Hans/Oberreuther, Heinrich (eds.): Pluralismus. Stuttgart: Klett 1978.

Massing, Peter: Interesse und Konsensus. Zur Rekonstruktion und Begründung normativkritischer Elemente neopluralistischer Demokratietheorie. Stuttgart: Leske 1978.

Pirker, Theo: Die verordnete Demokratie. Grundlagen und Erscheinungen der Restauration. Berlin: Olle & Wolter 1977.

Schwan, Alexander: Grundwerte der Demokratie. Orientierungsversuche im Pluralismus. Munich: Piper 1978.

Schwan, Alexander: Politische Philosophie im Zeichen des Pluralismus. Situationsanalyse, Kritik, Entwurf. Munich: Piper 1978.

Sontheimer, Kurt: Ist unsere Demokratie überfordert?, in: Aus Politik und Zeitgeschichte B 50/77, 1977, pp. 3-12.

Teubner, Gunther: Organisationsdemokratie und Verbandsverfassung. Tübingen: Mohr 1978.

Socialism

Butterwegge, Christoph: Der Bernstein-Boom in der SPD. Grundlagen, Geschichte und Funktion der gegenwärtigen Revisionismus-Renaissance, in: Blätter, 1978, pp. 579-592.

Fenner, Christian et al.: Zur Einführung in die Theorie des demokratischen Sozialimus. Frankfurt et al.: EVA 1977.

Günsche, Karl-Ludwig et al.: Kleine Geschichte der Sozialistischen Internationale. Bonn-Bad Godesberg: Neue Gesellschaft 1977.

Hirsch, Helmut: Der 'Fabier' Eduard Bernstein — Zur Entwicklungsgeschichte des evolutionären Sozialismus. Berlin-Bonn: J.H.W. Dietz 1977.

Jochheim, Gernot: Antimilitaristische Aktionstheorie, Soziale Revolution und Soziale Verteidigung. Zur Entwicklung der Gewaltfreiheitstheorie in der europäischen antimilitaristischen und sozialistischen Bewegung 1890-1940, unter bes. Berücksichtigung der Niederlande. Assen et al.: Van Gorcum; Frankfurt: Hag & Herchen 1977.

Lammich, Siegried: Grundzüge des sozialistischen Parlamentarismus. Baden-Baden: Nomos 1977.

Loth, Wilfried: Sozialimus und Internationalismus. Die französischen Sozialisten und die Nachkriegsordnung Europas 1940-1950. Stuttgart: DVA 1977.

Meyer, Ahlrich: Frühsozialismus. Theorien der sozialen Bewegung 1789-1848. Freiburg et al.: Alber 1977.

Meyer, Thomas: Bernsteins konstruktiver Sozialismus: Eduard Bernsteins Beitrag zur Theorie des Sozialismus. Berlin, Bad Godesberg: Dietz 1977.

Papcke, Sven: Der Revisionismusstreit und die politische Theorie der Reform. Stuttgart: Kohlhammer 1978.

Uellenburg, Wolfgang/Eppe, Heinrich: 70 Jahre Sozialistische Jugendinternationale, in: Aus Politik und Zeitgeschichte B 35/77, 1977, pp. 38-47.

Marxism, Communism

Bischoff, Joachim (ed.): Grundbegriffe des Marxismus. Hamburg: VSA 1978.

Botz, Gerhard et al.: Im Schatten der Arbeiterbewegung. Zur Geschichte des Anarchismus in Österreich und Deutschland. Vienna: Europaverlag 1977.

Flechtheim, Ossip K.: Von Marx bis Kolakowski. Sozialismus oder Untergang in der Barbarei? Frankfurt: EVA 1978.

Grebing, Helga: Der Revisionismus. Von Bernstein bis zum 'Prager Frühling'. Munich: Beck 1977.

Hornung, Klaus: Der faszinierende Irrtum. Karl Marx und die Folgen. Freiburg i. B.: Herder 1978.

Kraus, Rainer: Die Imperialismusdebatte zwischen Vladimir I. Lenin und Karl Kautsky: Eine vergleichende Analyse ihrer Theorien. Frankfurt et al.: Lang 1978.

Leonhard, Wolfgang: Kommunistische Diskussionen über Sozialismus-Modelle, in: OE, 1978, pp. 101-114.

Lösche, Peter: Anarchismus. Darmstadt: Wissenschaftliche Buchgesellschaft 1977.

Oelmüller, Willi (ed.): Weiterentwicklungen des Marxismus. Darmstadt: Wissenschaftliche Buchgesellschaft 1977.

Paul, Hans-Holger: Marx, Engels und die Imperialismustheorie der II. Internationale. Hamburg: VSA 1978.

Rock, Martin: Anarchismus und Terror. Ursprünge und Strategien. Trier: Spee-Verlag 1977.

Rothe, Valentine: Der russische Anarchismus und die Rätebewegung 1905. Frankfurt: Campus 1978.

Schäfer, Ingo: Mao Tse-Tung. Eine Einführung in sein Denken. Munich: Beck 1978.

Spieker, Manfred: Demokratie oder Diktatur? Zur Ideologie des Eurokommunismus, in: PVS, 1978, pp. 23-47.

Steitz, Walter: Einführung in die politische Ökonomie des Marxismus. Paderborn: Schöningh 1977.

Sternstein, Wolfgang: Marx, Lenin, Mao: Darstellung und Kritik der marxistischen Gesellschaftsanalyse. Frankfurt: Haag & Herchen 1978.

Vogel, Angela: Der deutsche Anarcho-Syndikalismus. Genese und Theorie einer vergessenen Bewegung. Berlin: Kramer 1977.

Zimmermann, Rüdiger: Der Leninbund: Linke Kommunisten in der Weimarer Republik. Düsseldorf: Droste 1978.

Nationalism, Fascism

Anderbrügge, Klaus: Völkisches Rechtsdenken. Zur Rechtslehre in der Zeit des Nationalsozialismus. Berlin: Duncker & Humblot 1978.

Berlin, Jörg et al.: Neofaschismus in der Bundesrepublik. Aktivität, Ideologie und Funktion rechtsextremer Gruppen, in: Blätter, 1978, pp. 528-554.

Dann, Otto (ed.): Nationalismus und sozialer Wandel. Hamburg: Hoffmann & Campe 1978.

Hennig, Eike: Bürgerliche Gesellschaft und Faschismus in Deutschland. Ein Forschungsbericht. Frankfurt: Suhrkamp 1977.

Rumpf, Helmut: Carl Schmitt und der Faschismus, in: Staat, 1978, pp. 223-243.

Thamer, H.-U./Wippermann, W.: Faschistische und neofaschistische Bewegungen. Probleme empirischer Faschismusforschungen. Darmstadt: Wissenschaftliche Buchgesellschaft 1977.

Winkler, Heinrich August: Revolution, Staat, Faschismus. Zur Revision des Historischen Materialismus: Göttingen: Vandenhoeck & Ruprecht 1978.

Winkler, Heinrich August (ed.): Nationalismus. Königstein/T.: Athenäum et al. 1978.

Wolffsohn, Michael: Linker und rechter Nationalsozialismus, in: ZfP, 1977, pp. 56-80.

Totalitarianism, Authoritarianism

Liberalism

Müller, J. Baptist: Liberalismus und Demokratie. Studien zum Verhältnis von Politik und Wirtschaft im Liberalismus. Stuttgart: Klett-Cotta 1978.

von Thadden, Rudolf (ed.): Die Krise des Liberalismus zwischen den Weltkriegen. Göttingen: Vandenhoeck & Ruprecht 1978.

Conservatism

Bamberg, Hans-Dieter: Die Deutschland-Stiftung e.V.: Studien über Kräfte der 'demokratischen Mitte' und des Konservatismus in der Bundesrepublik Deutschland. Meisenheim: Hain 1978.

Saage, Richard: Konservatismus und Faschismus. Anmerkungen zu Ernst Forsthoffs Entwicklung vom 'Totalen Staat' zum 'Staat der Industriegesellschaft', in: PVS, 1978, pp. 254-268.

Theories of Political Systems (State, Power, Legitimacy)

Axt, Heinz-Jürgen: Staat, multinationale Konzerne und politische Union in Westeuropa. Ein Beitrag zur Staatstheorie und Analyse regionaler Integration. Cologne: Pahl-Rugenstein 1978.

Badura, Peter: Staat, Recht und Verfassung in der Integrationslehre, in: Staat, 1977, pp. 305-325.

Böckenförde, Ernst-Wolfgang: Der Staat als sittlicher Staat. Berling: Duncker & Humblot 1978.

Brandes, Volkhard (ed.): Staat. Cologne et al.: EVA 1977.

Fach, Wolfgang/Degen, Ulrich (eds.): Politische Legitimität. Frankfurt et al.: Campus 1978.

Graf Kielmansegg, Peter/Matz, Ulrich (eds.): Die Rechtfertigung politischer Herrschaft. Doktrinen und Verfahren in Ost und West. Freiburg et al.: Alber 1978.

Grieffenhagen, Martin (ed.): Zur Theorie der Reform. Heidelberg: C. F. Müller 1978.

Hennen, Manfred/Prigge, Wolfgang-Ulrich: Autorität und Herrschaft. Darmstadt: Wissenschaftliche Buchgesellschaft 1977.

Hess, Henner: Die Entstehung zentraler Herrschaftsinstanzen durch die Bildung klientelärer Gefolgschaft. Zur Diskussion um die Entstehung staatlich organisierter Gesellschaften, in: KZfSS, 1977, pp. 762-778.

Kaiser, Hans-Rainer: Staat und gesellschaftliche Integration. Zur Analyse und Kritik des Staatsbegriffs bei Jürgen Habermas und Claus Offe. Marburg: VAG 1977.

Kriele, Martin: Legitimitätsprobleme der Bundesrepublik. Munich: Beck 1977.

Laufer, Heinz: Der sozialisierte Mensch. Die Gefährdung der personalen Existenz in der demokratisch regierten Industriegesellschaft. Stuttgart: Seewald 1977.

Oberreuther, Heinrich: Notstand und Demokratie: Vom monarchischen Obrigkeits- zum demokratischen Rechtsstaat. Munich: tuduv 1978.

Preuß, Ulrich K.: Legalität — Loyalität — Legitimität, in: Lev., 1977, ppl. 450-466.

Priester, Karin: Zur Staatstheorie bei Antonio Gramsci, in: Argument 104, 1977, pp. 515-532.

Rodenstein, Marianne: Bürgerinitiativen und politisches System: Eine Auseinandersetzung mit soziologischen Legitimationstheorien. Lahn-Gießen: Focus 1978.

Quaritsch, Helmut (ed.): Die Selbstdarstellung des Staates. Berlin: Duncker & Humblot 1977.

Sauer, Dieter: Staat und Staatsapparat. Ein theoretischer Ansatz. Frankfurt: Campus 1978.

Schmidtchen, Gerhard: Ist Legitimität meßbar?, in: ZParl, 1977, pp. 232-241.

Schneider, Hans-Dieter: Sozialpsychologie der Machtbeziehungen. Stuttgart: Enke 1978.

Schütte, Helmuth: Resultate und Kritik der neueren staatstheoretischen Diskussion, in: Argument 104, 1977, pp. 533-545.

Weede, Erich: Politische Kultur, Institutionalisierung und Prätorianismus: Überlegungen zur Theorie und empirischen Forschungspraxis, in: KZfSS, 1977, pp. 411-437, pp. 657-676.

Wege, Joachim: Positives Recht und sozialer Wandel im demokratischen und sozialen Rechtsstaat. Berlin: Duncker & Humblot 1977.

Political Development and Changes (Crisis, Violence and Revolution)

Agermüller, Hans-Heinrich et al.: Allgemeine Krise des Kapitalismus. Triebkräfte und Erscheinungsformen in der Gegenwart. Frankfurt: Marxistische Blätter 1976.

Allemann, Fritz René: Wie wirksam ist Terrorismus?, in: EA, 1978, pp. 343-358.

Altvater, Elmar: Politische Implikationen der Krisenbereinigung — Überlegungen zu den Austerity-Tendenzen in Westeuropa, in: Prokla 32/1978, pp. 43-72.

Bartol, Gerda: Ideologie und studentischer Protest. Untersuchungen zur Entstehung deutscher Studentenbewegungen im 19. und 20. Jahrhundert. Munich: Verlag Dokumentation 1977.

Binder, Sepp: Terrorismus. Herausforderung und Antwort. Bonn: Verlag Neue Gesellschaft 1978.

Breuer, Stefan: Die Krise der Revolutionstheorie. Negative Vergesellschaftung und Arbeitsmetaphysik bei Herbert Marcuse. Frankfurt: Syndicat 1977.

Engel-Janosi, Friedrich et al. (eds.): Gewalt und Gewaltlosigkeit. Probleme des 20. Jahrhunderts. Munich: Oldenbourg 1977.

Fetscher, Iring: Terrorismus und Reaktion. Cologne et al.: EVA 1977.

Funke, Manfred: Terrorismus — Ermittlungsversuch zu einer Herausforderung, in: Aus Politik und Zeitgeschichte B 41/77, 1977, pp. 29-44.

Funke, Manfred (ed.): Terrorismus. Untersuchungen zur Struktur und Strategie revolutionärer Gewaltpolitik. Kronberg, Ts.: Athenäum 1977; Düsseldorf: Droste 1977.

Funke, Manfred (ed.): Extremismus im demokratischen Rechtsstaat. Düsseldorf: Droste 1978.

Funke, Manfred: Extremismus und offene Gesellschaft, in: Aus Politik und Zeitgeschichte B 37/1978, pp. 3-21.

Gebhardt, Jürgen: Strukturprobleme einer Revolutionstheorie, in: ZfP, 1977, pp. 32-55.

Geissler, Heiner (ed.): Der Weg in die Gewalt. Geistige und gesellschaftliche Ursachen des Terrorismus und seine Folgen. Munich: Olzog 1978.

Grahn, Werner/Wagner, Ingo: Rechtliche und soziale Gleichheit im Klassenkampf. Frankfurt: Marxistische Blätter 1977.

Grossarth-Maticek, Ronald: Anfänge anarchistischer Gewaltbereitschaft in der Bundesrepublik Deutschland. Bonn-Bad Godesberg: Hohwacht 1976.

Holz, Hans Heinz: Hat der Terrorismus eine theoretische Basis?, in: Blätter, 1978, pp. 317-329.

Jahrbuch für Politik 8: Die RAF und die Linke. Zur Verbreitung des 'Modell Deutschland' in Europa. Berlin: Wagenbach 1978.

Käsler, Dirk: Revolution und Veralltäglichung. Eine Theorie postrevolutionärer Prozesse. Munich: Nymphenburger Verlagsbuchhandlung 1977.

Langguth, Gerd: Die Protestbewegung in der Bundesrepublik Deutschland 1968-1976. Cologne: Wissenschaft & Politik 1976.

Müller, Gernot et al.: Ökonomische Krisentendenzen im gegenwärtigen Kapitalismus. Frankfurt et al.: Campus 1978.

Paschen, Joachim: Demokratische Vereine und preußischer Staat. Entwicklung und Unterdrückung der demokratischen Bewegung während der Revolution von 1848/49. Munich: Oldenbourg 1977.

Pfromm, Hans-Adam (ed.): Krise und Reform in der Industriegesellschaft. Frankfurt/-Main: EVA 1976, 2 vols.

Rammstedt, Otthein: Soziale Bewegung. Frankfurt: Suhrkamp 1978.

Roloff, Ernst-August (ed.): Aggression, Gewalt, Krieg. Stuttgart: Metzler 1978.

Schwind, Hans-Dieter (ed.): Ursachen des Terrorismus in der Bundesrepublik Deutschland. Berlin et al.: de Gruyter 1978.

Seifert, Michael J.: Sozialer Konflikt. Eine Analyse der Entstehungsbedingungen politischer Bewegungen. Frankfurt: Lang 1978.

Wassmund, Hans (ed.): Revolutionstheorien. Eine Einführung. Munich: Beck 1978.

Wehler, Hans-Ulrich (ed.): 200 (Zweihundert) Jahre amerikanische Revolution und moderne Revolutionsforschung. Göttingen: Vandenhoeck & Ruprecht 1976.

Widmaier, Ulrich: Politische Gewaltanwendung als Problem der Organisation von Interessen. Eine Querschnittsstudie der soziopolitischen Ursachen gewaltsamer Konfliktaustrangung innerhalb von Nationalstaaten. Königstein/Ts.: Athenäum 1978.

Wiswede, Günter: Sozialer Wandel: Zur Erklärungskraft neuerer Entwicklungs- und Modernisierungstheorien. Darmstadt: Wissenschaftliche Buchgesellschaft 1978.

Wördemann, Franz: Terrorismus. Motive, Täter, Strategien. Munich: Piper 1977.

Zimmermann, Ekkhart: Soziologie der politischen Gewalt. Darstellung und Kritik vergleichender Aggregatdatenanalysen aus den USA. Stuttgart: Enke 1977.

Zimmermann, Ekkart (ed.): Makropolitische Konfliktforschung, in: OVS, 1978, pp. 455-600 (special issue).

C. GOVERNMENT AND POLITICS

The Political System (Theoretical and Comparative Studies)

Armanski, Gerhard et al. (eds.): Klassenbewegung, Staat und Krise. Konflikte im öffentlichen Dienst Westeuropas und der USA. Berlin: Olle & Wolter 1977.

Flora, Peter/Alber, Jens/Kohl, Jürgen: Zur Entwicklung der westeuropäischen Wohlfahrtsstaaten, in: PVS, 1977, pp. 707-772.

Steffani, Winfried: Parlamentarismus in den EG-Staaten und demokratisches Defizit der europäischen Institutionen, in: ZParl, 1978, pp. 233-253.

The Political System of the FGR

Bernewitz, Ernst Heinrich von (ed.): Wirtschaft und Politik verstehen. Didaktisches

Sachbuch zur Vorgeschichte und Geschichte der Bundesrepublik. Erläuterungen, Materialien, Arbeitsvorschläge. Reinbek: Rowohlt 1978.

Blanke, Bernhard et al.: Die Linke im Rechtsstaat, vol. 1: Bedingungen sozialistischer Politik, 1945-1965. Berlin: Rotbuch Verlag 1976.

Borsdorf, Ulrich/Niethammer, Lutz (eds.): Zwischen Befreiung und Besatzung. Analysen des US-Geheimdienstes über Positionen und Strukturen deutscher Politik 1945. Wuppertal: Hammer 1976.

Esche, Falk et al.: Parteiendemokratie, Wahlen und Parteien in der Bundesrepublik Deutschland. Hamburg: Hoffmann & Campe 1978.

Grube, Frank/Richter, Gerhard (eds.): Der SPD-Staat. Munich: Piper 1977.

Hennis, Wilhelm et al. (eds.): Regierbarkeit. Studien zu ihrer Problematisierung. Stuttgart: Klett-Cotta 1977.

Hurwitz, Harold: Antikommunismus und amerikanische Demokratisierungsvorhaben im Nachkriegsdeutschland, in: Aus Politik und Zeitgeschichte B 29/1978, pp. 29-46.

Kaelble, Hartmut et al.: Probleme der Modernisierung in Deutschland. Sozialhistorische Studien zum 19. u. 20. Jh. Opladen: Westdeutscher Verlag 1978.

Kühnl, Reinhard/Hardach, Gerd (eds.): Die Zerstörung der Weimarer Republik. Cologne: Pahl-Rugenstein 1977.

Leisewitz, André: Klassen in der Bundesrepublik Deutschland heute. Frankfurt: Marxistische Blätter 1977.

Lompe, Klaus: Einführung in das politische System der Bundesrepublik. Kronberg/Ts.: Athenäum 1978.

Oppermann, Thomas: Staatliche Einheit oder innere Freiheit? Zu den langfristigen Perspektiven der nationalen Frage in Deutschland, in: EA, 1978, pp. 681-692.

Pankoke, Eckart et al.: Neue Formen gesellschaftlicher Selbststeuerung in der Bundesrepublik Deutschland. Diskussion an Beispielen aus den Bereichen Bildung, Soziale Sicherung und kommunale Selbstverwaltung. Göttingen: Schwartz 1975.

Pilz, Frank: Das sozialstaatliche System der Bundesrepublik Deutschland. Grundzüge der Sozial- und Gesellschaftspolitik. Munich et al.: Reinhardt 1978.

Rudzio, Wolfgang: Die organisierte Demokratie. Parteien und Verbände in der Bundesrepublik. Stuttgart: Metzler 1977.

Rupp, Hans Karl: Politische Geschichte der Bundesrepublik Deutschland. Eine Einführung in ihre Entstehung und Entwicklung. Stuttgart: Kohlhammer 1978.

Scharf, Claus/Schröder, Hans-Jürgen (eds.): Politische und ökonomische Stabilisierung Westdeutschlands 1945-1949. 5 Beiträge zur Deutschlandpolitik der Westlichen Alliierten. Wiesbaden: Steiner 1977.

Schissler, Jakob: Zu einigen Problemen der politischen Kultur der Bundesrepublik Deutschland, in: ZfP, 1978, pp. 154-167.

Schmidt, Manfred G.: Die 'Politik der inneren Reformen' in der Bundesrepublik Deutschland 1969 — 1976, in: PVS, 1978, pp. 201-253.

Schwickert, Reinhard/Wolffsohn, Michael: Das Weimarer und Bonner Parteiensystem: Vergleiche und Modellkonstruktionen, in: ZParl, 1978, pp. 534-555.

Thaysen, Uwe: Bürgerinitiativen, Parlamente und Parteien in der Bundesrepublik. Eine Zwischenbilanz (1977), in: ZParl, 1978, pp. 87-103.

Constitutional Problems

Arnim, Hans Herbert von: Gemeinwohl und Gruppeninteressen. Die Durchsetzungsschwäche allgemeiner Interessen in der pluralistischen Demokratie. Ein Beitrag zu verfassungsrechtlichen Grundfragen der Wirtschaftsordnung. Frankfurt: Metzner 1977.

Böckenförde, Ernst-Wolfgang/Stern, Klaus: Die Ergebnisse der Enquete-Kommission Verfassungsreform und die verfassungsrechtliche Fortentwicklung der Bundesrepublik. Cologne: Grote 1977.

Brandt, Edmund: Vorzeitige Beendigung der Wahlperiode durch Parlamentsbeschluß, Minderheitsregierung und Gesetzgebungsnotstand. Zu den Vorschlägen der Enquete-Kommision 'Verfassungsreform' des Deutschen Bundestages, in: ZfP 1977, pp. 350-362.

Friedrich, Manfred (ed.): Verfassung. Beiträge zur Verfassungstheorie. Darmstadt: Wissenschaftliche Buchgesellschaft 1978.

Hrbek, Rudolf: Das deutsche Wahlgesetz zum Europäischen Parlament in der Parteienkontroverse, in: ZParl, 1978, pp. 168-179.

Isensee, Josef: Wirtschaftsdemokratie — Wirtschaftsgrundrechte — Soziale Gewaltenteilung. Verfassungsrechtliche Aspekte der unternehmerischen Mitbestimmung, in: Staat, 1978, pp. 161-182.

Kröger, Klaus: Grundrechtstheorie als Verfassungsproblem. Baden-Baden: Nomos 1978.

Kübler, Friedrich et al.: Mitbestimmung als gesetzgebungspolitische Aufgabe. Zur Verfassungsmäßigkeit des Mitbestimmungsgesetze 1976. Baden-Baden: Nomos 1978.

Lautner, Gerd: Die freiheitliche demokratische Grundordnung. Versuch einer Inhaltserklärung ihrer vom BVG aufgeführten Elemente. Kronberg/Ts.: Athenäum 1978.

Lehmbruch, Gerhard: Verfassungspolitische Alternativen der Politikverflechtung. Bemerkungen zur Strategie der Verfassungsreform, in: ZParl, 1977, pp. 461-474.

Murswieck, Dietrich: Die verfassunggebende Gewalt nach dem Grundgesetz für die Bundesrepublik Deutschland. Berlin: Duncker & Humblot 1978.

Rack, Manfred: Die Verfassung als Maßstab: Eine argumentationstheoretische Untersuchung am Beispiel des Problems der Verfassungsmäßigkeit nichtfiskalischer Abgaben. Berlin: Duncker & Humblot 1978.

Römer, Peter et al. (eds.): Der Kampf um das Grundgesetz. Über die politische Bedeutung der Verfassungsinterpretation. Frankfurt: Syndikat 1977.

Schlothauer, Reinhold: Die Verhängung des permanenten Ausnahmezustandes im Wege der Verfassungsinterpretation, in: Lev., 1977, pp. 538-551.

Stern, Klaus: Das Staatsrecht der Bundesrepublik Deutschland, Vol. 1. Munich: Beck 1977.

Vogt, Karl Herbert: Die Reform des Staatschaftungsrechts in Deutschland und die Französische 'Responsabilité de la Puissance Publique', in: Die Verwaltung, 1978, pp. 57-70.

Wedel, Henning von: Das Verfahren der demokratischen Verfassunggebung. Dargestellt am Beispiel Deutschlands 1848/49, 1919, 1948/49. Berlin: Duncker & Humblot 1976.

Federalism

Kirsch, Guy (ed.): Föderalismus. Stuttgart et al.: G. Fischer 1977.

Konegen, Norbert: Föderatives System und Bildungsplanung: Die öffentliche Bildungsplanung im Bereich von Regierung und Verwaltung der Bundesrepublik Deutschland als sektorales und regionales Koordinationsproblem im Rahmen der seit 1967 entwickelten Verfassungslage. Berlin: Dialogus Mundi 1978.

Stettner, Rupert: Neues Leben für den Föderalismus? Gedanken zu den Empfehlungen der Enquete-Kommission Verfassungsreform für eine Neuregelung der Gesetzgebungskompetenzen von Bund und Ländern, in: ZfP 1977, pp. 152-162.

Zeh, Wolfgang: Spätföderalismus: Vereinigungs- oder Differenzierungsföderalismus? Zur Arbeit der Enquete-Kommission an ihrem schwierigsten Objekt. in: ZParl, 1977, pp. 475-490.

The Powers

Executive

Bruche, Gert/Jáklie, Zóltan: Die Subventionsberichte der Bundesregierung, in: Lev., 1978, pp. 220-249.

Feuchte, Paul: Prognose, Vorsorge und Planung bei der Genehmigung industrieller Anlagen. Gesichtspunkte zum Beurteilungsspielraum der Exekutive, in: Die Verwaltung, 1977, pp. 291-311.

Wilhelmi, Hans-Herbert: Entscheidungsprozesse in der staatlichen Bildungsfinanzierung: ein interdisziplinärer Beitrag zur Erforschung der finanzpolitischen Willensbildung in der Exekutive. Berlin: Duncker & Humblot 1977.

Legislative

Ahrweiler, Georg: Zur Krise des Parlamentarismus, in: Blätter, 1978, pp. 681-698.

Bach, Wolfgang: Geschichte als politisches Argument. Eine Untersuchung an ausgewählten Debatten des Deutschen Bundestages. Stuttgart: Klett-Cotta 1977.

Botzenhart, Manfred: Deutscher Parlamentarismus in der Revolutionszeit 1848-1850. Düsseldorf: Droste 1977.

Brodersen, Carsten: Rechnungsprüfung für das Parlament in der konstitutionellen Monarchie. Berlin: Duncker & Humblot 1977.

Hartenstein, Frank-Helmut: Der Wehrbeauftragte des Deutschen Bundestages: Zuständigkeit und Befugnisse im Rahmen der parlamentarischen Kontrolle der Bundeswehr. Frankfurt: Lang 1977.

Hömig, Dieter: Zur parlamentarischen Kontrolle der Nachrichtendienste, in: Aus Politik und Zeitgeschichte B 42/77, 1977, pp. 15-31.

Hofmann, Rupert: Abgeordnetenfreiheit und parlamentarischer Abstimmungsmodus, in: ZfP, 1978, pp. 32-56.

Karpen, Ulrich: Parlamentarische Kontrolle der Regierungsplanung am Beispiel der Hochschulplanung, in: ZfP, 1977, pp. 262-290.

Klatt, Hartmut: Parlamentsreform in der Bundesrepublik. Reformvorhaben und Zielvorstellungen. Opladen: Leske 1978.

Lutterbeck, Bernd: Parlament und Information: eine informationstheoretische und verfassungsrechtliche Untersuchung. Munich: Oldenbourg 1977.

Müller, Emil-Peter: Die sozio-ökonomische und verbandliche Struktur des VIII. Deutschen Bundestages. Cologne: Deutscher Instituts-Verlag 1977.

Nahamowitz, Peter: Gesetzgebung in den kritischen Systemjahren 1967-69. Eine Rekonstruktion spätkapitalistischen Staatshandelns. Frankfurt: Campus 1978.

Plagemann, Hermann: Mehr parlamentarische Kontrolle durch Untersuchungsausschüsse. Zu den Empfehlungen der Enquete-Kommission Verfassungsreform, in: ZParl, 1977, pp. 242-251.

Rauh, Manfred: Die parlamentarisierung des Deutschen Reiches. Düsseldorf: Droste 1977.

Schrode, Klaus: Beamtenabgeordnete in Landtagen der Bundesrepublik Deutschland. Eine Untersuchung über das parlamentarische Verhalten von Abgeordneten in den Landtagen von Baden-Württemberg, Hessen und Rheinland-Pfalz, die in der öffentlichen Verwaltung tätig sind. Heidelberg: Winter 1977.

Schüttemeyer, Suzanne: Funktionsverluste des Bundestages durch die europäische Integration?, in: ZParl, 1978, pp. 261-278.

Widder, Helmut: Organisationsprobleme im parlamentarischen Regierungssystem: Zur Frage der Funktionsfähigkeit parlamentarischer Kollegien. Salzburg et al.: Pustet 1977.

Judiciary

Breuer, Stefan: Politik und Recht im Prozeß der Rationalisierung, in: Lev., 1977, pp. 53-99.

Eckertz,Rainer: Die Kompetenz des Bundesverfassungsgerichts und die Eigenheit des Politischen, in: Staat, 1978, pp. 183-203.

Häberle, Pater (ed.): Verfassungsgerichtsbarkeit. Darmstadt: Wissenschaftliche Buchgesellschaft 1977.

Hannover, Heinrich (ed.): Klassenherrschaft und Politische Justiz. Plädoyers für ein demokratisches Recht. Hamburg: VSA 1978.

Müller, Teresa: Die Haltung der Parteien zu den Problemen von Strafe und Strafvollzug. Frankfurt: Lang 1977.

Paech, Norman: Gesinnungsjustiz. Zur politischen Justiz der Radikalenverfolgung, in: Blätter, 1978, pp. 699-711.

Zachert, Ulrich et al.: Die Aussperrung. Zur rechtlichen Zulässigkeit und praktischen Durschsetzungsmöglichkeit eines Aussperrungsverbots. Cologne: Bund-Verlag 1978.

Freedom and Civil Rights

Blau, Joachim: Zum Ausbau des staatlichen Repressionsapparates seit Ende der sechziger Jahre. Frankfurt; IMSF 1977.

Brückner, Joseph A./Schmitt, Hans Theo: Verfassungsschutz und innere Sicherheit. Wuppertal: Deutscher Consulting Verlag 1977.

Cramer, Dettmar: Bürgerrechte '77. Cologne: Verlag Wissenschaft & Politik 1977.

Funke, Klaus-Detlef/Theilen, Ernst (eds.): Pressefreiheit und Mitbestimmung. Bonn-Bad Godesberg: Neue Gesellschaft 1977.

Gerlach, Johann W.: Radikalenfrage und Privatrecht. Zur politischen Freiheit in der Gesellschaft. Tübingen: Mohr 1978.

Günther, Hartmut et al.: Geschichte, politische Funktion und Arbeitsweise des Verfassungsschutzes, in: Blätter, 1977, pp. 1094-1115.

Guggenberger, Bernd: Bürgerinitiativen in der Parteiendemokratie. Stuttgart: Kohlhammer 1978.

Guggenberger, Bernd/Kempf, Udo (eds.): Bürgerinitiativen und repräsentatives System. Opladen: Westdt. Verlag 1978.

Heidelmeyer, Wolfgang (ed.): Die Menschenrechte. Erklärungen, Verfassungsartikel, Internationale Abkommen. Paderborn: Schöningh 1977.

Hieber, Lutz: Vermittlung wissenschaftlichen Wissens in Bürgerinitiativen, in: Blätter, 1978, pp. 353-360.

Huber, Wolfgang et al.: Menschenrechte. Perspektiven einer menschlichen Welt. Stuttgart et al.: Kreuz 1977.

Klier, Gerhard: Gewissensfreiheit und Psychologie. Der Beitrag der Psychologie zur Normbereichsanalyse des Grundrechts der Gewissensfreiheit. Berlin: Duncker & Humblot 1978.

Korinek, Karl: Das Petitionsrecht im demokratischen Rechtsstaat. Tübingen: Mohr 1977.

Leuenberger, Theodor: Die Ohmacht des Bürgers. Plädoyer für eine nachmoderne Gesellschaft. Frankfurt: S. Fischer 1977.

Pelinka, Anton: Bürgerinitiativen — gefährlich oder notwendig? Freiburg: Ploetz 1978.

Perels, Joachim (ed.): Grundrechte als Funktion der Demokratie. Frankfurt: Suhrkamp 1978.

Ridder, Helmut: Vom Wendekreis der Grundrechte, in: Lev., 1977, pp. 467-521.

Public Policy

Economic System and Economic Policy

Albuschkat, Harald: Globalsteuerung und Regelmechanismen als alternative stabilisierungspolitische Lenkungsmöglichkeiten in der Marktwirtschaft, in: Verwaltung, 1978, pp. 173-195.

Ambrosius, Gerold: Die Durchsetzung der Sozialen Marktwirtschaft in Westdeutschland 1945-1949. Stuttgart: Deutsche Verlags-Anstalt 1977.

Baisch, H. et al.: Die Wirtschaftskrise in der BRD. Eine Auseinandersetzung mit den Analysen des Sachverständigenrats zur Begutachtung der wirtschaftlichen Entwicklung, in: Lev., 1977, pp. 163-209.

Van der Bellen, Alexander: Öffentliche Unternehmen zwischen Markt und Staat. Cologne: Kiepenheuer & Witsch 1977.

Bernholz, Peter: Politische Ökonomie 3: Kapitalistische und sozialistische Marktwirtschaft. Tübingen: Mohr 1978.

Beyme, Klaus von et al.: Wirtschaftliches Wachstum als gesellschaftliches Problem. Königstein/Ts.: Athenäum 1978.

Biehl, Dieter et al.: Konjunkturelle Wirkungen öffentlicher Haushalte. Tübingen: Mohr 1978.

Bolz, Klaus et al.: Wirtschaftssysteme: Marktwirtschaft, Kapitalismus. Planwirtschaft, Sozialismus. Munich: Ehrenwirth 1978.

Bott, Helmut: Der Anteil staatlich-administrierter Preise am Preisindex der Lebenshaltung Eine empirsche Untersuchung für die Periode 1950 bis 1973. Göttingen: Schwartz 1976.

Brümmerhoff, Dieter: Zur Beeinflussung der Verteilung der Jahres- und Lebenseinkommen durch die Finanzpolitik. Tübingen: Mohr 1977.

Buchbinder, Fritz: Budgetpolitik. Wiesbaden: Gabler 1978.

Cassel, Dieter: Einkommenspolitik. Kritische Analyse eines umstrittenen stabilitätspolitischen Konzepts. Cologne: Kiepenheuer & Witsch 1977.

Dobias, Peter: Theorie und Praxis der Planwirtschaft. Paderborn: Schöningh 1977.

Elsenhans, Harmut (ed.): Migration und Wirtschaftsentwicklung. Frankfurt: Campus 1978.

Finking, Gerhard: Grundlagen der sektoralen Wirtschaftspolitik. Cologne: Bund-Verlag 1978.

Föppl, Christine: Die Vollbeschäftigungsformel. Wirksame Rezepte gegen die Arbeitslosigkeit. Frankfut; Fischer 1978.

Friedrich, Horst: Globalsteurerung, Wettbewerbspolitik und Investitionslenkung. Munich: Ehrenwirth 1978.

Gesamtreproduktionsprozess der BRD 1950-1975. Kritik der volkswirtschaftlichen Gesamtrechnung. Projekt Klassenanalyse. West Berlin: VSA 1976.

Glastetter, Werner: Die wirtschaftliche Entwicklung der Bundesrepublik Deutschland im Zeitraum 1950 bis 1975. Befunde und Aspekte. Berlin et al.: Springer 1977.

Grauhan, Rolf-Richard/Hickel, Rudolf: Krise des Steuerstaats? Widersprüche und Perspektiven, in: Aus Politik und Zeitgeschichte B 46/77, 1977, pp. 3-20.

Grauhan, Rolf-Richard/Hickel, Rudolf (eds.): Krise des Steuerstaats? Widersprüche, Perspektiven, Ausweichstrategien. Opladen: Westdeutscher Verlag (Leviathan special issue) 1978.

Groth, Klaus: Die Krise der Staatsfinanzen. Systematische Überlegungen zur Krise des Steuerstaates. Frankfurt: Suhrkamp 1978.

Handl, Johann: Klassenlagen und Sozialstruktur. Empirische Untersuchung für die BRD. Frankfurt et al.: Campus 1977.

Hartwich, Hans-Hermann: Wendepunkte des Wirtschaftssystems. Die Bundesrepublik Deutschland 1946-1949, 1966-1969, 1977-1978. Stuttgart: Leske 1978.

Heilmann, Martin: Die Umverteilungswirkungen der Einkommensteuerreform 1975. Göttingen: Schwartz 1976.

Herder-Dorneich, Philipp: Strukturwandel und soziale Ordnungspolitik. Cologne: Bachem 1977.

Hildebrandt, Eckart: Betriebliche Personalpolitik als Spaltungsstrategie des Kapitals — Kapitalistische Betriebspolitik und Gegenwehr in der Bundesrepublik 1974-1976, in: Prokla 26, 1977, pp. 151-191.

Huber, Joseph/Kosta, Jiri (eds.): Wirtschaftsdemokratie in der Diskussion. Cologne/Frankfurt: EVA 1978.

Huppertz, Paul-Helmut: Gewaltenteilung und antizyklische Finanzpolitik. Ein Beitrag zur Theorie institutioneller Bedingungen der Stabilisierungspolitik in der BRD. Baden-Baden: Nomos 1977.

Kock, Heinz et al.: Stabilitätspolitik. Göttingen: Schwartz 1976.

Krupp, Hans-Jürgen/Glatzer, Wolfgang (eds.): Umverteilung im Sozialstaat. Empirische Einkommensanalysen für die BRD. Frankfurt et al.: Campus 1978.

Loesch, Achim von: Die gemeinwirtschaftliche Unternehmung. Vom antikapitalistischen Ordnungsprinzip zum marktwirtschaftlichen Regulativ. Cologne: Bund-Verlag 1977.

Markmann, Heinz/Simmert, Diethard (eds.): Krise der Wirtschaftspolitik. Cologne: Bund-Verlag 1978.

Martiny, Anke: Marktmacht und Manipulation. Sind die Verbraucher Objekt oder Subjekt unserer Wirtschaftsordnung? Frankfurt et al.: EVA 1977.

Meinhold, Helmut: Fiskalpolitik durch sozialpolitische Parafisci. Tübingen: Mohr 1976.

Novy, Klaus: Strategien der Sozialisierung. Die Diskussion der Wirtschaftsreform in der Weimarer Republik. Frankfurt: Campus 1978.

Paschke, Jörg-Volker: Wettbewerb und Wirtschaftspolitik: Analyse der Bedeutung des Wettbewerbs in der Wirtschaftspolitik am Beispiel der sozialen Marktwirtschaft Erhards und der globalgesteuerten Marktwirtschaft Schillers. Frankfurt et al.: Lang 1977.

Piel, Manfred/Simmert, Diethard B.: Probleme der Staatsverschuldung, in: Aus Politik und Zeitgeschichte, B 42/1978, pp. 3-19.

Projekt Klassenalayse: Der Staat in der BRD. Ökonomische Grundlagen und Entwicklungstendenzen 1950-1976. Hamburg: Verlag für das Studium der Arbeiterbewegung 1978.

Projekt Klassenanalyse: Materialien zur Klassenstruktur der BRD, part 2: Grundriß der Klassenverhältnisse 1950-1970. Hamburg: VSA 1978.

Ribhegge, Hermann: Rationale Einkommenspolitik aus der Sicht der neuen politischen Ökonomie. Ein Beitrag zur Kooperation in der Wirtschaftspolitik. Tübingen: Mohr 1978.

Röper, Burckhart et al.: Theorie und Praxis der gemeinwirtschaftlichen Konzeption. Eine Analyse am Beispiel gemeinwirtschaftlicher Unternehmen. Göttingen: Schwartz 1976.

Ronge, Volker: 'Solidarische' Selbstorganisation der Wirtschaft — Eine Alternative zur Politisierung im Spätkapitalismus, in: Lev., 1978, pp. 176-202.

Semmler, Willi: Zur Theorie der Reproduktion und Akkumulation: Bemerkungen zu neueren multisektoralen Ansätzen sowie Überlegungen zum Verhältnis von privatem und staatlichem Sektor. Berlin: Olle & Wolter 1977.

Der Staat in der BRD. Ökonomische Basis und Entwicklungstendenzen, 1950-1976. Projekt Klassenanalyse. Westberlin: VSA 1977.

Starbatty, Joachim: Stabilitätspolitik in der freiheitlichsozialstaatlichen Demokratie. Baden-Baden: Nomos 1977.

Streißler, Erich: Zur Relativierung des Zieles der Geldwertstabilität. Göttingen: Schwartz 1976.

Strümpel, Burkhard: Die Krise des Wohlstands. Das Modell einer humanen Wirtschaft. Stuttgart et al.: Kohlhammer 1977.

Stumpf, Harald: Ein Wachstumskonzept und seine Grenzen. Zum Bericht der Kommission für wirtschaftlichen und sozialen Wandel, in: Aus Politik und Zeitgeschichte B 32/77, 1977, pp. 24-39.

Thomas, Rüdiger: Sozialisierungsmodelle. Demokratischer und marxistischer Sozialismus. Opladen: Westdeutscher Verlag 1977.

Ulrich, Peter: Die Großunternehmung als quasi-öffentliche Institution. Eine politische Theorie der Unternehmung. Stuttgart: Poeschel 1977.

Vilmar, Fritz: Wirtschaftsdemokratie und Humanisierung der Arbeit. Systematische Integration der wichtigsten Konzepte. Cologne et al.: EVA 1978.

Voigt, Rüdiger: Finanzsystem und Lebensqualität. Zur Bedeutung der Finanzverfassung im Sozialstaat, in: Aus Politik und Zeitgeschichte B 46/77, 1977, pp. 21-53.

Wagner, Wolf: Verelendungstheorie — die hilflose Kapitalismuskritik. Frankfurt: Fischer Taschenbuch Verlag 1976.

Waschke, Hildegard: Zentrale wirtschaftspolitische Beratungsgremien im Ausland. Eine Skizze der Wirtschaftsräte in Frankreich, Italien, den Niederlanden, Belgien, Luxemburg, Dänemark, Großbritannien, Kanada and USA. Cologne: Deutscher Institut-Verlag 1977.

Werner, Josua: Verteilungspolitik. Stuttgart: Gustav Fischer 1978.

Winter, Gerd (ed.): Sozialisierung von Unternehmen. Bedingungen und Begründungen. Cologne: EVA 1978.

Wirtschaftlicher und sozialer Wandel in der Bundesrepublik Deutschland. Gutachten der Kommission für wirtschaftlichen und sozialen Wandel. Göttingen: Schwartz 1977.

Zapf, Wolfgang (ed.): Lebensbedingungen in der Bundesrepublik Sozialer Wandel und Wohlfahrtsentwicklung. Frankfurt: Campus 1977.

Zinn, Karl Georg: Preissystem und Staatsinterventionismus. Cologne: Bund-Verlag 1978.

Social Policy

Alber, Jens: Regierungen, Arbeitslosigkeit und Arbeitslosenschutz: Zur Entwicklung der Arbeitslosenversicherung in Westeuropa, in: KZSS, 1978, pp. 726-760.

Baethge, Martin et al.: Sozialpolitik und Arbeiterinteresse. Eine empirische Untersuchung der Bedingungen und Grenzen staatlicher Arbeitsförderungspolitik und ihrer Verarbeitung durch die betroffenen Arbeitskräfte- am Beispiel Umschulung. Frankfurt: aspekte 1976.

Breddemann, Jeannette et al.: Sozialliberale Gesundheitspolitik in der Krise. Zum Krankenversicherungs-Kostendämpfungsgesetz, in: Argument 104, 1977, pp. 504-514.

Bujard, Otker/Lange, Ulrich: Armut im Alter. Ursachen, Erscheinungsformen, politisch-administrative Reaktionen. Weinheim et al.: Beltz 1978.

Fenner, Christian et al. (eds.): Unfähig zur Reform? Eine Bilanz der inneren Reformen seit 1969. Cologne: EVA 1978.

Fuhrke, Monika: Sozialpolitische Reformen oder Austeritypolitik in der Krise? Zur Kritik neuerer Theorieansätz der Sozialpolitik, in: Prokla 33, 1978, pp. 3-35.

Häussler, Siegfried: Gesundheitspolitik — Reform durch Zwang oder Einsicht? Cologne: Deutsche Instituts-Verlga 1976.

Hugger, Werner: Gesamtplanung und Reform des Gesundheitswesens der Bundesrepublik Deutschland. Frankfurt: Lang 1977.

Jurczik, Karin: Frauenarbeit und Frauenrolle. Zum Zusammenhang von Familienpolitik und Frauenerwerbstätigkeit in Deutschland von 1918-1975. Frankfurt et al.: Campus 1977 (second edition).

Köhler, Ernst: Arme und Irre. Die liberale Fürsorgepolitik des Bürgertums. Berlin: Wagenbach 1977.

Kramer, Johannes/Zimmer, Richard: Rentenversicherung — Krise ohne Ende?, in: Aus Politik und Zeitgeschichte B 50/77, 1977, pp. 13-31.

Krupp, Hans-Jürgen: Sozialpolitik und Sozialberichterstattung. Frankfurt et al.: Campus 1977.

Laufer, Heinz et al.: Freizeitpolitik von Bund, Ländern und Gemeinden. Göttingen: Schwartz 1976.

Liebel, Manfred: Produktivkraft Jugend. Über aktuelle und historische Aspekte der Arbeiterjugenfrage im Kapitalismus. Frankfurt: Jugen & Pol. 1976.

Metz, Hubert (ed.): Reform des Gesundheitssystems. Berlin: de Gruyter 1977.

Meyer/Thiele/Volkholz: Gesundheitsversorgung. Daten des Gesundheitssystems der BRD. Hamburg: VSA 1978.

Molitor, Bruno: Sozialpolitik auf den Prüfstand. Hamburg: Verl. Weltarchiv 1976.

Otten, Albert: Die Negative Einkommensteuer als soziapolitische Alternative. Diskussionsstand und Erfahrungen in den USA und eine Analyse für die BRD. Frankfurt et al.: Lang 1977.

Pfaff, Martin/Voigtländer, Hubert (eds.): Sozialpolitik im Wandel. Von der selektiven zur integrierten Sozialpolitik. Bonn: Neue Gesellschaft 1978.

Sengenberger, Werner (ed.): Der gespaltene Arbeitsmarkt. Probleme der Arbeitsmarktsegmentation. Frankfurt et al.: Campus 1978.

Sozialpolitik als soziale Kontrolle. Starnberger Studien 2. Frankfurt: Suhrkamp 1978.

Standfest, Erich (ed.): Sozialpolitik und Selbstverwaltung. Zur Demokratisierung des Sozialstaates. Cologne: Bund Verlag 1977.

Tallen, Hermann: Die Auseinandersetzung über § 218 StGB. Zu einem Konflict zwischen der SPD und der Katholischen Kirche. Munich: Schöningh 1977.

Weger, Hans-Dieter: Kritische Bilanz der Sozialpolitik. Cologne: Deutscher Instituts-Verlag 1977.

Zapf, Wolfgang (ed.): Gesellschaftspolitische Zielsysteme. Frankfurt: Campus 1976.

Educational Policy and Science Policy

Altendorf, Hans et al.: Arbeiterkinder an den Hochschulen. Soziale Selektion, materielle Lage, Ausbildungsförderung. Cologne: EVA 1978.

Bromann, Manfred: Bildungsplanung in der Bundesrepublik Deutschland. System und Grundlagen. Opladen: Westdeutscher Verlag 1978.

Fleischhut, Jens: Staatliche Forschungsförderung: Struktur und Funktion der Staatsausgaben für Forschung und Entwicklung. Meisenheim: Hain 1978.

Gehring, hansjörg: Amerikanische Literaturpolitik in Deutschland 1945-1953. Ein Aspekt des Re-Education-programms. Stuttgart: DVA 1976.

Gensch, Rainer: Forschungspolitik und 'gesellschaftlicher Bedarf'. Das Beispiel Altersforschung, in: Lev., 1977, pp. 210-238.

Hauff, Volker: Damit der Fortschritt nicht zum Risiko wird. Forschungspolitik als Zukunftsgestaltung. Stuttgart: Bonn aktuelle 1978.

Heymann, Klaus-Dieter/Karcher, Wolfgang (eds.): Das Scheitern der Hochschulreform. Fallstudie zur Gesamthochschulplanung in Baden-Württemberg 1968-1975. Weinheim et al.: Beltz 1976.

Hüfner, Klaus et al.: Konjunkturen und Bildungspolitik in der Bundesrepublik Deutschland, Vol. 1.: Der Aufschwung (1960-1967). Stuttgart: Klett 1977.

Kuper, Ernst: Demokratisierung von Schule und Schulverwaltung. Munich: Ehrenwirth 1977.

Maier, Hans: Anstösse: Beiträge zur Kultur- und Verfassungspolitik. Stuttgart: Seewald 1978.

Michalsky, Helga: Bildungspolitik und Bildungsreform in Preußen. Die Bedeutung des Unterrichtswesens als Faktor sozialen und politischen Wandels beim Übergang von der ständischen zur bürgerlich-liberalen Gesellschaft. Weinheim et al.: Beltz 1978.

Reidegeld, Eckhart: Krise, Verwaltungshandeln und Wissenschaftspolitik, in: Lev., 1977, pp. 28-52.

Sanders, Hermann: Bildungsökonomie und Bildungsplanung. Frankfurt: Campus 1978.

Schallenberger, Horst (ed.): Der Staat als Träger von Bildung und Wissenschaft: Analyse und Kritik von Trends in der Bildungs- und Wissenschaftspolitik. Ratingen: Henn 1977.

Stachelsky, Friedrich von: Außenwirtschaftliche Bestimmungsfaktoren der staatlichen Forschungspolitik in der Bundesrepublik Deutschland. Berlin: Duncker & Humblot 1978.

Environmental Policy

Bahl, Volker: Staatliche Politik am Beispiel der Kohle. Frankfurt et al.: Campus 1977.

Bungarten, Harald H.: Umweltpolitik in Westeuropa. EG, internationale Organisationen und nationale Umweltpolitiken. Bonn: Europa Union Verlag 1978.

Deubner, Christian: Die Atompolitik der westdeutschen Industrie und die Gründung von Euratom. Frankfurt et al.: Campus 1977.

Ehrenstein, Dieter von (ed.): Energiebedarf und Energiebedarfsforschung. Referate u. Ergebnisse einer Tagung des BMFT in Zusammenarbeit mit dem Projekt 'Kernenergie' der Universität Bremen. Villingen: Neckar-Verlag 1977.

Gerau, Jürgen: Zur politischen Ökologie der Industrialisierung des Umweltschutzes, in: Lev., 1977, pp. 239-270.

Gunst, Dietrich: Biopolitik zwischen Macht und Recht. Mainz: v. Hase & Koehler 1978.

Horn, Manfred: Die Energiepolitik der Bundesregierung von 1958 bis 1972. Zur Bedeutung der Penetration ausländischer Ölkonzerne in der Energiewirtschaft der BDR für die Abhängigkeit interner Strukturen und Entwicklungen. Berlin: Duncker & Humblot 1977.

Jänicke, Martin (ed.): Umweltpolitik. Beiträge zur Politologies des Umweltschutzes. Opladen: Leske & Budrich 1978.

Lienemann, Wolfgang et al. (eds.): Alternative Möglichkeiten für die Energiepolitik. Argumente und Kritik. Opladen: Westdeutscher Verlag 1978.

Mayer-Tasch, Peter Cornelius: Das umweltrechtliche Genehmigungsverfahren. Rechtspolitische Überlegungen zu seiner Demokratisierung und Liberalisierung, in: Aus Politik und Zeitgeschichte B 17/1978, pp. 20-38.

Meyer-Renschhausen, Martin: Energiepolitik in der BRD von 1950 bis heute. Analyse und Kritik. Cologne: Pahl-Rugenstein 1977.

Müller, Harald: Energiepolitik, Nuklearexport und die Weiterverbreitung von Kernwaffen: Analyse und Dokumentation. Frankfurt: Haag & Herchen 1978.

Müller-Wenk, Rudi: Die ökologische Buchhaltung. Ein Informations- und Steuerungsinstrument für umweltkonforme Unternehmenspolitik. Frankfurt: Campus 1978.

Radkau, Joachim: Die Kalkulation des Unberechenbaren. Zur Entwicklungs- und Wirkungsweise des industriellen Kernenergie-Interesses in der BRD, in: Blätter, 1978, pp. 1440-1466.

Ravens, Karl: Wohnungs- und Städtebaupolitik in der sozialen Demokratie. Bonn: Neue Gesellschaft 1977.

Schaaf, Peter: Ruhrbergbau und Sozialdemokratie. Die Energiepolitik der Großen Koalition 1966-1969. Marburg: VAG 1978.

Stamer, Peter: Orientierungslinien der Umweltpolitik. Göttingen: Vandenhoeck & Ruprecht 1977.

Strasser, Johano: Die Zukunft der Demokratie. Grenzen des Wachstums, Grenzen der Freiheit? Reinbek: Rowohlt 1977.

Technologie und Politik. Das Magazin zur Wachstumskrise. Ed. Freimut Duve. Reinbek: Rowholt.
6. Technologiepolitik in Lateinamerika. 1976.
7. Atomenergie/Brokdorf/Unterelbe. 1977.
8. Die Zukunft der Arbeit. 1. 1977.

Infrastructural Policy

Ahner, Dirk: Arbeitsmarkt und Lohnstruktur: Zum Einfluß von Aufbau und Funktionsweise des Arbeitsmarktes auf die Lohnstruktur. Tübingen: Mohr 1978.

Albrecht, Ulrich et al. Arbeitsplätze durch Rüstung? Warnung vor falschen Hoffnungen. Reinbek: Rowohlt 1978.

Arbeitskreis Politische Ökonomie: Der Arbeitsmarkt in der BRD — Plädoyer für eine kurzfristige Beschäftigungspolitik, in: Lev., 1978, pp. 415-463.

Besters, Hans (ed.): Strukturpolitik, wozu? Technokratischer Interventionismus versus marktwirtschaftliche Ordnungspolitik. Baden-Baden: Nomos 1978.

Bombach, Gottfried et al. (eds.): Probleme des Strukturwandels und der Strukturpolitik. Tübingen: Mohr 1977.

Bosch, Gerhard: Arbeitsplatzverlust. Die sozialen Folgen einer Betriebsstillegung. Frankfurt et al.: Campus 1978.

Bruche, Gert: Elektrizitätsversorgung und Staatsfunktion. Das Regulierungssystem der öffentlichen Elektrizitätsversorgung in der BRD. Frankfurt et al.: Campus 1977.

Buttler, Günter: Bevölkerung und Arbeitsmarkt bis zum Jahr 2000. Cologne. Deutscher Instituts-Verlag 1977.

Eckey, Hans-Friedrich: Grundlagen der regionalen Strukturpolitik. Cologne: Bund-Verlag 1978.

Egle, Franz et al.: Verdeckte Arbeitslosigkeit. Probleme der Messung in der Bundesrepublik. Göttingen: Schwartz 1976.

Epping, Günter: Bodenmarkt und Bodenpolitik in der Bundesrepublik Deutschland. Berlin: Duncker & Humblot 1977.

Esser, Josef et al.: Strukturelle Arbeitslosigkeit und politisches Konfliktpotential. Die Krise der saarländischen Stahlindustrie, in: Prokla, 2/1978, pp. 115-137.

Freiburghaus, Dieter: Dynamik der Arbeitslosigkeit. Untersuchungen von Umschlagsprozeß und Dauerverteilung der Arbeitslosigkeit in der Bundesrepublik 1966-1977. Königstein/Ts.: Athenäum 1978.

Güther, Bernd: Infrastruktur und Staat. Zur Entwicklung der allgemeinen Produktionsbedingungen in der BRD 1950-1975. Marburg: VAG 1977.

Hammer, Hans: Wirkungen politischer Maßnahmen zur Lenkung der Ausländerbeschäftigung. Göttingen: Schwartz 1976.

Hochschule für Wirtschaft und Politik (ed.): Arbeitsmarktpolitik. Opladen: Westdeutscher Verlag 1978.

Kappe, Dieter: Politik und Bevölkerung. Königstein/Ts.: Athenäum et al. 1978.

Leenen, Wolf Rainer: Bevölkerungspolitik in der Bundesrepublik Deutschland — eine neue gesellschaftspolitische Aufgabe?, in: Aus Politik und Zeitgeschichte B 21/1978, pp. 3-19.

Matthöfer, Hans: Huamnisierung der Arbeit und Produktivität in der Industriegesellschaft. Cologne: EVA 1977.

Naschold, Frieder: Alternative Raumpolitik. Ein Beitrag zur Verbesserung der Arbeits- und Lebensverhältnisse. Kronberg/Ts.: Athenäum 1978.

Neuloh, Otto (ed.): Soziale Innovation und sozialer Konflikt. Göttingen: Vandenhoeck & Ruprecht 1977.

Offe, Claus (ed.): Opfer des Arbeitsmarktes. Zur Theorie der strukturierten Arbeitslosigkeit. Neuwied et al.: Luchterhand 1977.

Rasmussen, Thomas: Entwicklungslinien des Dienstleistungssektors. Internationaler Strukturvergleich und Perspektiven für die BRD. Göttingen: Vandenhoeck & Ruprecht 1977.

Rumpf, Hans et al.: Technologische Entwicklung, Vol. 1. Göttingen: Schwartz 1976.

Schmid, Günther: Strukturierte Arbeitslosigkeit in der Bundesrepublik. Kronberg: Athenäum 1978.

Strangmeier, Reinhard L. F.: Der Arbeitsmarkt für Akademiker. Soziale Struktur und Steuerung. Frankfurt: Campus 1978.

Tjaden, K. H.: Territorialstruktur und antikapitalistische Reformpolitik, in: Argument 107, 1978, pp. 29-41.

Unrein, Hans: Arbeitslosigkeit. Cologne: Wissenschaft und Politik 1978.

Voss, Gerhard: Sektorale Strukturpolitik. Anspruch und Praxis. Cologne: Deutscher Instituts-Verlag 1977.

Wacker, Ali (ed.): Vom Schock zum Fatalismus? Soziale und psychische Auswirkungen der Arbeitslosigkeit. Frankfurt et al.: Campus 1978.

Wilkenloh, Freidhelm: Probleme und Bedingungen einer zielorientierten Politik unter besonderer Berücksichtigung des Sektors Verkehr, in: Verwaltung, 1977, pp. 433-449.

Zinn, Karl Georg (ed.): Strategien gegen die Arbeitslosigkeit. Frankfurt: EVA 1977.

Developmental Policy

Public Administration

General and Comparative Studies

Bessert-Nettelbeck, Joachim et al.: Die Skrupel des Wissenschaftlers beim Politik-Beraten. Linke Wirtschaftswissenschaftler und das Problem der Arbeitslosigkeit, in: Lev., 1977, pp. 578-596.

Bethge, Herbert: Das Hausrecht der öffentlichen Hand im Dilemma zwischen öffentlichem Recht und Privatrecht, in: Verwaltung, 1977, pp. 313-3321.

Böhret, Carl (ed.): Verwaltungsreformen und Politische Wissenschaft. Zur Zusammenarbeit von Praxis und Wissenschaft bei der Durchsetzung und Evaluierung von Neuerungen. Baden-Baden: Nomos 1978.

Bohle, Martin: Leistung, Erfolg und Leistungskonflikte in bürokratischen Organisationen. Ein empirischer Vergleich zwischen Beamten und Angestellten der Privatwirtschaft in der BRD. Meisenheim a. Gl.: Hain 1977.

Franz, Günther (ed.): Verwaltungsgrenzen in der Bundesrepublik Deutschland seit Beginn des 19. Jahrhunderts. Hannover: H. Schroedel 1977.

Guilleaume, Emil: Politische Entscheidungsfunktion und Urteilsvermögen, in: Verwaltung, 1977, pp. 273-290.

Guilleaume, Emil: Politische Entscheidungsfunktion und politischer Wille, in: Verwaltung, 1978, pp. 293-308.

Hesse, Wolfgang: Reformpolitik und Sozialwissenschaften — Wo entstehen staatliche Innovationsprogramme und wie können die Sozialwissenschaften zu ihrer Entwicklung beitragen? in: Aus Politik und Zeitgeschichte B 39/77, 1977, pp. 15-24.

Hollihn, Frank: Partizipation und Demokratie. Bürgerbeteiligung am kommunalen Planungsprozeß? Baden-Baden: Nomos 1978.

Jarass, Hans D.: Die Innovationsfähigkeit von Bürokratien, in: Verwaltung, 1978, pp. 27-42.

Mayntz, Renate: Soziologie der öffentlichen Verwaltung. Heidelberg et al.: C. F. Müller 1978.

Morsey, Rudolf (ed.): Verwaltungsgeschichte. Aufgaben, Zielsetzungen, Beispiel. Berlin: Duncker & Humblot 1977.

Pankoke, Eckart: Verwaltungssoziologie: Einführung in Probleme öffentlicher Verwaltung. Stuttgart: Kohlhammer 1977.

Skarpelis-Sperk, Sigrid: Soziale Rationierung öffentlicher Leistungen. Frankfurt: Campus 1978.

Steinberg, Rudolf: Faktoren bürokratischer Macht, in: Verwaltung, 1978, pp. 309-334.

Treiber, Hubert: Programmentwicklung als politischer Prozeß. Zum Verhältnis von Bürokratie und politischer Führung aus der Sicht der empirischen Verwaltungswissenschaft, in: ZfP, 1977, pp. 213-239.

Treutner, Erhard: Rechtsstaat und situative Verwaltung: Zu einer sozialwissenschaftlichen Theorie administrativer Organisationen. Frankfurt: Campus 1978.

Wagener, Frido (ed.): Regierbarkeit? Dezentralisation? Entstaatlichung? Bericht über die verwaltungswissenschaftliche Fachtagung der Deutschen Sektion des Internationalen Instituts für Verwaltungswissenschaften in Hamburg vom 9. bis 11. Juni 1976. Bonn: Eigenverlag der Deutschen Sektion 1976.

Waterkamp, Rainer: Handbuch Politische Planung. Opladen: Leske 1978.

Wordelmann, Peter: Simulation von Systemveränderungen: Möglichkeiten und Grenzen einer Planungsmethode, dargestellt am Beispiel des Ausbildungssektors. Frankfurt et al.: Lang 1978.

Planning

Brünner, Christian: Politische Planung im parlamentarischen Regierungssystem. Dargestellt am Beispiel der mittelfristigen Finanzplanung. Vienna etc.: Springer 1978.

Denso, Jochen et al.: Verwaltungseffizienz und Motivation. Anreize zur wirtschaftlichen Verwendung öffentlicher Mittel durch die Titelverwalter. Göttingen: Schwartz 1976.

Dietzel, Gottfried, T. W.: Wissenschaft und staatliche Entscheidungsplanung. Rechts- und Organisationsprobleme der wissenschaftlichen Politikberatung. Berlin: Duncker & Humblot 1978.

Dillkofer, Heidelore: Geschäftsverteilung als Prozeß zur Regelung von Zuständigkeiten im Bereich der Ministerialverwaltung, in: Verwaltung, 1978, pp. 133-172.

Eberwein, Wolf-Dieter: Aussenpolitik und Verwaltung. Umweltveränderung, organisatorsiche Anpassung und Funktionswandel des Auswärtigen Amtes, in: Verwaltung, 1978, pp. 439-470.

Fischer, Jürgen: Staatliche Planung und Demokratie: Möglichkeiten und Grenzen demokratischer Planungsorganisation. Frankfurt: Haag & Herchen 1978.

Garlichs, Dietrich/Müller, Edda: Eine neue Organisation für das Bundesverkehrsministerium, in: Verwaltung, 1977, pp. 343-362.

Gotthold, Jürgen: Stadtentwicklung zwischen Krise und Planung. Cologne: Kiepenheuer & Witsch 1978.

Häußermann, Hartmut: Die Politik der Bürokratie. Einführung in die Soziologie der staatlichen Verwaltung. Frankfurt: Campus 1977.

Hoffmann-Nowotny, Hans-Joachim (ed.): Politisches Klima und Planung. Soziale Indikatoren. Konzepte und Forschungsansätze, vol. 5. Frankfurt et al.: Campus 1977.

Hübener, Arend et al.: Erfolgskontrolle politischer Planung. Göttingen: Schwartz 1976.

Jäger, Peter: Öffentlich-Wirtschaftliche Effizienzkriterien der Verwaltungsautomation, in: Verwaltung, 1977, pp. 469-485.

Knoepfel, Peter: Demokratisierung der Raumplanung. Berlin: Duncker & Humblot 1977.

König, Herbert: Dynamische Verwaltung. Bürokratie zwischen Politik and Kosten. Stuttgart: Bonn aktuell 1977.

König, Klaus (ed.): Koordination und integrierte Planung in den Staatskanzleien. Vorträge und Diskussionsbeiträge der verwaltungswissenschaftlichen Arbeitstagung 1975 der Hochschule für Verwaltungswissenschaften Speyer. Berling: Duncker & Humblot 1976.

Lüder, Klaus/Budäus, Dietrich: Effizienzorientierte Haushaltsplanung und Mittelbewirtschaftung. Göttingen: Schwartz 1976.

Olivet, Peter: Die Organisation der Organisation der öffentlichen Verwaltung in der Bundesrepublik Deutschland: Aufbau von Arbeitsweise der zentralen Organisationsstellen in der öffentlichen Verwaltung der Bundesrepublik Deutschland. Berlin: Duncker & Humblot 1978.

Schaft, Wolfgang: Die mehrjährige Finanzplanung der Bundesländer. Hamburg: Weltarchiv 1976.

Schimanke, Dieter: Verwaltungsreform Baden-Württemberg: Verwaltungsinnovation als politisch-administrativer Prozess. Berlin: Duncker & Humblot 1978.

Scholz, Gotthard: Organisationsuntersuchungen in der Bundesministerialverwaltung, in: Verwaltung, 1977, pp. 333-342.

Vitzthum, Wolfgang Graf: Parlament und Planung. Zur verfassungsgerechten Zuordnung der Funktionen von Bundesregierung und Bundestag bei der politischen Planung. Baden-Baden: Nomos 1978.

Wittkämper, Gerhard, W.: Funktionale Verwaltungsreform. Eine systematische Darstellung von Hauptproblemen mit Dokumenten. Bonn-Bad Godesberg: Godesberger Taschenbuchverlag 1978.

Civil Service

Dammann, Klaus, et al.: Weiterbildung für den öffentlichen Dienst. Entwicklung staatlicher Aufgaben, Qualifikationsentwicklung und Tendenzen der Weiterbildung. Göttingen: Schwartz 1976.

Hepp, Robert: Amtsprestige oder Sozialprestige? Die Polizei zwischen Staat und Gesellschaft, in: ZfP, 1977, pp. 122-151.

König, Klaus/Kroppenstedt, Franz: Neutralisierung der Bürokratie. Zum Problem von Spitzenorganisationen auf Zeit im öffentlichen Dienst, in: ZfP, 1977, pp. 240-261.

Kugele, Dieter: Der politische Beamte. Entwicklung, Bewährung und Reform einer politisch-administrativen Institution. Munich: Tuduv 1978 (second edition).

Lohmar, Ulrich: Staatsbürokratie: Das hoheitliche Gewerbe. Deutsche Aspekte eines neuen Klassenkampfes. Munich: Goldmann 1978.

Roos, Wolfgang/Penth, Boris: Rationalisierung bei der Deutschen Bundespost, in: Prokla, 2/1978, pp. 151-169.

Wilhelm, Theodor: Staatsbewußtsein, Staatsbeamte, Lehrerschaft, in: Aus Politik und Zeitgeschichte B 41/77, 1977, pp. 3-28.

Wunder, Bernd: Die Rekrutierung der Beamtenschaft in Deutschland. Eine historische Betrachtung, in: Lev., 1977, pp. 360-377.

Local Government

Aich, Prodosh (ed.): Wie demokratisch ist Kommunalpolitik? Gemeindeverwaltung zwischen Bürgerinteressen und Mauschelei. Sozialgeschichte aus vertraulichen Kommunalakten. Reinbek: Rowohlt 1977.

Gotthold, Jürgen: Die Funktion der Gemeinden im gesamtstaatlichen Planungsprozeß, in: PVS, 1978, pp. 343-371.

Haasis, Hans-Arthur: Kommunalpolitik und Machtstruktur: Eine Sekundäranalyse deutscher empirischer Gemeindestudien. Frankfurt: Haag & Herchen 1978.

Kevenhörster, Paul (ed.): Lokale Politik unter exekutiver Führerschaft. Meisenheim: Hain 1977.

Kevenhörster, Paul/Wollmann, Hellmut (eds.): Kommunalpolitische Praxis und lokale Politikforschung. Berlin: Deutsches Institut für Urbanistik 1978.

Marquardt, Karlheinz: Computersimulation der Folgen kommunalpolitischer Entscheidungen. Freizeit-Stadtentwicklung-Politik. Frankfurt: Haag & Herchen 1976.

Rammstedt, Otthein (ed.): Bürgerbeteiligung und Bürgerinitiativen. Legitimation und Partizipation in der Demokratie angesichts gesellschaftlicher Konfliktsituationen. Villingen: Neckar-Verlag 1977.

Siewert, H.-Jörg: Verein und Kommunalpolitik, in: KZfSS, 1977, pp. 487-510.

Zeilinski, Heinz: Kommunale Selbstverwaltung und ihre Grenzen. Über den Einfluß von Staat und Wirtschaft auf die Gemeinden. Frankfurt et al.: Campus 1977.

D. POLITICAL PROCESS

Political Influences and Trends

Interest Groups

Berg, Wilfried: Verbände in der parlamentarischen Demokratie, in: Verwaltung, 1978, pp. 71-83.

Biervert, Bernd et al. (eds.): Verbraucherpolitik in der Marktwirtschaft. Reinbek: Rowohlt 1978.

Briem, Jürgen: Der SDS. Die Geschichte des bedeutendsten Studentenverbandes der BRD seit 1945. Frankfurt: päd. extra Buchverlag 1976.

Brockmann, Heinz Wilhelm (ed.): Kirche und moderne Gesellschaft. Duesseldorf: Patmos-Verlag 1976.

Bubholz, Edwin H.: Zwang zur Freiheit. Verbände, Staat, Individuum. Tübingen: Mohr 1977.

Denzler, Georg (ed.): Kirche und Staat auf Distanz. Historische und aktuelle Perspektiven. Munich:. Kösel 1977.

Dettling, Warnfried (ed.): Macht der Verbände — Ohnmacht der Demokratie? Beiträge zur Theorie und Politik der Verbände. Munich: Olzog 1976 .

Fichter, Tilman et al.: Kleine Geschichte des SDS. Der Sozialistische Deutsche Studentenbund von 1946 bis zur Selbstauflösung. Berlin: Rotbuch Verlag 1977.

Göbel, Uwe: Die Studentenbewegung und ihre Folgen: Die politische Situation an den Hochschulen zwischen 1967 und 1977. Cologne: Deutscher Instituts-Verlag 1977.

Huber, Wolfgang: Evangelische Kirche und politische Öffentlichkeit, in: Aus Politik und Zeitgeschichte B 29-30/77, 1977, pp. 3-11.

Kögler, Alfred: Die Entwicklung von 'Randgruppen' in der BRD. Göttingen: Schwartz 1976.

Minte, Horst: Zusammenhänge von Arbeit und Konsum als Problem einer aktiven Verbraucherpolitik, in: Aus Politik und Zeitgeschichte B 24/1978, pp. 3-13.

Neumann, Lothar, F.: Politik und Verbraucher. Königstein/Ts.: Athenäum et al. 1978.

Otto, Karl A.: Vom Ostermarsch zur APO. Geschichte der außerparlamentarischen Opposition in der BRD 1960-1970. Frankfurt: Campus 1977.

Raschke, Peter: Vereine und Verbände. Zur Organisation von Interessen in der Bundesrepublik Deutschland. Munich: Juventa Verlag 1978.

Schmidt, Walter: Gesellschaftliche Machtbildung durch Verbände, in: Staat, 1978, pp. 244-271.

Scholder, Klaus: Die Kirchen und das Dritte Riech, Vol. 1: Vorgeschichte und Zeit der Illusionen 1918-1934. Frankfurt et al.: Propyläen 1977.

Schröder, Heinjo: Vorschläge zur Transparenz des Verbandseinflusses auf die Gesetzgebung, in: ZParl, 1977, pp. 491-506.

Schuller, Wolfgang: Probleme historischer Korruptionsforschung, in: Staat, 1977, pp. 373-392.

Stitzel, Michael: Unternehmerverhalten und Gesellschaftspolitik. Stuttgart et al.: Kohlhammer 1977.

Vollrath, Ernst: Korruption in der Politik und Korruption der Politik, in: ZfP, 1977, pp. 333-341.

von Voss, Rüdiger (ed.): Staatsführung, Verbandsmacht und innere Souveränität. Von der Rolle der Verbände, Gewerkschaften und Bürgerinitiativen in der Politik. Stuttgart: Bonn aktuell 1977.

Trade Unions and Labour Movement

Abendroth, Michael et al.: Hafenarbeiterstreik 1978: Zum Konfliktpotential der Hafenarbeiter, in: Lev., 1978, pp. 286-313.

Adam, Hermann: Probleme der Vermögensbildung aus der Sicht der Gewerkschaften, in: Aus Politik und Zeitgeschichte B 36/77, 1977, pp. 3-16.

Borsdorf, Ulrich et al. (eds.): Grundlagen der Einheitsgewerkschaft. Historische Dokumente und Materialien. Cologne et al.: EVA 1977.

Borsdorf, Ulrich (ed.): Gewerkschaftliche Politik: Reform aus Solidarität. Zum 60. Geburtstag von Oskar Vetter. Cologne: Bund-Verlag 1977.

Briefs, Ulrich: Neue Technologien als Herausforderung für die Gewerkschaften, in: Blätter, 1978, pp. 1179-1197.

Dammann, Klaus: Tarifvertrag und Arbeitskampf. Rechtliche Rahmenbedingungen aktiver Lohnpolitik. Cologne: Pahl-Rugenstein 1977.

Deppe, F./Fülberth, G./Harrer, J. (eds.): Geschichte der deutschen Gewerkschaftsbewegung. Cologne: Pahl-Rugenstein 1977.

Dzielak, Willi et al.: Belegschaften und Gewerkschaft im Streik. Am Beispiel der Chemischen Industrie. Frankfurt et al.: Campus 1978.

Engelhardt, Ulrich: 'Nur vereinigt sind wir stark'. Die Anfänge der deutschen Gewerkschaftsbewegung 1862/63 bis 1869/70. Stuttgart: Klett-Cotta 1977, 2 vols.

Erd, Rainer: Verrechtlichung industrieller Konflikte. Normative Rahmenbedingungen des dualen Systems der Interessenvertretung. Frankfurt: Campus 1978.

Euler, Hanns Peter: Das Konfliktpotential industrieller Arbeitsstrukturen. Analyse der technischen und sozialen Ursachen. Opladen: Westdeutscher Verlag 1977.

Frauenkron, Karl-Peter/Gerl, Siegfried: Die Vermögensbildung der Arbeitnehmer in der Gesetzgebung des Deutschen Bundestages, in: Aus Politik und Zeitgeschichte B 36/77, 1977, pp. 36-45.

Fröhlich, Dieter: Die Arbeiterschaft — 'Bestandsmasse' oder 'Durchgangsmasse'?, in: KZfSS, 1978, pp. 283-304.

Geffken, Rolf: Gewerkschaften und Arbeitsrecht, in: Sopo 44, 1978, pp. 49-66.

Gege, Maximilian: Die Funktion des Wirtschaftsausschusses im Rahmen der wirtschaftlichen Mitbestimmung: Eine Untersuchung der rechtlichen Ausgestaltung und Funktionsfähigkeit des Ausschusses in der Praxis. Frankfurt: Haag & Herchen 1977.

Gewerkschaftsstaat oder Unternehmerstaat. Cologne: Bund-Verlag 1976.

Hagelstange, Thomas: Gewerkschaftsentwicklung und Krisen in der BRD, in: Argument 109/1978, pp. 357-372.

Hochgürtel, Gerhard/Stiegler, Barbara: Die Aufgaben des DGB an der Basis. Zum Berufsbild des DGB-Sekretärs. Bonn: Verlag Neue Gesellschaft 1978.

Horke, Gertraud: Soziologie der Gewerkschaften. Vienna: Europaverlag 1977.

Jacobi, Otto et al. (eds.): Arbeiterinteressen gegen Sozialpartnerschaft. Kritisches Gewerkschaftsjahrbuch 1978/79. Berlin: Rotbuch 1978.

Jacobi, Otto et al. (eds.): Gewerkschaftspolitik in der Krise. Berlin: Rotbuch Verlag 1978.

Jühe, Reinhard et al.: Gewerkschaften in der Bundesrepublik Deutschland. Daten, Fakten, Strukturen. Cologne: Deutscher Instituts-Verlag 1977.

Kleßmann, Christoph et al.: Streiks und Hungermärsche im Ruhrgebiet 1946-1948. Frankfurt et al.: Campus 1977.

Knebel, Jürgen:Koalitionsfreiheit und Gemeinwohl: zur verfassungsrechtlichen Zulässigkeit staatlicher Einwirkungen auf die tarifautonome Lohngestaltung. Berlin: Duncker & Humblot 1978.

Kraft, Alfons: Die Arbeiterselbstverwaltung im Spanungsverhältnis von Gesellschafts- und Arbeitsrecht. Cologne: Heymann 1978.

Lang, Werner: Kooperative Gewerkschaften und Einkommenspolitik. Das Beispiel Österreichs. Frankfurt: Lang 1978.

Leineweber, Bernd: Intellektuelle Arbeit und kritische Theorie: Eine Untersuchung zur Geschichte der Theorie in der Arbeiterbewegung. Frankfurt: Verlag Neue Kritik 1977.

Lichte, Rainer: Betriebsalltag von Industriearbeitern. Konflikthandeln einer Belegschaftsgruppe vor und während einer Betriebsstillegung. Frankfurt et al.: Campus 1978.

Meyer, Regine: Streik und Aussperrung in der Metallindustrie. Analyse der Streikbewegung in Nordwürttemberg-Nordbaden 1971. Marburg: VAG 1977.

Mitscherlich, Matthias: Das Arbeitskampfrecht der Bundesrepublik Deutschland und die Europäische Sozialcharta. Baden-Baden: Nomos 1976.

Molitor, Bruno: Lohnpolitik und Arbeitsmarkt. Hamburg: Verlag Weltarchiv 1977.

Müller-Jentsch, Walther: Die Neue Linke und die Gewerkschaften, in: Das Argument 107, 1978, pp. 17-28.

Neusüß, Christel: Produktivkraftentwicklung, Arbeiterbewegung und Schranken sozialer Emanzipation, entwickelt anhand der Rätediskussion und der Rationalisierungsdebatte der 20er Jahre, in: Prokla, 2/1978, pp. 75-113.

Oppolzer, Alfred (ed.): Humanisierung der Lohnarbeit? Der Kampf um die Arbeitsbedingungen. Berlin: Argument-Verlag 1977.

Pfromm, Hans-Adam: Solidarische Lohnpolitik. Zur wirtschaftlichen und sozialen Problematik tariflicher Lohnstrukturnivellierung. Cologne et al.: EVA 1978.

Pinl, Claudia: Das Arbeitnehmerpatriarchat. Die Frauenpolitik der Gewerkschaften. Cologne: Kiepenheuer & Witsch 1977.

Projektgruppe Gewerkschaftsforschung Tarifpolitik 1977. Frankfurt: Campus 1978.

Recht auf Arbeit — eine politische Herausforderung. Neuwied et al.: Luchterhand 1978.

Röhrich, Wilfried: Revolutionärer Syndikalismus. Ein Beitrag zur Sozialgeschichte der Arbeiterbewegung. Darmstadt: Wiss. Buchges. 1977.

Schachtschneider, Karl Albrecht: Imperative Lohnleitlinien unter dem Grundgesetz, in: Staat, 1977, pp. 493-520.

Schäfter, Heinz: Probleme der Lohn- und Tarifpolitik im Übergang zu den achtziger Jahren, in: Argument 109, 1978, pp. 347-356.

Scharpf, Fritz W.: Autonome Gewerkschaften und staatliche Wirtschaftspolitik: Probleme einer Verbändesgesetzgebung. Frankfurt: Otto-Brenner-Stiftung 1978.

Teschner, Eckart: Lohnpolitik im Betrieb: Eine empirische Untersuchung in der Metall-, Chemie-, Textil- und Tabakindustrie. Frankfurt et al.: Lang 1977.

Ullmann, Peter: Tarifverträge und Tarifpolitik in Deutschland bis 1914: Entstehung und Entwicklung, interessenpolitische Bedingungen und Bedeutung des Tarifvertragswesens für die sozialistischen Gewerkschaften. Frankfurt et al.: Lang 1977.

Vilmar, Fritz: Politik und Mitbestimmung: Kritische Zwischenbilanz — integrales Konzept. Kronberg: Athenaüm 1977.

Wehling, Hans-Georg (ed.): Arbeitskonflikte in der Bundesrepublik. Opladen: Leske 1978.

Weiß, Gerhard: Die ÖTV. Politik und gesellschaftliche Konzeptionen der Gewerkschaft ÖTV von 1966 bis 1976. Marburg: VAG 1978.

Weiß-Hartmann, Anne: Der Freie Gewerkschaftsbund Hessen 1945-1949. Marburg: VAG 1977.

Zacher, Hans F.: Staat und Gewerkschaften: zur Doppelverfassung einer Arbeitnehmergesellschaft. Heidelberg, Karlsruhe: Müller 1977.

Rural Influences

Promotional Groups

Thiel, Gerhard: Techniker und Ingenieure in der Bundesrepublik Deutschland. Veränderte Arbeitsbedingungen, Ausbildung, Organisationen einer Arbeitnehmergruppe. Cologne: EVA 1977.

Military Influences

Bielfeldt, Carola: Rüstungspolitik und Rüstungskomplex in der Bundesrepublik Deutschland. Frankfurt/M: 1976.

Bielfeldt, Carola: Rüstungsausgaben und Staatsinterventionismus. Das Beispiel der BRD 1950-1071. Frankfurt et al.: Campus 1977.

Grünewald, Guido: Abrüstung und Arbeitsplatzsicherung. Zur Diskussion über Rüstungskonversion und Arbeitslosigkeit, in: Blätter, 1978, pp. 657-680.

Krölls, Albert: Wehrdienstnovelle im Verfassungskonflikt, in: Demokratie und Recht 4/1977, pp. 388-402.

Mechtersheimer, Alfred: Rüstung und Politik in der Bundesrepublik. MRCA TORNADO. Geschichte und Funktion des größen westeuropäischen Rüstungsporgramms. Bad Honnef: OSang Verlag 1977.

Meyer, Peter: Kriegs- und Militärsoziologie. Opladen/Wiesbaden: Westdeutscher Verlag 1977.

Mutz, Reinhard: Sicherheitspolitik und demokratische Öffentlichkeit in der BRD. Probleme der Analyse, Kritik und Kontrolle militärischer Macht. Munich et al.: Oldenbourg 1978.

Nagel, Ernst-Josef/Starkulla, Heinz W.: Einstellungen von Wehrdienstverweigerern und Soldaten. Eine empirische Untersuchung. Munich: Kaiser; Mainz: Grünewald 1977.

Schrader, Rudolf: Naturwissenschaft und Militärstrategie, in: AP, 1978, pp. 199-208.

von Schubert, Klaus (ed.): Sicherheitspolitik der Bundesrepublik Deutschland. Dokumentation 1945-1977. Cologne: Wiss. & Pol. 1978.

Seidelmann, Reimund: Bundeswehr, Innere Führung und Demokratische Gesellschaft, in: Frankfurter Hefte 8/1977, pp. 22-32.

Zoll, Ralf et al. (eds.): Bundeswehr und Gesellschaft. Ein Wörterbuch. Opladen: Westdeut. Verlag 1977.

Zoll, Ralf: Militär und Gesellschaft in der Bundesrepublik Deutschland. Zum Problem der Legitimität von Streitkräften, in: Aus Politik und Zeitgeschichte B 36/1978, pp. 24-46.

National Minorities and Racial Factors

Sallen, Herbert A.: Zum Antisemitismus in der Bundesrepublik Deutschland. Konzepte, Methoden und Ergebnisse der empirischen Antisemitismusforschung. Frankfurt: Haag and Herchen 9177.

Political Parties

Brun, Rudolf (ed.): Der grüne Protest: Herausforderung durch die Umweltparteien. Frankfurt: Fischer TB-Verlag 1978.

Deppe, Rainer et al.: Sozialdemokratie und Klassenkonflikte: Metallarbeiterstreik, Betriebskonflikt, Mieterkampf. Frankfurt: Campus 1978.

Eisner, Freya: Das Verhältnis der KPD zu den Gewerkschaften in der Weimarer Republik. Cologne et al.: EVA 1977.

Focke, Franz: Sozialismus aus christlicher Verantwortung. Die Idee eines christlichen Sozialimus in der katholisch-sozialen Bewegung und in der CDU. Wuppertal: Hammer 1978.

Friedmann, Peter (ed.): Materialien zum politischen Richtungsstreit in der deutschen Sozialdemokratie 1890-1917. Berlin: Ullstein 1978, 2 vols.

Gollwitzer, Heinz (ed.): Europäische Bauernparteien im 20. Jahrhundert. Stuttgart et al.: G. Fischer 1977.

Hahn, Karl Josef et al.: Zusammenarbeit der Parteien in Westeuropa. Auf dem Weg zu einer neuen politischen Infrastruktur? Bonn: Europa Union Verlag 1976.

Hartmann, Jürgen: Strukturprobleme christdemokratischer Parteien in Europa, in: ZfP, 1978, pp. 175-193.

Hebel-Kunze, Bärbel: SPD und Faschismus. Zur politischen und organisatorischen Entwicklung der SPD 1932-1935. Frankfurt: Röderbeg 1977.

Heß, Jürgen C.: 'Das ganze Deutschland soll es sein'. Demokratischer Nationalismus in der Weimarer Republik am Beispiel der Deutschen Demokratischen Partei. Stuttgart: Klett-Cotta 1978.

Huster, Ernst-Ulrich: Die Politik der SPD 1945-1950. Frankfurt et al.: Campus 1978.

Jesse, Eckhard: Die Parteien der Bundesrepublik Deutschland und das Wahlrecht. Wahlrechtsausgestaltung zwischen politischer Oppurtunität und demokratischer Legitimität, in: Aus Politik und Zeitgeschichte B 51/1977, pp. 3-23.

Jüttner, Alfred/Liese, Hans J.: Taschenbuch der Europäischen Parteien und Wahlen. Munich: OLzog 1977.

Kastendiek, Hella: Arbeitnehmer in der SPD: Herausbildung und Funktion der Arbeitsgemeinschaft für Arbeitnehmerfragen (AfA). Berlin: Verlag Die Arbeitswelt 1978.

Kremendahl, Hans: Nur die Volkspartei ist mehrheitsfähig. Zur Lage der SPD nach der Bundestagswahl 1976. Bonn-Bad Godesberg: Neue Gesellschaft 1977.

Küpper, Jost: Die SPD und der Orientierungsrahmen '85. Bonn-Bad Godesberg: Neue Ges. 1977.

Lehnert, Detlef: Reform und Revolution in den Strategiediskussionen der klassischen Sozialdemokratie. Bonn-Bad Godesberg: Verlag Neue Gesellschaft 1977.

Ley, Richard: Föderalismusdiskussion innerhalb der CDU, CSU: von der Parteigründung bis zur Verabschiedung des Grundgesetzes. Mainz: v. Hase und Koehler 1978.

Marten, Heinz-Georg: Die unterwanderte FDP: politischer Liberalismus in Niedersachsen, Aufbau und Entwicklung der Freien Demokratischen Partei 1945-1955. Göttingen: Musterschmidt 1978.

Mittmann, Ursual: Fraktion und Partei. Ein Vergleich von Zentrum und Sozialdemokratie im Kaiserreich. Düsseldorf: Droste 1976.

Morsey, Rudolf: Der Untergang des politischen Katholizismus. Die Zentrumspartei zwischen christlichem Selbstverständnis und 'Nationaler Erhebung' 1932/33. Stuttgart et al.: Belser 1977.

Müller, Emil-Peter: Die Jugendorganisationen der politischen Parteien. Cologne: Deutscher Instituts-Verlag 1978.

Naßmacher, Karl-Heinz (ed.): Kommunalpolitik und Sozialdemokratie. Der Beitrag des demokratischen Sozialismus zur kommunalen Selbstverwaltung. Bonn-Bad Godesberg: Neue Ges. 1977.

Oberndörfer, Dieter (ed.): Sozialistische und kommunistische Parteien in Westeuropa. Opladen: Leske 1978.

Parteien-Jahrbuch: Dokumentation und Analyse der Entwicklung des Parteiensystems der Bundesrepublik Deutschland. Meisenheim: Hain 1978.

Rabe, Bernd: Der sozialdemokratische Charakter. Drei Generationen aktiver Parteimitglieder in einem Arbeiterviertel. Frankfurt et al.: Campus 1978.

Raschke, Joachim: Organisierter Konflikt in westeuropäischen Parteien. Eine vergleichende Analyse parteiinterner Oppositionsgruppen. Opladen: Westdeutscher Verlag 1977.

Raschke, Joachim (ed.): Die politischen Parteien Westeuropas. Geschichte-Programme-Praxis. Ein Handbuch. Reinbek: Rowohlt 1978.

Reichart-Dreyer, Ingrid: Werte, Systeme, Programme, Modell, Praxis und Alternativen politischer Willensbildung und Programmatik entwickelt am Beispiel der CDU. Bonn: Eichholz 1977.

Rengstorf, E.-V.: Links-Opposition in der Weimarer SPD. Die 'Klassenkampf-Gruppe' 1928-1931. Hannover: SOAK 1976.

Schmitz, Kurt Th.: Deutsche Einheit und Europäische Integration. Der sozialdemokratische Beitrag zur Außenpolitik der BRD unter besonderer Berücksichtigung des programmatischen Wandels einer Oppositionspartei. Bonn: Verlag Neue Gesellschaft 1978.

Stuby, Gerhard: Die 'Staatskrise' in der BRD und der Stellenwert der innerparteilichen Auseinandersetzungen in der SPD, in: Blätter, 1977, pp. 793-809.

Vieregge, Henning von: Parteistiftungen. Zur Rolle der Konrad-Adenauer-, Friedrich-Ebert-, Friedrich-Naumann- und Hanns-Seidel-Stiftung im politischen System der BRD. Baden-Baden: Nomos 1977.

Wilker, Lothar: Die Sicherheitspolitik der SPD 1956 — 1966. Zwischen Wiedervereinigungs- und Bündnisorientierung. Bonn-Bad Godesberg: Neue Gesellschaft 1977.

Wittemann, Klaus Peter: Kommunistische Politik in Westdeutschland nach 1945. Der Ansatz der Gruppe Arbeiterpolitik. Darstellung ihrer grundlegenden politischen Auffassungen und ihrer Entwicklungen zwischen 1945 und 1952. Hannover: SOAK 1977.

Zeuner, Bodo: 'Solidarität' mit der SPD oder Solidarität der Klasse? Zur SPD-Bindung der DGB-Gewerkschaften, in: Prokla 26, 1977, pp. 3-32.

Political Socialization

Claussen, Bernhard: Politische Bildung und Frauenemanzipation: Theoretische Grundlagen, empirische Befunde, curriculares Material. Frankfurt: Haag and Herchen 1978.

Grosser, Dieter: Kompendium Didaktik politische Bildung. Munich: Ehrenwirth 1977.

Hättich, Manfred: Rationalität als Ziel politischer Bildung: Eine Einführung. Munich: Olzog 1977.

Harten, Hans-Christian: Kognitive Sozialisation und politische Erkenntnis. Piagets Entwicklungspsychologie als Grundlage einer Theorie der politischen Bildung. Weinheim et al.: Beltz 1977.

Koch-Hillebrecht, Manfred: Das Deutschenbild: Gegenwart, Geschichte, Psychologie. Munich: Beck 1977.

Pawelka, Peter: Politische Sozialisation. Wiesbaden: Akademische Verlagsgesellschaft 1977.

Preuss-Lausitz, Ulf et al. (eds.): Fachunterricht und politisches Lernen. Beiträge zur erfahrungsorientierten politischen Bildung an Gesamtschulen. Weinheim et al.: Beltz 1976.

Schiele, Siegfried/Schneider, Herbert (eds.): Das Konsensproblem in der politischen Bildung. Stuttgart: Klett 1977.

Schmiederer, Rolf: Politische Bildung im Interesee der Schüler. Cologne et al.: Europäische Verlagsanstalt 1977.

Schulze, Gerhard: Politisches Lernen in der Alltagserfahrung. Eine empirische Analyse. Munich: Juventa 1977.

Schwonke, Martin: Sozialisation und Sozialstruktur. Stuttgart: Metzler 1977.

Wasmund, Klaus: Politische Orientierung Jugendlicher: Eine empirische Untersuchung zur politischen Sozialisation in der 9. Klasse der Hauptschule. Munich: Vögel 1977.

Zängle, Michael: Einführung in die politische Sozialisationsforschung. Paderborn: Schöningh 1978.

Elite Recruitment

Lipp, Wolfgang: Bürokratische, partizipative und Kaderorganisation als Instrumente sozialer Steuerung. Typenanalyse und Leistungsvergleich, in: Die Verwaltung, 1978, pp. 3-25.

Pumm, Günter: Kandidatenauswahl und innerparteiliche Demokratie in der Hamburger SPD: Eine empirische Untersuchung der Kandidatennominierungen für die Bundestagswahl 1969, der Bürgerschaftswahl 1970, des Senats und der Deputationen. Frankfurt et al.: Lang 1977.

Schössler, Dietmar/Weede,Erich: West German Elite Views on National Security and Foreign Policy Issues. Kronberg: Athenäum 1978.

Mass Media and Political Communication

Decker, Horst (ed.): Einführung in die Kommunkationswissenschaft: Der Prozeß der politischen Meinungs- und Willensbildung. Munich: Verl. Dok. 1976.

Decker, Horst et al.: Politische Kommunikation. Eine Einführung. Berlin: Spies 1976.

Hackforth, Josef: Massenmedien und ihre Wirkungen. Kommunikationspolitische Konsequenzen für den publizistischen Wandel. Literatur Expertise — Bibliographie. Göttingen: Schwartz 1976.

Koch-Hillebrecht, Manfred: Das Deutschland-Bild. Gegenwart, Geschichte, Psychologie. Munich: Beck 1977.

Mast, Claudia: Politische Öffentlichkeit: Untersuchung einer Parteiensendung des Zweiten Deutschen Fernsehens. Osnabrück: Fromm 1978.

Menke-Glückert, Peter: Der Medienmarkt im Umbruch. Eine aktueller Leitfaden. Frankfurt: Metzner 1978.

Noelle-Neumann, Elisabeth et al.: Streitpunkt lokales Pressemonopol. Düsseldorf: Droste 1977.

Noll, Jochen: Die deutsche Tagespresse. Ihre wirtschaftliche und redaktionelle Struktur. Frankfurt et al.: Campus 1977.

Paeffgen, Manfred: Das Bild Schwarz-Afrikas in der öffentlichen Meinung der BRD 1949-1972. Munich: Weltforum Verlag 1976.

Ronneberger, Franz: Kommunikationspolitik, vol. 1: Institutionen, Prozesse, Ziele. Mainz: v. Hase und Koehler 1978.

Schenk, Michael: Publikums- und Wirkungsforschung. Theoretische Ansätze und empirische Befunde der Massenkommunikationsforschung. Tübingen: Mohr 1978.

Steininger, Rolf: Deutschlandfunk — die Vorgeschichte einer Rundfunkanstalt 1949-1961. Ein Beitrag zur Innenpolitik der Bundesrepublik Deutschland. Berlin: Volker Spieß 1977.

Steinmüller, Wilhelm (ed.): Informationsrecht und Informationspolitik. Munich: Oldenbourg 1976.

Representation and Elections

Backhaus, Jürgen et al. (eds.): Partizipation in Betrieb und Gesellschaft. Frankfurt: Campus 1978.

Berger, Manfred et al.: Die Bundestagswahl 1976: Politik und Sozialstruktur. Oder: Wider die falsche Einheit der Wahlforschung, in: ZParl, 1977, pp. 197-231.

Biege, H. P. et al.: Zwischen Persönlichkeitswahl und Parteientscheidung. Kommunales Wahlverhalten im Lichte einer Oberbürgermeisterwahl. Meisenheim: Hain 1978.

Büsch, Otto et al. (eds.): Wählerbewegung in der deutschen Geschichte. Analysen und Berichte zu den Reichstagswahlen 1871-1933. Berlin: Colloquium Verlag 1978.

Buse, Michael et al.: Determinanten politischer Partizipation. Theorieansatz und empirische Überprüfung am Beispiel der Stadtsanierung Andernach. Meisenheim a. Gl.: Hain 1978.

Dienel, Peter C.: Die Planungszelle. Der Bürger plant seine Umwelt. Eine Alternative zur Establishment-Demokratie. Opladen: Westdeutscher Verlag 1978.

Horn, Wolfgang: Kandidaten im Wahlkampf: Kandidatenauslese, Wahlkampf und lokale Presse 1975 in Essen. Meisenheim: Hain 1978.

Kaase, Max (ed.): Wahlsoziologie heute. Analysen aus Anlaß der Bundestagswahl 1976 (Im Auftrag der Deutschen Vereinigung für Politische Wissenschaft), in: PVS 2/3, 1977, pp. 141-704.

Kaltefleiter, Werner: Vorspiel zum Wechsel: eine Analyse der Bundestagswahl 1976. Berlin: Duncker & Humblot 1977.

Kanitz, Horst (ed.): Kommunales Wahlverhalten. Bonn: Eichholz-Verlag 1976.

Matthöfer, Hans (ed.): Bürgerbeteiligung und Bürgerinitiativen. Villingen: Neckar-Verlag 1977.

Müller, Gerd: Das Wahlplakat. Pragmatische Untersuchungen zur Sprache in der Politik am Beispiel von Wahlplakaten aus der Weimarer Republik und der Bundesrepublik. Tübingen: Niemeyer 1978.

Nohlen, Dieter: Wahlsysteme der Welt. Daten und Analysen. Ein Handbuch. Munich: Piper 1978.

Oberndörfer, Dieter (ed.): Wählerverhalten in der Bundesrepublik Deutschland. Studien zu ausgewählten Problemen der Wahlforschung aus Anlaß der Bundestagswahl 1976. Berling: Duncker & Humblot 1978.

Area Studies

West European Countries

France

Baron, Stefan: Das Volksfrontbündnis und die Entwicklung des Parteiensystems in Frankreich. Cologne et al.: Heymanns 1977.

Breuer, Stafan: Stalinismuskritik von links? Marginalien zur Kontroverse über die Diktatur des Proletariats in der Kommunistischen Partei Frankreichs, in: Lev., 1977, pp. 378-399.

Kimmel, Adolf: Die V. Republik am Wendepunkt?, in: ZfP, 1978, pp. 57-91.

Schabert, Tilo: Ansätze zu einer Phänomenologie der politischen Parteien in Frankreich, in: ZfP, 1978, pp. 357-376.

Woyke, Wichard: Frankreichs Parteiensystem vor den Wahlen, in: AP, 1978, pp. 3-14.

Great Britain

Birke, Adolf M.: Pluralismus und Gewerkschaftsautonomie in England. Entstehungsgeschichte eine politischen Theorie. Stuttgart: Klett-Cotta 1978.

Dahrendorf, Ralf: Großbritannien — Modell oder Sonderfall, in: EA 6/1977, pp. 157-170.

Hartmann, Jürgen: Aspekte der 'britischen Krise', in: Aus Politik und Zeitgeschichte B 45/1977, pp. 21-37.

Italy

Albers, Detlev: Demokratie und Sozialismus in Italien. Der 'historische Kompromiß' und die Strategie der Parteien und Gewerkschaften. Frankfurt: Campus 1978.

Alf, Sophie: Leitfaden Italien. Vom antifaschistischen Kampf zum Historischen Kompromiß. Berlin: Rotbuch Verlag 1977.

Genth, Renate/Altvater, Elmar: Politische Konzeptionen und Schwierigkeiten der KPI in der Krise — ein Aufriß von Problemen einer Strategie der Arbeiterbewegung, in: Prokla 26, 1977, pp. 77-108; Prokla 27, 1977, pp. 103-118.

Italien. Geschichte, Ökonomie, Politik. Berlin: Olle & Wolter 1977.

Mangeng, Elisabeth: Der Anachronismus in Theorie und Strategie der Kommunistischen Partei: Italienische Arbeitswissenschaft gegen Theorie des Stamokap. Lahn-Gießen: Focus-Verlag 1977.

Timmermann, Heinz: Die KPI — Profil einer eurokommunistischen Partei in der Regierungsmehrheit, in: OE, 1978, pp. 415-428; pp. 511-523.

Spain

Franz, Hans-Werner/Tovar, Santiago (eds.): Gewerkschaftsbewegung in Spanien. Auf dem Weg zur Einheit? West Berlin: VSA 1976.

Lorenzen, Ebba: Presse unter Franco. Zur Entwicklung publizistischer Institutionen und Prozesse im politischen Kräftespiel. Munich: Verl. Dok. 1978.

Maier, Lothar: Spaniens Weg zur Demokratie. Meisenheim: Hain 1977.

Meyer, Heinz/Woyke, Wichard: Spanien — eine politische Länderkunde. Opladen: Leske 1978.

Spanien. Die zweite Revolution? West Berlin: Olle & Wolter 1976.

Other Countries

Eichenberger, Kurt: Zusammen- und Gegenspiel repräsentativer und plebiszitärer Komponenten im schweizerischen Regierungssystem, in: ZParl, 1977, pp. 318-333.

Gruner, Erich: Die eidgenössische Bundesversammlung als Milizparlament, in: ZParl, 1977, pp. 351-356.

Hübner, Hans: Portugal: Prüfstein der Demokratie? Cologne: Kiepenheuer & Witsch 1976.

Kerr, Henry H.: Die Struktur der Opposition in der schweizerischen Bundesversammlung, in: ZParl, 1977, pp. 357-367.

Mez, Lutz: Ziviler Widerstand in Norwegen. Frankfurt: Haag und Herchen 1976.

Mühll, Urs von der: Die Unterentwicklung Portugals. Von der Weltmacht zur Halbkolonie Englands. Frankfurt et al.: Campus 1978.

Petersen, Herbert: Schweden — Die 'politische Wende' findet nicht statt, in: Aus Politik und Zeitgeschichte B 45/1977, pp. 38-44.

Portugal, Grenzen der Revolution? West Berlin: Olle & Wolter 1976.

Riklin, Alois: Die Funktion des schweizerischen Parlaments im internationalen Vergleich, in: ZParl, 1977, pp. 368-385.

van Schendelen, M.P.C.M.: Informations- und Entscheidungsprozesse im niederländischen Parlament im Rahmen einer Repräsentationstheorie, in: ZParl, 1977, pp. 252-266.

Schmid, Gerhard: Föderalismus und Ständerat in der Schweiz, in: Zparl, 1977, pp. 334-350.

Wenturis, Nikolaus: Die soziopolitischen und ökonomischen Strukturen Griechenlands im Hinblick auf seine Integration in die EG. Frankfurt et al.: Lang 1977.

The USA and Canada

Hartmann, Jürgen: Kontinuität und Wandel in den Beziehungen des amerikanischen Kongresses zum Präsidenten der USA (1947-1977), in: ZParl, 1977, pp. 507-524.

Köpp, Klaus: Wahlkreiseinteilung durch Richterspurch? Berlin: Duncker & Humblot 1978.

Maassen, Bernd: Der US-Supreme-Court im gewaltenteilenden amerikanischen Regierungssystem: (1783-1972). Frankfurt et al.: Lang 1977.

Matthias, Helmut: US-Präsidenten und Wirtschaftspolitik, in: AP, 1978, pp. 27-37.

Merkl, Peter/Raabe, Dieter: Politische Soziologie der USA. Wiesbaden: Akademische Verlagsgesellschaft 1977.

SOCIALIST SYSTEMS

Comparison of Capitalist and Socialist Systems and Theoretical Discussions of Research on Socialist Systems

Bartsch, Günther: Wende in Osteuropa? Revolution und Gegenrevolution in Osteuropa seit 1948. Krefeld: Sinus-Verlag 1977.

Brunner, Georg/Kaschkat, Hannes: Wandel und Verharrung in den politischen Systemen des sowjetischen Hegemonialbereichs, in: ZfP, 1977, pp. 363-388.

Gramatzki, Hans-Erich et al.: Arbeiterselbstverwaltung und Mitbestimmung in den Staaten Osteuropas. Hannover: Fackelträger Verlag 1977.

Haffner, Friedrich: Die ökonomischen Grundzüge der 'entwickelten sozialistischen Gesellschaft', in: OE, 1978, pp. 586-603.

Hensel, Karl Paul: Systemvergleich als Aufgabe. Aufsätze und Vorträge, ed. Hannelore Hamel. Stuttgart: G. Fischer 1977.

Höhmann, Hans-Hermann (ed.): Arbeitsmarkt und Wirtschaftsplanung. Beiträge zur Beschäftigungsstruktur und Arbeitskräftepolitik in Osteuropa. Cologne et al.: Europäische Verlagsanstalt 1977.

Meissner, Boris: Elemente des Wandels in der östlichen Welt. Cologne: Markus Verlag 1976.

Meyer, Gert: Sozialistische Systeme. Theorie- und Strukturanalyse. Ein Studienbuch. Stuttgart: Leske 1978.

Pelikan, Jiri/Wilke, Manfred (eds.): Menschenrechte. Eine Jahrbuch zu Osteuropa. Reinbek: Rowohlt 1977.

Schroeder, F.-Ch./Meissner, Boris (eds.): Verfassungs- und Verwaltungsreformen in den sozialistischen Staaten. Berlin: Duncker & Humblot 1978.

Sikora, Franz: Sozialistische Solidarität und nationale Interessen: Polen, Tschechoslowakei, DDR. Cologne: Verlag Wissenschaft und Politik 1978.

Timmermann, Heinz: Moskau, Peking und die Eurokommunisten, in: OE, 1978, pp. 167-174.

Wädekin, Karl-Eugen: Sozialistische Agrarpolitik in Osteuropa. Vol. 2: Entwicklung und Probleme 1960-1976. Berlin: Duncker & Humblot 1978.

Comparisons between the two German States

Behr, Wolfgang: Grundlagen der Politik in der Bundesrepublik Deutschland und in der DDR. Ein Systemvergleich, in: Aus Politik und Zeitgeschichte B 9/1978, pp. 3-28.

Hemal, Hannelore (ed.): BRD-DDR. Die Wirtschaftssysteme. Soziale Markwirtschaft und Sozialistische Planwirtschaft im Systemvergleich. Munich: Beck 1977.

Wilkens, Herbert: Das Sozialprodukt der Deutschen Demokratischen Republik im Vergleich mit dem der Bundesrepublik Deutschland. Berlin: Duncker & Humblot 1976.

The Political System of the GDR

Biermann, Wolfgang: Demokratisierung in der DDR? Ökonomische Notwendigkeiten, Herrschaftsstrukturen, Rolle der Gewerkschaften 1961-1977. Cologne: Wissenschaft und Politik 1978.

Bust-Bartels, Axel: Die Entwicklung ausgewählter Arbeitsbedingungen in der DDR, in: Prokla 27, 1977, pp. 41-75.

Damus, Renate: Der reale Sozialismus als Herrschaftssystem am Beispiel der DDR. Kritik der nachkapitalistischen Gesellschaft. Giessen: Focus-Verlag 1978.

Deutschland-Archiv (Special Issue): Kultur und Gesellschaft in der DDR. Zehnte Tagung zum Stand der DDR-Forschung in der Bundesrepublik 31. Mai bis 3. Juni 1977.

Dietz, Raimund: Investitionspolitik in der DDR, in: DA, 1978, pp. 390-401.

Eisenfeld, Bernd: Kriegsdienstverweigerung in der DDR, ein Friedensdienst?: Genesis, Befragung, Analyse, Dokumente. Frankfurt: Haag and Herchen 1978.

Glaeßner, Gert-Joachim: Herrschaft durch Kader. Leitung der Gesellschaft und Kaderpolitik in der DDR am Beispiel des Staatsapparates. Opladen: Westdeutscher Verlag 1977.

Glaeßner, Gert-Joachim: Bildungsökonomie und Bildungsplanung. Vorüberlegungen zu einer Analyse der gesellschaftlichen und politischen Funktion von Bildungsprozessen in der DDR, in: DA, 1978, pp. 937-956.

Glaeßner, Gert-Joachim/Rudolph, Irmhild: Macht durch Wissen. Zum Zusammenhang von Bildungspolitik, Bildungssystem und Kaderqualifizierung in der DDR. Eine politisch-soziologische Untersuchung. Opladen: Westdeutscher Verlag 1978.

Grätz, Frank: Ideelle Stimuli in der DDR-Wirtschaft, in: DA, 1977, pp. 1071-1079.

Grebing, Helga: Die intellektuelle Opposition in der DDR seit 1956. Ernst Bloch — Wolfgang Harich — Robert Havemann, in: Aus Politik und Zeitgeschichte B 45/1977, 3-19.

Gurtz, Johannes: Der Staatshaushalt der DDR. Grundriß. Berlin: Die Wirtschaft 1977.

Klein, Werner: Wirtschaftspolitische Aspekte der Dezentralisierung in der DDR, in: DA, 1978, pp. 36-51.

Körner, Ulrich: Materielle Stimulierung in der DDR. Zur Entwicklung der Planung und Bildung des Prämienfonds, in: DA, 1977, pp. 1080-1092.

Krebs, Christian: Zur aktuellen Situation der DDR-Landwirtschaft. Produktionsziele, Betriebstrukturen und Musterstatuten, in: DA, 1977, pp. 1051-1071.

Lambrecht, Horst: Die Landwirtschaft der DDR vor und nach ihrer Umgestaltung im Jahre 1960. Berlin: Duncker & Humblot 1977.

Lammich, Siegfried: Die DDR und die übrigen sozialistischen Länder Europas. Ein verfassungsrechtlicher Vergleich, in: DA, 1978, pp. 52-62.

Lapp, Peter Joachim: Zur Geschichte der Regierung der DDR, in: DA, 1977, pp. 835-848.

Lieser-Triebnigg, Erika: Das neue Arbeitsgesetzbuch der DDR, in: DA, 1977, pp. 1268-1289.

Ludz, Peter Christian: Die Neuordnung der Führungsspitze der DDR. Beweggründe und Auswirkungen der Machtkonzentration bei Erich Honecker, in: EA 4/1977, pp. 113-120.

Maaß, Hans-Christian 'Genossenschaftliche Demokratie' in der DDR. Entwicklung eines Begriffs, in: DA, 1977, pp. 724-731.

Neugebauer, Gero: Partei und Staatsapparat in der DDR. Opladen: Westdeutscher Verlag 1978.

Riedel, Heide: Hörfunk und Fernsehen in der DDR. Funktion, Struktur und Programm des Rundfunks in der DDR. Cologne: Braun 1977.

Schäfer, Hans-Peter: Chancengleichheit und Begabtenförderun in der DDR, in: DA, 1977, pp. 818-828.

Scherzinger, Angela: Zur Planung, Organisation und Lenkung von Forschuing und Entwicklung in der DDR. Aspekte des wissenschaftlich-technischen Fortschritts. Berlin: Duncker & Humblot 1977.

Schneider, Eberhard (ed.): SED — Programm und Status von 1976. Text, Kommentar, Didaktische Hilfen. Opladen: Leske 1977.

Staritz, Dietrich: Zum Verhältnis von Planungssystem und Partizipation in der DDR, in: DA, 1978, pp. 1049-1070.

Werner, Steffen: Kybernetik statt Marx. Politische Ökonomie und marxistische Philosophie in der DDR unter dem Einfluß der elektronischen Datenverarbeitung. Stuttgart: Bonn aktuell 1977.

Winter, Helmut: Außenwirtschaftsplanung und betriebliche Ergebnisrechnung in der DDR, in: DA, 1977, pp. 1185-1200.

Berlin

The Soviet Union

von Borcke, Astrid: Sowjetsystem und öffentliche Meinung, in: Aus Politik und Zeitgeschichte B 13/1978, pp. 13-31.

Borst, Gert et al.: Militärwesen in der Sowjetunion. Munich: Bernard & Graefe 1977.

Brahm, Heinz: Sowjetische Intellektuelle über die 'chinesische Gefahr'. Ein gestaffeltes System der Informierung, in: OE, 1978, pp. 150-166.

Brahm, Heinz et al.: Sowjetische Politik heute. Probleme und Alternativen, in: Aus Politik und Zeitgeschichte, B 40/1978, ppl. 3-13.

Brockmann, Jürgen: Die Differenzierung der sowjetischen Sozialstruktur. Wiesbaden: Harrassowitz 1978.

Brunner, Georg: Politische Soziologie der UdSSR, 2 vols. Wiesbaden: Akademische Verlagsgesellschaft 1977.

Eichwede, Wolfgang et al.: 60 Jahre Sowjet-Rußland. Hannover: Niedersächsische Landeszentrale für politische Bildung 1977.

Fischer, Alexander: Politik, Strategie und Rüstung in der Sowjetunion. Munich: Bernard & Graefe 1977.

Gumpel, Werner (ed.): Arbeits- und Sozialpolitik in der Sowjetunion. Munich: Olzog 1976.

Haffner, Friedrich: Systemkonträre Beziehungen in der sowjetischen Planwirtschaft. Ein Beitrag zur Theorie der mixed economy. Berlin: Duncker & Humblot 1978.

Heiter, Heinrich: Vom friedlichen Weg zum Sozialismus zur Diktatur des Proletariats: Wandlungen der sowjetischen Konzeption der Volksdemokratie 1945-49. Frankfurt: Haag und Herchen 1977.

Liely, Helmut: Die Landbevölkerung der UdSSR. Demographische und sozioökonomische Strukturmerkmale, in: OE, 1978, pp. 236-249.

Luchterhandt, Otto: Die Grundrechte in der neuen sowjetischen Unionsverfassung, in: OE, 1978, pp. 28-40.

Martiny, Albrecht: Probleme des Einzelhandels und des tertiären Sektors in der Sowjetunion, in: OE, 1978, pp. 385-397.

Masuch, Michael: Das Problem der Erklärung des 'Stalinismus', in: Argument 106, 1977, pp. 826-843.

Meissner, Boris: Die politischen Aspekte der neuen Bundesverfassung der Sowjetunion, in: EA 22/1977, pp. 800-810.

Meissner, Boris: Partei, Staat und Nation in der neuen Verfassung der UdSSR, in: OE, 1978, pp. 3-17.

Meyer, Gerd: Bürokratischer Sozialismus. Eine Analyse des sowjetischen Herrschaftssystems. Stuttgart- Bad Canstatt: Frommann-Holzboog 1977.

Meyer, Gert: Industrialisierung, Arbeiterklasse und Stalinherrschaft in der UdSSR, in: Argument, 106, 1977, pp. 844-859; 107, 1978, pp. 42-59; 108, pp. 202-221.

Meyer, Gert: Aufgaben der sowjetischen Gewerkschaften, in: Blätter, 1978, pp. 89-105.

Mitter, Wolfgang: Pädagogische Forschung und Bildungspolitik in der Sowjetunion: Organisation, Gegenstand, Methoden. Weinheim: Beltz 1978.

Sowjetunion 1976/77. Innenpolitik, Wirtschaft, Außenpolitik. Munich: Hanser 1977.

Stehr, Uwe: Stereotype Merkmale sowjetischer Politikanalysen. Dargestellt am Beispiel von RGW-Interpretationen, in: OE, 1978, pp. 524-537.

Tatur, Melanie: Ansätze zur Partizipation von Arbeitern an Verwaltungsfunktionen im sowjetischen Industriebetrieb, in: OE, 1978, pp. 318-337.

Teckenberg, Wolfgang: Die soziale Struktur der sowjetischen Arbeiterklasse im internationalen Vergleich. Auf dem Wege zur industrialisierten Ständegesellschaft? Munich et al: Oldenbourg 1977.

Teckenberg, Wolfgang: Prestigerangordnungen, berufliche Bewertungen und Präferenzen in der UdSSR, in: KZfSS, 1977, pp. 731-761.

Thalheim, Karl C.: Die Wirtschaft in der neuen Verfassung der UdSSR, in: OE, 1978, pp. 18-27.

Westen, Klaus: Das Rätesystem in der neuen sowjetischen Verfassung, in: OE, 1978, pp. 41-48.

Other Socialist Systems
East European Socialist Countries

Adamicek, Josef: Entwicklung des gesellschaftlichen Konsums in der CSSR. Berlin: Duncker & Humblot 1977.

Bosl, Karl (ed.): Die erste tschechoslowakische Republik als multinationaler Parteienstaat. Munich: Oldenbourg 1978.

Grothusen, Klaus-Detlev et al.: Rumänien. Göttingen: Vandenhoeck & Ruprecht 1977.

Hoppe, Hans-Joachim: Todor Shiwkow. Eine politische Biographie, in: OE, 1978, pp. 399-408.

Müller, Adolf: Die Tschechoslowakei auf der Suche nach Sicherheit. Berlin: Berlin-Verlag 1977.

Rafael, Edgar R.: 'Entwicklungsland' Rumänien. Zur Geschichte der 'Umdefinierung' eines sozialistischen Staates. Munich: Odlenbourg 1977.

Schnur, Roman (ed.): Probleme der Gesetzlichkeit im Staatsapparat der Volksrepublik Polen. Berlin: Duncker & Humblot 1977.

Sikora, Franz': Sozialistische Solidarität und nationale Interessen. Polen, Tschechoslowakei, DDR. Cologne: Wissenschaft und Politik 1977.

Tschechoslowakei. Munich: Hanser 1977.

Zotschew, Theordor D.: Bevölkerungs- und Wohnungsprobleme in Bulgarien, in: OE, 1978, pp. 409-414.

Yugoslavia

Haberl, Othmar Nikola: Parteiorganisation und nationale Frage in Jugoslawien. Wiesbaden: Harassowitz 1976.

Cuba

Furtak, Robert: Kuba: Institutionalisierung eines revolutionären Systems, in: OE, 1978, pp. 494-510.

China

Domes, Jürgen, Das politische System der Volksrepublik China. Grundzüge und Perspektiven, in: Staat, 1978, pp. 73-95.

Fischer, Harald et al.: China: das neue Selbstbewußtsein, Gesellschaft, Erziehung, Bevölkerung. Munich: Piper 1978.

Franz, Helmut (ed.): China unter neuer Führung: Hintergründe und Analysen zur Entwicklung von Gesellschaft, Wirtschaft, Wissenschaft und Kultur nach dem Sturz der 'Viererbande' im Herbst 1976. Bochum: Studienverl. Brockmeyer 1978.

Hoffmann, Rainer: Maos Rebellen. Sozialgeschichte der chinesischen Kulturrevolution. Hamburg: Hoffmann & Campe 1977.

Juttka-Reisse, Rosemarie: Geschichte und Struktur der chinesischen Gesellschaft. Stuttgart-Bad Canstatt: Frommann-Holzboog 1977.

Kühner, Hans: Abenteur der Dialektik in China: die Wandlungen des Basis-Überbau-Begriffs auf dem Weg zur 'Kulturrevolution'. Munich: tuduv 1977.

Lorenz, Richard (ed.): Umwälzung einer Gesellschaft. Zur Sozialgeschichte der chinesischen Revolution (1911-1949). Frankfurt: Suhrkamp 1977.

Mehnert, Klaus: Kampf um Maos Erbe. Stuttgart: Deutsche Verlagsanstalt 1977.

Manzel, Ulrich: Theorie und Praxis des chinesischen Entwicklungsmodells. Ein Beitrag zum Konzept autozentrierter Entwicklung. Opladen: Westdeutscher Verlag 1978.

Developing Countries

Latin America

Bennholdt-Thomsen, Veronika von (ed.): Lateinamerika. Analysen und Berichte. Vol. 1: Kapitalistische Entwicklung und politische Repression; vol. 2: Internationale Verflechtung und soziale Kämpfe. Berlin: Olle & Wolter 1977, 1978.

Berger, Manfredo: Bildungswesen und Dependenzsituation. Eine empirische Darstellung der Beziehungen zwischen Bildungswesen und Gesellschaft in Brasilien. Munich: Fink 1977.

Buck, Karl-Hermann: Die Sozialistische Partei Chiles 1933-1973. Geschichte, Programme, Sozialstruktur. Frankfurt: Haag & Herchen 1977.

Freitag, Barbara: Die brasilianische Bildungspolitik. Munich: Fink 1977.

Grabendorff, Wolf et al.: Brasilien: Entwicklungsmodell und Außenpolitik. Munich: Fink 1977.

Kellenbenz, H. et al. (eds.): Lateinamerika. Studien I. Munich: Fink 1977.

Mansilla, Hugo C. F.: Der südamerikanische Reformismus: Nationalistische Modernisierungsversuche in Argentinien, Bolivien und Peru. Rheinstetten: Schindele 1977.

Möller, Alois: Städtische Marginalität und Militärregierung in Peru. Göttingen: Eichhorn 1977.

Münster, Arno: Argentinien. Guerilla und Konterrevolution. Arbeiterkämpfe gegen oligarchische Diktatur und Gewerkschaftsbürokratie. Munich: Trikont 1977.

Oberndörfer, Dieter (ed.): Kommunalverwaltung in Mittelamerika: eine Studie über die Hauptstädte Guatemalas und El Salvadors. Mainz: v. Hase und Koehler 1977.

Stanchina, Peer Christopher: Staat und Kirche in Mexiko. Munich: Beck 1978.

Africa

Brückner, Reinhard: Südafrikas schwarze Zukunft. Die Jugendunruhen seit 1976, ihre Ursachen und Folgen. Frankfurt: Lembeck 1977.

Duve, Freimut (ed.): Kap ohne Hoffnung oder die Politik der Apartheid. Reinbek: Rowohlt 1978.

Halback, Axel J.: Die Zukunft Südafrikas: Möglichkeiten eines inneren Wandels, in: EA 13/1977, pp. 409-418.

Hanf, Theodor et al.: Südafrika: Friedlicher Wandel? Möglichkeiten demokratischer Konfliktregelung. Eine empirische Untersuchung. Munich: Kaiser; Mainz: Math.-Grünewald-Verlag 1978.

Hanf, Theodor/Weiland, Heribert: Konkordanzdemokratie für Südafrika? Zur Bedeutung der neueren verfassungspolitischen Debatte, in: EA, 1978, pp. 755-770.

Höpker, Wolfgang (ed.): Südafrika auf der Waage. Ein Subkontinent zwischen Evolution und Revolution. Cologne: Wiss. & Pol. 1978.

Kühlein, Conrad: Die Auswirkungen der Revolution in Äthiopien auf die Lage am Horn von Afrika, in: EA, 1978, pp. 135-144.

Leistner, G. M. Erich: Südafrika. Schwarz und Weiß im Wirtschaftsprozeß. Hamburg: Weltarchiv 1977.

Niemann, Rolf: Von Rhodesien zu Zimbabwe. Emanzipation der Afrikaner durch Guerillakampf oder Verfassungskonferenz. Frankfurt/Main: Haag & Herchen 1976.

Noller, Jost F.: Theorie und Praxis der Apartheid. Eine Analyse der Grundlagen und Bedingungen der Politik der 'Getrennten Entwicklung' in Südafrika. Frankfurt et al.: Lang 1977.

Nuscheler, Franz/Ziemer, Klaus: Die Wahl der Parlamente und anderer Staatsorgane. Vol. 2: Afrika. Politische Repräsentation in Afrika. Berlin: de Gruyter 1978.

Ortlieb, Heinz-Dietrich/Spandau, Arnt (eds.): Südafrika. Revolution oder Evolution? Studien zur Lebenslage der Schwarzen. Hamburg: Weltarchiv 1977.

Rädel, Fritz E.: Aufstieg oder Ausbeutung der Schwarzafrikaner? Einkommens- und Verbrauchsstrukturen in Südafrika. Hamburg: Weltarchiv 1978.

Reuke, Ludger: Befreier und Erlöser? Militär und Entwicklung in Ghana. Bonn-Bad Godesberg: Neue Ges. 1976.

Runge, Erika: Südafrika-Rassendiktatur zwischen Elend und Widerstand. Protokolle und Dokumentation zur Apartheid. Reinbek: Rowohlt 1976.

Seelow, Frank: Geld und Geldpolitik im unterentwickelten Kapitalismus Afrikas. Unter besonderer Berücksichtigung d. historischen Herausbildung der Geldverfassung in ehemals Britisch-Westafrika. Meisenheim a. Gl.: Hain 1977.

von Schack, Alard: Schwarzafrika und sein 'weißer' Norden, in: AP, 1977, pp. 102-114.

Scholler, Heinrich: Verfassungsrecht und Verfassungspolitik in Äthiopien seit 1974, in: ZfP, 1977, pp. 402-420.

Ziemer, Klaus: Politische Parteien im frankophonen Afrika. Kronberg/Ts.: Hain 1978.

Arab Countries and the Middle East

Ansprenger, Franz: Juden und Araber in Einem Land. Die politischen Beziehungen der beiden Völker im Mandatsgebiet Palästina und im Staat Israel. Munich: Kaiser; Mainz: Grünewald 1978.

Bechtoldt, Heinrich: Der Dualismus in der türkischen Politik, in: AP, 1977, pp. 405-423.

Diskin, Abraham/Wolffsohn, Michael: Das Ende des Dominanzpartei-Systems: Israels Wahlen vom 17. Mai 1977, in: PVS, 1977, pp. 773-841.

Haritz, Detlef: Der Bürgerkrieg im Libanon. Offenbach: Verlag 2000, 1977.

Orland, Nachum: Israels Revisionisten: die geistigen Väter Menachim Begins. Munich: tuduv 1978.

Röper, Erich: Rechtsfragen bei der Entstehung Israels, in: Aus Politik und Zeitgeschichte B 18/1978, pp. 3-21.

Wehling, Gerd-Rudolf: Die politischen Parteien im Verfassungs system Israels. Berlin: Duncker & Humblot 1977.

Weiher, Gerhard: Militär und Entwicklung in der Türkei 1945-1973. Ein Beitrag zur Untersuchung der Rolle des Militärs in der Entwicklung der Dritten Welt. Opladen: Leske 1978.

Asia

Dohmen, Holger/Weggel, Oskar: Indochina seit der Stunde Null, in: EA, 1978, pp. 21-32.

Domes, Jürgen: Aspekte des politischen Systems der Republik China auf Taiwan, in: ZfP, 1978, pp. 255-278.

Sembdner, Friedrich: Das kommunistische Regierungssystem in Vietnam. Cologne: Wissenschaft und Politik 1978.

Simon, Walter: Japan — die patriarchalische Variante. Besonderheiten in den Beziehungen zwischen Kapital und Arbeit, in: Blätter, 1978, pp. 1343-1357.

Wontroba, Gerd/Menzel, Ulrich: Stagnation und Unterentwicklung in Korea. Von der Yi-Dynastie zur Peripherisierung unter japanischer Kolonialherrschaft. Meisenheim: Hain 1978.

E. INTERNATIONAL RELATIONS

General Studies on Theory and Methodology

Bühl, Walter L.: Transnationale Politik. Internationale Beziehungen zwischen Hegemonie und Interdependenz. Stuttgart: Klett-Cotta 1978.

Kindermann, Gottfried-Karl (ed.): Grundelemente der Weltpolitik. Eine Einführung. Munich: Piper 1977.

Mommsen, Wolfgang J.: Imperialismus. Seine geistigen, politischen und wirtschaftlichen Grundlagen. Ein Quellen- und Arbeitsbuch. Hamburg: Hoffmann & Campe 1977.

Röhrich, Wilfried: Politik und Ökonomie der Weltgesellschaft. Das internationale System. Reinbek: Rowohlt 1978.

Simonis, Georg: Außenpolitik und Abschreckung. Ansätze zu einer kritischen Theorie des internationalen Systems. Frankfurt: Campus 1977.

Woyke, Wichard (ed.): Handwörterbuch internationale Politik. Opladen: Leske & Budrich 1977.

States in International Affairs: Their Foreign Relations

General

Böhnke, Rolf: Nationale Sicherheit und multinationale Unternehmen, in: PVS 1/1977, pp. 3-24.

Deutsch, Karl W. (ed.): Außenpolitik und Öffentlichkeit in der direkten Demokratie. Ein Gespräch mit Experten. Bern/Stuttgart: Haupt 1977.

Gerdes, Dirk: Legitimationsprobleme und Außenpolitik. Ein Unterrichtsmodell für die Sekundarstufe. Stuttgart: Metzler 1978.

Gunst, Dietrich: Außenpolitik zwischen Macht und Recht. Mainz: Von Hase & Koehler 1977.

Hasse, Rolf: Wirtschaftliche Sanktionen als Mittel der Außenpolitik. Das Rhodesien-Embargo. Berlin: Duncker & Humblot 1977.

Kammler, Hans: Staatenkonkurrenz, Machtverteilung, Imperialismus, in: ZfP 4/1978, pp. 327-348.

Kuper, Ernst: Entspannungspolitik. Mittel der Herrschaftssicherung oder Ursache von permanentem Legitimationsdruck?, in: Neue Politische Literatur 2/1978, pp. 145-157.

Schreiber, Manfred (ed.): Zwischen Sicherheit und Freiheit. Munich: Olzog 1977.

FRG

Baring, Arnulf/Sase, Masamori (eds.): Zwei zaghafte Riesen? Deutschland und Japan seit 1945. Stuttgart/Zürich: Belser 1977.

Baumann, Hans: Außenhandel, Direktinvestitionen und Industriestruktur der deutschen Wirtschaft. Eine Untersuchung ihrer Entwicklung unter Berücksichtigung der Wechselkursänderungen. Berlin: Duncker & Humblot 1977.

Beitel, Werner/Nötzhold, Jürgen: Deutsch-sowjetische Wirtschaftsbeziehungen in der Zeit der Weimarer Republik. Eine Bilanz im Hinblick auf gegenwärtige Probleme. Baden-Baden: Nomos 1978.

Benz, Wolfgang/Graml, Hermann (eds.): Aspekte deutscher Außenpolitik im 20. Jahrhundert. Aufsätze Hans Rothfels zum Gedächtnis. Stuttgart: DVA 1976.

Bley, Helmut et al.: Afrika und Bonn. Versäumnisse und Zwänge deutscher Afrika-Politik. Reinbek: Rowohlt 1978.

Blumenwitz, Dieter: Die beiden deutschen Staaten in den Vereinten Nationen, in: ZfP 2/1977, pp. 101-121.

Blumenwitz, Dieter et al.: Partnerschaft mit dem Osten. 10 Beiträge zur Lage Deutschlands nach den Verträgen. Munich: Lurz 1976.

Brauch, Hans-Günter: Abrüstungsamt der Bundesregierung, Ein Vorschlag für eine aktive Friedenspolitik, in: Aus Politik und Zeitgeschichte B 8/1978, pp. 17-29.

Briessen, Fritz van: Grundzüge der deutsch-chinesischen Beziehungen. Darmstadt: Wissenschaftliche Buchgesellschaft 1977.

Bruns, Wilhelm: Deutsch-deutsche Beziehungen. Prämissen, Probleme, Perspektiven. Opladen: Leske & Budrich 1978.

Bruns, Wilhelm: Die beiden deutschen Staaten in der UNO, in: Aus Politik und Zeitgeschichte B 12/1978, pp. 19-31.

Bruns, Wilhelm: Von der Konfrontation zur Kooperation? Die deutsch-deutschen Beziehungen seit dem Grundlagenvertrag, in: Neue Politische Literatur 2/1978, pp. 158-171.

Dams, Theodor/Grohs, Gerhard (eds.): Kontroversen in der internationalen Rohstoffpolitik. Ein Beitrag zur Rohstoffpolitik der BRD nach UNCTAD IV. Munich: Kaiser; Mainz: Grünewald-Verlag 1977.

Ebert, Theodor: Verteidigungspolitik aus der Sicht der Ökologiebewegung, in: Gewaltfreie Aktion, 35/36, 1978, pp. 77-86.

Engels, Benno/Laaser, Ullrich (eds.): Deutsche Bildungshilfe in der zweiten Entwicklungsdekade. Eine Zwischenbilanz. Munich: Weltforum-Verlag 1978.

Forndran, Erhard/Golczewski, Frank/Riesenberger, Dieter (eds.): Innen- und Außenpolitik unter nationalsozialistischer Bedrohung. Determinanten internationaler Beziehungen in historischen Fallstudien. Opladen: Westdeutscher Verlag 1977.

Friedensanalysen 7: Jungsozialisten und Jungdemokraten zur Friedens- und Sicherheitspolitik. Frankfurt: Suhrkamp 1977.

Geisler, Wolff: Die militärische Zusammenarbeit zwischen BRD und RSA im atomaren und konventionellen Bereich, in: Blätter 2/1978, pp. 166-185.

Genscher, Hans-Dietrich: Deutsche Außenpolitik. Stuttgart: Bonn aktuell 1977.

Haftendorn, Helga (ed.): Verwaltete Außenpolitik. Sicherheits- und entspannungspolitische Entscheidungsprozesse in Bonn. Cologne: Wissenschaft und Politik 1978.

Hoebrink, Hein: Westdeutsche Wiedervereinigungspolitik 1949-1961. Meisenheim a. Glan: Hain 1978.

Jacobsen, Hans-Adolf: Fünf Jahre Warschauer Vertrag. Versuch einer Bilanz der Beziehungen zwischen der BRD und der Volksrepublik Polen 1970-1975. Berlin: Berlin Verlag 1976.

Jacobsen, Hans-Adolf: Von der Strategie der Gewalt zur Politik der Friedenssicherung. Beiträge zur deutschen Geschichte im 20. Jahrhundert. Düsseldorf: Dorste 1977.

Geißler, Heiner (ed.): Sicherheit für unsere Freiheit. Zur verteidigungspolitischen Lage der Bundesrepublik Deutschland. Stuttgart: Bonn aktuell 1978.

Jahrbuch für Friedens- und Konfliktforschung, Bd. 5: Rüstung und Militär in der Bundesrepublik Deutschland. Wiesbaden: Westdeutscher Verlag 1977.

Jungnickel, Rolf/Krägenau, Henry/Lefeldt, Mathias/Holthus, Manfred: Der Einfluß der multinationalen Unternehmen auf Außenwirtschaft und Branchenstruktur in der Bundesrepublik Deutschland. Hamburg: Verlag Weltarchiv 1977.

Klingshirn, Agnes/Kramer, Dieter: Kultureller Austausch oder Strategie der außenpolitischen Einwirkung? Probleme der auswärtigen Kulturpolitik der BRD, in: Blätter 6/1978, pp. 737-751.

Knapp, Manfred et al.: Die USA und Deutschland: 1918-1975. Deutsch-amerikanische Beziehungen zwischen Rivalität und Partnerschaft. Munich: Beck 1978.

Knapp, Manfred: Bonn — Washington. Kooperation und Konkurrenz, in: AP 4/1978, pp. 385-398.

Knorr, Lorenz: Bonner Politik gegen Sicherheit und Zusammenarbeit. Wie steht es mit der Verwirklichung der Beschlüsse der Konferenz über Sicherheit und Zusammenarbeit in Europa? Frankfurt: Marxistische Blätter 1976.

Kreile, Michael: Die Bundesrepublik Deutschland — eine 'economie dominante' in. Westeuropa?, in: Aus Politik und Zeitgeschichte B 26/1978, pp. 3-17.

Lauk, Kurt J.: Kernwaffen und eine Diplomatie der Friedenssicherung. Die Notwendigkeit nuklearer Absicherung der Bundesrepublik Deutschland, in: Beiträge zur Konfliktforschung 4/1977, pp. 117-138.

Michalka, Wolfgang (ed.): Nationalsozialistische Außenpolitik. Darmstadt: Wissenschaftliche Buchgesellschaft 1978.

Moersch, Karl: Kurs-Revision: Deutsche Politik nach Adenauer. Frankfurt: Societäts-Verlag 1978.

Müller-Link, Horst: Industrialisierung und Außenpolitik. Preußen-Deutschland und das Zarenreich 1860-1890. Göttingen/Zürich: Vandenhoeck & Ruprecht 1977.

Mutz, R.: Sicherheitspolitik und demokratische Öffentlichkeit in der BRD. Probleme der Analyse, Kritik und Kontrolle militärischer Macht. Munich: Oldenbourg 1978.

Offenheit gegen Offenheit. Meinungen, Kontroversen, Dialoge. Bundesrepublik Deutschland — Sowjetunion. Cologne: Pahl-Rugenstein 1978.

Oldenburg, Fred/Meier, Christian: Die deutsch-russischen Beziehungen im Zeichen des Breshnew-Besuchs, in: OE 10/1978, pp. 855-875.

Olle, Werner/Schoeller, Wolfgang: Auslandsproduktion und strukturelle Arbeitslosigkeit — Zur Entwicklung der westdeutschen Direktinvestionen im Ausland (1974 bis 1976), in: Prokla 29, 1977, pp. 101-124.

Opitz, Reinhard (ed.): Europastrategien des deutschen Kapitals. 1900-1945. Cologne: Pahl-Rugenstein 1978.

Oppermann, Thomas: Staatliche Einheit oder innere Freiheit? Zu den langfristigen Perspektiven der nationalen Frage in Deutschland, in: EA 21/1978, pp. 681-692.

Overesch, Manfred: Gesamtdeutsche Illusion und westdeutsche Realität. Von den Vorbereitungen für einen deutschen Friedensvertrag zur Gründung des Auswärtigen Amtes der BRD 1946-1949/51. Düsseldorf: Droste 1978.

Peisert, Hans-Gert: Die auswärtige Kulturpolitik der Bundesrepublik Deutschland: Sozialwissenschaftliche Analysen und Planungsmodelle. Stuttgart: Klett-Cotta 1978.

Pfister, Hermann (ed.): Polen und Deutsche. Der lange Weg zu Frieden und Versöhnung. Waldkirch: Waldkircher Verlagsgesellschaft 1977.

Piontkowitz, Heribert: Anfänge westdeutscher Außenpolitik. 1946-1949. Das deutsche Büro für Friedensfragen. Stuttgart: DVA 1978.

Ress, Georg: Die Rechtslage Deutschlands nach dem Grundlagenvertrag vom 21. Dezember 1972. Heidelberg: Springer 1978.

Röhrs, Hermann: Deutsche Entwicklungshilfe in der afghanischen Lehrerausbildung. Königstein/Ts.: Hain 1978.

Scharf, Claus/Schröder, Hans-Jürgen (eds.): Politische und ökonomische Stabilisierung Westdeutschlands: 1945-1949. 5 Beiträge zur Deutschlandpolitik der westlichen Alliierten. Wiesbaden: Steiner 1977.

Schmitz, K.Th.: Deutsche Einheit und Europäische Integration. Der sozialdemokratische Beitrag zur Außenpolitik der Bundesrepublik Deutschland unter besonderer Berücksichtigung des programmatischen Wandels einer Oppositionspartei. Bonn: Verlag Neue Gesellschaft 1978.

Schneider, Herbert/Uffelmann, Uwe (eds.): Zur Außenpolitik der Bundesrepublik Deutschland. Ein Reader für den historisch-politischen Unterricht. Paderborn: Schöningh 1977.

Schubert, Klaus von: Sicherheitspolitik der Bundesrepublik Deutschland. Dokumentation 1945-1977, 2 vols. Cologne: Verlag Wissenschaft und Politik 1978.

Schulz, Hans-Jürgen: Militarismus und Kapitalismus in der Bundesrepublik. Frankfurt: ISP-Verlag 1977.

Schwarz, Hans-Peter: Brauchen wir ein neues deutschland-politisches Konzept?, in: EA 11/1977, pp. 327-338.

Stachelsky, Friedrich von: Außenwirtschaftliche Bestimmungsfaktoren der staatlichen Forschungspolitik der Bundesrepublik Deutschland. Berlin: Duncker & Humblot 1978.

Thiel, Elke: Dollar-Dominanz, Lastenteilung und amerikanische Truppenpräsenz in Europa. Zur Frage kritischer Verknüpfungen währungs- und stationierungspolitischer Zielsetzungen in den deutsch- amerikanischen Beziehungen. Baden-Baden: Nomos 1978.

Urban, Sabine M.-L./Brost, Franz F./Villot, J.-Gérard: Die westdeutschen Unternehmen und der französische Markt. Meisenheim a. Glan: Hain 1977.

Weede, Erich/Schössler, Dietmar: Abschreckung und Entspannung. Hypothesen westdeutscher Eliten und ihre Bewährung in der quantitativen Forschung, in: Beiträge zur Konfliktforschung 3/1978, pp. 59-80.

Wendt, Hans/Lorenz, Jürgen: Internationale Bindungen und Beziehungen: der Bundestag im Geflecht der Europa-Parlamente und internationaler Parlamentariergruppen. Bonn: A-Z-Studio 1978.

Wilker, Lothar: Die Sicherheitspolitik der SPD 1956-1966. Zwischen Wiedervereinigungs- und Bündnisorientierung. Bonn-Bad Godesberg: Verlag Neue Gesellschaft 1977.

Wirtschaftsbeziehungen zu Südafrika. Südafrikanischer Kirchenrat und Evangelische Kirche in Deutschland zur Frage von Investitionen in Südafrika. Frankfurt: Lembeck 1978.

GDR

Arons, Renée/Tiedtke, Juttá: Die Entspannungspolitik der UdSSR und der DDR am Beispiel der KSZE-Initiativen. Frankfurt: HSFK-Studies 19/1977.

Bruns, Wilhelm: Die UNO-Politik der DDR. Stuttgart: Bonn aktuell 1978.

Bruns, Wilhelm: Die Außenpolitik der DDR als Forschungsgegenstand, in: Neue Politische Literatur 4/1977, pp. 503-515.

Jansen, Bernhard: BRD und DDR nach Abschluß des Grundlagenvertrages. Baden-Baden: Nomos 1977.

Kregel, Bernd: Außenpolitik und Systemstabilisierung in der DDR. Opladen: Leske & Budrich 1979.

Lambrecht, Horst: Der Handel der Deutschen Demokratischen Republik mit der Bundesrepublik Deutschland und den übrigen OECD-Ländern. Eine vergleichende Betrachtung des Westhandels der DDR in den Jahren 1965-1975. Berlin: Duncker & Humblot 1977.

Lieser-Triebnigg, Erika: Das Recht des Außenhandels in der DDR: Organisation und Arbeitsweise. Cologne: Verlag Wissenschaft und Politik 1978.

Löwis, Henning von: Das politische und militärische Engagement der Deutschen Demokratischen Republik in Schwarzafrika. Ein Überblick 1953-1978, in: Beiträge zur Konfliktforschung 1/1978, pp. 5-54.

Ludz, Peter C.: Die DDR zwischen Ost und West. Politische Analysen 1961 bis 1976. Munich: Beck 1977.

Mahnke, Hans Heinrich: Die neuen Freundschafts- und Beistands-Verträge der DDR, in: DA 11/1977, pp. 1160-1184.

von Plate, Bernard: DDR-Außenpolitik Richtung Afrika und Araber, in: AP 11/1978, pp. 73-83.

Rahn, Günter: Das Feindbild der NVA in der sozialistischen Wehrerziehung, in: DA 5/1977, pp. 495-505.

Schweisfurth, Theodor: Die Freundschafts- und Beistandsverträge der DDR aus dem Jahre 1977, in: EA 18/1978, pp. 599-608.

Timmermann, Heinz: Ost-Berlins Beziehungen zu Jugoslawien und 'Eurokommunisten', in: DA 10/1977, pp. 949-965.

United States

Böge, Wolfgang: Die USA und der Kampf um die Unabhängigkeit Angloas: 1940-1964. Hamburg: Lüdke 1978.

Brauch, Hans-Günter: Neue Weltwirtschaftsordnung und die USA, in: AP 2/1978, pp. 173-186.

Brock, Lothar: Die Funktion der OAS für die Rechtfertigung der Lateinamerika-Politik der USA, in: PVS 1/1978, pp. 3-22.

Cziempiel, Ernst-Otto: Amerika und seine Umwelt. Außenpolitik der USA in den siebziger Jahren (IV), in: Neue Politische LIteratur 4/1978, pp. 432-449.

Fink, Matthias: Nationales Interesse und Entwicklungshilfe: John F. Kennedy's 'Alliance for Progress'. Munich: Minerva 1978.

Garbuny, Siegfried: Neue Beziehungen: USA und Lateinamerika, in: AP 2/1978, pp. 145-158.

Grabendorff, Wolf: Lateinamerika und die Vereinigten Staaten, in: EA 14/1977, pp. 433-440.

Grabendorff, Wolf: Erdrückende Nachbarschaft: Mexikos Beziehungen zu den USA, in: Verfassung und Recht in Übersee 3/1977, pp. 441-459.

Grabendorff, Wolf: Das interamerikanische Verhältnis seit dem Amtsantritt Carters, in: Aus Politik und Zeitgeschichte B 33-34/1977, pp. 29-38.

Greiner, Bernd: Konturen der Außenpolitik Präsident Carters, in: Blätter 8/1977, pp. 948-968.

Hacke, Christian: John F. Kennedy und die Kuba-Krise 1962. Zur Revision und Bestandsaufnahme der Ereignisse vor 15 Jahren, in: Aus Politik und Zeitgeschichte B 33-34/1977, pp. 39-54.

Hansen, Niels: Der Einfluß ethnischer Minderheiten auf die Außenpolitik der Vereinigten Staaten, in: EA 17/1977, pp. 551-560.

Knorr, Lorenz: Friedliche oder feindliche Koexistenz? Zur veränderten Globalstrategie der USA, Blätter 3/1978, pp. 274-289.

Rode, Reinhard: US—Handelspolitik in der Ära Nixon/Ford. Außenpolitik der USA in den siebziger Jahren (I), in: Neue Politische Literatur 3/1977, pp. 346-360.

Krell, Gert: Internationale Rüstungsdynamik und amerikanische Rüstungspolitik. Außenpolitik der USA in den siebziger Jahren (III), in: Neue Politische Literatur 1/1978, pp. 53-70.

Kubbig, Bernd W.: Grundsätze und Widersprüche der amerikanischen Nonproliferationspolitik, in: Blätter 4/1978, pp. 440-460.

Müller, Harald: Energiepolitik: Ein neuer Bereich der Außenpolitik — Außenpolitik der USA in den siebziger Jahren (II), in: Neue Politische Literatur, 4/1977, pp. 484-502.

Niess, Frank: Amerikanische Außenpolitik. Analysen und Materialien für den Unterricht. Düsseldorf: Schwann 1977.

Rode, Reinhard: Die Handelspolitik der USA in den siebziger Jahren: ein freihändlerisch-protektionistisches Verwirrspiel?, in: PVS 3/1978, pp. 315-342.

Schweigler, Gebhard: Die amerikanische Entspannungspolitik: Wandel oder Kontinuität?, in: EA 22/1977, pp. 791-799.

Schweigler, Gebhard: Politikwissenschaft und Außenpolitik in den USA. Am Beispiel der europäischen-amerikanischen Beziehungen. Munich: Oldenbourg 1977.

Steinberg, Rudolf: Präsident und Außenpolitik. Aussenpolitische Entscheidungsfindung des Präsidenten der USA im Spannungsfeld von Kongreß, Bürokratie und öffentlicher Meinung, in: Staat 3/1977, pp. 327-358.

Taft, Philipp: Gewerkschaftliche Außenpolitik. Das Beispiel der amerikanischen Gewerkschaften. Frankfurt: Europäische Verlagsanstalt 1975.

Velbinger, Hartmut: Eindämmung und Entspannung: George F. Kennan und die amerikanische Strategie in den 70er Jahren. Munich: tuduv 1977.

Volger, Gernot: Die Zahlungsbilanzpolitik der Vereinigten Staaten. Dominanz und Dependenz im internationalen Währungssystem. Berlin: Duncker & Humblot 1976.

Witt, Peter: Die internationale Energiepolitik der USA und Präsident Carters nationales Energieprogramm, in: EA 18/1977, pp. 586-594.

Wolf, Dieter O. A./Dauses, Manfred A.: Die Kriegsrechte in den Vereinigten Staaten. Analyse der verfassungsrechtlichen und politischen Auseinandersetzung zwischen Präsident und Kongreß um die 'War Powers'. Berlin/Munich: Duncker & Humblot 1978.

USSR

Aichinger, Wilfred: Sowjetische Österreichpolitik 1943-1945. Vienna: Österreichische Gesellschaft für Zeitgeschichte 1977.

Hoensch, Jörg: Sowjetische Osteuropapolitik 1945-1975. Kronberg/Ts.: Athenäum 1977.

Fischer, Alexander/Bertram, Christoph/Domes, Jürgen et al.: Politik, Strategie und Rüstung der Sowjetunion. Munich: Bernard & Graefe 1977.

Gathen, Heinz von zur: Änderungen in der Militärdoktrin der Sowjetunion?, in: Europäische Wehrkunde 9/1978, pp. 437-447.

Geyer, Dietrich: Der russische Imperialismus. Göttingen: Vandenhoeck & Ruprecht 1977.

Geyer, Dietrich/Meissner, Boris (eds.): Osteuropa-Handbuch — Sowjetunion. Außenpolitik III: Völkerrechtstheorie und Vertragspolitik. Cologne/Vienna: Böhlau 1977.

Kühne, Winrich: Grundtendenzen der sowjetischen Außenpolitik im südlichen Afrika, in: Aus Politik und Zeitgeschichte, B 46/1978, pp. 19-31.

Melchers, K.: Sowjetunion in Afrika. Cologne: Verlag Internationale Solidarität 1978.

Meissner, Boris: Der auswärtige Dienst der UdSSR, in: AP 1/1977, pp. 47-61.

Meissner, Boris: Breshnjew-Verfassung und Moskauer Außenpolitik, in: AP 3/1978, pp. 256-272.

Nolte, Hans-Heinrich: Gruppeninteressen und Außenpolitik: Die Sowjetunion in der Geschichte internationaler Beziehungen. Göttingen: Musterschmidt 1979.

Oldenburg, Fred: Konsens und Dissens in den jugoslawisch-sowjetischen Beziehungen, in: Beiträge zur Konfliktforschung 3/1977, pp. 77-130.

Pilster, Hans-Christian: Friede und Gewalt. Der militärische Aspekt der sowjetischen Koexistenzpolitik. Stuttgart: Seewald 1977.

Pruck, Erich, F.: Zivilverteidigung in der Sowjetunion, in: OE 12/1977, pp. 1057-1068.

Pruck, Erich, F.: Aus dem Wehrbereich der Sowjetunion (1977), in: OE 9/1978, pp. 820-831.

Royen, Christoph: Die sowjetische Koexistenzpolitik gegenüber Westeuropa. Voraussetzungen, Ziele, Dilemmata. Baden-Baden: Nomos 1978.

Schneider, Eberhard: Die sowjetische Vietnampolitik 1975/76, in: AP 1/1977, pp. 15-33.

Tomson, Edgar: Kriegsbegriff und Kriegsrecht in der Sowjetunion. Berlin: Berlin-Verlag 1979.

China

Eberhard, Wolfram: China und seine westlichen Nachbarn. Darmstadt: Wissenschaftliche Buchgesellschaft 1978.

Glaubitz, Joachim: Der chinesisch-japanische Friedens- und Freundschaftsvertrag, in: EA 20/1978, pp. 649-658.

Höpker, Wolfgang: Die Politik Chinas in Afrika. Zentrales Motiv ist der Konflikt mit Moskau, in: Beiträge zur Konfliktforschung 3/1978, pp. 81-94.

Optiz, Peter J.: Chinas Außenpolitik. Ideologische Prinzipien — strategische Konzepte. Zürich: Edition Interform 1977.

Opitz, Peter J.: Westeuropa in der Globalstrategie Pekings. Einige Anmerkungen anläßlich der Unterzeichung des Handelsvertrages zwischen der EG und der Volksrepublik China, in: ZfP 3/1978, pp. 223-238.

Pfeifenberger, Werner: Die UNO-Politik der Volksrepublik China. Konstanz: E. Reusch 1978.

Ruge, G.: Begegnung mit China. Eine Weltmacht im Aufbruch. Düsseldorf: Econ 1978.

Rummel, Reinhardt: Die Fixierung Chinas auf Westeuropa, in: AP 3/1978, pp. 273-286.

Strupp, Michael: Chinas Grenzen mit Birma und mit der Sowjetunion. Völkerrechtliche Theorie und Praxis der Volksrepublik China. Hamburg: Institut für Asienkunde 1978.

Wettig, Gerhard: Chinesische Bedrohungsvorstellungen im Verhältnis zur Sowjetunion, in: Aus Politik und Zeitgeschichte B 1/1978, pp. 48-53.

Other Countries

Ahrens-Thiele, Dagmar: Japans Rohstoffpolitik im Kräftefeld Moskau-Peking. Hamburg: Institut für Asienkunde 1977.

Braun, Dieter: Indiens erweiterter Wirkungsradius. Internationale Aspekte der veränderten Konstellation in Südasien, in: EA 1/1978, pp. 11-20.

Dauth, Jürgen: Das 'Dritte China'. Die chinesischen Minderheiten in Südostasien, in: Aus Politik und Zeitgeschichte B 40/1978, pp. 15-29.

Dohmen, Holger/Weggel, Oskar: Indochina in der Stunde Null, in: EA 1/1978, pp. 21-32.

Grabendorff, Wolf/Nitsch, Manfred: Brasilien: Entwicklungsmodell und Außenpolitik. Munich: Fink 1977.

Handke, Werner: Japans weltwirtschaftliche Optionen, in: AP 2/1977, pp. 147-160.

Hofmann, Michael: Perus Außenbeziehungen unter der Militärregierung. Frankfurt: Haag & Herchen 1978.

Kühnlein, Conrad: Die Auswirkungen der Revolution in Äthiopien auf die Lage am Horn von Afrika, in: EA 5/1978, pp. 135-144.

Laumer, Helmut: Japans wirtschaftliche Verflechtung mit Südostasien. Hamburg: Institut für Asienkunde 1977.

Meissner, Boris: Oststaaten und europäische Sicherheit. Cologne: Wissenschaft und Politik 1977.

Müller, Adolf: Die Tschechoslowakei auf der Suche nach Sicherheit. Berlin: Berlin Verlag 1977.

Münchhausen, Thankmar Freiherr von: Kolonialismus und Demokratie. Die französische Algerienpolitik von 1945-1962. Munich: Weltforum 1977.

Niedhart, Gottfried: Großbritannien und die Sowjetunion 1934-1939. Munich: Fink 1977.

Schütze, Walter: Neue Tendenzen der französischen Europa- und Sicherheitspolitik nach den Wahlen vom März 1978, in: EA 23/1968, pp. 771-782.

Steinbach, Udo: Irans regionale und internatinale Rolle, in: Orient 2/1978, pp. 118-138.

Steinbach, Udo: Perspektiven der türkischen Außen- und Sicherheitspolitik, in: EA 14/1978, pp. 431-440.

Topp, Horst-Dieter: Die albanische Außenpolitik: Ziele, Determinanten und Entwicklung, in: EA 3/1978, pp. 75-82.

Weggel, Oskar: Sri Lanka. Konfliktpotential und Außenpolitik. Hamburg: Institut für Asienkunde 1978.

Woker, Daniel: Die skandinavischen Neutralen. Prinzip und Praxis der schwedischen und finnischen Neutralität. Bern/Stuttgart: Haupt 1978.

Wolffsohn, Michael: Israels zweite Staatsgründung. Außenpolitische Folgen der Wahlen in Israel, in: EA 18/1977, pp. 603-612.

International Politics

General Studies

Dönhoff, Marion Gräfin/Kaiser, Karl et al.: Die internationale Politik 1970-1972. Jahrbuch des Forschungsinstituts der Deutschen Gesellschaft für Auswärtige Politik. Vienna/Munich: Oldenbourg 1978.

Gröner, Helmut/Schüller, Alfred (eds.): Internationale Wirtschaftsordnung. Stuttgart/New York: Fischer 1978.

Institut für Wissenschaft und Politik (ed.): Polarität und Interdependenz. Beiträge zu Fragen der Internationalen Politik. Baden-Baden: Nomos 1978.

Internationales Institut für den Frieden, Vienna (ed.): Wissenschaftliches Symposium Internationale Zusammenarbeit zur Lösung der Globalen Probleme für die Erhaltung des Friedens. Vienna: Verlag Gazzetta 1977.

Jacobsen, Hans-Adolf: Der Weg zur Teilung der Welt. Politik und Strategie von 1939 bis 1945. Koblenz: Verlag Wehr und Wissen 1977.

Krippendorff, Ekkehart: Die Entstehung des internationalen Systems, in: Neue Politische Literatur 1/1977, pp. 36-48.

Küng, Emil: Weltwirtschaftspolitik. Tübingen: Mohr 1978.

Mickel, Wolfgang, W.: Konfliktfeld: Internationale Politik. Darmstadt/Neuwied: Luchterhand 1974.

Niedhart, Gottfried: Weltherrschaft versus World Appeasement, in: Neue Politische Literatur 3/1978, pp. 281-291.

Weltmarkt und internationale Beziehungen. Frankfurt: Institut für Marxistische Studien und Forschungen 1976.

Basic Aspects of International Politics

Andersen, Uwe: Das internationale Währungssystem zwischen Nationaler Souveränität und Supranationaler Integration. Entwicklungstendenzen seit Bretton Woods im Spannungsfeld der Interessen. Berlin: Duncker & Humblot 1977.

Aschinger, Franz E.: Das neue Währungssystem: von Bretton Woods bis zur Dollarkrise 1977. Frankfurt: Knapp 1978.

Dicke, Detlev Christian: Die Intervention mit wirtschaftlichen Mitteln im Völkerrecht — zugleich ein Beitrag zu den Fragen der wirtschaftlichen Souveränität. Baden-Baden: Nomos 1978.

Donges, Jürgen B.: Die Welthandelsordnung am Scheidewege. Weitere Liberalisierung oder neuer Protektionismus?, in: EA 7/1978, pp. 197-204.

Fisch, J.: Krieg und Frieden im Friedensvertrag. Eine universalgeschichtliche Studie über Grundlagen und Formenlehre des Friedensschlusses. Stuttgart: Klett-Cotta 1978.

Hagen, Johann, J.: Internationalisierung des Kapitals und Souveränität der Staaten, in: Blätter 1/1977, pp. 80-93.

Hankel, Wilhelm: Weltwirtschaft. Vom Wohlstand der Nationen heute. Düsseldorf: Econ 1977.

Hankel, Wilhelm: Die Dollarschwäche — Gründe und Hintergründe. Zur Neuorientierung der deutschen Wirtschaftspolitik: Exportsubstitution und atlantische Kooperation, in: Aus Politik und Zeitgeschichte B12/1978, pp. 3-18.

Hellmann, Rainer: Dollar, Gold und Schlange. Die letzten Jahre von Bretton Woods. Baden-Baden: Nomos 1976.

Kewenig, Wilhelm A. (ed.): Völkerrecht und internationale wirtschaftliche Zusammenarbeit. Referate und Diskussion eines Symposiums. Berlin: Duncker & Humblot 1978.

Kreile, Michael: Internationale Währungspolitik und Weltwährungskrise, in: Neue Politische Literatur 4/1978, pp. 464-487.

Leithäuser, Gerhard: Der Internationale Währungsfonds (IWF) und die eingeschränkte Souveränität nationalstaatlicher Wirtschaftspolitik in seinem Einflußbereich, in: Blätter 3/1978, pp. 290-306.

Thiel, Elke: Reform des internationalen Währungssystems?, in: AP2/1977, pp. 135-146.

Tomuschat, Christian/Schmidt, Reine: Der Verfassungsstaat im Geflecht der internationalen Beziehungen. Berlin: de Gruyter 1978.

Wenger, Siegfried: Außenhandel auf dem kapitalistischen Weltmarkt. Gesetzmäßigkeiten und Tendenzen. Berlin: Verlag Die Wirtschaft 1978.

Zumpfort, Wolf-Dieter: Untersuchungen zum Wachstum des Eurodollarmarktes. Tübingen: Mohr 1977.

Configurations of International Politics

East-West Relations

Abschreckung und Entspannung. 25 Jahre Sicherheitspolitik zwischen bipolarer Konfrontation und begrenzter Kooperation. Berlin: Duncker & Humblot 1977.

Baudissin, Wolf Graf von: Sicherheitspolitik im Entspannungsprozeß. Partnerschaft trotz Antagonismus, in: Blätter 6/1977, pp. 697-700.

Bethlen, Stefan Graf (ed.): Osthandel in der Krise. Munich: Olzog 1976.

Blumenwitz, Dieter et al.: Die KSZE (Konferenz über Sicherheit und Zusammenarbeit in Europa) und die Menschenrechte. Politische und rechtliche Überlegungen zur 2. Etappe. Berlin: Duncker & Humblot 1977.

Czempiel, Ernst-Otto: Die Vereinigten Staaten von Amerika und die Entspannung. Menschenrechte und Rüstungspolitik im Ost-West-Konflikt, in: Aus Politik und Zeitgeschichte B 37/1977, pp. 3-17.

Delbrück, Jost/Ropers, Norbert/Zellentin, Gerda (eds.): Grünbuch zu den Folgewirkungen der KSZE. Cologne: Wissenschaft und Politik 1977.

Ehrhardt, Carl A.: EWG und RGW kommen sich nur langsam häher, in: AP 2/1977, pp. 161-176.

Fischer, Per: Das Ergebnis von Belgrad. Das KSZE-Folgetreffen in seiner Bedeutung für den Entspannungsprozeß, in: EA 8/1978, pp. 221-230.

Franzmeyer, Fritz: Zum Stand der wirtschaftspolitischen Beziehungen zwischen RGW und EG, in: EA 1/1977, pp. 9-17.

Guz, E./Weseloh, H. A.: KSZE-Belgrad. Das erste Folgetreffen der Konferenz über Sicherheit und Zusammenarbeit in Europa. Stuttgart: Bonn aktuell 1978.

Jacobsen, Hans-Adolf: Erfordernisse einer künftigen realen Entspannungspolitik in Europa. Sechs Perspektiv-Thesen, in: Beiträge zur Konfliktforschung 1/1978, pp. 55-70.

Jansen, Bernhard: EWG und DDR nach Abschluß des Grundlagenvertrages. Baden-Baden: Nomos 1977.

Große-Jütte, Annemarie/Jütte, Rüdiger (eds.): Entspannung ohne Frieden. Versäumnisse europäischer Politik. Frankfurt: S. Fischer 1977.

Kaiser, Karl/Kreis, Karl Markus (eds.): Sicherheitspolitik vor neuen Aufgaben. Frankfurt: Metzner 1977.

Kaltenbrunner, G.-K.: Strategie der Feigheit? Wie lange wird der Westen noch frei sein? Freiburg: Herder 1977.

Kiersch, Gerhard/Seidelmann, Reimund (eds.): Sicherheit und Entspannung in Europa. Die Antwort des demokratischen Sozialismus. Cologne: EVA 1977.

Kreile, Michael: Osthandel und Ostpolitik. Baden-Baden: Nomos 1978.

Kriele, Martin: Die Menschenrechte zwischen Ost und West. Cologne: Wissenschaft und Politik 1977.

Lebahn, Axel: RGW und EG — Faktoren des Ost-West-Handels, in: AP 2/1978, pp. 123-144.

Mai, Gunther: Westliche Sicherheitspolitik im Kalten Krieg. Der Korea-Krieg und die deutsche Wiederbewaffnung 1950. Boppard: Harald Boldt 1977.

Meissner, Boris: Der sowjetische Nationsbegriff und die Frage des Fortbestands der deutschen Nation, in: EA 10/1977, pp. 315-324.

Müller, Friedemann: Sicherheitspolitische Aspekte der Ost-West-Wirtschaftsbeziehungen, in: Aus Politik und Zeitgeschichte B 37/1977, pp. 30-38.

Nolte, Ernst: Marxismus, Faschismus, kalter Krieg. Stuttgart: DVA 1977.

Optiz, Reinhard: Die Neutronenbombe, die BRD und Europa, in: Blätter 9/1977, pp. 1048-1074.

Oststaaten und KSZE: Analysen und Dokumentation. Cologne: Wissenschaft und Politik 1977.

Portes, Richard: Osteuropas Westschulden — keine Einbahnstrasse, in: Europäische Rundschau 4/1977, pp. 91-12.

Raven, Wolfram von: Abschreckung gegen Einschüchterung. Die Notlage des Nordatlantikpaktes, in: Politische Studien 233, 1977, pp. 234-246.

Ruehl, Lothar: Europas Sicherheitsprobleme im Mittelmeerraum, in: EA2 1978, pp. 33-42.

Schenk, Karl-Ernst/Czege, Andreas Wass von: Technologietransfer durch Ost-West-Kooperation. Theoretische Überlegungen und Erfahrungen der Praxis. Stuttgart/New York: Gustav Fischer 1978.

Schwarz, Hans-Peter: Zwischenbilanz der KSZE. Stuttgart: Seewald 1977.

Schwarz, Klaus-Dieter (ed.): Sicherheitspolitik. Analysen zur politischen und militärischen Sicherheit. Bad Honnef: Osang 1977.

Steinhoff, J.: Wohin treibt die Nato? Probleme der Verteidigung Westeuropas. Munich: Deutscher Taschenbuch Verlag 1978.

Stratmann, K.-Peter: Nato-Strategie in der Krise? Militärische Optionen von Nato und Warschauer Pakt in Mitteleuropa. Baden-Baden: Nomos 1978.

Stratmann, K.-Peter: Schwächen der NATO-Verteidigung und Angriffs-Optionen des Warschauer Pakts. Kritische Anmerkungen zur derzeitigen 'Strategiedebatte', in: Aus Politik und Zeitgeschichte B 37/1977, pp. 18-29.

Tiedtke, S.: Die Warschauer Vertragsorganisation. Zum Verhältnis von Militär- und Entspannungspolitik in Osteuropa. Munich/Vienna: Oldenbourg 1978.

Well, Günther van: Belgrad 1977. Das KSZE-Folgetreffen und seine Bedeutung für den Entspannungsprozeß, in: EA 18/1977, pp. 577-585.

Welter, Ferdinand: Belgrad 1977. Der Westen mit Blick auf die KSZE-Nachfolgekonferenz, in: Beiträge zur Konfliktforschung 3/1977, pp. 67-76.

Wettig, Gerhard: Östliche Entspannungspolitik zwischen Zusammenarbeit und Abgrenzung, in: Aus Politik und Zeitgeschichte B 19/1977, pp. 33-38.

Wettig, Gerhard: Die Warschauer-Paktstaaten auf der Belgrader KSZE-Folgekonferenz, in: OE 5/1978, pp. 473-493.

Wettig, Gerhard: Sicherheitspolitik und KSZE-Treffen Belgrad, in: AP 3/1978, pp. 287-296.

Woyke, Wichard: Die Nato in den siebziger Jahren. Eine Bestandsaufnahme. Opladen: Leske und Budrich 1977.

Zieger, G. Die Integration im Warschauer Pakt. Berlin: Berlin Verlag 1977.

North-South Relations

Bandulet, B.: Schnee für Afrika. Entwicklungshilfe: Vergeudete Milliarden. Munich: Herbig 1978.

Baron, Stefan/Glismann, Hans H./Stecher, Bernd: Internationale Rohstoffpolitik. Ziele, Mittel, Kosten. Tübingen: Mohr 1977.

Bergsten, C. Fred: Ein umfassendes Programm für internationale Rohstofffragen, in: EA 20/1977, pp. 711-720.

Betz, Joachim: Die Internationalisierung der Entwicklungshilfe. Baden-Baden: Nomos 1978.

Beyfuss, Jörg: Außenhandel mit Entwicklungsländern: Entwicklung und Perspektiven. Cologne: Deutscher Instituts-Verlag 1978.

Boeck, Klaus: Die währungspolitischen Forderungen der Entwicklungsländer zur Schaffung einer neuen Weltwirtschaftsordnung. Hamburg: Verlag Weltarchiv 1978.

Bremer Gesellschaft für Wirtschaftsforschung (ed.): Auswertung der Dokumentation der vierten Welthandels-und Entwicklungskonferenz Nairobi 1976. Baden-Baden: Nomos 1978.

Burchard, Hans-Joachim: Nord-Süd-Dialog — und wie weiter?, in: AP 4/1977, pp. 393-404.

Corea, G./Knirsch, P./Nerlich, U. et al.: Umstrittene Weltwirtschaftsordnung. Zürich: Schulthess Polygraphischer Verlag 1977.

Dams, Theodor: Weltwirtschaft im Umbruch: Konfrontation oder Kooperation mit der Dritten Welt? Würzburg: Ploetz 1978.

Donndorf, Hans-Michael: Formen der internationalen Zusammenarbeit auf dem Energierohstoff- Sektor. Auf der Suche nach Uran. Göttingen: Schwartz 1977.

Duttweiler, Rudolf: Internationale Investitionsfinanzierung und Zahlungsbilanz: ein Beitrag zur Außenverschuldungsproblematik der Entwicklungsländer. Diessenhofen: Rüegger 1978.

Emmerich, Klaus: Ist Nord-Süd-Entspannung möglich? Eine neue Politik für eine neue Front. Zürich: Edition Interform 1978.

Esters, Günther (eds.): Nord-Süd-Politik. Überlegungen zu aktuellen wirtschaftlichen Problemen. Bonn- Bad Godesberg: Verlag Neue Gesellschaft 1977.

Fröbel, Folker/Heinrichs, Jürgen/Kreye, Otto: Die neue internationale Arbeitsteilung. Strukturelle Arbeitslosigkeit in den Industrieländern und die Industrialisierung der Entwicklungsländer. Reinbek: Rowohlt 1977.

Gerth-Wellmann, Hella: Die EG und die Dritte Welt. Wem nützt das Lomé-Abkommen?, in: Blätter 12/1978, pp. 1429-1440.

Hager, Wolfgang: Eine internationale Getreidereserve als Beitrag zur politischen und wirtschaftlichen Stabilität, in: EA 9/1977, pp. 271-278.

Hartmann, Gode: Nationalisierung und Enteignung im Völkerrecht: völkerrechtliche Probleme der politischen und ökonomischen Beziehungen zwischen den westlichen Industrienationen und Entwicklungsländern im Lichte neuerer Rechtsentwicklungen in den Vereinten Nationen. Berlin: Duncker & Humblot 1977.

Hedrich, Manfred/Ropp, Klaus Frhr von der: Lomé II im Lichte der Erfahrungen mit Lomé I, in: AP 3/1978, pp. 297-312.

Institut für Europäische Politik (ed.): Europa und der Nord-Süd-Dialog: eine erste Bilanz der Pariser Konferenz über Internationale Wirtschaftliche Zusammenarbeit. Bonn Europa Union 1977.

Internationale Verschuldung: Entwicklungstendenzen, Risiken, Risikopolitik, in: Außenwirtschaft 12/1978, pp. 1-232.

Jenisch, Uwe: UN-Seerechtskonferenz vor der 7. Session, in: AP 1/1978, pp. 45-62.

Kappeler, Dietrich: Wie verletzlich sind die Erdölproduzenten des Persischen Golfes gegenüber Maßnahmen der OECD-Staaten?, in: EA 18/1977, pp. 595-602.

Kebschull, Dietrich/Michalski, Wolfgang et al. (eds.): Die neue Weltwirtschaftsordnung. Beiträge zu ausgewählten Forderungen der Entwicklungsländer. Hamburg: Verlag Weltarchiv 1977.

Klein, Hans-Günther: Entwicklungshilfe: Spezifische Äußerungsform internationaler Politik. Baden-Baden: Nomos 1977.

Kollatz, Udo: Entwicklungszusammenarbeit — Lehrstück praktischer Politik, in: Aus Politik und Zeitgeschichte B 50/1978, pp. 3-24.

Matthíes, Volker: Neue Weltwirtschaftsordnung. Hintergründe, Positionen, Argumente. Leverkusen: Leske & Budrich 1978.

Matzke, Otto: Nahrung als weltpolitisches Machtinstrument?, in: EA 5/1977, pp. 123-134.

Matzke, Otto: Ist eine Welternährungskrise vermeidbar?, in: AP 3/1977, pp. 284-299.

Matzke, Otto: Das Welternährungsproblem aus sozialer, ökonomischer und politischer Sicht, in: Aus Politik und Zeitgeschichte B 27/1978, pp. 3-23.

Matzke, Otto: Anhaltende Kontroverse über einen gemeinsamen Rohstoff-Fonds, in: Aus Politik und Zeitgeschichte B 44/1977, pp. 43-54.

Metzger, Dorothea: Konflikt und Allianz in der internationalen Rohstoffwirtschaft, das Beispiel Kupfer. Bonn: Progress-Dritte-Welt-Verlag 1977.

Ostrowsky, Jürgen: NATO-Politik in Afrika, in: Blätter 7/1978, pp. 793-804.

Petersen, Hans J.: Die Verschuldung der Entwicklungsländer als Problem der Nord-Süd-Beziehungen, in: EA 21/1978, pp. 693-702.

Ruge, M. Der Beitrag von UNCTAD zur Herausbildung des Entwicklungsvölkerrechts. Frankfurt: Haag & Herchen 1976.

Schmidt, Rudolf: Nord-Süd-Dialog und neue Weltwirtschaftsordnung, in: AP 3/1977, pp. 273-283.

Schönfeld, Roland: Der Ostblock im Nord-Süd-Konflikt, in: ZfP 4/1977, pp. 389-401.

Schulz, Manfred (ed.): Europäische Gemeinschaft und Entwicklungsländer: die ungleichen Partner. Frankfurt/Berlin/Munich: Diesterweg 1978.

Schumacher, Dieter: Entwicklungshilfe und internationale Arbeitsteilung: Ableitung sektoraler Schwerpunkte mit Hilfe der linearen Programmierung am Beispiel der Republik Korea. Berlin: Duncker & Humblot 1977.

Seitz, Konrad: Die Verhandlungen über einen gemeinsamen Rohstoff-Fonds, in: Wirtschaftsdienst 2/1978, pp. 93-97.

Senft, J.: Entwicklungshilfe oder Entwicklungspolitik. Münster: Regensberg 1978.

Solomon, Norman B./Schuhmacher, Erwin: Technologietransfer. Europas Industrie zieht um. Cologne: Diederichs 1977.

Studier, Alphons: Die UNO-Seerechtskonferenz und die Problematik einer neuen Weltwirtschaftsordnung, in: Blätter 8/1977, pp. 1014-1024.

Tetzlaff, Rainer: Die Weltbank. Funktionsweise, Machtverhältnisse und politische Bedeutung für die Dritte Welt, in: Aus Politik und Zeitgeschichte B 42/1978, pp. 20-31.

Tietzel, Manfred: Internationale Rohstoffpolitik. Eine Analyse rohstoffpolitischer Aspekte des Nord-Süd-Dialogs. Bonn — Bad Godesberg: Verlag Neue Gesellschaft 1977.

Tinbergen, J. (ed.): Der Dialog Nord-Süd. Informationen zur Entwicklungspolitik. Cologne: Europäische Verlagsanstalt 1977.

Tüttenberg, Elke: Der Beitrag der Staaten des Ostblocks zur Wirtschaft der Entwicklungsländer Afrikas. St. Augustin: Institut für Internationale Solidarität der Konrad-Adenauer-Stiftung 1977.

Unger, Karl: Die EG und die Entwicklungsländer, Das Abkommen von Lomé als Grundstein einer neuen Weltwirtschaftsordnung?, in: Blätter 3/1977, pp. 301-317.

Vitzthum, Wolfgang Graf: Neue Weltwirtschaftsordnung und neue Weltmeeresordnung. Innere Widersprüche bei zwei Ansätzen zu sektoralen Weltordnungen, in: EA 15/1977, pp. 455-468.

Weise, Herbert: Die neue Weltwirtschaftsordnung und ihre finanziellen Implikationen für die sozialistischen Industrieländer, in: Osteuropa-Wirtschaft 1/1978, pp. 46-57.

Wegener, Henning: Sozialistische Länder und neue Weltwirtschaftsordnung, in: EA 10/1977, pp. 293-302.

Weggel, Oskar: China seit der Kulturrevolution: Entwicklungsenthusiasmus und Farbwechsel, in: EA 13/1978, pp. 387-396.

Wessels, Wolfgang (ed.): Europa und der Nord-Süd-Dialog. Eine erste Bilanz der Pariser Konferenz über internationale wirtschaftliche Zusammenarbeit. Bonn: Europa-Union 1977.

Wirths, Willi: Ernährungssituation. Datenanalyse zur Versorgung der Erdbevölkerung. Paderborn: Schöningh 1978.

Wir wollen die Herren unserer Länder sein? Die 3. Welt im Kampf für die neue Weltwirtschaftsordnung. Cologne: Verlag Internationale Solidarität 1977.

Wissenschaftlicher Beirat beim Bundesministerium für Wirtschaftliche Zusammenarbeit (ed.): Auf dem Weg zu einer neuen Weltwirtschaftsordnung. Stuttgart: Klett 1978.

Other

Dettke, D.: Allianz im Wandel. Amerikanisch-europäische Sicherheitsbeziehungen im Zeichen des Bilateralismus der Supermächte. Frankfurt: Metzner 1976.

Ehrenberg, Eckehardt/Mallmann, Wolfgang: Rüstung und Wirtschaft am Golf. Iran und seine Nachbarn (1965-1978). Hamburg: Mitteilungen des Deutschen Orient-Instituts 1978.

Ernst, Wolfgang: Japan — Rätsel ohne Lösung? Zur neueren Entwicklung der europäisch-japanischen Beziehungen, in: EA 21/1977, pp. 760-772.

Grosser, Alfred: Das Bündnis. Die westeuropäischen Länder und die USA seit dem Krieg. Munich: Hanser 1978.

Großmann, Bernhard: Japan und die Volksrepublik China als Wirtschaftspartner, in: EA 22/1978, pp. 711-724.

Heinzlmeir, Helmut: Der Konflikt am Horn von Afrika, in: Aus Politik und Zeitgeschichte B 16/1978, p. 3-16.

Herlt, Rudolf: Der Dollarschock: Seine Folgen und die Aussichten zu seiner Überwindung, in: EA 11/1978, pp. 313-322.

Kade, Gerhard: Die Bonner Gipfelkonferenz der 'Großen Sieben' und die Widersprüche zwischen Westeuropa und den USA, in: Blätter 8/1978, pp. 912-926.

Kaiser, Karl/Schwarz, H.-P. (eds.): Amerika und Westeuropa. Gegenwarts- und Zukunftsprobleme. Stuttgart: Belser 1977.

Kaiser, Karl: Auf der Suche nach einer Welt-Nuklearordnung. Zum Hintergrund deutsch-amerikanischer Divergenzen, in: EA 5/1978, pp. 153-172.

Knapp, Manfred: Das Deutschlandproblem und die Ursprünge des Europäischen Wiederaufbauprogramms, in: PVS 1/1978, pp. 48-65.

Kubbig, Bernd W.: Energie und Sicherheit für Westeuropa. Optionen, Konflikte, Perspektiven, in: Aus Politik und Zeitgeschichte B 5/1978, pp. 3-35.

Lindner, Roland: Europäische Politik für Forschung und Bildung. Baden-Baden: Nomos 1977.

Matthies, Volker: Der Grenzkonflikt Somalias mit Äthiopien und Kenya. Analyse eines zwischenstaatlichen Konflikts in der Dritten Welt. Hamburg: Institut für Afrika-Kunde 1977.

Schaetzel, J. Robert: Ein Bündnis geht aus den Fugen — Amerika und die Europäische Gemeinschaft. Düsselford: Econ 1977.

Schweinfurth, Ulrich: Neu-Staaten und Supermächte im Pazifik, in: AP 2/1977, pp. 202-213.

Steinbach, Udo: Arabische Politik rund um das Horn von Afrika, in: AP 3/1977, pp. 300-311.

Steuber, Ursel: Internationale Banken: Auslandsaktivitäten von Banken bedeutender Industrieländer. Hamburg: Verlag Weltarchiv 1977.

Thiel, Elke: Zur Rolle Japans in der wirtschaftlichen Zusammenarbeit der westlichen Industrieländer. Internationale Sicherheitspolitik als Aufgabe, in: Aus Politik und Zeitgeschichte B 47/1978, pp. 29-38.

Issues of International Politics

Armaments, Arms Control and Disarmament

Aboltin, Wladimir et al.: Wirtschaftliche Folgen einer Abrüstung. Berlin: Berlin-Verlag 1977.

Abrüstung und Rüstungskontrolle. Dokumente zur Haltung der Bundesrepublik Deutschland. Bonn: Köllen Druck & Verlag 1978.

Baumann, Gerhard: Die Neutronenwaffe als sicherheitspolitisches Instrument, in: Politische Studien 240, 1978, pp. 385-398.

Booß, Bernhelm: Cruise Missiles. Wunderwaffe oder teurer Wahnsinn?, in: Blätter 1/1978, pp. 18-33.

Bredow, Wilfred von: Abrüstungspolitik und Rüstungstechnologie. Wie kann man das Tempo rüstungstechnologischer Neuentwicklungen drosseln?, in: Blätter 10/1978, pp. 1170-1179.

Bredow, Wilfried/Kade, Gerhard (eds.): Abrüstung. Politische Voraussetzungen, sozioökonomische Folgen, Aufgaben der Wissenschaftler. Cologne: Pahl-Rugenstein 1978.

Citron, Klaus J.: Die Sondergeneralversammlung der Vereinten Nationen für Abrüstung. Rückblick, Ergebnisse und Perspektiven, in: EA 19/1978, pp. 630-640.

Czerwick, Erwin/Müller, Harald: Rüstungskonzerne, ökonomisches Interesse und das Konzept des 'militärisch-industriellen Komplexes', in: Friedensanalysen 6/1977, pp. 153-177.

Forstmeier, Friedrich/Volkmann, Hans-Erich (eds.): Kriegswirtschaft und Rüstung 1939-1945. Düsseldorf: Droste 1977.

Institut für Internationale Politik und Wirtschaft der DDR: Dokumente zur Abrüstung 1917-1976. Frankfurt: Marxistische Blätter 1978.

Grünewald, Guido: Abrüstung und Arbeitsplatzsicherung. Zur Diskussion über Rüstungskonversion und Arbeitslosigkeit, in: Blätter 6/1978, pp. 657-680.

Guha, Anton-Andreas: Die Neutronenbombe — oder: Die Perversion menschlichen Denkens. Frankfurt: Fischer 1977.

Haftendorn, Helga: Der internationale Rüstungstransfer. Motive, Folgen, Kontrollmöglichkeiten, in: EA 11/1978, pp. 331-340.

Huffschmid, Jörg: Ökonomie der Abrüstung, in: Blätter 5/1977, pp. 532-551.

Kade, Gerhard: Die Sondertagung der UNO-Generalversammlung zur Abrüstung. Eine vorläufige Bilanz, in: Blätter 7/1978, pp. 780-784.

Klein, Peter: Weltproblem Abrüstung: Politische und ökonomische Probleme des Ringens um Rüstungsbegrenzung und Abrüstung. Frankfurt: Marxistische Blätter 1979.

Krell, Gert: Rüstungsdynamik und Rüstungskontrolle. Die gesellschaftlichen Auseinandersetzungen um SALT in den USA 1969-1975. Frankfurt: Haag & Herchen 1977.

Krell, Gert/Schlotter, Peter: Zur Diskussion über die taktischen Nuklearwaffen in Europa: Analyse und Dokumentation. Frankfurt: Haag & Herchen 1977.

Lauk, Kurt L.: Kernwaffen und die Diplomatie der Friedenssicherung, in: Beiträge zur Konfliktforschung 4/1977, pp. 117-136.

Lock, Peter/Wulf, Herbert: Wachstum durch Rüstung? Zum Zusammenhang von wirtschaftlicher und militärischer Sicherheit, in: Blätter 4/1977, pp. 413-433.

Mechtersheimer, Alfred: Rüstung und Politik in der Bundesrepublik. MRCA Tornado. Geschichte und Funktion des größten westeuropäischen Rüstungsprogramms. Bad Honnef: Osang 1977.

Medick, Monika: Waffenexporte und auswärtige Politik. Gesellschaftliche Interessen und politische Entscheidungen. Meisenheim: Hain 1977.

Mies, Ulrich Franz Josef: Destablisierungsfaktoren des gegenwärtigen Abschreckungssystems: Die Implikationen der 1974er Modifikation der US-Nuklearstrategie für die global-strategische Stabilität. Frankfurt: Haag & Herchen 1979.

Müller, Harald: Energiepolitik, Nuklearexport und die Weiterverbreitung von Kernwaffen. Analyse und Dokumentation. Frankfurt: Haag & Herchen 1978,

Nerlich, Uwe: Die Politik des Streitkräfteabbaus in Europa. Vorschläge für eine politische Neuorientierung der MBFR-Verhandlungen, in: EA 7/1977, pp. 197-204.

Neuhold, Hanspeter: Aberüstung und Rüstungskontrolle — Theoretische Perspektiven und aktuelle Rivalitäten, in: Österreichische Zeitschrift für Außenpolitik 2/1978, pp. 89-111.

Wolff, Claudia et al.: Neutronenbombe, in: Vorgänge 33, 1978, ppl. 67-80.

Opel, Manfred: Zur Diskussion um die Neutronenwaffe, in: Aus Politik und Zeitgeschichte B 8/1978, pp. 3-16.

Opitz, Reinhard: Die Neutronenbombe, die BRD und Europa, in: Blätter 9/1977, pp. 1048-1075.

Pander, Joachim von: Die Sicherheitskontrolle nach dem Nichtverbreitungsvertrag in den EG-Staaten. Cologne: Heymanns 1978.

Pordzik, Wolfgang: SALT II im Kreuzfeuer der Kritik. Zur inneramerikanischen Kontroverse über die Sicherheitspolitik der Regierung Carter, in: EA 16/1978, pp. 517-526.

Preuschen, Rüdiger von: Nichtverbreitungspolitik und Nuklearexport, in: Recht der Internationalen Wirtschaft 12/1977, pp. 741ff.

Rodejohann, Jo: Militärische Aspekte der Auseinandersetzung um die Neutronenwaffe (ERW). Eine Zwischenbilanz, in: Blätter 8/1978, pp. 926-937.

Ruehl, Lothar: Die Wiener Verhandlungen über einen Truppenabbau in Mitteleuropa. Stand und Aussichten, in: EA 13/1977, pp. 399-408.

Schilling, Walter: Rüstungskontrolle im strategischen Bereich — falsch programmiert?, in: Liberal 7/1978, pp. 485-494.

Schlaich, Gerog Joachim: Der Stand der weltweiten multilateralen Abrüstungsbemühungen. Die Verhandlungen im Genfer Abrüstungsausschuß (CCD) und die Abrüstungsdebatte der Vereinten Nationen, in: EA 22/1977, pp. 781-790.

Schulte, Ludwig: Die unbewältigte Krise. Alternative Modelle zur Nato-Verteidigung, in: Beiträge zur Konfliktforschung 2/1978, pp. 19-40.

Schulz, Hans-Juergen: Militarismus und Kapitalismus in der Bundesrepublik. Frankfurt: ISP 1977.

Schulz, Karl-Ernst (ed.): Militär und Ökonomie. Beiträge zu einem Symposium. Göttingen: Vandenhoeck & Ruprecht 1977.

Sucharipa, Ernst: Die Sondergeneralversammlung der Vereinten Nationen über Abrüstung (23 Mai-30 Juni 1978), in: Österreichische Zeitschrift für Außenpolitik 2/1978, pp. 112-133.

Walpuski, Günter/Wolf, Dieter O.A.: Der 'Militärisch-Industrielle Komplex', in: Aus Politik und Zeitgeschichte B 14/78 1978, pp. 23-38.

Woyke, Wichard: Die Nato in den siebziger Jahren. Eine Bestandsaufnahme. Leverkusen: Leske & Budrich 1977.

Underdevelopment and Development Strategies

Baars, Gerald: Dezentralisierung als Entwicklungsstrategie? Das Beispiel Tanzanias, in: Internationales Afrikaforum 1/1977, pp. 50-59.

Bennholdt-Thomsen, Veronika et al. (eds.): Lateinamerika. Analysen und Berichte. Berlin: Olle & Wolter 1978.

Bosse, Hans: Verwaltete Unterentwicklung. Funktionen und Verwertung der Bildungsforschung in der staatlichen Entwicklungspolitik. Frankfurt: Suhrkamp 1978.

Büttner, F./Lindenberg, K./Reuke, L./Sielaff, R.: Reform in Uniform? Militärherrschaft und Entwicklung in der Dritten Welt. Bonn-Bad Godesberg: Verlag Neue Gesellschaft 1976.

Dohmen, Holger/Machetzki, Rüdiger/Weggel, Oskar: Malaysia — Vietnam — Birma. Drei mögliche Wege für Südostasien?, in: Aus Politik und Zeitgeschichte B 10/1977, pp. 3-37.

Elsenhans, Hartmut: Algerien. Koloniale und postkoloniale Reformpolitik. Hamburg: Institut für Afrikakunde 1977.

Esser, Klaus: Lateinarmerika. Industrialisierungsstrategien und Entwicklung. Frankfurt: Suhrkamp 1978.

Evers, Tilmann Tönnies: Bürgerliche Herrschaft in der Dritten Welt. Zur Theorie des Staates. in: ökonomisch unterentwickelten Gesellschaftsformationen. Cologne/Frankfurt: Europäische Verlagsanstalt 1977.

Entwicklungsprobleme der arabischen Erdölstaaten: Hamburg: Mitteilungen des Deutschen Orient-Institutes 1977.

Goldschmidt, Dietrich (ed.): Technologie in Entwicklungsländern: Möglichkeiten eigenständiger Entwicklung, Probleme des Transfers, neue Wege der der Ausbildung, Chancen wirtschaftlicher Zusammenarbeit. Jahrestagung der Vereinigung Deutscher Wissenschaftler. Munich: Weltforum-Verlag 1978.

Hanisch, Rolf: Der Handlungsspielraum eines Landes der Peripherie im internationalen System. Das Beispiel Ghanas. Saarbrücken: Verlag der SSIP-Schriften 1975.

Heller, Mute: Die Rolle der Sozialwissenschaften im Entwicklungsprozeß. Betrachtungen zur 'Entwicklungspolitik' im Mittleren Osten anläßlich eines Internationalen Kongresses in Kairo, in: Dritte Welt 2-3/1977, pp. 136-158.

Hennicke, P.: Die entwicklungstheoretischen Konzeptionen Mao Tse-tungs. Historische Grundlagen und sozialökonomische Bedingungen der Entwicklungspolitik der Volksrepublik China 1927-1957. Munich: Minerva 1978.

Jaeger, Franz: Welthandel und Wachstum: Chance für die 3. und 4. Welt? Diessenhofen: Rüegger 1977.

Jaenecke, Heinrich: Die weißen Herren. 300 Jahre Krieg und Gewalt in Süd-Afrika. Munich: Bertelsmann 1977.

Keferstein, Klaus: Förderung des Außenhandels unter Entwicklungsländern, eine entwicklungspolitische Alternative? Frankfurt: Haag & Herchen 1978.

Kimmig, Karl-Heinz: Die Industriereform in Peru: sozioökonomische und politische Aspekte des Strukturwandels im Industriesektor unter der Militärregierung Velasco Alvarado. Meisenheim am Glan: Hain 1978.

Klein, Heinz Günther: Entwicklungshilfe: Spezifische Äusserungsform internationaler Politik. Eine Analyse d. Kontextes, d. Merkmale u. Wirkungen praktizierter Entwicklungshilfepolitik u. Skizzierung d. Möglichkeiten u. Grundvoraussetzungen autonomiefördernder entwicklungshilfepolitischer Zusammenarbeit. Baden-Baden: Nomos 1977.

Kley, Gisbert (ed.): Marktwirtschaft und Weltwirtschaft: Probleme einer marktwirtschaftlichen Entwicklungspolitik. Heidelberg/Hamburg: von Decker 1978.

Krockow, Christian Graf von: China als Entwicklungsland. Versuch zum Verstehen, in: Aus Politik und Zeitgeschichte B 1/1978, pp. 3-20.

Mansilla, H. C. F.: Entwicklung als Nachahmung. Vorarbeiten zu einer kritischen Theorie der Modernisierung. Königstein/Ts.: Hain 1978.

Menzel, Ulrich: Theorie und Praxis des chinesischen Entwicklungsmodells. Ein Beitrag zum Konzept autozentrierter Entwicklung. Opladen: Westdeutscher Verlag 1978.

Mühll, Urs von der: Die Unterentwicklung Portugals. Von der Weltmacht zur Halbkolonie Englands. Frankfurt/New York: Campus 1978.

Nohlen, Dieter/Nuscheler, Franz (eds.): Handbuch der Dritten Welt, Vol. 4: Unterentwicklung und Entwicklung in Asien. Hamburg: Hoffmann & Campe 1978.

Opitz, Peter, J.: Et tu, China? Entwicklungstendenzen der chinesischen Politik seit dem Tod Mao-Tse-tungs, in: Aus Politik und Zeitgeschichte B 1/1978, pp. 21-47.

Pfennig, Werner/Voll, Klaus: Entwicklungsprobleme und Lösungsversuche in der Volksrepublik China. Maos Erbe im Widerspruch. Berlin: Dialogus mundi 1977.

Pohl, Heinrich: Strategien regionaler Bildungs- und Entwicklungsplanung. in: Lateinamerika. Munich: Fink 1977.

Puhle, Hans-Jürgen (ed.): Lateinamerika. Historische Realität und Dependencia-Theorien. Hamburg: Hoffmann & Campe 1978.

Riegel, Klaus-Georg: Politische Soziologie unterindustrialisierter Gesellschaften. Wiesbaden: Akademische Verlagsgesellschaft 1976.

Robbe, M.: Dritte Welt, Asyl der Armen? Bemerkungen zum Verständnis und Selbstverständnis der nationalen Befreiungsbewegungen. Berlin: Union 1977.

Ropp, Klaus von der/Waller, Peter Paul: Die Entwicklungsperspektiven für Zimbabwe, in: AP 4/1978, pp. 463-476.

Rothermund, Dietmar: Europa und Asien im Zeitalter des Merkantilismus. Darmstadt: Wissenschaftliche Buchgesellschaft 1978.

Schwefel, Dieter: Grundbedürfnisse und Entwicklungspolitik. Baden-Baden: Nomos 1978.

Senghaas, Dieter: Gibt es eine entwicklungspolitische Alternative für die Dritte Welt?, in: Aus Politik und Zeitgeschichte B 7/1978, pp. 3-18.

Skriver, Ansgar: Das Konzept der Hilfe ist falsch. Entwicklung in Abhängigkeit. Wuppertal: Hammer 1977.

Tetzlaff, Rainer: Ein Wendepunkt in der internationalen Entwicklungsdiskussion? Kritische Anmerkungen zum 'Dag Hammarskjöld-Bericht 1976', in: Friedensanalysen 4/1977, pp. 201-208.

Thesing, Josef (ed.): Politik und Entwicklung in Lateinamerika. Beiträge zu den zentralen Problemen des Kontinents. Mainz: v. Hase & Koehler 1976.

Timmler, Markus: Von der Entwicklungshilfe zur Entwicklungspolitik, in: AP 2/1978, pp. 159-172.

Timmler, Markus: Die Entwicklungsländer suchen den Alleingang, in: AP 3/1978, pp. 313-327.

Urff, Winfried von (ed.): Wachstum, Einkommensverteilung und Beschäftigung in Entwicklungsländern. Berlin: Duncker & Humblot 1978.

Veit, Winfried: Nationale Emanzipation. Entwicklungsstrategie und Außenpolitik in Tropisch Afrika — die Beispiele Elfenbeinküste und Guinea. Munich: Weltforum- Verlag 1978.

Wolff, Jürgen H.: Planung in Entwicklungsländern. Eine Bilanz aus politik- und verwaltungswissenschaftlicher Sicht. Berlin: Duncker & Humblot 1977.

Wontroba, Gerd/Menzel, Ulrich: Stagnation oder Unterentwicklung in Korea. Königstein/Ts.: Hain 1978.

Other

Bungarten, Harald H.: Umweltpolitik in Westeuropa. EG, internationale Organisationen und nationale Umweltpolitiken. Bonn: Europa Union 1978.

Dauses, Manfred A./Wolf, Dieter O. A.: Weltraum und Sicherheit, in: Aus Politik und Zeitgeschichte B 14/1978, pp. 3-21.

Füllenbach, Josef: Umweltschutz zwischen Ost und West. Umweltpolitik in Osteuropa und gesamteuropäische Zusammenarbeit. Bonn: Europa Union 1977.

Kapp, Karl William: Sozioökonomische Entwicklung und Umwelt. Neue internationale Perspektiven, in: Aus Politik und Zeitgeschichte B 7/1978, pp. 19-28.

Kubbig, Bernd W.: Energie und Sicherheit für Westeuropa. Optionen, Konflikte, Perspektiven, in: Aus Politik und Zeitgeschichte B 5/1978, pp. 3-35.

Tscharner, Benedikt von/Madöry, Robert: Das Internationale Energieprogramm. Eine Zwischenbilanz, in: Außenwirtschaft 4/1977, pp. 311-339.

Transnational Relations and Politics

Multinational Corporations

Axt, Heinz-Jürgen: Sozialpartnerschaft als Modell für Europa? 'Dreierkonferenzen' als Konzertierte Aktion auf EG-Ebene, in: Blätter 4/1977, pp. 455-469.

Barnet, Richard Josef: Die Krisenmacher: die Multinationalen und die Verwandlung des Kapitalismus. Rebeck bei Hamburg: Rowohlt 1977.

Biermann, Herbert: Wirtschaftspolitische Theorie der multinationalen Unternehmen. Stuttgart: Gustav Fischer 1978.

Breidenstein, Gerhard: Internationale Konzerne. Arbeitsbuch für Schule, Gewerkschaften, politische Gruppen. Reinbek: Rowohlt 1978.

Däubler, Wolfgang/Wohlgemuth, Karl (eds.): Transnationale Konzerne und Weltwirtschaftsordnung. Baden-Baden: Nomos 1978.

Eli, Max/Sogo, Shosha: Strukturen und Strategien japanischer Welthandelsunternehmungen. Düsseldorf/Vienna: Econ 1977.

Froemer, Friedhelm (ed.): Multinationale Unternehmen: eine Bestandsaufnahme mit Einführung und Dokumentation der Meinungen, Förderungen und Vereinbarungen. Leverkusen: Heggen 1977.

Holtz, Uwe: Europa und die Multis. Chance für die Dritte Welt? Baden-Baden: Nomos 1978.

Jungnickel, Rolf et al.: Einfluß multinationaler Unternehmen auf Außenwirtschaft und Branchenstruktur der Bundesrepublik Deutschland. Hamburg: Verlag Weltarchiv 1977.

Koopmann, Georg: Multinationale Unternehmen in Kolumbien. Hamburg: Verlag Weltarchiv 1978.

Kramer, Heinz: Die Rolle der Sozialpartner im Entscheidungsprozeß der EG, in: Aus Politik und Zeitgeschichte B 22/1977, pp. 23-45.

Krosigk, Friedrich von: Multinationale Unternehmen und die Krise in Europa: eine Untersuchung zum ökonomischen Strukturwandel und seinen politischen Folgen im Rahmen des europäischen Regionalismus. Königstein/Ts.: Athenäum 1978.

Link, Werner: Deutsche und amerikanische Gewerkschaften und Geschäftsleute 1945-1976. Eine Studie über transnationale Beziehungen. Düsseldorf: Droste 1978.

Lorenz, Peter: Multinationale Unternehmen sozialistischer Länder. Baden-Baden: Nomos 1978.

Matthies, Klaus: Transnationale Unternehmen in Mexiko. Hamburg: Verlag Weltarchiv 1977.

Mirow, Kurt Rudolf: Die Diktatur der Kartelle. Zum Beispiel Brasilien. Material zur Vermachtung des Weltmarktes. Reinbek: Rowohlt 1977.

International Trade Unions

Kendall, Walter: Gewerkschaften in Europa. Die europäische Arbeiterbewegung von den Anfängen bis zur Gegenwart. Hamburg: Hoffmann & Campe 1977.

Nagels, Karl-Heinz: Industrielle Demokratie in Europa. Mitbestimmung und Kontrolle in der Europäischen Aktiengesellschaft. Frankfurt/New York: Campus 1977.

Nagels, Karlheinz: Überbetriebliche Partizipation von Arbeitnehmern in Europa. Frankfurt/New York: Campus 1978.

Steiert, Rudolf: Die Entwicklung transnationaler Strukturen der Gewerkschaftsbewegung in der Europäischen Gemeinschaft, in: ZParl, 1978, pp. 215-232.

Tudyka, Kurt P. et al.: Macht ohne Grenzen und grenzenlose Ohnmacht. Arbeitnehmerbewußtsein und die Bedingungen gewerkschaftlicher Gegenstrategien in multinationalen Konzernen. Frankfurt/New York: Campus 1978.

Waschke, Hildegard: Supra-nationale Gewerkschaftspolitik: Ziele und Wege der internationalen Gewerkschaftsbewegung. Cologne: Deutscher Instituts-Verlag 1978.

Other

Burkhardt, Barbara/Schumann, Wolfgang: Die transnationalen Verbandszusammenschlüsse der Landwirtschaft und des Handels, in: Zparl, 1978, pp. 200-214.

Gresch, Norbert: Transnationale Parteienzusammenarbeit in der EG. Baden-Baden: Nomos 1978.

Höhne, Hansjoachim: Report über Nachrichtenagenturen. Bd 1: Die Situation auf den Nachrichtenmärkten der Welt. Baden-Baden: Nomos 1976.

Hrbek, Rudolf: Parteibünde in der Europäischen Gemeinschaft auf dem Weg zu programmatischem Profil, in: EA 10/1978, pp. 299-310.

Kimmel, Adolf (ed.): Eurokommunismus. Die kommunistischen Parteien Frankreichs, Italiens, Spaniens und Portugals, Cologne: Böhlau 1977.

Koschwitz, Hansjürgen: 'Freiheit der Information' oder 'Kommunikationsimperialismus'? Konfliktwirkungen publizistischer Medien im Verhältnis von Industrie- und Entwicklungsländern, in: Aus Politik und Zeitgeschichte B 15/1977, pp. 11-38.

Picht, Robert (ed.): Kulturpolitik für Europa. Planansätze europäischer Stiftungsarbeit. Bonn: Europa Union 1977.

Schmidt, Robert H.: Grenzüberschreitende Publizistik in Rundfunk, Tagespresse und Zeitschriften der Großregion Saarland — Westpfalz — Lothringen — Luxemburg — Trier. Spiegel und Motor der Zusammenarbeit. Saarbrücken: Die Mitte 1978.

Stammen, Theo (ed.): Parteien in Europa. Nationale Parteiensysteme — Transnationale Parteienbeziehungen — Konturen eines europäischen Parteiensystems. Munich: Beck 1978.

Steinkühler, Manfred (ed.): Eurokommunismus im Widerspruch. Analyse und Dokumentation. Cologne: Wissenschaft und Politik 1977.

Steuber, Ursel: Internationale Bankenkooperation: deutsche Banken in internationalen Gruppen. Frankfurt: Knapp 1977.

Timmermann, Heinz (ed.):. Eurokommunismus. Fakten, Analysen, Interviews. Frankfurt: Fischer 1978.

International Organization and Integration

General Studies

Wiegand, Gerd: Organisatorische Aspekte der internationalen Verwaltung von Entwicklungshilfe: ein Beitrag zur Organisationsanalyse internationaler Organisationen am Beispiel der UNDP und der Weltbank. Berlin: Duncker & Humblot 1978.

The United Nations System

Brinkmann, Matthias: Majoritätsprinzip und Einstimmigkeit in den Vereinten Nationen: Konsequenzen und Grenzen staatlicher Gleichberechtigung in der Generalversammlung. Frankfurt: Haag & Herchen 1978.

Fahl, Gundolf: Der UNO-Sicherheitsrat. Analyse und Dokumentation nach dreißigjährigem Bestehen. Berlin: Berlin Verlag 1978.

Gössner, Rolf: Die Vereinten Nationen und die Menschenrechte, in: Blätter 1/1978, pp. 33-47.

Haase, Winfrid: Die Internationale Arbeitsorganisation (IAO). Nach dem Austritt der USA sind die Probleme nicht kleiner geworden, in: Beiträge zur Konfliktforschung 1/1978, pp. 71-92.

Handbuch Vereinte Nationen. Munich: Verlag Dokumentation 1977.

Harding, Leonhard: Die Südafrikapolitik der UNO und der Kirchen. Munich: Kaiser: Mainz: Grünewald 1977.

Krökel, Michael: Die Bindungswirkung von Resolutionen des Sicherheitsrates der V.N. gegenüber Mitgliedsstaaten. Berlin: Duncker & Humblot 1977.

Küpper, C. (ed.): Die friedenssichernde Funktion der UN am Beispiel des Nahost-Konflikts und des Nord-Süd-Problems. Opladen: Leske & Budrich 1977.

Lagoni, Rainer: Die Vereinten Nationen und der internationale Terrorismus, in: EA 6/1977, pp. 171-180.

Matzke, Otto: Probleme der Restrukturierung des Wirtschafts- und Sozialbereichs des UN-Systems, in: Beiträge zur Konfliktforschung 4/1978, pp. 5-33.

Neuhold, Hanspeter: Internationale Konflikte — verbotene und erlaubte Mittel ihrer Austragung: Versuche einer transdisziplinären Betrachtung der Grundsätze des Gewalt- und Interventionsverbots sowie der friedlichen Streitbeilegung im Lichte der UN-Prinzipien deklaration 1970 und der modernen Sozialwissenschaften. Wien/New York: Springer 1977.

Scheuner, U.: Die Vereinten Nationen als Faktor der internationalen Politik. Düsseldorf: Westdeutscher Verlag 1976.

Unser, Günther: Die UNO: Aufgaben und Struktur der Vereinten Nationen. Munich/-Vienna: Olzog 1978.

Watzke, Wolfgang: Was ist eine Aggression? Zur Genesis der Definition bei den Vereinten Nationen, in: Beiträge zur Konfliktforschung 4/1978, pp. 105-156.

West European Organizations

Aigner, Heinrich: Finanzkontrolle der Europäischen Gemeinschaften: Entwicklung und Perspektiven, in: Zparl, 1978, pp. 186-192.

Aron, R.: Plädoyer für das dekadente Europa. Berlin: Ullstein 1978.

Axt, Heinz-Jürgen: Staat, multinationale Konzerne und politische Union in Westeuropa. Cologne: Pahl-Rugenstein 1977.

Axt, Heinz-Jürgen: Stahlkrise und westeuropäische Integration. Die Krise — Hemmnis oder Triebkraft der Verflechtung?, in: PVS 2/1978, pp. 157-200.

Axt, Heinz-Jürgen: Direktwahlen zum Europäischen Parlament — ein Weg zu mehr Demokratie?, in Blätter 9/1978, pp. 1098-1111.

Baumgartner, Dirk: Institutionelle Aspekte des AKP-EWG-Abkommens von Lomé, in: Europarecht 2/1978, pp. 105-221.

Beutler, Bengt/Bieber, Roland/Pipkorn, Jörn/Streil, Jochen; Die Europäische Gemeinschaft. Rechtsordnung und Politik. Baden-Baden: Nomos 1978.

Buck, Karl H.: Griechenland und die Europäische Gemeinschaft. Erwartungen und Probleme des Beitritts. Bonn: Europa Union 1978.

Busch, Klaus: Die Krise der Europäischen Gemeinschaft. Cologne: EVA 1978.

Busch, Klaus: Die Europäische Gemeinschaft in der Krise — die Ursachen des Scheiterns der Wirtschafts- und Währungsunion, in: Prokla 1/1978, pp. 95-132.

Claus, Burghard/Eßer, Klaus/Heimpel, Christian: Zur Erweiterung der EG in Süd-Europa. Berlin: Deutsches Institut für Entwicklungspolitik 1977.

Deubner, Christian: Die Atompolitik der westdeutschen Industrie und die Gründung von Euratom. Frankfurt/New York: Campus 1977.

Deubner, Christian et al.: Die Erweiterung der Europäischen Gemeinschaft nach Süden, in: Aus Politik und Zeitgeschichte 38/1978, pp. 3-20.

Deubner, Christian: Die Expansion der westdeutschen Industrie und die Gründung von Euratom, in: Lev. 1978, pp. 250-285.

Dunsch, Jürgen: Die Europapolitik der britischen Labour party 1970-1975; innerparteiliche Meinungsbildung und parteioffizielle Konzeptionen. Bad Honnef: Bock u. Herchen 1978.

Dürr, Ernst et al.: Wirtschafts- und gesellschaftspolitische Ordnungsprobleme der Europäischen Gemeinschaft. Baden-Baden: Nomos 1978.

Eßer,Klaus et al.: Europäische Gemeinschaft und süd-europäische Beitrittsländer. Anforderungen an die Integrationsfähigkeit. Berlin: Deutsches Institut für Entwicklungspolitik 1978.

Esternauer, F.: Die europäische Gemeinschaft und Österreich. Vienna: Braunmüller 1978.

Esterbauer, F.: Europäische Union — föderalistisch-demokratische Grundzüge. Vienna: Braunmüller 1978.

Everling, Ulrich: Möglichkeiten und Grenzen der Europa-Politik. Zum Stand der europäischen Integration, in: EA 4/1978, pp. 101-110.

Geiger, Rudolf: Außenbeziehungen der Europäischen Wirtschaftsgemeinschaft und auswärtige Gewalt der Mitgliedsstaaten. Zur Entwicklung der Rechtssprechung des Europäischen Gerichtshofes zu den Vertragsschlußkompetenzen der EWG, in: Zeitschrift für ausländisches öffentliches Recht und Völkerrecht 3-4/1977, pp. 640-666.

Groeben, Hans von der/Möller, Hans (eds.): Möglichkeiten und Grenzen einer Europäischen Union. Berichte einer Arbeitsgemeinschaft im Zentrum für interdisziplinäre Forschung in Bielefeld. Baden-Baden: Nomos 1978.

Gruner, Joachim: Probleme einer zweiten Erweiterungsrunde der EG, in: IPW-Berichte 1/1978, pp. 19-27.

Haferkamp, Wilhelm: Chancen und Risiken der zweiten EG-Erweiterung, in: EA 19/1977, pp. 617-626.

Hallstein, Walter: Europa und die Banken. Commerzbank 1977.

Harbrecht, Wolfgang: Die europäischen Gemeinschaften. Stuttgart: Gustav Fischer 1978.

Hartwig, Klaus Dieter: Verteidigungspolitik als Moment der westeuropäischen Integration. Frankfurt: Haag & Herchen 1977.

Hasenpflug, Hajo/Kohler, Beate (eds.): Die Süd-Erweiterung der Europäischen Gemeinschaft. Wende oder Ende der Integration? Hamburg: Verlag Weltarchiv 1977.

Hengsbach, Friedhelm: Die Assoziierung afrikanischer Staaten an die Europäische Gemeinschaft. Eine Politik raumwirtschaftlicher Integration? Baden-Baden: Nomos 1977.

Höhn, J.: Außenpolitik der EG-Staaten: Im Fall der KSZE. Geschichte, Struktur, Entscheidungsprozesse, Aktionen, Möglichkeiten und Grenzen. Munich: tuduv 1978.

Industrie- und Handelskammer Berlin (ed.): Perspektiven der europäischen Integration. Chancen Berlins. Berlin-Besuch des Präsidenten der EG-Kommission und Vortrag vor der IHK-Berlin. Berlin: 1978.

Jansen, Jürgen: Britische Konservative und Europa. Debattenaussagen im Unterhaus zur westeuropäischen Integration 1945-1972. Baden-Baden: Nomos 1978.

Kasten Hans: Die europäische Wirtschaftsintegration. Grundlagen. Munich: Fink 1978.

Klank, Wilfried: Zur verstärkten Rüstungskooperation in Westeuropa, in: Militärgeschichte 1/1978, pp. 74-85.

Klingelhöfer, Wolf-Dieter: Grundlagen einer rationalen Kreditpolitik in der Europäischen Gemeinschaft. Berlin: Duncker & Humblot 1978.

Koester, Ulrich: EG-Agrarpolitik in der Sackgasse: divergierende nationale Interessen bei der Verwirklichung der EGW-Agrarpolitik. Baden-Baden: Nomos 1977.

Koppe, Karheinz: Mehr Europa — weniger Bürokratie. Eine Gemeinschaft erstickt an sich selbst. Kronberg/Ts.: Athenäum 1978.

Kramer, Heinz/Rummel, Reinhardt: Gemeinschaftsbildung Westeuropas in der Außenpolitik. Zur Tragfähigkeit der Europäischen Zusammenarbeit (EPZ). Baden-Baden: Nomos 1978.

Kramer, Heinz: Ziele und Verhalten der Sozialpartner in Westeuropa als Faktoren für die Gemeinschaftsbildung. Ebenhausen: Stiftung Wissenschaft und Politik 1977.

Lahnstein, Manfred: Über die Währungsunion zur Wirtschaftsunion?, in: EA 9/1978, pp. 263-270.

Lindemann, Beate: EG-Staaten und Vereinte Nationen. Die politische Zusammenarbeit der Neun in den UN-Hauptorganen. Munich: Oldenbourg 1978.

Lipgens, Walter: Die Anfänge der europäischen Einigungspolitik 1945-1950, vol. 1: 1945-1947. Stuttgart: Klett 1977.

Lutz, Christian: Von der Wirtschaftsgemeinschaft zur Europäischen Union. Plädoyer für eine Verfassungs- Revolution. Bonn Europa Union 1977.

Michaelis, Hans: Energiemarkt und Energiepolitik in einer Europäischen Union. Frankfurt: Metzner 1976.

Morawitz, Rudolf: Die wirtschaftlichen Probleme eines Beitritts Griechenlands zur Europäischen Gemeinschaft, in: EA 8/1977, pp. 249-258.

Müller-Graf, Peter-Christian: Die Direktwahl des europäischen Parlaments. Genese und Perspektiven. Tübingen: Mohr 1977.

Oppermann, Thomas (ed.): In welches Europa führen die Direktwahlen? Perspektiven künftiger Verantwortung. Tübinger Europa-Colloquium aus Anlaß des 500 jährigen Jubiläums der Eberhard-Karls-Universität. Berlin: Duncker & Humblot 1978.

Pfeffer, Joachim: Der rechtliche Rahmen des Wirtschaft verkehrs mit den RGW-Ländern. Cologne: Heymanns 1978.

Picht, Robert (ed.): Deutschland, Frankreich, Europa. Bilanz einer schwierigen Partnerschaft. Munich: Piper 1978.

Randzio-Plath, Christa: Europa — eine Chance für Frauen? Der Kampf um die Gleichstellung ist nicht verloren. Baden-Baden: Nomos 1978.

Rattinger, Hans et al.: Mandatsverteilung im europäischen Parlament nach der Direktwahl: Eine Simulationsstudie. Berlin: Duncker & Humblot 1978.

Roemheld, Lutz: Integraler Föderalismus: Modell für Europa; ein Weg zur personalen Gruppen gesellschaft, Vol. 1: Geschichtliche Entwicklung: Munich: Vögel 1977.

Rogalla, Dieter: Beamtenmitsprache im Neuner-Europa. Eine vergleichende Untersuchung zum Personalvertretungsrecht in den Zentralbehörden der Mitgliedstaaten und der Europäischen Gemeinschaften. Baden-Baden: Nomos 1978.

Rummel, Reinhardt: Die europäische politische Zusammenarbeit als Ansatz gemeinsamer Außenpolitik der Neun. Ebenhausen: Stiftung Wissenschaft und Politik 1977.

Rummel, Reinhardt: Zur Zukunft der Europäischen Politischen Zusammenarbeit (EPZ). Zwischen Diplomatie-Club und gemeinsamem Entscheidungszentrum, in: Aus Politik und Zeitgeschichte 38/1978, pp. 21-35.

Sasse, Christoph: Eine Gemeinschaft — Neun Legitimitäten. Eine Skizze zur Machtverteilung in der EG, in: ZParl 1978, pp. 254-260.

Seitz, Konrad: Die Europäische Gemeinschaft in einer Welt des Übergangs. Die Aufgaben Europas bei der Gestaltung einer kooperativen Weltordnung, in: EA 16/1978, pp. 495-506.

Schmeder, Winfried: Die Rechtsangleichung als Integrationsmittel der Europäischen Gemeinschaft. Cologne: Heymanns 1978.

Schneider, Heinrich/Wessels, Wolfgang (eds.): Auf dem Weg zur Europäischen Union? Diskussionbeiträge zum Tindemans-Bericht. Bonn: Europa Union Verl. 1977.

Schoneweg, Egon: Neue Aspekte institutionalisierter Interessenvertretung in der EG, in: ZParl 1978, pp. 192-200.

Schulz, Eberhard (ed.): Die Ostbeziehungen der Europäischen Gemeinschaft. Von nationalstaatlicher Politik zu gemeinsamer Verantwortung. Munich/Vienna: Oldenbourg 1977.

Schüttemeyer,Suzanne/Thaysen, Uwe: Das Europabewußtsein 1977/78, in: ZParl 1978, pp. 159-165.

Steinbach, Udo: Auf dem Weg nach Europa? Die Beziehungen zwischen der Türkei und der Europäischen Gemeinschaft durchlaufen eine kritische Phase, in: Orient 1/1977, pp. 79-101.

Strizek, Helmut/Hammers-Strizek, Gisel: Europäische Einigung. Bilanz und Perspektiven. Bonn: Verlag Neue Gesellschaft 1978.

Volle,Angelika: Wie gemeinschaftlich ist die Fischereipolitik der Europäischen Gemeinschaft?, in: EA 3/1977, pp. 73-84.

Weissenberg, Paul: Die Kompetenz der Europäischen Wirtschaftsgemeinschaft zum Abschluß von Handels- und Kooperationsabkommen gemäß Art. 113 EWG-Vertrag. Berlin: Duncker & Humblot 1978.

Wenturis, Nikolaus: Die soziopolitischen und ökonomischen Strukturen Griechenlands im Hinblick auf seine Integration in die EG. Eine Modell-Skizze von Kern-Peripherie — Relationen. Frankfurt: Lang 1977.

Woyke, Richard: Europawahl '79: Daten, Fakten, Probleme. Opladen: Leske & Budrich 1978.

Zuleeg, Manfred: Der Verfassungsgrundsatz der Demokratie und die Europäischen Gemeinschaft, in: Staat 1/1977, pp. 27-47.

Other

Hedrich, Manfred/v.d. Ropp, Klaus Frhr.: Chancen regionaler Integration in West-Afrika, in: AP 1/1978, pp. 84-97.

Kappeler, Dietrich: Territorialkonflikte in Afrika und die Grundsätze der Organisation der Afrikanischen Einheit, in: EA 17/1978, pp. 561-570.

Machowski, Heinrich: Außenwirtschaftspolitische Ziele der RGW-Länder im neuen Planjahrfünft 1976-80, in: EA 3/1977, pp. 85-94.

Pritzel, Konstantin: Möglichkeiten und Grenzen gesamteuropäischer Zusammenarbeit. Politische und wirtschaftliche Aspekte der Verhandlungen EG/RGW, in: DA 8/1978, pp. 829-848.

Sikora, Franz: Sozialistische Solidarität und nationale Interessen. Polen. Tschechoslowakei, DDR. Cologne: Wissenschaft und Politik 1977.

Stehr, Uwe: Sozioökonomische Bedingungen des Außenverhaltens der RGW-Staaten. Frankfurt: 1977.

PEACE RESEARCH

General Studies

Brauch, Hans Günter: Entwicklungen und Ergebnisse der Friedensforschung, in: Neue Politische Literatur 2/1977, pp. 174-201; 1/1978, pp. 71-104; 3/1977, pp. 385-414; 4/1977, pp. 516-535.

Broschat, Monika: Erzeihung zum Frieden: Auseinandersetzung mit friedenspädagogischen Konzepten in der Bundesrepublik Deutschland. Frankfurt/Bern/Las Vegas: Lang 1978.

Groneymeyer, Reimer: Frieden. Baden-Baden: Signal Verlag 1978.

Groten, Hubert: Friedensforschung — Anspruch und Praxis. Studien zur Realisationsmöglichkeit des positiven Friedensbegriffs. Baden-Baden: Nomos 1977.

Holl, Karl: Historische Friedensforschung, in: Neue Politische Literatur 2/1977, pp. 202-212.

Kempf, Wilhelm: Konfliktlösung und Aggression: zu der Grundlegung einer psychologischen Friedensforschung. Bern: Huber 1978.

Kühnlein, Gertrud: Die Entwicklung der kritischen Friedensforschung in der Bundesrepublik Deutschland: Untersuchung und Kritik einer neuen Wissenschaft. Frankfurt: Haag & Herchen 1978.

Küpper, Christel (ed.): Friedenserziehung. Ein Handbuch. Schriften zur politischen Didaktik. Leverkusen: Leske & Budrich 1978.

Küpper, Christel (ed.): Friedenserziehung. Eine Einführung. Munich: 1977.

Landeszentrale für politische Bildung des Landes Nordrhein-Westfalen (ed.): Erziehung für den Frieden. Probleme des Friedens in der einen Welt. Cologne: Wissenschaft und Politik 1977.

Mushkat, Mario'n: Rückständigkeit, Entwicklungshilfe und Friedensforschung, in: ZfP 2/1978, pp. 194-216.

Nähring, Hannelore: Friedenserziehung: Analyse friedenspädagogischer Literatur und theoretischer Grundlegung für die Planung von Curricula zur Friedenserziehung. Hamburg: Lüdke 1977.

Topical Studies

Friedensanalysen 4: Schwerpunkt: Friedensbewegung. Frankfurt: Suhrkamp 1977.

Friedensanalysen 6: Schwerpunkt: Gewalt, Sozialisation, Aggression. Frankfurt: Suhrkamp 1977.

Friedensanalysen 8: Kriege und Bürgerkriege der Gegenwart. Frankfurt: Suhrkamp 1978.

Gugel, Günther: Friedenserziehung und Jugendarbeit: theoretische Überlegungen, praktische Ansätze. Zorneding bei Munich: Seewann 1977.

Hornung, Volker: Wirtschaftlicher Boykott als gewaltfreies Mittel in Bürgerrechtsbewegungen. Fallstudien zur amerikanischen Bürgerrechts und Landarbeiterbewegung. Frankfurt: Haag & Herchen 1979.

Kunstleben, Franz et al.: 'und ich geh doch zur Bundeswehr!' Planung, Dokumentation und Analyse eines Unterrichtsprojekts im Rahmen schulnaher Curriculumentwicklung. Waldkirch: Waldkircher Verlagsgesellschaft 1976.

Luber, Burkhard/Bloech, Falk (eds.): Frieden auf dem Land. Eine Dokumentation über vier Jahre regionale Friedensarbeit aus Anlaß des 30 jährigen Bestehens des Internationalen Freundschaftsheimes. Waldkirch: Waldkircher Verlagsgesellschaft 1978.

Lutz, Dieter/Schierholz, Henning: Friedens- und Abrüstungspolitik. Bausteine für eine politische Bildungsarbeit. Waldkirch: Waldkircher Verlagsgesellschaft 1978.

Otten, Hendrik: Wehrdienst — organisierte Aggression, Zivildienst — organisierte Friedenserziehung? Eine didaktische Skizze für die Sekundarstufe II und Erwachsenenbildung, in: Politische Didaktik 1/1978, pp. 63-72.

Roloff, Ernst-August: Aggression — Gewalt — Krieg. Vorüberlegungen zu einem fächerübergreifenden Stufenkonzept, in: Politische Didaktik 1/1978, pp. 2-17.

Schmölz, Frank-Martin (ed.): Christlicher Friedensbegriff und europäische Friedensordnung. Munich/Mainz: Kaiser/Grünewald 1977.

Simma, Bruno/Schenk, Dieter: Friedliche Streiterledigung in Europa. Überlegungen zum schweizerischen KSZE-Vorschlag, in: EA 14/1978, pp. 419-430.

Timmermann, Heinrich: Friedenssicherungsbewegungen in den Vereinigten Staaten von Amerika und Großbritannien während des Ersten Weltkrieges. Frankfurt/Bern/Las Vegas: Lang 1978.

NOTES ON CONTRIBUTORS

Ulrich Albrecht is Professor of Political Science at the Free University of Berlin. In his research he has focused on the political economy of armament dynamics and, in particular, on processes of arms transfers from developed to developing countries. His publications include *Der Handel mit Waffen* (1971) and *Politik und Waffengeschäfte* (1972); and, as co-author, *Rüstung und Unterentwicklung* (1976) and *Arbeitsplätze durch Rüstung* (1978).

Klaus von Beyme is Professor of Political Science at the University of Heidelberg. His books include *Interessengruppen in der Demokratie* (1969), *Die parlamentarischen Regierungssysteme in Europa* (1970), *Die Politischen Theorien der Gegenwart* (1972), *Ökonomie und Politik im Sozialismus* (1975), *Gewerkschaften und Arbeitsbeziehungen in kapitalistischen Ländern* (1977), *Sozialismus oder Wohlfahrsstaat* (1977) and *Das Politische System der Bundesrepublik* (1979).

Klaus Jürgen Gantzel is Professor of Political Science at the University of Hamburg. For many years he has been the research co-ordinator of the division on international relations (Sektion Internationale Politik) of the German Political Science Association. He has published two books, *System und Akteur* (1972) and, as co-author, *Konflikt, Eskalation, Krise* (1972) and he has edited numerous volumes with papers prepared for the meetings of the Sektion Internationale Politik.

Gisela Gantzel-Kress is a free-lance political scientist and author living in Hamburg.

Helga Haftendorn is Professor of International Relations at the Free University of Berlin. Her areas of main interest are German foreign policy, problems of arms control, and American foreign policy. Her books include *Militärhilfe und Rüstungsexporte der Bundesrepublik Deutschland* (1971), *Abrüstungs- und Entspannungspolitik zwischen Sicherheitsbefriedigung und Friedenssicherung* (1974) and, as co-author, *Verwaltete Außenpolitik* (1978).

Joachim Krause is a Research Associate at the Stiftung Wissenschaft und Politik — Research Institute for International Affairs, Ebenhausen. He has co-authored the book *Verwaltete Außenpolitik* (1978).

Michael Kreile is Assistant Professor of Political Science at the University of Heidelberg. His research interests include the foreign policies of industrialized countries and the surge of Eurocommunism, especially in Italy. He has published a book *Osthandel und Ostpolitik* (1978).

Ekkehart Krippendorff is Professor of Political Science at the John F. Kennedy Institute for North American Studies of the Free University of Berlin. His publications in the field of international relations include *Die amerikanische Strategie* (1970), *Internationales System als Geschichte* (1975) and *Internationale Beziehungen als Wissenschaft* (1977).

Volker Rittberger is Professor of Political Science at the University of Tübingen and Special Fellow of the United Nations Institute for Training and Research (UNITAR). His publications include *Evolution and International Organisation* (1973) and, as co-author, *Konflikt, Eskalation Krise* (1972), *Abrüstungspolitik und Grundgesetz* (1976) and *Abrüstungsplanung in der Bundesrepublik* (1979).

Frieder Schlupp is a research associate and lecturer in the Department of Political Science of the University of Konstanz. His main research interest centres on the analysis of international economic and political relations of developed capitalist countries. He is a co-author of *Die Internationalisierung des Kapitals* (1979) and has published several articles on related topics.

Gebhard Schweigler is a senior research specialist at the Research Institute of the German Society for Foreign Policy in Bonn. His publications include *Nationalbewußsein in der BRD und der DDR* (1973), *National Consciousness in Divided Germany* (1975) and *Politikwissenschaft und Außenpolitik in den USA* (1977).

Lothar Wilker is Assistant Professor of International Relations at the Free University of Berlin. He has published *Sicherheitspolitik der SPD 1956-1966* (1977) and, as co-author, *Verwaltete Außenpolitik* (1978).